Body Image, Eating Disorders, and Obesity in Youth

SECOND EDITION

Body Image, Eating Disorders, and Obesity in Youth

Assessment, Prevention, and Treatment

SECOND EDITION

Edited by Linda Smolak and J. Kevin Thompson

American Psychological Association • Washington, DC

First Printing November 2008
Second Printing October 2009

Published by
American Psychological Association
750 First Street, NE
Washington, DC 20002
www.apa.org

To order
APA Order Department
P.O. Box 92984
Washington, DC 20090-2984
Tel: (800) 374-2721; Direct: (202) 336-5510
Fax: (202) 336-5502; TDD/TTY: (202) 336-6123
Online: www.apa.org/books/
E-mail: order@apa.org

In the U.K., Europe, Africa, and the Middle East, copies may be ordered from
American Psychological Association
3 Henrietta Street
Covent Garden, London
WC2E 8LU England

Typeset in Goudy by SquareOne Publishing Partners, Boston, MA

Printer: United Book Press, Baltimore, MD
Cover Designer: Mercury Publishing Services, Rockville, MD
Technical/Production Editor: Emily Welsh

The opinions and statements published are the responsibility of the authors, and such opinions and statements do not necessarily represent the policies of the American Psychological Association.

Library of Congress Cataloging-in-Publication Data
Body image, eating disorders, and obesity in youth : assessment,
prevention, and treatment / edited by Linda Smolak and J. Kevin
Thompson. -- 2nd ed.
    p. cm.
Includes bibliographical references and index.
ISBN-13: 978-1-4338-0405-2
ISBN-10: 1-4338-0405-0
1. Eating disorders in adolescence. 2. Body image in adolescence. 3.
Body image disturbance. 4. Obesity in adolescence. I. Smolak, Linda,
1951- II. Thompson, J. Kevin.

RJ506.E18B635 2009
618.92'8526--dc22

                        2008023404

British Library Cataloguing-in-Publication Data
A CIP record is available from the British Library.

Printed in the United States of America
Second Edition

CONTENTS

CONTENTS

CONTRIBUTORS

Drew A. Anderson, PhD, University at Albany, State University of New York

Eileen Anderson-Fye, EdD, Case Western Reserve University, Cleveland, OH

Katherine W. Bauer, MS, University of Minnesota, Minneapolis

Leann L. Birch, PhD, Pennsylvania State University, University Park

Simone Blaney, PhD, La Trobe University, Bundoora, Australia

Canice E. Crerand, PhD, The Children's Hospital of Philadelphia, Philadelphia, PA

Lisa Diewald, MS, RD, LDN, University of Pennsylvania, Philadelphia

Myles S. Faith, PhD, University of Pennsylvania School of Medicine, Philadelphia

Jennifer O. Fisher, PhD, Temple University, Philadelphia, PA

Debra L. Franko, PhD, Northeastern University, Boston, MA

Jessica B. Edwards George, PhD, University of Massachusetts Medical School, Worcester

Jess Haines, PhD, MHSc, RD, Harvard Medical School, Boston, MA

Leslie J. Heinberg, PhD, Cleveland Clinic Lerner College of Medicine of Case Western Reserve University; Cleveland Clinic Foundation, Cleveland, OH

Kate E. Holt, PhD, Deakin University, Burwood, Australia

Alison L. Infield, BA, University of Pennsylvania School of Medicine, Philadelphia

Julia Kerns, BA, University of Pennsylvania School of Medicine, Philadelphia

Eve Kutchman, MEd, Rainbow Babies and Children's Hospital, Cleveland, OH

Jenn Laheta, MEd, Duke University School of Nursing, Durham, NC

Bryan Lask, MD, Ulleval University Hospital, Oslo, Norway; Great Ormond Street Hospital for Children, London, England; Huntercombe Hospitals, England

Jason M. Lavender, MA, University at Albany, State University of New York

Sarah Lawhun, MEd, RD, LD, Rainbow Babies and Children's Hospital, Cleveland, OH

Michael P. Levine, PhD, FAED, Kenyon College, Gambier, OH

Marita P. McCabe, PhD, Deakin University, Burwood, Australia

Suzanne M. Milnes, MA, University at Albany, State University of New York

Alexander J. Mussap, PhD, Deakin University, Burwood, Australia

Dianne Neumark-Sztainer, MPH, PhD, University of Minnesota, Minneapolis

Susan Paxton, PhD, La Trobe University, Bundoora, Australia

Lina A. Ricciardelli, PhD, Deakin University, Burwood, Australia

Megan Roehrig, PhD, Yale University, New Haven, CT

David B. Sarwer, PhD, University of Pennsylvania School of Medicine, Philadelphia

Angela M. Simmons, PhD, University at Albany, State University of New York

Megan M. Sinton, PhD, Washington University in St. Louis, St. Louis, MO

Linda Smolak, PhD, Kenyon College, Gambier, OH

Steffanie Sperry, MA, University of South Florida, Tampa

J. Kevin Thompson, PhD, University of South Florida, Tampa

Beth Watkins, PhD, St George's University of London, England

Eleanor H. Wertheim, PhD, La Trobe University, Bundoora, Australia

Tovah Yanover, PhD, University of South Florida, Tampa

PREFACE

Much has happened since the first volume of *Body Image, Eating Disorders, and Obesity in Youth* was published in 2001. Since that time, there has been an explosion of research output in these three areas. A search of index terms in PsycINFO comparing the number of published articles in this period with the immediately preceding 7 years indicated a 100% increase in the number of articles on the topic of childhood or adolescent body image; a 96% increase in articles on childhood or adolescent eating disorders; and a staggering 504% increase in the number of published papers on childhood or adolescent obesity. Clearly, the time is right for a reanalysis of existing findings in light of the recent literature.

The goal for this new edition is to assimilate the recent information into a form that is easily accessible for researchers, clinicians, and students. Our inspiration, as noted in the preface to the previous volume, is provided by not only the interest and support of our colleagues, but our own personal experiences (and those of our colleagues) with the many young girls and boys who struggle with body image and weight-related problems.

Finally, on a much more personal note, both of us have encountered situations with our own children and grandchildren related to body image, eating, and weight issues, and these continue to not only fuel our motivation to remain active in this area but also provide unique anecdotes that affect our perspectives. In our first book, Kevin noted that his daughter Carly (who was

2 at the time and is now 9) had not discovered Barbie dolls. Until she was about 3, he tried providing competing dolls and also used psychoeducational tactics ("Barbie is really very thin; she is not like most girls or women"), but after one long discussion, he repented when Carly said "I know Barbie is too skinny, but I like her anyway" (apparently, too much psychoeducation is contraindicated). Kevin's son Jared (now 11) had discovered barbells at age 4 but not the fashion pressures of middle school, until now—Kevin is sure of this because he recently spent 2 hours at a clothing store while his son tried on shirt after shirt after shirt. (Jared finally agreed that three were acceptable.)

Linda's children are now too old to provide new stories about body image in childhood or adolescence. However, buying things for her grand-children has been startling. She thought—or hoped—that there might have been a decline in gendered body image messages for young children over the past 25 years. In Buckeye country, where Linda lives, little girls are still given pom-poms as props by photographers and the boys are given footballs. One of the most popular movies is *High School Musical*, in which the hero is a basketball player and the heroine is a cheerleader. Research continues to demonstrate that cheerleading is associated with the thin ideal and eating problems, whereas football (and, to a lesser extent, other sports) is associated with drive for muscularity and steroid and food supplement use. Yet, it is apparently important that we teach our girls and boys early on that these are valuable roles.

We hope that this new volume stimulates even more research in the areas of body image, eating disorders, and obesity in youth. Our thanks go out to our wonderful contributors for their excellent chapters and we send our thoughts and encouragement to the young people and their families who struggle with the problems addressed in this book. We also thank the American Psychological Association for its continued interest in these topics. Our hope is that the reader will find something useful that will have a positive impact on the understanding, prevention, and treatment of body image, eating disorders, and obesity.

We would also like to extend our thanks to people who were inspirational and supportive to us. Linda would like to thank her Kenyon College family, particularly Michael Levine, Sarah Murnen, and Dana Krieg for their support and for interesting discussions on body image and eating topics. As always, her family—particularly her children Marlyce, Jesse, and Meghan and her grandchildren Sabrina, Nathan, and Isabel—provided motivation and inspiration. Finally, Linda's husband, Jim Keeler, was unfailing (yet again) in his support of this work. Kevin would like to thank his children who, as noted previously, continue to provide personal experiences that inform professional work. He would also like to thank his wife, Veronica, and some very special collaborators over the years, including Leslie Heinberg, Stacey Dunn, Tom Cash, Myles Faith, David Sarwer, Susan Paxton, Rachel Calogero, and the many graduate student colleagues who make all of the research possible.

I

INTRODUCTION

BODY IMAGE, EATING DISORDERS, AND OBESITY IN CHILDREN AND ADOLESCENTS: INTRODUCTION TO THE SECOND EDITION

LINDA SMOLAK AND J. KEVIN THOMPSON

There has been a dramatic increase in research addressing body image, eating disorders, and obesity in adolescents and children since the publication of the first edition of this book in 2001. Important new breakthroughs have been made in the understanding of body image issues and eating disturbances, and much new information has appeared regarding risk factors, prevention, and treatment options. Additionally, since the first edition of this volume, the increased prevalence of obesity in childhood and adolescence has emerged as a major public health issue, leading to a host of new guidelines for assessment, treatment, and the detection of risk (Barlow & Expert Committee, 2007; Davis et al., 2007; Spear et al., 2007). The prevalence of obesity in childhood and adolescence has increased from approximately 5% from 1963 to 1970 to 17% from 2003 to 2004 (Ogden et al., 2006). Obesity in childhood and adolescence is associated with both short- and long-term health problems (e.g., Baird et al., 2005; Freedman, Mei, Srinivasan, Berenson, & Dietz, 2007; Nader et al., 2006; D. Thompson et al., 2007; Xanthakos & Inge, 2007) and severe psychosocial consequences because these individuals are often stigmatized and marginalized as a result of their weight (Puhl & Latner, 2007). A renewed and active focus on obesity, however, should not distract from the need to address eating disturbances in childhood and adolescence. When one considers prevalence rates inclusive of subclinical cases along with individuals diagnosed with eating disorders

(Thompson & Smolak, 2001), the rates of between 10% and 15% approach the current figure of 17% for obesity. Additionally, eating disturbances are associated with a variety of health problems and have one of the highest mortality rates of any psychiatric disorder. Arguably, when considered in tandem, eating disorders and obesity may be the most pressing health-related conditions affecting America's youth.

As with the first edition, it is important and appropriate to consider the triumvirate of body image issues, eating problems, and obesity within one volume. Eating disorders and obesity represent the two ends of a weight-related clinical disturbance. Body image issues, certainly one of the core etiological features of eating disorders, are also intimately connected to the psychological health and psychosocial functioning of overweight and obese individuals. Additionally, eating disorders and obesity are health concerns that share similar causal features, developmental issues, and potential preventive approaches.

First, depression appears to be a risk factor for both obesity and eating disorders in adolescence (e.g., Stice, Presnell, Shaw, & Rohde, 2005). Dieting appears to contribute to bulimia nervosa (BN) and anorexia nervosa (AN), as well as to obesity (Field et al., 2007; Neumark-Sztainer, Wall, et al., 2006; Stice, 2002; Stice et al., 2005), although the link between dieting and obesity may be stronger for girls than for boys (Field et al., 2007). Second, both eating disorders and obesity entail developmental patterns and childhood behaviors that can continue into adulthood. Thus, developmental psychopathology models are applicable to both (e.g., Levine & Smolak, 2006). This is not to say that obesity represents a form of psychopathology; rather the emphasis is on pathways from childhood to adulthood and how they may converge or diverge to reach particular end points. Third, eating disorders and obesity involve poor nutrition and, often, a lack of or an excess of exercise. Thus, prevention efforts may target healthy nutrition and exercise patterns in order to address both eating disorders and obesity (e.g., Irving & Neumark-Sztainer, 2002).

In the remainder of this chapter, we introduce each of the three major topics of the book, providing an overview that provides general background information useful for framing the succeeding chapters. We close with a discussion of the content of the chapters included in this edition, providing a roadmap for the organization of the book.

BODY IMAGE

Body image can broadly be defined as the subjective evaluation of one's appearance, in contrast with physical attractiveness, which is an external or objective rating of appearance (J. Thompson, Heinberg, Altabe, & Tantlefff-Dunn, 1999). *Body image disturbance* is a rather broad umbrella term that consists of several dimensions, including affective, cognitive, behavioral, and perceptual components. Much of the work in the area of eating disorders and obesity focuses on the evaluation of a specific dimension referred to as weight and/or body shape dissatisfaction. Body dissatisfaction is evident by the early elementary school years and perhaps even during the preschool years (Smolak, 2004). Both boys and girls show body dissatisfaction, although the nature and patterns of this problem are gendered, with boys being more concerned with muscularity than girls, although some boys also worry about being too fat (J. Thompson & Cafri, 2007). Girls, on the other hand, primarily tend to be concerned about being or becoming overweight (Smolak, 2004).

Body dissatisfaction is fairly common in both childhood and adolescence. Studies frequently find that about 40% of late elementary school-age girls (Grades 4 and 5; approximately 9–11 years old) are worried that they are either fat or will become fat (Smolak, Levine, & Schermer, 1998). Although girls are more likely than boys to report being concerned about being overweight, both are similar in terms of overall body esteem in childhood. Furthermore, if the boys who worry about being too fat are combined with the boys who worry about not being muscular enough, the percentage of adolescent boys who are body dissatisfied is often comparable to the percentage of dissatisfied girls (Ricciardelli & McCabe, 2007).

Why is body dissatisfaction in younger individuals important? Adolescents with higher levels of body dissatisfaction are at risk for poor self-esteem and depression (e.g., Stice & Bearman, 2001; Wichstrom, 1999). They are more likely to develop eating problems, such as unhealthy weight-control behaviors (e.g., self-induced vomiting, laxative use) in girls and binge eating in boys (Neumark-Sztainer, Paxton, et al., 2006). Even in childhood, girls who are body dissatisfied are more likely to diet, a behavior associated with both eating disorders and obesity (J. Thompson et al., 1999). They are less likely to engage in healthy exercise (e.g., Neumark-Sztainer, Paxton, et al., 2006). Higher body dissatisfaction may also be associated with a poor outcome in the treatment of eating disorders (Gowers & Bryant-Waugh, 2004). Middle and high school-age boys who are concerned about their muscularity are more likely to use food supplements and steroids (Smolak, Murnen, & Thompson, 2005). Thus, body dissatisfaction may create a myriad of problems (see Ricciardelli, McCabe, Mussap, & Holt, chap. 4, this volume; Wertheim, Paxton, & Blaney, chap. 3, this volume). It is particularly troublesome that body dissatisfaction may continue over time. This may be truer of adolescents than of younger children, however, there is some evidence suggesting constancy even in elementary school-age children (Davison, Markey, & Birch, 2003; Paxton, Eisenberg, & Neumark-Sztainer, 2006).

A variety of influences on body image have been identified, including media images and messages, parental and peer modeling and comments, and even toys (Cafri, van den Berg, & Thompson, 2006; Dittmar, Halliwell, & Ive, 2006). Understanding these and other risk factors will help in the prevention (Levine & Smolak, chap. 11, this volume) and treatment of body image problems and will thereby potentially reduce eating disorders, steroid abuse, and obesity in adolescents and adults.

EATING DISORDERS

As noted earlier, eating disturbances occur frequently in childhood and adolescence. Indeed, both AN and BN have peak ages of onset during adolescence (Bryant-Waugh, 2006). It is very difficult to ascertain the incidence and prevalence of eating disorders and other eating problems in children and adolescents (Bryant-Waugh, 2006). However, among those admitted to psychiatric inpatient units, eating disorders may be the most common diagnosis for adolescents and the second most common diagnosis for children of all ages (O'Herlihy et al., 2004). Definitions of AN and BN from the fourth edition, text revision of the *Diagnostic and Statistical Manual of Mental Disorders* (DSM–IV–TR; American Psychiatric Association, 2000) note criteria related to restrictive eating, body image disturbances, menstrual dysfunction, binge eating, and purging activity. However, as Watkins and Lask (chap. 2, this volume) discuss, there are a number of problems with applying these definitions to anyone other than adult women. Thus, one reason for studying eating disorders in childhood and adolescence is to understand the presentation of eating problems during these developmental periods.

There are a variety of differences in the presentation of eating disorders depending on developmental level. For instance, Peebles, Wilson, and Lock (2006) found that children (<13 years old) were more likely to be diagnosed with eating disorder not otherwise specified (EDNOS) than were adolescents. The tendency to diagnose children with EDNOS may be attributable to definitional categories that make it difficult for children to meet all of their criteria or it may represent a true difference in the nature of eating disorders (Bryant-Waugh, 2006; Gowers & Bryant-Waugh, 2004). Children are also less likely than adolescents to be diagnosed with BN and to exhibit bulimic behavior, including binge eating and diet pill or laxative use (Peebles et al., 2006). On the other hand, children showed relatively high levels of anorexic behaviors, including more rapid weight loss as well as a lower weight relative to ideal body weight when compared with adolescents (Peebles et al., 2006). Additionally, AN is more common than BN in prepubertal children, a trend that is the reverse of that in adult women (Bryant-Waugh, 2006).

Because children and adolescents are still developing physically, eating disorders may be particularly dangerous. For example, severe restrictive eating appears to interfere with bones that are actively growing during this time. Active treatment may not prevent this serious problem (Stone et al., 2006). It is possible that neurological development is similarly vulnerable (see Smolak, chap. 7, this volume). Additionally, as Watkins and Lask note (chap. 2, this volume), it is possible that there are serious eating problems that occur in children that are not currently included in any diagnostic scheme. This may well mean that children are not appropriately diagnosed and treated for their eating problems. Failure to diagnose and treat an eating problem early in its development may reduce the child's chances for recovery (American Academy of Pediatrics, 2003). Furthermore, as Sperry and colleagues note (chap. 13, this volume), although there has been significant progress in the evaluation of treatments for eating disorders in adolescents since 2001, there is still little work with children. Additionally, many of the medications commonly used with adults have not been thoroughly evaluated in children.

OBESITY

As Kutchman, Lawhun, Laheta, and Heinberg point out (chap. 8, this volume), childhood obesity is frequently treated as a public health emergency and an epidemic, primarily because of the increase of childhood obesity in recent years. As noted earlier, childhood and adolescent obesity is currently around 17% (Ogden et al., 2006). Overweight is typically defined as between the 85th and 95th body mass index (BMI) percentile using the Centers for Disease Control and Prevention (CDC) growth charts (see Faith, Kerns, & Diewald, chap. 14, this volume, for more information on BMI cutoffs). Among children and adolescents, obesity is defined as BMI at the 95th percentile or higher. Recent research suggests that BMI at the 99th percentile or higher constitutes "extreme obesity" and that 4% of children (2 million) fit this category (Xanthakos & Inge, 2007). Children in ethnic minority groups are particularly at risk. For example, using CDC standards, nearly two thirds of Cree Indian preschoolers in Quebec, Canada, are overweight (Willows, Johnson, & Ball, 2007) and Hispanic preschool children in the United States are more likely to be overweight than White or Black children (Kimbro, Brooks-Gunn, & McLanahan, 2006; Whitaker & Orzol, 2006).

In the obesity literature on adults, there is considerable debate as to the meaning of the "overweight" category (BMI 25–30). Although medical organizations continue to suggest that being overweight is dangerous (Eckel, Kahn, Robertson, & Rizza, 2006), some research indicates that overweight adults appear to actually have lower morbidity rates than thin or average-weight adults (Romero-Corral et al., 2006). However, mortality in nonsmoking adults with a BMI of 30 or more is about 30% higher than in nonsmokers with a BMI of 20; nonsmoking adults with a BMI of 40 or more have mortality rates of approximately 100% higher (Wadden, Brownell, & Foster, 2002).

Just as the meaning of overweight status in adulthood has been debated, the usefulness of weight categories for children has been questioned. Some authors argue that the categories not only have the potential to be stigmatizing, but that they are uninformative and misleading (Berg, 2004). For example, fat is more clearly associated with health problems than weight *per se* is (Berg, 2004). Fully one third of children with a 95th percentile BMI do not have excess adiposity. If one looks at the "at risk" for overweight category (85th–94th percentile) only 13% have excess adiposity (Freedman et al., 2007). When risk factors for cardiovascular disease (e.g., levels of triglycerides, low-density lipoprotein, and high-density lipoprotein cholesterol) were examined, 25% of children (ages 5–17) in the 25th BMI percentile or below had at least one risk factor compared to 51% of those in the 85th to 94th percentile and 70% of those in the 95th percentile. Thus, although there is clearly a relationship between risk and BMI, nearly 50% of individuals "at risk for overweight" had no risk factors, whereas 25% of the thinnest children did (Freedman et al., 2007). Additionally, the CDC standards yield more liberal estimates of overweight and obesity in children when compared with International Obesity Task Force (IOTF) standards (Willows et al., 2007). This also means it is easier for children to become overweight under CDC standards. For example, in a study of Cree Indian children, 4.9% of those who were normal weight at age 3 were categorized as overweight at age 5 using IOTF criteria compared with14.9% when CDC standards were employed (Willows et al., 2007).

However, there is increased risk for cardiovascular problems and adult obesity in CDC-defined overweight children (e.g., Freedman et al., 2007; Nader et al., 2006; D. Thompson et al., 2007). Such risks begin to be evident as early as elementary school (e.g., D. Thompson et al., 2007). Furthermore, when considering the heaviest children, those at or above the 99th percentile in BMI for age and sex, the risk becomes clearer. Fully 92% of children with BMIs of 99th to 99.4 percentiles have excess adiposity as do 98% of those with BMIs in at least the 99.5 percentile. In the Freedman et al. (2007) study, all of the children who were in the 99th percentile became obese adults and 88% of them had early adult BMIs of 35 or greater.

The causes of childhood obesity are multifaceted (see Kutchman, Lawhun, Laheta, & Heinberg, chap. 8, this volume). However, although individual characteristics such as genetics do play a role, it is noteworthy that community characteristics also play a role. For example, living in a community where there are venues for exercise and physical activities, such as gyms, as well as the ability to see people biking or walking within the neighborhood, is associated with a lower BMI in sixth-grade girls (Evenson, Scott, Cohen, & Voorhees, 2007). This suggests that the ecological approach to prevention that is gaining attention in the eating disorders field (e.g., Levine & Smolak, 2006) may also be tenable for the prevention and treatment of obesity. This is an interesting area for future research.

THIS EDITION

The goal of this edition is to provide descriptions of (a) the nature of body image, eating disorders, and obesity among children and adolescents; (b) the likely causes and outcomes of these problems; and (c) treatments and prevention programs for these problems. The chapters in this book are research-oriented, providing empirically based accounts of body image, eating disorders, and obesity in youth. Within this framework, the authors also provide suggestions for the direction and design of future research, along with practical guidelines for assessment, prevention, and treatment.

Foundations

The first section of this book provides basic etiological and descriptive information about body image, eating disorders, and obesity in children and adolescents. In chapter 1, Jennifer Fisher, Meghan Sinton, and Leann Birch provide a developmental approach to the earliest roots of eating problems. They describe experiences in infancy and the preschool years that might lay the foundations for a variety of later eating problems. This will be the first exposure to this literature for many readers. It is an exciting chapter because of the possibilities it raises for parental education and early prevention efforts.

Beth Watkins and Bryan Lask (chap. 2) discuss the intricacies of defining eating disorders in children. They describe the difficulties inherent in this process given the *DSM–IV–TR* criteria. They also use the Great Ormand Street criteria to articulate eating disorders that might be exclusive to children. Determining definitions of disorders is crucial for effective treatment as well as for the willingness of insurance companies to reimburse for treatment.

Two chapters describing body image problems in children and adolescents follow. In the first edition of this book, both genders were addressed in the same chapter. However, the growth in attention to the body image concerns of boys necessitates separate chapters for body image issues in this edition. In chapter 3, Eleanor Wertheim, Susan Paxton, and Simone Blaney provide the chapter concerning girls; whereas in chapter 4, Lina Ricciardelli, Marita McCabe, Alexander Mussap, and Kate Holt discuss boys. The differences in body image concerns for boys and girls might be viewed as underscoring the role of gender and other sociocultural factors in defining ideal body types. There has been enormous growth in the literature concerning gendered-body image; these chapters not only capture these advances but also highlight new directions for research in these areas.

The next two chapters further emphasize the role of societal demands and definitions in not only body image but also in eating disorders and obesity. Debra Franko and Jessica Edwards George (chap. 5) describe minority group differences among U.S. children and adolescents in these phenomena. Again, awareness of such differences is crucial in developing effective treatment and prevention programs. In chapter 6, Eileen Anderson-Fye provides an informative cross-cultural look at these issues. This topic is a new addition to the second edition, reflecting the growth of cross-cultural data.

This section ends with a consideration of the risk and protective factors involved in the etiology of body image, eating disorders, and obesity in children and adolescents. Some of these issues were touched on in the earlier chapters. Chapter 7 by Linda Smolak provides additional information about risk and protection for body image and eating problems. Eve Kutchman, Sarah Lawhun, Jenn Laheta, and Leslie Heinberg (chap. 8) report up-to-date information about risk and protective factors for the development of obesity. These chapters provide valuable leads for potential sites of intervention in both treatment and prevention.

Assessment, Prevention, and Treatment

With the descriptions and etiological roots of children's body image, eating disorders, and obesity in place, the contributions move on to more specialized topics. We begin with two chapters describing assessment. Assessment of childhood and adolescent body image and eating disorders presents a variety of challenges, not the least of which are the developmental changes in cognition and self. In chapter 9, Tovah Yanover and J. Kevin Thompson provide descriptions of available body image assessment tools. Drew Anderson, Jason Lavender, Suzanne Milnes, and Angela Simmons (chap. 10) do the same for eating disorders instruments. Both chapters provide essential information for clinicians and for researchers attempting to develop new measures.

We have mentioned several times that the diagnostic and etiological information provided in the foundational chapters is essential to the development of effective prevention programs. Prevention programs may well provide the best hope for addressing the health threats posed by body image, eating, and obesity-related problems. In chapter 11, Michael Levine and Linda Smolak describe recent programs for the prevention of body image and eating problems. Katherine Bauer, Jess Haines, and Dianne Neumark-Sztainer follow in chapter 12, with a discussion on the efforts to prevent obesity among children and adolescents. Both chapters discuss the important movement to coordinate eating disorders and obesity prevention.

Prevention is not always available or effective and so treatment becomes a necessity. Research concerning the treatment of eating-disordered children and adolescents is severely limited. Steffanie Sperry, Megan Roehrig, and J. Kevin Thompson (chap. 13) provide a description of the available treatments for eating disorders in childhood and adolescence as well as of some of the special problems faced by treatment providers. In chapter 14, Myles Faith, Julia Kerns, and Lisa Diewald describe treating the difficult, but not intransigent, problem of childhood obesity.

Finally, David Sarwer, Alison Infield, and Canice Crerand (chap. 15) discuss the research on the often controversial topic of plastic surgery for adolescents. Again, extant literature is limited and Sarwer and his colleagues describe not only what is known but what needs to be learned.

It is evident that reducing eating disorders and obesity in adulthood requires a thorough understanding of the nature, etiology, treatment, and prevention of these problems in childhood and adolescence. It is also essential that we find ways to reduce the suffering of children and adolescents facing eating disorders and obesity. We hope that this edition will be helpful in generating the research that will lead to solutions to these pressing problems.

REFERENCES

American Academy of Pediatrics. (2003). Policy statement: Identifying and treating eating disorders. *Pediatrics, 111,* 204–211.

American Psychiatric Association. (2000). *Diagnostic and statistical manual of mental disorders* (4th ed., text rev.). Washington, DC: Author

Baird, J., Fisher, D., Lucas, P., Kleijnen, J., Roberts, H., & Law, C. (2005). Being big or growing fast: Systematic review of size and growth in infancy and later obesity. *BMJ* 331:929, doi:10.1136/bmj.38586.411273.E0.

Barlow, S. E., & Expert Committee. (2007). Expert committee recommendations regarding the prevention, assessment, and treatment of child and adolescent overweight and obesity: Summary report. *Pediatrics, 120,* S164–S192.

Berg, F. (2004). *Underage and overweight: America's childhood obesity crisis—What every family needs to know.* New York: Hatherleigh Press.

Bryant-Waugh, R. (2006). Eating disorders in children and adolescents. In S. Wonderlich, J. Mitchell, M. de Zwaan, & H. Steiger (Eds.), *Annual review of eating disorders, Part 2—2006* (pp. 131–144). Oxford, England: Radcliffe.

Cafri, G., van den Berg, P., & Thompson, J. K. (2006). Pursuit of muscularity in adolescent boys: Relations among biopsychosocial variables and clinical outcomes. *Journal of Clinical Child and Adolescent Psychology, 353,* 283–291.

Davis, M. M., Gance-Cleveland, B., Hassink, S., Johnson, R., Paradis, G., & Resnicow, D. (2007). Recommendations for prevention of childhood obesity. *Pediatrics, 120,* S229–S253.

Davison, K. K., Markey, C. N., & Birch, L. L. (2003). A longitudinal examination of patterns in girls' weight concerns and body dissatisfaction from ages 5 to 9 years. *International Journal of Eating Disorders, 33,* 320–332.

Dittmar, H., Halliwell, E., & Ive, S. (2006). Does Barbie make girls want to be thin? The effect of experimental exposure to images of dolls on the body image of 5–8-year-old girls. *Developmental Psychology, 42,* 283–292.

Eckel, R., Kahn, R., Robertson, R. M., & Rizza, R. (2006). Preventing cardiovascular disease and diabetes: A call to action from the American Diabetes Association and the American Heart Association. *Circulation, 113*, 2943–2946.

Evenson, K., Scott, M., Cohen, D., & Voorhees, C. (2007). Girls' perception of neighborhood factors on physical activity, sedentary behavior, and BMI. *Obesity, 15*, 430–445.

Field, A. E., Aneja, P., Austin, S. B., Shrier, L., de Moor, C., & Gordon-Larsen, P. (2007). Race and gender differences in the association of dieting and gains in BMI among young adults. *Obesity, 15*, 456–464.

Freedman, D. S., Mei, Z., Srinivasan, S., Berenson, G., & Dietz, W. (2007). Cardiovascular risk factors and excess adiposity among overweight children and adolescents: The Bogalusa Heart Study. *Journal of Pediatrics, 150*, 12–17.

Gowers, S., & Bryant-Waugh, R. (2004). Management of child and adolescent eating disorders: The current evidence base and future directions. *Journal of Child Psychology and Psychiatry, 45*, 63–83.

Irving, L. M., & Neumark-Sztainer, D. (2002). Integrating primary prevention of eating disorders and obesity: Feasible or futile? *Preventive Medicine, 34(3)*, 299–309.

Kimbro, R., Brooks-Gunn, J., & McLanahan, S. (2006). Racial and ethnic differentials in overweight and obesity among 3-year-old children. *American Journal of Public Health, 97(2)*, 298–305.

Levine, M. P., & Smolak, L. (2006). *The prevention of eating problems and eating disorders: Theory, research, and practice.* Mahwah, NJ: Erlbaum.

Nader, P. R., O'Brien, M., Houts, R., Bradley, R., Belsky, J., Crosnoe, R., et al. (2006). Identifying risk for obesity in early childhood. *Pediatrics, 118*, e594–e601.

Neumark-Sztainer, D., Paxton, S., Hannan, P. J., Haines, J., & Story, M. (2006). Does body satisfaction matter: Five-year longitudinal associations between body satisfaction and health behaviors in adolescent females and males. *Journal of Adolescent Health, 39*, 244–251.

Neumark-Sztainer, D., Wall, M., Guo, J., Story, M., Haines, J., & Eisenberg, M. (2006). Obesity, disordered eating, and eating disorders in a longitudinal study of adolescents: How do dieters fare five years later? *Journal of the American Dietetic Association, 106*, 559–568.

O'Herlihy, A., Worrall, A., Lelliott, P., Jaffa, T., Mears, A., Banerjee, S., & Hill, P. (2004). Characteristis of the residents of in-patient child and adolescent mental health services in England and Wales. *Clinical Child Psychology and Psychiatry, 9*, 579–588.

Ogden, C. L., Carroll, M. D., Curtin, L. R., McDowell, M. A., Tabak, C. J., & Flegal, K. M. (2006). Prevalence of overweight ad obesity in the United States, 1999-2004. *JAMA, 295*, 1549–1555.

Paxton, S. J., Eisenberg, M. E., & Neumark-Sztainer, D. (2006). Prospective predictors of body dissatisfaction in adolescent girls and boys: A five-year longitudinal study. *Developmental Psychology, 42*, 888–899.

Peebles, R., Wilson, J. L., & Lock, J. D. (2006). How do children with eating disorders differ from adolescents with eating disorders at initial evaluation? *Journal of Adolescent Health, 39*, 800–805.

Puhl, R., & Latner, J. D. (2007). Stigma, obesity and the health of the nation's children. *Psychological Bulletin, 133*, 557–580.

Ricciardelli, L. A., & McCabe, M. P. (2007). Pursuit of muscularity among adolescents. In J. K. Thompson & G. Cafri (Eds.), *The muscular ideal: Psychological, social, and medical perspectives* (pp. 199–216). Washington, DC: American Psychological Association.

Romero-Corral, A., Montori, V. M., Somers, V. K., Korinek, J., Thomas, R. J., Allison, T. G., et al. (2006). Association of bodyweight with total mortality and with cardiovascular events in coronary artery disease: A systematic review of cohort studies. *The Lancet, 368,* 666–678.

Smolak, L. (2004). Body image in children and adolescents: Where do we go from here? *Body Image, 1,* 15–28.

Smolak, L., Levine, M. P., & Schermer, F. (1998). Lessons from lessons: An evaluation of an elementary school program. In G. Noordenbos & W. Vandereycken (Eds.), *The prevention of eating disorders* (pp. 137–172). London: Athlone Press.

Smolak, L., Murnen, S. K., & Thompson, J. K. (2005). Sociocultural influences and muscle building in adolescent boys. *Psychology of Men and Masculinity, 6,* 223–239.

Spear, B. A., Barlow, S. E., Ervin, C., Ludwig, D. S., Saelens, B. E., Schetzina, K. E., & Taveras, E. M. (2007). Recommendations for treatment of child and adolescent overweight and obesity. *Pediatrics, 120,* S254–S288.

Stice, E. (2002). Risk and maintenance factors for eating pathology: A meta-analytic review. *Psychological Bulletin, 128,* 825–848.

Stice, E., & Bearman, S. K. (2001). Body-image and eating disturbances prospectively predict increases in depressive symptoms in adolescent girls: A growth curve analysis. *Developmental Psychology, 37,* 597–607.

Stice, E., Presnell, K., Shaw, H., & Rohde, P. (2005). Psychological and behavioral risk factors for obesity onset in adolescent girls: A prospective study. *Journal of Counseling and Clinical Psychology, 73,* 195–202.

Stone, M., Brody, J., Kohn, M., Clarke, S., Madden, S., & Cowell, C. (2006). Bone changes in adolescent girls with anorexia nervosa. *Journal of Adolescent Health, 39,* 835–841.

Thompson, D., Obarzanek, E., Franko, D. L., Barton, B. A., Morrison, J., Biro, F., et al. (2007). Child overweight and cardiovascular disease risk factors: The National Heart, Lung, and Blood Institute Growth and Health Study. *The Journal of Pediatrics, 150,* 18–25.

Thompson, J. K., & Cafri, G. (Eds.). (2007). *The muscular ideal: Psychological, social, and medical perspectives.* Washington, DC: American Psychological Association.

Thompson, J. K., Heinberg, L. J., Altabe, M. N., & Tantleff-Dunn, S. (1999). *Exacting beauty: Theory, assessment, and treatment of body image disturbance.* Washington, DC: American Psychological Association.

Thompson, J. K., & Smolak, L. (2001). Body image, eating disorders, and obesity in youth—The future is now. In J. K. Thompson & L. Smolak (Eds.), *Body image, eating disorders, and obesity in children: Theory, assessment, treatment, and prevention* (pp. 1–18). Washington, DC: American Psychological Association.

Wadden, T., Brownell, K. D., & Foster, G. D. (2002). Obesity: Responding to the global epidemic. *Journal of Consulting and Clinical Psychology, 70,* 510–525.

Whitaker, R. C., & Orzol, S. M. (2006). Obesity among US urban preschool children: Relationships to race, ethnicity, and socioeconomic status. *Archives of Pediatric and Adolescent Medicine, 160*, 578–584.

Wichstrom, L. (1999). The emergence of gender differences in depressed model during adolescence. *Developmental Psychology, 35*, 232–245.

Willows, N., Johnson, M., & Ball, G. (2007). Prevalence estimates of overweight and obesity in Cree preschool children in Northern Quebec according to international and US reference criteria. *American Journal of Public Health, 97*, 311–316.

Xanthakos, S. A., & Inge, T. H. (2007). Extreme pediatric obesity: Weighing the health dangers. *Journal of Pediatrics, 150*, 3–5.

II

FOUNDATIONS

1

EARLY PARENTAL INFLUENCE AND RISK FOR THE EMERGENCE OF DISORDERED EATING

JENNIFER O. FISHER, MEGHAN M. SINTON, AND LEANN L. BIRCH

Influences within the family environment have a profound effect on the development of eating patterns needed to sustain healthy development in infants and children. Early familial influences provide a basis for emerging individual differences among children concerning food selection and food-intake patterns. Parents play a pivotal role in providing early dietary experiences, including the modeling and reinforcing of eating behaviors and attitudes, and in shaping the contexts in which eating occurs. It is through such parental influence that, in conjunction with infant and child characteristics, disordered eating may emerge.

In this chapter, we examine the familial factors influencing the development of food preferences, food selection, and the regulation of food intake from infancy (birth–2 years) through early childhood (ages 2–5). We also examine early indicators of, and parental influence on, disordered eating during early (ages 2–5) and middle (ages 5–9) childhood.

Role of Maternal Diet in Taste and Flavor Experiences in Utero

The transition to solid foods, or perhaps an infant's experience with being breast- or formula-fed, is often considered an individual's earliest dietary experience. However, the first dietary experiences, in fact, appear to occur before birth. Amniotic fluid surrounds the fetus to maintain fetal temperature, to serve as a buffer and as a vehicle for fetal movement. With the emergence of swallowing and taste mechanisms between gestation Weeks 12 and 14, the amniotic fluid also becomes a rich source of sensory exposure for the fetus (Liley, 1972). Mennella, Johnson, and Beauchamp (1995) found that the odor of garlic was detected in the amniotic fluid of four out of five women who consumed capsules containing garlic oil shortly before undergoing a routine amniocentesis. Although these "transmittable" flavors of the maternal diet are not well characterized, this evidence suggests that experience with dietary flavors begins as the fetus is exposed to tastes and flavors of the maternal diet *in utero*. Mennella and colleagues (Liem & Mennella, 2002; Mennella & Beauchamp, 2002; Mennella, Jagnow, & Beauchamp, 2001) controlled mothers' intake of carrots so that the vegetables were consumed during the last trimester of pregnancy, during the first weeks of breastfeeding, or not at all during either period. Mothers who consumed carrots during pregnancy or lactation had infants who responded more positively when carrots were introduced to the diet than did infants whose mothers had not consumed carrots during pregnancy or lactation. Thus, early flavor experience of the fetus and the infant appears to have lasting effects on preferences into childhood (Liem & Mennella, 2002; Mennella & Beauchamp, 2002).

Influence of Breast Milk and Formula

The choice to breast- or formula-feed may initiate very different trajectories with respect to emerging flavor preferences and regulation of energy intake. As indicated earlier, maternal dietary intake appears to impact flavors in breast milk. Work from Mennella and Beauchamp indicates that flavors such as garlic, vanilla, and alcohol can be detected in breast milk (Mennella & Beauchamp, 1991a, 1993). These findings indicate that the earliest infant diet, consisting solely of human breast milk, does provide the infant with varied flavor experience. In contrast, the flavor experiences of the formula-fed infant may be much more constant and less varied.

In addition to its influence on flavor experience and food acceptance, breast- versus bottlefeeding also provides distinctly different experiences with respect to the balance of control in feeding in the mother–infant dyad

(Taveras et al., 2004). As the breastfeeding mother does not have visual cues regarding the volume of any given feed, she may be much more dependent on and responsive to cues from the infant to initiate or terminate feeding (e.g., when the infant's sucking rate slows or stops). This is consistent with the finding that the volume of feeding in the breastfed infant is not constrained by milk availability (Dewey, Heinig, Nommsen, & Lonnerdal, 1991). In contrast, bottlefeeding provides the mother with relatively more information about the infant's intake. As a natural consequence, mothers who choose to bottlefeed may assume a more active role in determining when feeding begins and ends, as well as how much the infant consumes at each meal. Indeed, observations of mother–infant pairs at 1 week, 1 month, and 2 months of age revealed that mothers who bottlefed initiated a greater number of feeding starts and stops than mothers of breastfed infants (Wright, Fawcett, & Crow, 1980).

These differences between formula- and breastfed infants may be responsible for the protective effects of breastfeeding for obesity. Most recent epidemiological studies report a modest protective effect of breastfeeding on risk for obesity in children and adolescents (Arenz & von Kries, 2005; Elliott, Kjolhede, Gournis, & Rasmussen, 1997; Gillman et al., 2001), although other studies report null or short-term findings (Hediger, Overpeck, Kuczmarski, & Ruan, 2001; Michels et al., 2007). As breastfeeding may be a proxy for additional sociocultural and/or demographic factors that are associated with risk for overweight, Gillman and colleagues (2006) used a within-family approach to adjust for potential sociocultural factors, including maternal overweight, and, even when controlling for these additional factors, results continued to provide support for the hypothesis that breastfeeding is protective against overweight. Clearly, continued examination of the complex association between breastfeeding and risk for overweight, as well as the duration of this protection, is needed. Furthermore, there is little research examining whether such differences in early feeding experience might also alter risk for disordered eating.

Food Acceptance Patterns During the Transition to Solid Foods

The American Academy of Pediatrics recommends that solid foods be introduced when infants are between 4 and 6 months old, and although there is variability in the timing, introduction to the semisolid foods generally begins on average in the United States when infants are about 4 months old. Infants are born with a preference for sweet and a rejection of sour and bitter. A preference for the taste of salt is absent at birth but is present by about 4 months (Bartoshuk & Beauchamp, 1994). These taste preferences are unlearned, and have powerful effects on infants' reactions to their first solid foods. In general, sweet foods, such as juices or flavored yogurts, are more easily accepted relative to those containing bitter taste constituents.

Taste acceptance, however, may not readily translate into food acceptance; infants and young children tend to initially reject new foods. This "neo-phobic" response is thought to originate from learned safety behavior, where a tentative approach to new foods serves an adaptive role to guard against poisoning. Work by Kalat and Rozin (1973) indicates that the initial neo-phobia is reduced and the food is accepted as safe when repeated opportunities to consume a new food are not followed by illness. The powerful role of experience in food acceptance is underscored by the fact that repeated exposure even facilitates acceptance of foods containing disliked tastes. For example, Mennella and Beauchamp (1996a) observed that infants who were exposed to the bitter components of protein hydrolysate-based formulas were more likely to accept that type of formula at later points in infancy than were those infants who had not been exposed to the taste.

Thus, early repeated experience with flavors may play an important role in food acceptance during the transition to solid foods by modifying infants' response to novel foods. Exposing infants to a new food increases their acceptance of a similar food (Birch, Gunder, Grimm-Thomas, & Laing, 1998; Cooke, 2007; Maier, Chabanet, Schaal, Issanchou, & Leathwood, 2007; Sullivan & Birch, 1994). Maier et al. (2007) found that repeated exposure of infants to an initially disliked vegetable puree was associated with long-lasting acceptance and liking of the food. Similarly, Sullivan and Birch (1994) found acceptance of foods by 6-month-olds was enhanced by repeatedly providing those foods. This effect was most notable for breastfed infants, indicating that repeated exposure to flavors of the maternal diet may facilitate food acceptance by providing the infant with varied flavor experiences. To the extent that breastfed infants more readily accept solid foods, less maternal control and encouragement may be required to facilitate toddlers' consumption of new foods during this period. Additionally, infants who more readily accept new foods may be considered "easier" to feed, and elicit less maternal frustration and concern regarding feeding. Mothers who report concerns that the child eats few foods, is a picky eater, or doesn't eat enough are more likely to pressure the child to eat. Unfortunately, as described in a subsequent section, pressuring children to eat tends to have negative consequences, opposite to what is intended; pressuring children to eat tends to foster food dislikes and lower intakes of the foods children are pressured to eat (Birch, McPhee, Shoba, Steinberg, & Krehbiel, 1987; Galloway, Fiorito, Francis, & Birch, 2006).

EARLY CHILDHOOD

As they make the transition to the adult diet of their culture, children are exposed to vast amounts of information regarding the meaning of food and eating. Although young children consume approximately 30% of their energy intake from snacks (Stanek, Abbott, & Cramer, 1990), an increasing percentage of eating takes place in more structured settings that influence children's eating patterns and attitudes. In these contexts, children learn where eating is acceptable—whether eating always takes place at a family table, or may occur in other settings such as in front of a television, in one's room, or at the grocery store. Children also learn about the times of day when eating is appropriate, such as when dinner is eaten each night and whether eating a snack before bed is allowed. Information regarding the structure of eating occasions is also imparted and reinforced with the repeated experience of eating meals. Children learn manners and adopt cuisine rules regarding how foods are eaten—whether with a spoon or with their hands—and at what type of eating occasions those foods are consumed. For instance, children tend to prefer particular foods at the times of day when it is considered appropriate to eat those foods (Birch, Billman, & Richards, 1984). Children also learn these food rules change in different environments, such as at a daycare setting, or at a friend's house.

For most children, eating alone is much more novel than eating among other children and family members; children's food preferences and eating patterns develop in social environments. By eating with others, children come to learn which people are usually present at meals and how those individuals act and interact at meals. The impact of social influences on the development of children's food acceptance patterns is illustrated in work showing age-related changes in children's ideas about what foods are appropriate and inappropriate to eat. Rozin, Hammer, Oster, Horowitz, and Marmara (1986) found that older children were much less likely to consume culturally unacceptable combinations of foods, such as cookies with catsup, than their younger counterparts. Additionally, older children found nonfood substances, such as grasshoppers and dirt, less acceptable than younger children. Such findings suggest, given older children's greater exposure to and experience with eating behaviors with other adults and peers in social settings, along with increases in social referencing behaviors as children age, that social experiences influence ideas about what foods are acceptable to eat.

Social influences may modify children's food acceptance patterns via observational learning as well as through the direct interaction that social experiences provide. Addessi, Galloway, Visalberghi, and Birch (2005) found young children were more likely to accept and eat a novel food when an adult was present and eating the same food than when an adult was either present but not eating or present but eating a different food. Parents in particular make salient role models for the development of healthy eating patterns and acceptance of food in children. Work from Galloway, Fiorito, Lee, and Birch (2005), in which mothers who consumed more fruits and vegetables had daughters who ate more fruits and vegetables and were less likely to be picky eaters, specifically highlights the importance of maternal eating behavior on the development of healthy eating patterns and acceptance of foods in young girls. Parents and caregivers may serve as especially salient eating models because of their direct authority over the foods that come into the home, as well as many of the feeding decisions that affect the child. Children may also draw from the eating behavior of their siblings and peers as play behavior emerges and opportunities to eat with playmates and with peer groups in daycare settings increase. Birch (1980) found that exposing children to a peer group where members displayed a preference for a "disliked" vegetable facilitated their selection of the disliked vegetable. Similarly, Hendy and Raudenbush (2000) found peers to reduce the influence of teachers on preschool children's acceptance of new foods.

Parent–Child Balance in the Control of Eating

At the same time that children learn about eating by observing the behavior of others, changes begin to occur in the dynamics of their social interactions surrounding eating. It is in these early social interactions that one can see the beginnings of patterns that may either promote or protect children from elevated risk of the possible development of disordered eating. In particular, children become more independent and strive for greater autonomy and control over their eating. The developing ability to verbally articulate needs and wants about eating facilitates children's participation in eating decisions and children are increasingly able to express their views on food and eating. Although these changes reflect a growing self-sufficiency on the part of the child, the feeding interactions brought about with this stage of development do not necessarily make child feeding easier for parent or child.

The balance of parent–child control in feeding appears to have a formative influence on children's eating; the ability to self-regulate eating is determined, in part, by the extent to which parents provide structure in eating while also allowing the child a degree of autonomy in eating. At any point in development, large differences may exist among parents in the extent to which they allow the child to control eating, including the timing of meals, as well as what and how much is eaten. Costanzo and Woody (1985) contended that excessive control is imposed in feeding when that area of child behavior is important to the parent or is problematic for either parent or child. For example, societal values about thinness in females may cause parents of young girls to be particularly aware of what their own eating as well as that of their daughter means for the child's "risk" for developing eating and/or weight problems (Costanzo & Woody, 1984). As a consequence, parental influence in their daughters' eating may be especially heightened when parents perceive "risk." This perspective is supported by empirical work indicating that mothers' own restrained eating and their preschool-age daughters' overweight is positively associated with greater maternal control in feeding (Birch & Fisher, 2000; Francis, Hofer, & Birch, 2001).

Differences among parents in control of child feeding have important implications for the development of children's food preferences, selection, and intake regulation. For instance, young children possess the ability to adequately self-regulate energy intakes within a meal (Birch & Deysher, 1985, 1986) and over the course of the day (Birch, Johnson, Jones, & Peters, 1993; Shea, Stein, Basch, Contento, & Zybert, 1992), such that providing opportunities for children to control how much they eat can moderate the effects of large portion sizes on children's energy intake (Fisher, Rolls, & Birch, 2003). However, large individual differences in children's ability to regulate energy intake are apparent by the preschool period. These differences among children are traceable, in part, to differences among their parents in the amount of control imposed in child feeding. Johnson and Birch (1994) found that high levels of parental control in the feeding process were negatively associated with children's ability to regulate energy intake. These findings are consistent with the perspective that increasing amounts of parental control in feeding decrease children's opportunities to exercise and develop self-control in eating (Costanzo & Woody, 1985).

Consequences of Excessive Parental Control

Survey data indicate that parents often have good reason to exert control over their children's eating behavior; most children aged 2 to 19 fail to meet all guidelines specified by the food guide pyramid and have diets containing too much fat and sugar, with too many low nutrient-dense foods in particular (Kant, 2003), and too few fruits and vegetables (Krebs-Smith et al., 1996; Munoz, Krebs-Smith, Ballard-Barbash, & Cleveland, 1997). Among girls, diet quality declines over time (Mannino, Lee, Mitchell, Smiciklas-Wright, & Birch, 2004). Parental attempts to increase children's intake of nutrient-rich foods, such as fruits and vegetables, may be aimed at ensuring adequate nutrition to promote growth and well-being. Conversely, feeding practices that restrict children's intake of foods high in fat and sugar may occur in response to parental awareness of the health risks associated with overweight and early dieting behavior in children, both of which may exacerbate risk for continued overweight and/or disordered eating over time. Although both restricting access to unhealthy foods and encouraging intake of healthy ones may seem to be effective approaches to creating healthful eating patterns, excessive pressure and restriction in child feeding may have unintended negative effects on children's eating.

Restricting children's access to foods appears to paradoxically turn those foods into "forbidden fruits" in children's eating. Children's preferences are enhanced for foods that are offered as a reward for the completion of another task (Birch, Zimmerman, & Hind, 1980; Lepper, Sagotsky, Dafoe,

& Greene, 1982). Additionally, placing a preferred food in sight, but out of reach, decreases children's capacity to exercise self-control over obtaining that food (Mischel, Shoda, & Rodriguez, 1989). Although children's intake of restricted foods is limited while parental restriction is imposed, work by Fisher and Birch (1999a, 1999b) indicates that restriction may cause preschool-age children to have difficulty controlling their eating when restriction is not in effect and forbidden foods are present. Mothers' reports of restricting their preschool-age daughter's access to palatable snack foods were positively associated with daughters' intakes when given free access to those foods immediately after a meal (Fisher & Birch, 1999a). In experimental research, Fisher and Birch (1999b) reported that restricting children's access to a snack food increased their subsequent behavioral response to that food and promoted selection and intake.

Longitudinal data suggest enduring effects of early maternal restriction on daughter's risk for overeating and overweight. Faith et al. (2004) observed greater body mass index (BMI) scores at age 7 for those children whose parents had reported greater levels of restrictive feeding at age 5. Fisher and Birch (2002) found maternal restriction of daughter's intake at age 5 to predict daughter's eating during a free access procedure at age 7, even when controlling for girls' baseline (age 5) free access eating scores and BMI. Birch, Fisher, and Davison (2003) reported that greater maternal restriction of daughter's intake at age 5 continued to predict greater intake of food during a free access procedure when girls were age 9; these effects were most pronounced for girls initially classified as overweight at age 5. These studies indicate that restriction may diminish children's ability to self-control food intake if their own hunger and satiety cues take a secondary role to the availability of palatable, forbidden foods. Restriction of child intake then becomes a part of a cycle in which maternal feeding practices and daughters' (over)eating behaviors reinforce one another, leading to greater weight gain and higher restriction over time (Fisher & Birch, 2002). Finally, in addition to influencing overeating in children, parental control over a child's eating may also influence dietary restraint (Edmunds & Hill, 1999). Although some level of dietary restraint and dieting may be desirable in light of the rising rates of overweight among youth, self-initiated restraint or dieting appears to increase, as opposed to decrease, risk for weight gain and overweight in children and adolescents (Field et al., 2003; Goldschmidt, Aspen, Sinton, Tanofsky-Kraff & Wilfley, 2008; Tanofsky-Kraff et al., 2006). These complex associations among parental feeding practices, early emergence of problems in child intake and energy balance, and risk for overweight require further attention.

Finally, restriction of intake may result in children's concerns about consuming certain foods as well as negative self-evaluation. Work by Klesges, Stein, Eck, Isbell, and Klesges (1991) illustrates that even young children understand parental expectations for the limited consumption of certain foods; young children decreased food choices that were high in sugar when told that their mothers would be evaluating their food selections. Fisher and Birch (2000) found that parental restriction predicted how daughters felt about their eating; high that levels of restriction were associated with daughters' perceptions of eating too much, and feeling bad about it. Furthermore, restriction may cause children to equate their consumption of a forbidden or "bad-for-you" food with bad behavior (Fisher & Birch, 2000), leading to unhealthy attitudes toward eating and posing the risk that self-evaluation will become associated with eating and food. Thus, restricting children's access to foods may create an eating environment in which children are overtly focused on the restricted foods and their responses to restriction.

In contrast to the effects of restriction on children's eating, less is known about how parental pressure on children to eat may modify children's eating behavior. Available data indicate that pressure in feeding may ultimately discourage children's intake of "encouraged" foods. Children's preferences are decreased for foods that are used instrumentally (Birch, Marlin, & Rotter, 1984). Thus, pressuring children to eat their vegetables before they can leave the table or have dessert may serve to only decrease children's liking of those vegetables. In support of this, a recent experimental study found that children consumed less food and made more negative comments about the food when they were pressured to eat, in contrast with children who were not pressured to eat (Galloway et al., 2006). Other research suggests that parental pressure may reduce children's responsiveness to internal cues of hunger and satiety. Birch and colleagues (1987) demonstrated that children's ability to respond to the energy density of the foods they consume was diminished by adult directives to "clean their plates." Finally, recent work shows a negative association between parental pressure to eat and daughters' calcium (Birch, Fisher, Smiciklas-Wright, & Mitchell, 1999) and fruit and vegetable intake (Galloway et al., 2005). These studies, then, indicate that parental pressure to eat is associated with decreased intake of healthy foods that can foster healthy growth and development.

Intergenerational Transfer of Eating Attitudes and Behaviors

Parental influences on children's eating may not only affect their eating experience and development, but may also promote intergenerational transfer of eating behavior. Food selection and/or change in eating behaviors are influenced through experiences with different family members (Bove, Sobal, & Rauschenbach, 2003; Furst, Connors, Bisogni, Sobal, & Falk, 1996; Schafer, Schafer, Dunbar, & Keith, 1999) and children's nutrient intakes reflect the diets of their parents (da Veiga & Sichieri, 2006; Oliveria et al., 1992). Parents have the potential to shape these similarities by making the foods they consume available to their children, by serving as influential eating models, and by exerting control in child feeding. Studies examining multiple avenues of parental influence are needed to shed light on how eating behavior is transferred from one generation to the next.

Work from our laboratory indicates that parent–child similarities in problematic regulation of intake are present at an early point in development and particularly apparent for mothers and daughters. A study by Cutting, Fisher, Grimm-Thomas, and Birch (1999) provides evidence that mothers' influence on their preschool-age daughters' eating behavior may also convey information about how food intake is regulated. In that study, mothers' reports of their own disinhibited eating were positively associated with their preschool-age daughters' intake of foods eaten beyond fullness. In this procedure, daughters were given free access to a variety of energy-dense snack foods immediately after having eaten lunch. Intake by the daughters in this setting bore a resemblance to their mothers' reports of disinhibited eating: an enhanced responsiveness to external cues in eating.

Information about eating that is transferred from mother to child appears to extend well beyond that of what and how much is eaten. For example, two studies have observed similarities in mother–daughter levels of dietary restraint (Hill, Weaver, & Blundell, 1990; Ruther & Richman, 1993). These associations appear to emerge during middle childhood. Five-year-old daughters of mothers who engaged in unhealthy dieting behaviors were observed to have more weight concerns and were twice as likely to possess awareness of and knowledge about dieting than peers whose mothers had healthy diet behaviors (Abramovitz & Birch, 2000). The association between maternal restriction and the emergence of dieting in girls may also reflect maternal concern about, investment in, and reaction to daughter's overweight so that girls' weight status moderates the influence of maternal restriction on daughter's dieting behaviors (Francis et al., 2001; Sinton & Birch, 2005). These findings suggest that mothers shape their daughters' orientation to weight issues as well to the dieting "tools" used to act on those concerns.

The importance of maternal eating behaviors when considering children's disordered eating is further highlighted by several recent studies. Tiggemann and Lowes (2002) found a positive association between maternal dietary restraint and monitoring of daughter's intake. Similarly, Francis and Birch (2005) found mothers' preoccupation with weight and eating to be associated with attempts to restrict their daughters intake and to encourage their daughters weight loss. Greater restriction and encouragement of weight loss were then associated with greater dietary restraint in girls. Regarding the effect of maternal characteristics on the emergence of disordered eating in early childhood, longitudinal work from Stice, Agras, and Hammer (1999) indicated an effect for several maternal characteristics and behaviors, including body dissatisfaction, dieting, and bulimic symptoms, on young children's eating disturbances during the first 5 years of life.

Modeling and parenting influences on children's eating and weight problems may be particularly pronounced when energy-dense foods are involved. For example, parents who enjoy desserts high in fat may tend to keep these types of foods in the home thus their children observe their parents eating these foods. Children may come to believe that high-fat desserts constitute a focal part of the family dinner or of family time together, such as watching movies or playing board games. Additionally, children may observe that parents not only express liking for high-fat desserts, but may preferentially consume these foods. Because children readily form preferences for energy-dense foods (Johnson, McPhee, & Birch, 1991; Kern, McPhee, Fisher, Johnson, & Birch, 1993), repeated opportunities to consume high-fat dessert foods may enhance the effects of this particular parental modeling on children's intake of desserts high in fat. Research is needed to understand how the "family" diet interacts with parental eating behavior and feeding practices to shape eating and weight problems in children. Finally, during middle childhood, the characteristics of girls, especially their own weight status, weight concern, and self-evaluations, can also influence the developing control of food intake and may place girls at risk for disordered eating. Two recent studies highlight the effects of childhood overweight on the emergence of dieting (Sinton & Birch, 2005) and dietary restraint, disinhibited eating, and weight concerns (Shunk & Birch, 2004) in preadolescent girls. Sinton and Birch (2005) found the weight status of 5-year-old girls to independently and in interactions with their depression and self-concept predict dieting scores at age 9; these findings converge with earlier work indicating that overweight in girls is associated with negative self-evaluation and risk for disordered eating (Burrows & Cooper, 2002). Shunk and Birch (2004) noted that girls at risk for overweight at age 5 had greater dietary restraint, disinhibited eating, and concern about weight and body shape at age 9. Finally, recent work revealed that girls' weight status, weight concern, and negative affect at age 9 were associated with girls' self-reported dietary restraint, binge eating, emotional eating, and weight and appearance-related body dissatisfaction at ages 11 and 13. Taken together, findings suggest that individual characteristics in middle childhood do convey risk for several disordered eating behaviors during early adolescence (Sinton, 2006).

Because thinness and restrained eating are particularly valued in females, parents may perceive greater risk for their daughters than for their sons. It is clear that girls observe and emulate their mothers' eating and dieting behaviors, and that maternal dietary restraint and dieting history predicts their young daughters' knowledge about the links between dieting and weight control, why people diet, and what behaviors are associated with weight control. Later on, the emergence of dietary restraint among daughters is linked to their weight concerns and body satisfaction (Shunk

& Birch, 2004) and these self-evaluations and eating behaviors in daughters are shaped by parental input (Francis & Birch, 2005; Sinton, 2006).

CONCLUSION

Converging evidence indicates that healthful patterns of eating develop in environments that provide children with diverse experiences with flavors and foods, exposure to eating models who exhibit healthful eating patterns and flexible control over child eating, and repeated opportunities to make choices regarding what and how much to eat. In contrast, excessive parental control over or restriction of child feeding can elevate child risk for weight and eating problems as such control is associated with eating in the absence of hunger and negative self-evaluations in response to eating. Thus, parents should guide, as opposed to control, children's food selections, enabling children to develop healthy attitudes toward eating and to be able to respond to feelings of hunger and satiety. However, to date much of what we know about parental influence on early eating patterns and the risk for disordered eating has focused on young White girls. Future studies examining cultural and ethnic differences regarding the influence of parental feeding behaviors and eating attitudes are warranted, as are studies examining the emergence of early disordered eating behaviors in boys.

In conclusion, early eating experiences within the family environment have the potential to establish either healthy or unhealthy eating practices in children; such practices may influence risk for disordered eating in adolescence. Thus, although continued examination of the impact of these early eating experiences on the emergence of disordered eating is necessary, this view suggests that the etiology of eating problems may be found in children's earliest experiences with food and eating.

REFERENCES

Abramovitz, B. A., & Birch, L. L. (2000). Five-year-old girls' ideas about dieting are predicted by their mothers' dieting. *Journal of the American Dietetic Association, 100*(10), 1157–1163.

Addessi, E., Galloway, A. T., Visalberghi, E., & Birch, L. L. (2005). Specific social influences on the acceptance of novel foods in 2–5-year-old children. *Appetite, 45*(3), 264–271.

Arenz, S., & von Kries, R. (2005). Protective effect of breastfeeding against obesity in childhood: Can a meta-analysis of observational studies help to validate the hypothesis? *Advances in Experimental Medicine & Biology, 569*, 40–48.

Bartoshuk, L. M., & Beauchamp, G. K. (1994). Chemical senses. *Annual Review of Psychology, 45*, 419–449.

Birch, L. L. (1980). Effects of peer models' food choices and eating behaviors on preschoolers' food preferences. *Child Development, 51,* 489–496.

Birch, L. L., Billman, J., & Richards, S. S. (1984). Time of day influences food acceptability. *Appetite, 5,* 109–112.

Birch, L. L., & Deysher, M. (1985). Conditioned and unconditioned caloric compensation: Evidence for self-regulation of food intake by young children. *Learning and Motivation, 16,* 341–355.

Birch, L. L., & Deysher, M. (1986). Caloric compensation and sensory specific satiety: Evidence for self-regulation of food intake by young children. *Appetite, 7,* 323–331.

Birch, L. L., & Fisher, J. O. (2000). Mothers' child-feeding practices influence daughters' eating and weight. *American Journal of Clinical Nutrition, 71*(5), 1054–1061.

Birch, L. L., Fisher, J. O., & Davison, K. K. (2003). Learning to overeat: Maternal use of restrictive feeding practices promotes girls' eating in the absence of hunger. *American Journal of Clinical Nutrition, 78*(2), 215–220.

Birch, L. L., Fisher, J. O., Smiciklas-Wright, H., & Mitchell, D. (1999). Eat as I do not as I say: Parental influences on young girls' calcium intakes. *Faseb Journal, 13*(4), A593–A593.

Birch, L. L., Gunder, L., Grimm-Thomas, K., & Laing, D. G. (1998). Infants' consumption of a new food enhances acceptance of similar foods. *Appetite, 30*(3), 283–295.

Birch, L. L., Johnson, S. L., Jones, M. B., & Peters, J. C. (1993). Effects of a non-energy fat substitute on children's energy and macronutrient intake. *American Journal of Clinical Nutrition, 58*(3), 326–333.

Birch, L. L., Marlin, D. W., & Rotter, J. (1984). Eating as the "means" activity in a contigency: Effects on young children's food preferences. *Child Development, 55,* 431–439.

Birch, L. L., McPhee, L., Shoba, B. C., Steinberg, L., & Krehbiel, R. (1987). "Clean up your plate": Effects of child feeding practices on the conditioning of meal size. *Learning and Motivation, 18,* 301–317.

Birch, L. L., Zimmerman, S. I., & Hind, H. (1980). The influence of social-affective context on the formation of children's food preferences. *Child Development, 51,* 856–861.

Bove, C. F., Sobal, J., & Rauschenbach, B. S. (2003). Food choices among newly married couples: Convergence, conflict, individualism, and projects. *Appetite, 40*(1), 25–41.

Burrows, A., & Cooper, M. (2002). Possible risk factors in the development of eating disorders in overweight pre-adolescent girls. *International Journal of Obesity and Related Metabolic Disorders, 26*(9), 1268–1273.

Cooke, L. (2007). The importance of exposure for healthy eating in childhood: A review. *Journal of Human Nutrition and Dietetics, 20*(4), 294–301.

Costanzo, P. R., & Woody, E. Z. (1984). Parental perspectives on obesity in children: The importance of sex differences. *Journal of Social and Clinical Psychology, 2,* 305–313.

Costanzo, P. R., & Woody, E. Z. (1985). Domain-specific parenting styles and their impact on the child's development of particular deviance: The example of obesity proneness. *Journal of Social and Clinical Psychology, 3,* 425–445.

Cutting, T. M., Fisher, J. O., Grimm-Thomas, K., & Birch, L. L. (1999). Like mother, like daughter: Familial patterns of overweight are mediated by mothers' dietary disinhibition. *American Journal of Clinical Nutrition, 69*(4), 608–613.

da Veiga, G. V. & Sichieri, R. (2006). Correlation in food intake between parents and adolescents depends on socioeconomic level. *Nutrition Research, 26*(10), 517–523.

Dewey, K. G., Heinig, M. J., Nommsen, L. A., & Lonnerdal, B. (1991). Maternal versus infant factors related to breast-milk intake and residual milk volume—the Darling study. *Pediatrics, 87*(6), 829–837.

Edmunds, H., & Hill, A. J. (1999). Dieting and the family context of eating in young adolescent children. *International Journal of Eating Disorders, 25*(4), 435–440.

Elliott, K. G., Kjolhede, C. L., Gournis, E., & Rasmussen, K. M. (1997). Duration of breastfeeding associated with obesity during adolescence. *Obesity Research, 5*(6), 538–541.

Faith, M. S., Berkowitz, R. I., Stallings, V. A., Kerns, J., Storey, M., & Stunkard, A. J. (2004). Parental feeding attitudes and styles and child body mass index: Prospective analysis of a gene–environment interaction. *Pediatrics, 114*, e429–436.

Field, A. E., Austin, S. B., Taylor, C. B., Malspeis, S., Rosner, B., Rockett, H. R., et al. (2003). Relation between dieting and weight change among preadolescents and adolescents. *Pediatrics, 112*(4), 900–906.

Fisher, J. O., & Birch, L. L. (1999a). Restricting access to foods and children's eating. *Appetite, 32*(3), 405–419.

Fisher, J. O., & Birch, L. L. (1999b). Restricting access to palatable foods affects children's behavioral response, food selection, and intake. *American Journal of Clinical Nutrition, 69*(6), 1264–1272.

Fisher, J. O., & Birch, L. L. (2000). Parents' restrictive feeding practices are associated with young girls' negative self-evaluation of eating. *Journal of the American Dietetic Association, 100*(11), 1341–1346.

Fisher, J. O., & Birch, L. L. (2002). Eating in the absence of hunger and overweight in girls from 5 to 7 y of age. *American Journal of Clinical Nutrition, 76*(1), 226–231.

Fisher, J. O., Rolls, B. J., & Birch, L. L. (2003). Children's bite size and intake of an entree are greater with large portions than with age-appropriate or self-selected portions. *American Journal of Clinical Nutrition, 77*(5), 1164–1170.

Francis, L. A., & Birch, L. L. (2005). Maternal influences on daughters' restrained eating behavior. *Health Psychology, 24*(6), 548–554.

Francis, L. A., Hofer, S. M., & Birch, L. L. (2001). Predictors of maternal child-feeding style: Maternal and child characteristics. *Appetite, 37*(3), 231–243.

Furst, T., Connors, M., Bisogni, C. A., Sobal, J., & Falk, L. W. (1996). Food choice: A conceptual model of the process. *Appetite, 26*(3), 247–265.

Galloway, A. T., Fiorito, L., Francis, L. A., & Birch, L. L. (2006). "Finish your soup": Counterproductive effects of pressuring children to eat on intake and affect. *Appetite, 46*(3), 318–323.

Galloway, A. T., Fiorito, L., Lee, Y., & Birch, L. L. (2005). Parental pressure, dietary patterns, and weight status among girls who are "picky eaters." *Journal of the American Dietetic Association, 105*(4), 541–548.

Gillman, M. W., Rifas-Shiman, S. L., Berkey, C. S., Frazier, A. L., Rockett, H. R., Camargo, C. A. Jr., et al. (2006). Breast-feeding and overweight in adolescence. *Epidemiology, 17*(1), 112–114.

Gillman, M. W., Rifas-Shiman, S. L., Camargo, C. A., Jr., Berkey, C. S., Frazier, A. L., Rockett, H. R. H., et al. (2001). Risk of overweight among adolescents who were breastfed as infants. *Journal of the American Medical Association, 285*(19), 2461–2467.

Goldschmidt, A. B., Aspen, V. P., Sinton, M. M., Tanofsky-Kraff, M., & Wilfley, D. E. (2008). Disordered eating attitudes and behaviors in overweight youth. *Obesity, 16*(2), 257–264.

Hediger, M. L., Overpeck, M. D., Kuczmarski, R. J., & Ruan, W. J. (2001). Association between infant breastfeeding and overweight in young children. *Journal of the American Medical Association, 285*(19), 2453–2460.

Hendy, H. M., & Raudenbush, B. (2000). Effectiveness of teacher modeling to encourage food acceptance in preschool children. *Appetite, 34*(1), 61–76.

Hill, A. J., Weaver, C., & Blundell, J. E. (1990). Dieting concerns of 10-year-old girls and their mothers. *British Journal of Clinical Psychology, 29*, 346–348.

Johnson, S. L., & Birch, L. L. (1994). Parents' and children's adiposity and eating style. *Pediatrics, 94*(5), 653–661.

Johnson, S. L., McPhee, L., & Birch, L. L. (1991). Conditioned preferences- Young children prefer flavors associated with high dietary fat. *Physiology & Behavior, 50*(6), 1245–1251.

Kant, A. K. (2003). Reported consumption of low-nutrient-density foods by American children and adolescents: Nutritional and health correlates, NHANES III, 1988 to 1994. *Archives of Pediatric & Adolescent Medicine, 157*(8), 789–796.

Kalat, J. W., & Rozin, P. (1973). "Learned safety" as a mechanism of long-delay taste-aversion in rats. *Journal of Comparative and Psychological Psychology, 83*, 198–207.

Kern, D. L., McPhee, L., Fisher, J., Johnson, S., & Birch, L. L. (1993). The postingestive consequences of fat condition preferences for flavors associated with high dietary fat. *Faseb Journal, 7*(3), A90–A90.

Klesges, R. C., Stein, R. J., Eck, L. H., Isbell, T. R., & Klesges, L. M. (1991). Parental influence on food selection in young children and its relationship to childhood obesity. *American Journal of Clinical Nutrition, 53*, 859–864.

Krebs-Smith, S. M., Cook, D. A., Subar, A. F., Cleveland, L., Friday, J., & Kahle, L. L. (1996). Fruit and vegetable intakes of children and adolescents in the United States. *Archives of Pediatrics & Adolescent Medicine, 150*(1), 81–86.

Lepper, M. R., Sagotsky, G., Dafoe, J. L., & Greene, D. (1982). Consequences of superfluous social constraints: Effects on young children's social inferences and subsequent intrinsic interest. *Journal of Personality and Social Psychology, 42*, 51–65.

Liem, D. G., & Mennella, J. A. (2002). Sweet and sour preferences during childhood: Role of early experiences. *Developmental Psychobiology, 41*, 388–395.

Liley, A. W. (1972). Disorders of amniotic fluid. In N. S. Assali (Ed.), *Pathophysiology of gestation: Fetal placental disorders* (Vol. 2). San Diego, CA: Academic Press.

Maier, A., Chabanet, C., Schaal, B. Issanchou, S., & Leathwood, P. (2007). Effects of repeated exposure on acceptance of initially disliked vegetables in 7-month old infants. *Food Quality and Preference, 18*(8), 1023–1032.

Mannino, M., Lee, Y., Mitchell, D. C., Smiciklas-Wright, H., & Birch, L. L. (2004). The quality of girls' diets declines and tracks across middle childhood. *International Journal of Behavioral Nutrition and Physical Activity, 1*(1), 5–10.

Mennella, J. A., & Beauchamp, G. K. (1991a). Maternal diet alters the sensory qualities of human-milk and the nursling's behavior. *Pediatrics, 88*(4), 737–744.

Mennella, J. A., & Beauchamp, G. K. (1991b). The transfer of alcohol to human milk—Effects on flavor and the infant's behavior. *New England Journal of Medicine, 325*(14), 981–985.

Mennella, J. A., & Beauchamp, G. K. (1993). The effects of repeated exposure to garlic-flavored milk on the nursling's behavior. *Pediatric Research, 34*(6), 805–808.

Mennella, J. A., & Beauchamp, G. K. (1994). The infant's response to flavored milk. *Infant Behavior & Development, 17,* 819.

Mennella, J. A., & Beauchamp, G. K. (1996). Developmental changes in the acceptance of protein hydrolysate formula. *Journal of Developmental and Behavioral Pediatrics, 17*(6), 386–391.

Mennella, J. A., & Beauchamp, G. K. (2002). Flavor experiences during formula feeding are related to preferences during childhood. *Early Human Development, 68,* 71–82.

Mennella, J. A., Jagnow, C. P., & Beauchamp, G. K. (2001). Prenatal and postnatal flavor learning by human infants. *Pediatrics, 107,* E88.

Mennella, J. A., Johnson, A., & Beauchamp, G. K. (1995). Garlic ingestion by pregnant women alters the odor of amniotic fluid. *Chemical Senses, 20*(6), 192–192.

Michels, K. B., Willett, W. C., Graubard, B. I., Vaidya, R. L., Cantwell, M. M., Sansbury, L. B., & Forman, M. R. (2007). A longitudinal study of infant feeding and obesity throughout the life course. *International Journal of Obesity, 31*(7), 1078–1085.

Munoz, K. A., Krebs-Smith, S. M., Ballard-Barbash, R., & Cleveland, G. E. (1997). Food intakes of US children and adolescents compared with recommendations. *Pediatrics, 100*(3), 323–329.

Oliveria, S. A., Ellison, R. C., Moore, L. L., Gillman, M. W., Garrahie, E. J., & Singer, M. R. (1992). Parent–child relationships in nutrient intake: The Framingham Children's Study. *American Journal of Clinical Nutrition, 56*(3), 593–598.

Rozin, P., Hammer, L., Oster, H., Horowitz, T., & Marmara, V. (1986). The child's conception of food: Differentiation of categories of rejected substances in the 1.4 to 5 year age range. *Appetite, 7,* 141–151.

Ruther, N. M., & Richman, C. L. (1993). The relationship between mother's eating restraint and their children's attitudes and behaviors. *Bulletin of the Psychonomic Society, 31*(3), 217–220.

Schafer, R. B., Schafer, E., Dunbar, M., & Keith, P. M. (1999). Marital food interaction and dietary behavior. *Social Science and Medicine, 48,* 787–796.

Shea, S., Stein, A. D., Basch, C. E., Contento, I. R., & Zybert, P. (1992). Variability and self-regulation of energy-intake in young children in their everyday environment. *Pediatrics, 90*(4), 542–546.

Shunk, J. A., & Birch, L. L. (2004). Girls at risk for overweight at age 5 are at risk for dietary restraint, disinhibited overeating, weight concerns, and body dissatisfaction from 5 to 9 years. *Journal of the American Dietetic Association, 104*(7), 1120–1126.

Sinton, M. M. (2006). Individual and contextual influences on early adolescent girls' disordered eating (Doctoral Dissertation, The Pennsylvania State University, 2006). *Dissertation Abstracts International, 67*(8-B), 4741.

Sinton, M. M., & Birch, L. L. (2005). Weight status and psychosocial factors predict the emergence of dieting in preadolescent girls. *International Journal of Eating Disorders, 38*(4), 346–354.

Stanek, K., Abbott, D., & Cramer, S. (1990). Diet quality and the eating environment of preschool children. *Journal of the American Dietetic Association, 90*(11), 1582–1584.

Stice, E., Agras, W. S., & Hammer, L. D. (1999). Risk factors for the emergence of childhood eating disturbances: A five-year prospective study. *International Journal of Eating Disorders, 25*(4), 375–387.

Sullivan, S. A., & Birch, L. L. (1994). Infant dietary experience and acceptance of solid foods. *Pediatrics, 93*(2), 271–277.

Tanofsky-Kraff, M., Cohen, M. L., Yanovski, S. Z., Cox, C., Theim, K. R., Keil, M., et al. (2006). A prospective study of psychological predictors of body fat gain among children at high risk for adult obesity. *Pediatrics, 117*, 1203–1209.

Taveras, E. M., Scanlon, K. S., Birch, L. L., Rifas-Shiman, S. L., Rich-Edwards, J. W., & Gillman, M. W. (2004). Association of breastfeeding with maternal control of infant feeding at age 1 year. *Pediatrics, 114*(5), E577–E583.

Tiggemann, M., & Lowes, J. (2002). Predictors of maternal control over children's eating behaviour. *Appetite, 39*(1), 1–7.

Wright, P., Fawcett, J., & Crow, R. (1980). The development of differences in the feeding behavior of bottle and breastfed human infants from birth to two months. *Behavior Processes, 5*, 1–20.

2

DEFINING EATING DISORDERS IN CHILDREN

BETH WATKINS AND BRYAN LASK

More than 100 years ago, *The Lancet* published a brief report of a 7-year-old girl who was refusing food and suffering from severe emaciation (Collins, 1894), shortly followed by another report of an 11-year-old girl who eventually died of starvation after refusing food (Marshall, 1895). Collins suggested that there was a psychological component to the younger girl's food avoidance, whereas Marshall described the girl in his report as suffering from anorexia nervosa (AN). These constituted the first published scientific reports of eating disorders of childhood onset, and since then, eating disorders have been widely reported in children and adolescents (Bryant-Waugh & Lask, 2007).

DIFFICULTIES IN CLASSIFICATION

Although it is generally recognized that postpubertal adolescents present with eating disorders that are largely similar to those in adults, reports of childhood eating disorders tend to suggest a heterogeneous group (e.g., Fosson, Knibbs, Bryant-Waugh, & Lask, 1987; Gowers, Crisp, Joughin,

& Bhat, 1991; Higgs, Goodyer, & Birch, 1989; Jacobs & Isaacs, 1986). This raises questions about the applicability of existing accepted diagnostic criteria for eating disorders as stated in the fourth text revision of the *Diagnostic and Statistical Manual of Mental Disorders* (4th ed., text rev., *DSM–IV–TR*; American Psychiatric Association, 2000) or the 10th International Classification of Diseases and Health Problems (ICD-10; World Health Organization, 1992) to this population.

There remains confusion and uncertainty about the nature of childhood-onset eating disorders. First, there is a continuum of eating and feeding difficulties that can occur from birth onward. Infant feeding problems and subsequent weaning difficulties (which are discussed in detail in chapter 1) are relatively common, whereas food fads or highly selective eating patterns in preschool-age children are also commonly observed. In the majority of cases, these feeding and eating difficulties are not a cause for major concern, as they tend to be self-limiting, and the child's growth and development is generally unaffected (Pinhas, Steinegger, & Katzman, 2007). Developmentally, feeding problems may be appropriate, as they are a means of experimentation with new tastes and textures, and also enable children to test the impact of their behavior on their caregivers. Feeding difficulties tend to be considered "phases" that the child will outgrow, and indeed, this is generally the case (Bryant-Waugh & Lask, 2007). However, eating problems in older children should be taken more seriously, as feeding and eating problems are not developmentally normal in this age group. Additionally, the child's cognitive development is by then much more sophisticated, and eating problems may be related to underlying psychological issues.

The second reason for the uncertainty about the nature of these disorders is that there has been much confusion and inconsistency in the literature about the nature of eating difficulties in children. Some believe that eating disorders (i.e., AN and bulimia nervosa [BN]) that mostly occur in young women simply do not occur in children. According to Haslam (1986), "[AN] is really only a problem with adolescents, and there is virtually no chance at all of younger children having this condition" (p. 95). Similarly, it has been suggested that AN represents a maladaptive biological response to the growth changes of puberty (Crisp, 1983), which would preclude prepubertal children from having the disorder.

The third reason for confusion is that much of the published work on the subject of childhood-onset eating disorders has been based on clinical case reports, as there has been a lack of standardized instruments for the assessment of eating disorders in this age group. These clinical case reports have described children from the age of 8 years and older (e.g., Fosson et al., 1987; Gowers et al., 1991; Higgs et al., 1989; Jacobs & Isaacs, 1986), and, although many of the children included in these case series have received clinical diagnoses of an eating disorder, it has been difficult to demonstrate this on the basis of objective, reliable assessment because the necessary tools simply have not been available. However, this situation is now improving, as more measures of eating-disorder psychopathology and symptomatology are being developed and validated for use with children and adolescents (Watkins, 2007).

The final reason for the confusion is that for those who argue that AN does occur in children, uncertainty exists over whether the symptomatology of this particular disorder in childhood differs from the symptomatology in older adolescents and adults. This debate has been fueled by the fact that children who present with restricted eating and emaciation usually received a diagnosis of AN, despite being described as a heterogeneous group, as they often do not exhibit overvalued ideas regarding weight and shape (e.g., Fosson et al., 1987; Gowers et al., 1991; Higgs et al., 1989; Jacobs & Isaacs, 1986). A critical question raised by these cases of early onset is the precise nature of the central psychopathology. Given that AN, and to a far lesser extent, BN, are being diagnosed in children, many of whom are prepubertal, the question arises as to whether the core disturbances in cognitions concerning body weight and shape, which are the hallmark of the eating disorders of later onset (American Psychiatric Association, 2000), are manifested by these patients. The question of whether such overvalued ideas are present in children with eating disorders of early onset is not answered by the case series that have been reported to date. For example, Fosson et al. (1987) reported that only 56% of their patients with what they defined as early-onset AN gave a fear of fatness (a core diagnostic feature of AN) as their main reason for refusing food. Despite the methodological limitations of these studies (none has used systematic and standardized methods of assessment), the findings are suggestive of distinct subgroups within these younger patient samples, and are a clear illustration of why the notion that children could have AN has been queried. This raises the question of whether these children are being classified correctly. Indeed, it may be that clinicians are attempting a "best-fit" diagnosis in the absence of a taxonomy that accomodates the heterogeneity of childhood eating disorders. Thus, clarity and consistency in classification remains elusive.

Nicholls, Chater, and Lask (2000) argued that the use of current taxonomies may not be suitable for, or applicable to, children with eating disorders, as some of the fixed criteria of these diagnostic systems would preclude a child or young adolescent being diagnosed, and thus treated, appropriately. For example, one of the DSM–IV–TR diagnostic criteria for AN is amenorrhea, which only applies to postmenarcheal females. Although the DSM–IV–TR criteria do concede that menarche can be delayed in prepubertal females, it is impossible to know when an individual female would have started her menarche had she been of a healthy weight, and thus, this criteria seems impossible to apply. Additionally, for males, the DSM–IV– TR criteria suggest that low levels of serum testosterone should be observed in men with AN. However, this physical measure precludes a diagnosis of AN in prepubertal boys in whom one would expect to observe low levels of serum testosterone as a matter of course. These very specific criteria can be considered to automatically exclude both boys and premenarcheal girls from receiving a diagnosis of AN—indeed, these criteria also exclude some women who continue to menstruate at a very low weight. Another criterion for diagnosis in both the *DSM–IV–TR* and the ICD-10 is weighing less than 85% of expected body weight. This precludes children who were initially overweight but who have lost a significant amount of weight. Any significant weight loss during periods of expected growth, regardless of premorbid weight, and even if weight remains within the healthy range, should be treated with concern (Rome et al., 2003). It is important to note that although children who are obese may lose weight for positive health reasons during a period of expected growth because of either being on a self-directed or medically supervised weight-loss program, any unusual and sudden significant weight loss in these children should still be treated with concern.

Thus, a more appropriate, developmentally sensitive approach to classification of childhood eating disorders may be a system of "syndrome recognition guidelines," which would not only tackle the issues presented by the lack of applicability of current taxonomies, but also attend to the heterogeneity described in the literature. This idea was initially proposed by Fosson and colleagues in 1987, and developed to provide a set of criteria, which have been refined over time, and are referred to as the Great Ormond Street (GOS) criteria (Bryant-Waugh & Lask, 1995, 2007; Lask & Bryant-Waugh, 1992; see discussion later in this chapter).

The reliability of this system was investigated in a case note study conducted by Nicholls et al. (2000). Of the 226 children who had attended the eating disorders service at GOS Hospital, London between 1992 and 1998, 81 (ages 6–16 years), were randomly selected for this study. Each child's case notes were examined by two clinicians, who each made their diagnoses, blind to the other, according to three sets of diagnostic criteria, namely *DSM–IV–TR*, ICD-10, and the GOS. All children were given either an eating disorder diagnosis, or were rated as unclassifiable if their presentation did not fit the diagnostic criteria of the diagnostic systems. Interrater agreement was only demonstrated in 49.3% of cases using the ICD-10 diagnostic criteria. Agreement between the two clinicians using the *DSM–IV–TR* criteria was reasonably high at 77.8%, although this may have been aided by the limited number of categories (i.e., AN , BN, and eating disorder not otherwise specified [EDNOS]). However, 51.2% of children had been given a diagnosis of EDNOS, which suggests that a variety of pathologies may have been categorized in this way in the absence of alternatives. Nicholls et al. (2000) noted that disorders not included in classification systems may lead to them going unrecognized which, potentially, could have serious consequences. The greatest interrater agreement was found using the GOS criteria, with 85% of children receiving the same diagnosis from both clinicians. This was not suprising, as the GOS criteria have been specifically developed to reflect the heterogeneous presentation of childhood eating disorders. However, this finding suggests that these criteria provide a more reliable alternative to the diagnostic systems currently available.

With the advent of an adapted version of the Eating Disorder Examination (EDE; Fairburn & Cooper, 1993) for use with children (ChEDE; Bryant-Waugh, Cooper, Taylor, & Lask, 1996), and the availability of GOS criteria for more reliable clinical diagnosis, this issue of whether AN of early and later onset is comparable, and whether AN can be clearly differentiated from other childhood eating disorders, has been addressed (Cooper, Watkins, Bryant-Waugh, & Lask, 2002). Cooper and et al. found that the ChEDE profiles of the early-onset children were strikingly similar to those of participants with a later onset AN, suggesting that early-onset AN is of the same phenomenological form as that seen in adolesence and adulthood. Additionally, the study found that the ChEDE reliably discriminated between those who had received a clinical diagnosis of AN and those who had received a diagnosis of another childhood-onset eating disorder, reinforcing the suggestion that, as a whole, those with childhood eating disorders do indeed constitute a heterogeneous group, while lending support for the use of a more appropriate diagnostic system in this population.

The GOS criteria for eating disorders (see Exhibit 2.1) coupled with descriptions of childhood-onset eating disorders are presented here.

ANOREXIA NERVOSA

Although AN in children has been shown to be strikingly similar to that in older adolescents and adults (Cooper et al., 2002), there are some fundamental developmental differences. For example, children with AN often fail to maintain hydration (Irwin, 1981), and, as noted earlier, any weight loss, regardless of premorbid weight, during periods of expected growth should be treated with concern, even if the child remains within the healthy weight range (Rome et al., 2003).

There is little consistency in the literature to date with regard to terminology used to describe the onset of AN in children and adolescents under the age of 18 years. Some studies deem "early onset" to simply mean an onset under the age of 18 years (e.g., Eisler et al., 1997), whereas others describe those with an early onset to be aged 14 years or under (e.g., Matsumoto et al., 2001). Other studies attend to the pubertal status of the young person when applying the terms *early onset* or *late onset* (e.g., Cooper et al., 2002). Russell (1985) noted that it is wise to consider the onset of AN as early or late in terms of pubertal development rather than age, as the age at which a child goes through puberty varies from child to child, and puberty is a complex process that spans 2 to 3 years (Tanner, 1962).

Exhibit 2.1
Great Ormond Street Criteria for Rating Disorders

Anorexia nervosa
- Determined weight loss (e.g., through food avoidance, self-induced vomiting, excessive exercising, abuse of laxatives)
- Abnormal cognitions regarding weight and/or shape
- Morbid preoccupation with weight and/or shape, food and/or eating

Bulimia nervosa
- Recurrent binges and purges and/or food restriction
- Sense of lack of control
- Abnormal cognitions regarding weight and/or shape

Food avoidance emotional disorder
- Food avoidance
- Weight loss
- Mood disturbance
- No abnormal cognitions regarding weight and/or shape
- No preoccupations regarding weight and/or shape
- No organic brain disease, psychosis, illicit drug use, or prescribed drug-related side-effects

Selective eating
- Narrow range of foods (for at least 2 years)
- Unwillingness to try new foods
- No abnormal cognitions regarding weight and/or shape
- No morbid preoccupations regarding weight and/or shape
- Weight may be low, normal, or high

Functional dysphagia
- Food avoidance
- Fear of swallowing, choking, or vomiting
- No abnormal cognitions regarding weight and/or shape
- No morbid preoccupations with weight and/or shape

Pervasive refusal syndrome
- Profound refusal to eat, drink, walk, talk, or self-care
- Determined resistance to efforts to help

There have been no epidemiological studies that focus on early-onset AN. In adolescence, the prevalence rate of AN is estimated at 0.1% to 0.2% (Ben-Tovim & Morton, 1989; Whitaker et al., 1990), but this is almost certainly lower in children (Bryant-Waugh & Lask, 1995). A large-scale study of the incidence of AN in both children and adolescents, which screened the entire population of school-age children in Goteberg, Sweden, found an accumulated prevalence for AN (those who had or had had the disorder) of 0.84% (Rastam, Gillberg, & Garton, 1989). Although there is no firm evidence that there has been an increase in the incidence of early-onset childhood AN since the early 1960s, there appears to be more presentations to specialist clinics (Bryant-Waugh & Lask, 1995). However, this could be explained by a heightening awareness of the disorder over the years and better accessibility to services.

There is also the question of whether the severity of early-onset AN is similar to that seen in later onset, and findings are mixed. For example, one study addressing this question reported lower levels of purging behavior in those with an early onset of AN, and also reported that these patients were less likely to be extremely emaciated when compared with those patients with a later onset (Matsumoto et al., 2001). However, studies that used standardized assessment methods found similar severity levels in those with early-onset AN and those with later onset (Arnow, Sanders, & Steiner, 1999; Cooper et al., 2002).

Studies of AN in adults and adolescents have consistently shown that 90% to 95% of patients are female (Garfinkel & Garner, 1982). The picture is less clear in children and young adolescents. Swift (1982) reported similar sex ratios in childhood-onset AN to the adult and adolescent studies, finding an overall sex ratio of girls to boys of 9.5:1. However, some studies report as many as 19% to 30% are boys, although, as mentioned earlier, these samples were reporting children and young adolescents who may not have had weight and shape concerns (e.g., Fosson et al., 1987; Hawley, 1985; Higgs et al., 1989; Jacobs & Isaacs, 1986).

It has been noted clinically (Bryant-Waugh & Lask, 2007) that boys with AN tend to want to become more muscular, rather than lose weight and are more concerned about being "flabby" than fat. Although, like girls, they restrict their eating and often exercise excessively, they report concerns about being unhealthy rather than being unattractive were they to gain weight.

BULIMIA NERVOSA

BN is very rare in premenarcheal children, but when it does occur, it presents in a similar manner to that seen in adolescents and adults. It is characterized by episodes of overeating in which the sufferer experiences a loss of control, usually followed by compensatory behaviors such as self-induced vomiting, laxative abuse, excessive exercising, and periods of fasting or severe food restriction, which are intended to avoid weight gain. The weight and shape concerns characteristic of AN are also core features of BN. Individuals with BN often have very low self-esteem and may engage in deliberate self-harming behaviors, such as cutting (e.g., Ruuska, Kaltiala-Heino, Rantanen, & Koivisto, 2005).

Although rare, Bryant-Waugh and Lask (1995) reported that 10% of their referrals to a child and adolescent eating disorder specialist comprised of cases of BN with an onset younger than age 14. Cooper et al. (2002) reported five cases of premenarcheal BN, in a consecutive series of 88 children diagnosed with an eating disorder, whereas Bryant-Waugh and Lask (2007) reported a 7-year-old child who received a clinical diagnosis of BN. Many women with BN often report that their disorder started in early adolescence, and only present for treatment after having BN for a number of years, suggesting that it can remain "hidden" for many years. Although BN has been reported in men (e.g., Mitchell & Goff, 1984), there have been virtually no reports of this disorder in boys.

ATYPICAL CHILDHOOD-ONSET EATING DISORDERS

None of the "atypical" childhood-onset eating disorders have been well studied and their clinical features and nosological status are uncertain, although weight and shape concerns are not usually a feature of these disorders. What is known about these conditions is that there is dysfunctional behavior around food, although the fundamental psychological disturbance is unclear. Using *DSM–IV–TR* criteria, children with atypical eating disorders would usually receive a diagnosis of EDNOS. The advantage of using the GOS criteria is that they allow for more homogeneous categories, and thus better targeted treatment strategies (Rosen, 2003).

Food Avoidance Emotional Disorder

Food avoidance emotional disorder (FAED) was originally thought to be a primary emotional disorder where food avoidance was a prominent feature (Higgs et al., 1989). More recently, a study investigating comorbidity in early-onset eating disorders found that only 15% of children with FAED fulfilled diagnostic criteria for a noneating, emotional disorder (Watkins, Cooper, & Lask, 2003), suggesting that although there is some mood disturbance present, it is unlikely to constitute a primary affective disorder. Children with FAED present with symptoms similar to those seen in AN, in that they are usually significantly underweight and are restricting their food intake. However, they do not have the same preoccupation with weight and shape, nor do they have the distorted views of their own body that are characteristic of AN. Higgs et al. (1989) suggested that FAED may be an intermediate condition between AN and childhood emotional disorder (with no eating disorder); a partial syndrome of AN with an overall more favorable prognosis. However, this assertion has yet to be tested empirically.

There are no reports of the incidence, prevalence, or sex ratio of FAED. However, Cooper et al. (2002) reported that this was the most common diagnosis after AN in a consecutive series of 88 children presenting with childhood-onset eating disorders at two specialist clinics. Approximately 29% received a diagnosis of FAED. The ratio of girls to boys in this FAED group was 4:1.

Selective Eating

Children who are selective eaters have typically consumed a very narrow range of foods for at least 2 years and are unwilling to try new foods. They do not have a distorted body image nor the preoccupation with weight or shape characteristic of AN and BN. Growth and development in selective eaters does not appear to be affected by their eating habits, and they do not have a fear of choking or vomiting (Nicholls, Christie, Randall, & Lask, 2001). It has been suggested that selective eating may be a variant of normal eating behavior, a stereotyped behavior in a developmental disorder, or an emotional (phobic) disorder (Nicholls et al., 2001).

Again, there are no reports of the incidence, prevalence, or sex ratio of selective eating in the general population. However, Nicholls et al. (2001) and Cooper et al. (2002) found a sex ratio of boys to girls of around 4:1 in recent studies, suggesting that boys are far more likely to present with selective eating than girls.

Functional Dysphagia

The characteristic feature of functional dysphagia is a fear of swallowing, vomiting, or choking, for which there is usually an easily identifiable precipitant, such as having choked on a piece of food; having had traumatic gastrointestinal investigations; or experience of abuse that becomes associated with particular textures, tastes, or types of food (Bryant-Waugh & Lask, 2007). This makes the child anxious about, and resistant to, eating normally, resulting in a marked avoidance of food. These children do not have the characteristic weight and shape concerns seen in children with AN or BN. There has been very little reported about this disorder, and its incidence is unknown. Indeed, in a consecutive series of 88 children with childhood-onset eating disorders (Cooper et al., 2002), only 1 child received a diagnosis of functional dysphagia.

Pervasive Refusal Syndrome

Pervasive refusal syndrome (PRS) was first suggested by Lask, Britten, Kroll, Magagna, and Tranter (1991). They described a small case series of children who displayed a profound and pervasive refusal to eat, drink, walk, talk, or care for themselves in any way over a period of several months. These children usually present as underweight and often are dehydrated, but it is unclear whether they have distorted cognitions regarding weight and shape, as they are unwilling to communicate. An additional and striking feature is their determined resistance to any form of help. Lask et al. (1991) suggested that the condition may be understood as an extreme form of posttraumatic stress disorder. Further cases of children with this condition have been reported (e.g., McGowan & Green, 1998; Nunn & Thompson, 1996), with the hypothesis that pervasive refusal is a model of learned helplessness. One other case has since been reported in the literature (Taylor, Dosseter, Kilham, & Bernard, 2000), which casts doubt on this theory as the child was only 4 years old and would "not have the developmental capacity to sustain the cognitive generalization for helplessness" (p. 28). Clearly, there is much yet to be understood about this rare but life-threatening disorder. A fuller exposition of PRS has been provided by Lask (2004).

CONCLUSION

It is now widely accepted that eating disorders do occur in children. There is a growing literature on childhood-onset AN, and it appears that the core behavioral, psychological, and physical features are similar to those in adults. However, the differences between children and adults also need to be taken into account. As children have lower levels of body fat, they tend to become emaciated and suffer the effects of starvation far more quickly than adults, and this must be taken into account when considering treatment. Although cases of childhood-onset BN have been reported, they are so rare that empirical research is difficult. Clinical features reported regarding the atypical childhood-onset eating disorders generally concur, although empirical testing of these features is yet to be developed.

The literature to date gives a clear indication that there is a need both for consistency in the terminology used when describing eating disorders in children and adolescents, and for a diagnostic system that allows for description of atypical eating disorders of childhood and adolescence that is developmentally appropriate. Within the *DSM–IV–TR* categories, these children and adolescents with atypical eating disorders may be unclassifiable, as the alternative to a diagnosis of AN or BN is EDNOS, which fails to capture the qualitative differences presented in this group. Indeed, EDNOS suggests a quantitative difference from AN or BN rather than a qualitative one (Nicholls et al., 2000).

It is evident that clinicians need a clearer, more developmentally appropriate means of classifying childhood eating disorders, as the heterogeneity in the case series described here may be getting in the way of providing appropriate treatment.

REFERENCES

American Psychiatric Association. (2000). *Diagnostic and statistical manual of mental disorders* (4th ed., text rev.). Washington, DC: Author.

Arnow, B., Sanders, M., & Steiner, H. (1999). Premenarcheal versus post menarcheal anorexia nervosa: A comparison study. *Clinical Child Psychology and Psychiatry, 4*, 403–414.

Ben-Tovim, D. I., & Morton, J. (1989). The prevalence of anorexia nervosa. *New England Journal of Medicine, 320*, 736–737.

Bryant-Waugh, R. J., Cooper, P. J., Taylor, C. L., & Lask, B. D. (1996). The use of the Eating Disorder Examination with children: A pilot study. *International Journal of Eating Disorders, 19*, 391–497.

Bryant-Waugh, R., & Lask, B. (1995). Annotation: Eating disorders in children. *Journal of Child Psychology and Psychiatry, 36*, 191–202.

Bryant-Waugh, R., & Lask, B. (2007). Overview. In B. Lask & R. Bryant-Waugh (Eds.), *Anorexia nervosa and related eating disorders in childhood and adolescence* (35–50). London: Routledge.

Collins, W. J. (1894). Anorexia nervosa. *The Lancet, 1*, 202–203.

Cooper, P. J., Watkins, B., Bryant-Waugh, R., & Lask, B. (2002). The nosology of eating disorders of early onset. *Psychological Medicine, 32*, 873–880.

Crisp, A. H. (1983). Anorexia nervosa. *British Medical Journal (Clinical Research Edition), 287*, 855–858.

Eisler, I., Dare, C., Russell, G., Szmukler, G., le Grange, D., & Dodge, E. (1997). Family and individual therapy in anorexia nervosa. A 5-year follow-up. *Archives of General Psychiatry, 54*(11), 1025–30.

Fairburn, C. G., & Cooper, Z. (1993). The eating disorder examination (12th ed.). In C. G. Fairburn & G. T. Wilson (Eds.), *Binge eating: Nature, assessment and treatment* (pp. 317–360). New York: Guilford.

Fosson, A., Knibbs, J., Bryant-Waugh, R., & Lask, B. (1987). Early onset anorexia nervosa. *Archives of Disease in Childhood, 621*, 114–118.

Garfinkel, P. E., & Garner, D. M. (1982). *Anorexia nervosa: A multi-dimensional perspective*. New York: Basic Books.

Gowers, S., Crisp, A. H., Joughin, N., & Bhat, N. (1991). Premenarcheal anorexia nervosa. *Journal of Child Psychology and Psychiatry, 32*, 515–524.

Haslam, D. (1986). *Eat up! A parents guide to eating problems*. London: MacDonald.

Hawley, R. (1985). The outcome of anorexia nervosa in younger subjects. *British Journal of Psychiatry, 146*, 657–660.

Higgs, J., Goodyer, I., & Birch, J. (1989). Anorexia nervosa and food avoidance emotional disorder. *Archives of Disease in Childhood, 64*, 346–351.

Irwin, M. (1981). Diagnosis of anorexia nervosa in children and the validity of DSM–III. *American Journal of Psychiatry, 138*, 1382–1383.

Jacobs, B., & Isaacs, S. (1986). Pre-pubertal anorexia nervosa: A retrospective controlled study. *Journal of Child Psychology and Psychiatry, 27*, 237–250.

Lask, B. (2004). Pervasive refusal syndrome. *Advances in Psychiatric Treatment, 10*, 153–159.

Lask, B., Britten, C., Kroll, L., Magagna, J., & Tranter, M. (1991). Children with pervasive refusal. *Archives of Disease in Childhood, 66*, 866–869.

Lask, B., & Bryant-Waugh, R. (1992). Early-onset anorexia nervosa and related eating disorders. *Journal of Child Psychology and Psychiatry, 33*, 281–300.

Marshall, C. (1895). Fatal case in a girl aged 11 years. *The Lancet, 1*, 817.

Matsumoto, H., Takei, N., Kawai, M., Saito, F., Kachi, K., Ohashi, Y., et al. (2001). Differences of symptoms and standardized weight index between patients with early-onset and late-onset anorexia nervosa. *Acta Psychiatrica Scandinavica, 104*(1), 66–71.

McGowan, R., & Green, J. (1998). Pervasive refusal syndrome: A less severe variant with defined aetiology. *Clinical Child Psychology and Psychiatry, 3*, 583–589.

Mitchell, J. E., & Goff, G. (1984). Bulimia in male patients. *Psychosomatics, 25*, 909–913.

Nicholls, D., Chater, R., & Lask, B. (2000). Children into DSM don't go: A comparison of classification systems for eating disorders in childhood and early adolescence. *International Journal of Eating Disorders, 28*, 317–324.

Nicholls, D., Christie, D., Randall, L., & Lask, B. (2001). Selective eating: Symptom, disorder or normal variant. *Clinical Child Psychology and Psychiatry, 6*, 257–270.

Nunn, K. P., & Thompson, S. L. (1996). The pervasive refusal syndrome: Learned helplessness and hopelessness. *Clinical Child Psychology & Psychiatry, 1*, 121–132.

Pinhas, L., Steinegger, C., & Katzman, D. K. (2007). Clinical assessment and physical complications. In B. Lask & R. Bryant-Waugh (Eds.), *Anorexia nervosa and related eating disorders in childhood and adolescence* (pp. 98–124). London: Routledge.

Rastam, M., Gillberg, C., & Garton, M. (1989). Anorexia nervosa in a Swedish urban region: A population based study. *British Journal of Psychiatry, 155*, 642–646.

Rome, E. S., Ammerman, S., Rosen, D. S., Keller, R. J., Lock, J., Mammel, K. A., et al. (2003). Children and adolescents with eating disorders: The state of the art. *Pediatrics, 111*, 98–108.

Rosen, D. (2003). Eating disorders in children and young adolescents: Etiology, classification, clinical features and treatment. *Adolescent Medicine: State of the Art Reviews, 14*, 49–59.

Russell, G. F. M. (1985). Premenarcheal anorexia nervosa and its sequelae. *Journal of Psychiatric Research, 19*, 363–369.

Ruuska, J., Kaltiala-Heino, R., Rantanen, P., & Koivisto, A. (2005). Psychopathological distress predicts suicidal ideation and self-harm in adolescent eating disorder outpatients. *European Child & Adolescent Psychiatry, 14*, 276–281.

Swift, W. J. (1982). The long-term outcome of early onset anorexia nervosa: A critical review. *Journal of the American Academy of Child Psychiatry, 21*, 38–46.

Tanner, J. M. (1962). *Growth at adolescence*. Oxford, England: Blackwell Scientific.

Taylor, S., Dosseter, D., Kilham, H., & Bernard, E. (2000). The youngest case of pervasive refusal syndrome? *Clinical Child Psychology and Psychiatry, 5*, 23–29.

Watkins, B. (2007). Appendix: Assessment instruments and interviews. In B. Lask & R. Bryant-Waugh (Eds.), *Anorexia nervosa and related eating disorders in childhood and adolescence* (pp. 361–375). London: Routledge.

Watkins, B., Cooper, P., & Lask, B. (2003). *Co-morbidity in early onset eating disturbance*. Paper presented at the ninth annual meeting of the Eating Disorders Research Society, Ravello, Italy.

Whitaker, A., Johnson, J., Shaffer, D., Rapoport, J., Kalikow, K., Walsh, B. T., et al. (1990). Uncommon troubles in young people: Prevalence estimates of selected psychiatric disorders in a non-referred psychiatric population. *Archives of General Psychiatry, 47*, 487–496.

World Health Organization. (1992). *The ICD-10 classification of mental and behavioural disorders: Clinical descriptions and diagnostic guidelines*. Geneva, Switzerland: Author.

3

BODY IMAGE IN GIRLS

ELEANOR H. WERTHEIM, SUSAN J. PAXTON, AND SIMONE BLANEY

Positive body image plays a vital role in fostering healthy psychological and physical development in girls. Conversely, poor body image has a wide range of negative consequences. In this chapter we provide a general background about the nature of body image in girls and the consequences of poor body image. We describe epidemiological research and risk factors related to body image and body disturbance in girls. Models for the development of body image disturbance are also described. Finally, prospective research examining the negative consequences of body dissatisfaction and appearance concerns, particularly related to dieting, disordered eating, depression, and self-esteem, are reviewed.

OVERVIEW OF BODY IMAGE DISTURBANCE

Range of Body Image Disturbance

Body image is generally considered a multidimensional construct, covering cognitive, affective, and behavioral dimensions (Thompson, Heinberg,

47

Altabe, & Tantleff-Dunn, 1999). Dissatisfaction with one's body, an important element of body image, can range from a mild preference for different body characteristics to severe distress associated with extreme behaviors to change the body or avoid negative judgments. Furthermore, body image disturbance can vary depending on the specific body characteristic targeted, including concern over body shape, weight, various body parts, facial characteristics, fitness, and strength.

The vast majority of studies in girls have examined body weight and shape satisfaction, an interest that has arisen largely out of the association between body concerns and eating disorders. Therefore, this chapter focuses on girls' views of their size and weight and associated levels of body dissatisfaction. However, it should be noted that a range of other body image concerns do exist in girls. For example, one of every two Australian girls has reported not being happy with their skin (Goldstein, 2006).

Body Size Dissatisfaction Among Young Girls

Much of the research on body image in girls has examined the number of girls who would like to be thinner. Assessment methods include questionnaire or interview responses indicating that the individual would "prefer" to be thinner. Use of figural stimuli is also common, in which participants select their perceived current body size and also their ideal size from a series of increasingly large figures. Discrepancies between current and ideal ratings are taken to represent body dissatisfaction. See chapter 10 for details on assessment approaches.

Most studies using these techniques have found that a substantial proportion of girls prefer to be thinner, and this can occur in girls as young as 5 years old. Lowes and Tiggemann (2003) found 59% of 5- to 8-year-old girls chose an ideal figure that was smaller than their current figure. Most studies of preadolescent girls suggest that 40% to 50% would prefer to be thinner (e.g., McCabe & Ricciardelli, 2003; Rolland, Farnill, & Griffiths, 1997). Among adolescent girls, the proportion wanting to be thinner rises to more than 70% (Fear, Bulik, & Sullivan, 1996; Grigg, Bowman, & Redman, 1996; Paxton et al., 1991; Tiggemann & Pennington, 1990). In these studies, only a small proportion of girls reported preferring to be larger or to weigh more (e.g., 8% and 10%, respectively in Paxton et al., 1991; Truby & Paxton, 2002) and generally the girls who wanted to be larger were, in fact, underweight.

Although an ideal size thinner than one's current size reflects values, it does not necessarily indicate whether thinness is important to the person. Studies have therefore examined degree of body dissatisfaction and importance of a larger body size. Paxton et al. (1991) found that adolescent girls often thought being thinner would make them happier (57%), healthier (44%), and better looking (43%), and about 25% thought it would make them more successful and have more dates. Actively trying to lose weight, diet, or use more extreme methods such as vomiting or taking laxatives reflects yet greater importance of the concerns about weight. The age at which girls begin to take active steps to lose weight appears to be younger than initially thought. In a sample of 9-year-old girls ($N = 900$), 20% were already reporting trying to lose weight (Field et al., 1999). Use of more extreme methods are reported by a many girls, particularly adolescents, with 35% to 57% of girls reporting trying unhealthy weight-loss methods such as fasting, crash dieting, vomiting, or laxative use (Grigg et al., 1996; Maude, Wertheim, Paxton, Gibbons, & Szmukler, 1993; Neumark-Sztainer et al., 2002).

Another indicator of internalizing the thinness ideal involves how highly correlated one's body size is with one's body esteem. Many study findings in a range of age groups and ethnicities have suggested that larger girls tend to be more dissatisfied with their body and feel less good about themselves in general (Duncan, Al-Nakeeb, & Nevill, 2004; Paxton, Schutz, Wertheim, & Muir, 1999; Wertheim, Koerner, & Paxton, 2001).

At the far end of the continuum could be placed girls who are so concerned about various features that they undergo surgical or cosmetic procedures to change them. Sarwer (2001) reviewed this area, presenting evidence that a substantial number of adolescent girls, and at times even children, undergo procedures such as liposuction, nose reshaping, breast augmentation or reduction, facial implants, ear surgery, eyelid surgery, hair removal, and acne treatments (see also chap. 15, this volume).

Psychological Disorders Associated With Body Image Problems

Body dysmorphic disorder is an extreme form of body concern that includes a preoccupation and distress over an imagined defect or physical anomaly. Although most cases occur in adults, retrospective reports of adults with the disorder suggest as many as 70% report symptom onset in early or middle adolescence (Phillips & Diaz, 1997) and some cases have been reported in adolescents or even in children prior to adolescence (Albertini & Phillips, 1999; Phillips, Menard, & Fay, 2006). Anorexia nervosa (AN) and bulimia nervosa (BN) also can be seen as extreme manifestations of heightened concern with shape and weight, mostly affecting females. AN usually appears in early or later adolescence and BN in later adolescence, although younger children have been diagnosed (American Psychiatric Association, 2000).

Gender Differences

The thinness ideal appears to have different patterns for girls than boys, with the female gender being viewed as a strong risk factor for body image-related consequences in the form of eating disorders (Jacobi, Hayward, de Zwaan, Kraemer, & Agras, 2004). In the first few years of life, no major differences are apparent between prevalence rates of girls and boys in terms of wanting to be thinner (e.g., Lowes & Tiggemann, 2003), and although older studies have suggested a greater proportion of girls than boys want to be thinner, a review of recent studies (see chap. 4, this volume) concluded that the proportion of preadolescent boys reporting wanting to be thinner (27%–47%) was similar to that of preadolescent girls. However, a greater number of boys than girls want to be larger and particularly more muscular (e.g., Ricciardelli & McCabe, 2001b). In adolescence, body dissatisfaction is significantly greater in girls than boys (Knauss, Paxton, & Alsaker, 2007). More than 70% of girls report wanting to be thinner, including many in the normal weight range (e.g., Paxton et al., 1991). In contrast, the number of boys who are dissatisfied with their size tends to be more evenly split between wanting to be thinner and wanting to be larger and more muscular. Boys' body image issues are discussed in more detail in chapter 4.

Cultural and Ethnic Group Differences

Traditionally it has been thought that the drive for thinness is a Western phenomenon; however, increasing evidence suggests that the preference for a thin body and concern over a large size exists in children from various cultural groups. For example, studies of girls in Croatia (Markovic, Votava-Raic, & Nikolic, 1998), Iran (Nobakht & Dezhkam, 2000), and China (Huon, Mingyi, Oliver, & Xiao, 2002) suggest that dieting and a desire to be thinner appears across cultures. Differences also exist between ethnic groups within cultures, with African American adolescent girls reporting a larger ideal size and less body dissatisfaction than girls from other ethnic groups in the United States (Kelly, Wall, Eisenberg, Story, & Neumark-Sztainer, 2005; Neumark-Sztainer et al., 2002). For more details on ethnic and cross-cultural issues, see chapters 5 and 6.

RISK FACTORS FOR THE DEVELOPMENT OF BODY
DISSATISFACTION IN GIRLS

Researchers have explored factors that contribute to the development of body image and, in particular, body dissatisfaction. It is widely recognized that a range of factors are operative, and that a biopsychosocial approach in which physical characteristics, in conjunction with sociocultural influences, specific interpersonal experiences, and individual psychological character-istics combine to lead to the development of body concerns. Thus, although many studies examine individual factors, multifactorial models of contrib-uting factors in the development of body image have been developed which can be applied to both early childhood and adolescence (Cash & Pruzinski, 2002; Schutz, Paxton, & Wertheim, 2002; Smolak & Levine, 2001; Stice, 1994; van den Berg, Thompson, Obremski-Brandon, & Coovert, 2002).

Biological and Physical Factors

Biological and physical characteristics are generally included in models of body dissatisfaction. Although biological characteristics and neurobiological disorders can result in a direct experience of body disorientation, distortion, or discomfort (Wertheim, Paxton, & Blaney, 2004), most body image disturbances come about because the individual's body characteristics do not fit within culturally determined norms, the most commonly discussed of which involve body size and shape. Consistent with this idea, a higher weight to height ratio (body mass index [BMI]) that does not conform to the current beauty ideal is frequently observed to be a risk factor for development of body dissatisfaction (Field et al., 2001; Ohring, Graber, & Brooks-Gunn, 2002; Paxton, Eisenberg, & Neumark-Sztainer, 2006). Thus, particular physical characteristics are likely to become more salient as the child develops a sense of self versus others and sees the self in the context of her social environment.

Sociocultural Influences

Sociocultural influences have been shown to be significant in determining children's standards of beauty and in suggesting how important appearance should be to the child. These influences consist of the general social context, portrayed through media images and messages (Tiggemann, 2005), toys sold in shops (Dittmar, Halliwell, & Ive, 2006), and input from parents (Wertheim, Mee, & Paxton, 1999), peers (Clark & Tiggemann, 2006; Jones, Vigfusdottir, & Lee, 2004; Paxton et al., 1999), neighbors, schools, and medical practitioners. When a girl lives in a subculture that promotes an ideal body type that departs from her own, she is likely to become particularly vulnerable to internalizing these messages, with resultant body dissatisfaction. This state of affairs, in which the female ideal departs from one's actual body shape, has become prevalent in Western or Western-influenced cultures, laying the foundation for body dissatisfaction in many girls (Garner, Garfinkel, Schwartz, & Thompson, 1980; Thompson et al., 1999; Wiseman, Gray, Mosimann, & Athens, 1992).

Numerous studies of adolescent girls have demonstrated that exposure to idealized female media images results in a mean decrease in body satisfaction (e.g., Durkin & Paxton, 2002; Groesz, Levine, & Murnen, 2002). Girls who have an existing belief in the importance of appearance and high body comparison tendencies have been shown to be particularly vulnerable (Durkin, Paxton, & Sorbello, 2007).

Parental influences appear to be most important when parents, particularly mothers, actively encourage their daughter to lose weight or diet, or when they model observable behaviors, such as crash dieting (Benedikt, Wertheim, & Love, 1998; Wertheim et al., 1999). It is likely that parental behavior of this kind simultaneously reinforces the importance of appearance and thinness and the difficulties in achieving the beauty ideal.

Friends and peer influences can also have a profound impact on a girl's body image. Friendship groups share body attitudes (Paxton et al., 1999) and the importance that peers place on weight and eating is strongly related to weight concerns in elementary and middle school-age girls (Dohnt & Tiggemann, 2006; Taylor et al., 1998). Recent research has observed that having a friend who is dieting prospectively predicted the development of body concerns in early adolescent girls (Paxton, Neumark-Sztainer, Hannan, & Eisenberg, 2006). A growing body of research suggests that through appearance-related conversation (e.g., about clothes, weight, and diets), girls provide a "peer appearance culture" (Jones et al., 2004). These conversations often take the form of discussions known as "fat talk" in which girls develop a norm of concern about weight and shape and compare themselves to each other (Nichter, 2000; Wertheim, Paxton, Schutz, & Muir, 1997). Two mechanisms linking peer appearance culture and body concerns have been proposed. In one study, appearance schemas (i.e., cognitive structures concerning appearance that organize and determine the processing of self-related information; Cash & Labarge, 1996) mediated the relationship between peer appearance conversations and body esteem in 9- to 12-year-old girls (Clark & Tiggemann, 2007), whereas in a second study, social comparisons were found to mediate the relationship (Jones, 2004). Hence, the peer environment may increase the importance of weight or frequency of body comparisons that in turn increase body dissatisfaction.

Weight and appearance-related teasing and comments made by peers, parents, siblings, or other sources have been observed to be powerful negative influences on body image in girls, even after controlling for body size (Ata, Ludden, & Lally, 2007; Eisenberg, Neumark-Sztainer, & Story, 2003; Jones et al., 2004; Keery, Boutelle, van den Berg, & Thompson, 2005; Lunner et al., 2000; Paxton et al., 1999; Wade & Lowes, 2002; Wertheim et al., 2001). Over and above these separate influences, girls who are most vulnerable appear to live in an environment in which multiple sociocultural influences are advocating the thin ideal (Dunkley, Wertheim, & Paxton, 2001; Levine, Smolak, & Hayden, 1994; Taylor et al., 1998).

Individual Characteristics

Most theoretical models propose that certain individual characteristics make girls more likely to be influenced by societal ideals and messages. These characteristics include temperament and personality variables such as low self-esteem, depressed mood, global psychological functioning, and perfectionism (Wade & Lowes, 2002; Wertheim et al., 2004). They also include individual psychological processes such as placing a high value on thinness and appearance (holding appearance-related schemas or internalizing the thin ideal), and frequently comparing one's body with others' (Schutz et al., 2002; Thompson & Stice, 2001).

Low self-esteem and depressed mood are often correlated with body concerns in girls (Ohring et al., 2002; Paxton et al., 1999; Wade & Lowes, 2002). Cross-sectional path analysis and experimental studies suggest low self-esteem and depressive mood facilitate a belief in the importance of thinness, which increases vulnerability to dissatisfaction (Durkin et al., 2007). Paxton, Norris, Wertheim, Durkin, & Anderson, 2005). However, prospective support for low self-esteem and depressed mood as risk factors has been inconsistent. A 5-year study of early adolescent girls identified self-esteem as a risk factor for body dissatisfaction (Paxton, Eisenberg, et al., 2006). However, other studies have not found such a relationship over a shorter period (Button, Sonuga Barke, Davies, & Thompson, 1996). Furthermore, depressive symptoms have not been found to predict body dissatisfaction in girls (see Wertheim, Paxton, et al., 2004). The role of perfectionism has not been explored in depth. However, in a cross-sectional path analysis, perfectionism was associated with lower self-esteem and more overvaluation of weight and shape (Wade & Lowes, 2002).

Longitudinal studies of adolescent girls support the importance of several cognitive characteristics in predicting body concerns, including greater appearance-related schemas (Hargreaves & Tiggemann, 2002b), appearance comparison tendencies (Jones, 2004), and internalization of the thinness ideal (Thompson & Stice, 2001). Durkin and Paxton (2002) found that adolescent girls with higher scores on appearance comparison tendencies and internalization of the thin ideal responded more negatively after viewing idealized images of female beauty. Clark and Tiggemann (2007) observed that an appearance-related schema mediated the effect of media exposure on body concerns in 9- to 12-year-old girls. Hargreaves and Tiggemann (2002a) observed in adolescent girls that the effect of appearance-related television commercials on body image was partially moderated by appearance schema, concluding that exposure to appearance-related commercials acts by priming the appearance-related schema.

A Synthesized Model

Several theorists have offered multifactorial models of the development of body dissatisfaction that may be applied to early childhood and adolescence (Cash & Pruzinski, 2002; Durkin et al., 2007; Schutz et al., 2002; Stice, 1994; Thompson et al., 1999; van den Berg et al., 2002; Wade & Lowes, 2002). Figure 3.1 draws together findings from cross-sectional, experimental,

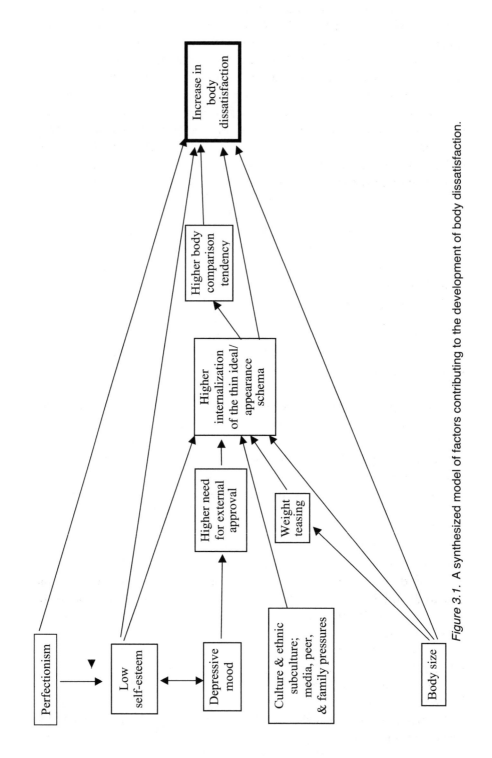

Figure 3.1. A synthesized model of factors contributing to the development of body dissatisfaction.

and longitudinal studies to form a synthesized model of factors contributing to the development of body dissatisfaction in girls. In this model, perfectionism contributes to vulnerability to low self-esteem and low self-esteem and depressive symptoms contribute to a need for approval from a girl's social environment. Low self-esteem may also lead directly to poor body image. A need for approval contributes to endorsement of socially espoused avenues to success, in particular an internalization of the thin ideal. Other factors may contribute to internalizing the thin ideal including culture and ethnic subculture; media, peer, and family appearance pressures; weight teasing; and larger body size. Higher internalization leads directly to body dissatisfaction and also indirectly to the body comparison process.

CONCEPTS FROM DEVELOPMENTAL MODELS

Two primary developmental phases have been discussed in the literature related to girls' body image: early childhood, when body ideals and concerns are likely to begin (Ricciardelli & McCabe, 2001a; Truby & Paxton, 2002) and the pubertal period, when dramatic changes in body characteristics, including size, take place as girls mature physically.

Early Childhood Development

The age at which body image concerns first appear is not completely clear because there have been few studies of preschool-age children. A study of 5- to 8-year-olds (Lowes & Tiggemann, 2003) suggested that whereas the mean scores for perceived current figure and ideal figure size did not differ significantly for 5-year-old girls, they did for older girls. Despite a small sample, the findings suggest that between ages 5 and 6 may be a threshold time of developing a preference for a thin ideal. By age 6 or 7, more than 50% of the girls in the study chose an ideal smaller than their current figure. The concept of dieting also developed over this period, with 7- to 8-year-olds understanding best what a diet is (Lowes & Tiggemann, 2003).

Another study (Davison, Markey, & Birch, 2003) compared 5-year-old girls to 7- and 9-year-olds, and also found higher body dissatisfaction in the older groups. BMI was also progressively more highly correlated with dissatisfaction in the older groups in this study. This pattern was replicated in a large sample in China. Li, Hu, Ma, Wu, and Ma (2005) found that the correlation between BMI and body dissatisfaction was not significant for girls aged 3 to 4 years old, significant but very low ($r = .14$) at 5 years old, and became increasingly large between 6 ($r = .28$) and 12 to 15 years ($r = .55–.57$). Therefore, the development of body dissatisfaction around weight and shape appears to emerge around the time children enter school. However, as discussed next, some of the foundations of these concerns may begin to develop earlier.

Early Stages in Developing Awareness of Body Stereotypes and Body-Related Stigma

One process that may be related to the emergence of body dissatisfaction is the development of an awareness of social stereotypes. It may not be until children understand that certain body types are socially preferred and others disliked or stigmatized, that they begin to apply the ideas to themselves. In a review of weight bias in children, Latner and Schwartz (2005) identified two strategies used to study weight bias in children: one in which a child rates the likeability of images of children of different weights, and one in which a child ascribes adjectives (e.g., "lazy," "cheats," "pretty") to silhouettes of children of different sizes.

Latner and Schwartz concluded that by 3 years old, children learn negative stereotypes about overweight individuals. For example, in a study by Cramer and Steinwert (1998), 3-year-olds were read a story about a mean child and then selected a picture of the mean child. The picture of the heaviest child was most frequently selected. These negative stereotypes intensify during childhood (Latner & Schwartz, 2005). Weight bias increases around the second grade (Brylinsky & Moore, 1994), intensifies during childhood (Wardle, Voltz, & Golding, 1995), and moderates somewhat in young adulthood (Latner, Stunkard, & Wilson, 2005). Stigmatization of overweight does not appear to be lessening despite the increasing proportion of young people who are heavy in the Western world. In fact, Latner and Stunkard (2003) observed an increased bias against the overweight child as compared with the 1960s. In this social environment it is not surprising that body image disturbance, especially among heavier children, continues to develop in childhood.

Puberty

During puberty, girls go through a period of dramatic change in their bodies, to which they must adjust over a short time span. Furthermore, girls may become concerned when noticing differences between their own rate and size of change compared with that of peers. When they are either early or late maturers, girls may compare themselves to others and notice they do not match the norm, which can be distressing at a time when "fitting in" is seen as important.

The pubertal transition may make girls more vulnerable to other risk factors. For example, menstrual status has been shown to be a moderator variable, with mother–child similarities in drive for thinness found in menstrual but not premenstrual girls (Sanftner, Crowther, Crawford, & Watts,

1996; Usmiani & Daniluk, 1997; Wertheim, Martin, Prior, Sanson, & Smart, 2002). Similarly, in a study by Smolak, Levine, and Gralen (1993), onset of dating was only found to be predictive of weight dissatisfaction when it was synchronous with menarche.

Longitudinal studies of pubertal development as a risk factor have reported mixed findings (Wertheim, Paxton, et al., 2004), however, there is some evidence that early menstrual onset predicts greater body dissatisfaction. This relationship appears to be mediated by the increases in body size, which occur around puberty (Kimm, Barton, Obarzanek, & Crawford, 1997; Wertheim et al., 2002). Therefore, it appears that during puberty, girls find themselves moving farther from the societal ideals of beauty, which can result directly in greater body concerns, or create a vulnerability to other forms of influence.

Longitudinal Research into Stability and Change in Body Image

Several longitudinal studies have examined whether body image disturbance is maintained over time (stability) and whether cross-sectional findings of greater body image disturbance in older age groups are replicated in prospective studies. In relation to stability, studies find that body concerns at one time point correlate with body concerns at a later time point, although the strength of the correlation differs across studies, and there appears some evidence of increasing correlations in older samples.

For example, Davison, Markey, and Birch (2003) found significant, but not particularly high, body dissatisfaction test–retest correlations between ages 5 and 7 of $r = .23$; and a slightly higher correlation of $r = .37$ between ages 7 and 9. In contrast, in an adolescent sample, Wertheim et al. (2001) found body dissatisfaction correlations over an 8-month period ranging from $r = .73$ to .75 in Grade 7 and 8 girls to .87 in Grade 10 girls, similar to other studies in this age group (Attie & Brooks-Gunn, 1989; Patton, Johnson-Sabine, Wood, Mann, & Wakeling, 1990). Santonastaso, Favaro, Ferrara, Sala, and Zanetti (1995) further found that 76% of 15- to 17-year-old girls with more severe body disturbances were similarly diagnosed 9 months later. Therefore, once established, in many girls body dissatisfaction appears to be maintained over time, and body dissatisfaction appears to be particularly stable once girls move into adolescence.

Above this basic stability, the question arises as to whether mean scores or percentages reporting body concerns in a particular sample increase over time, as one might expect from the many cross-sectional studies that find higher rates of body dissatisfaction in older girls. Although some prospective studies have found increases in body concerns or dieting over time (Eisenberg, Neumark-Sztainer & Paxton, 2006; Field et al., 2003), at least as many studies of various age groups and time spans have found that body concerns decreased over time (e.g,. Davison et al., 2003; Ohring et al.,

2002; Striegel-Moore et al., 2000). Some authors suggest that this decrease is an artifact of repeated testing in which girls may develop response biases, or lose interest in completing the same questions repeatedly. Partial support for these conjectures was found in Wertheim, Paxton, and Tilgner's (2004) reliability study in which current ideal difference scores decreased significantly over 2 weeks and 6 weeks for Grade 7 girls although there was no decrease over a 14-week period for grade-matched girls, or for any time span for the Grade 8 girls, suggesting an effect of repeated testing in some contexts. Further research is needed to examine the meaning of conflicting findings of cross-sectional and longitudinal research into changes in body image.

CONSEQUENCES OF BODY IMAGE DISTURBANCE

Body image disturbance in girls is increasingly being recognized as having the potential to contribute to the development of a range of behavioral and psychological problems. Longitudinal research has explored the role of body image disturbance as a risk factor for disordered eating symptoms, depressed mood and low self-esteem.

Body Image as a Prospective Predictor of Eating Disturbance

Different aspects of body image have been examined as prospective predictors of eating problems (see Table 3.1 for these studies). A first aspect could be labeled *weight and shape concerns*, which refers to discontent with one's body weight, shape, or size; in most measures this construct reflects a desire to be thinner. A second body image aspect examined may be labeled *general appearance concerns* (e.g., dissatisfaction with body appearance in general, not necessarily reflecting thinness concerns). Most longitudinal studies we examined (16 of 21) found that *weight and shape concerns* did predict increases in eating problems such as dieting, drive for thinness, bulimic symptoms, binge eating, compensatory behaviors, and partial syndrome BN over periods ranging from 8 months to 4 years (e.g., Field et al., 2001, 2002; Shaw, Stice, & Springer, 2004; Stice, Presnell, & Spangler, 2002). A small number (5 of 21), however, reported null effects, in which body concerns did not lead to increases in eating disorder symptoms (e.g., Leon, Fulkerson, Perry, & Early-Zald, 1995; Patton et al., 1990).

In contrast, in these longitudinal studies, *general appearance concerns* did not consistently predict eating problems. In a minority of studies (5 of 12), appearance concerns prospectively predicted eating problems (e.g., Attie & Brooks-Gunn, 1989; Friestad & Rise, 2004; Graber, Brooks-Gunn, Paikoff, & Warren, 1994; Neumark-Sztainer, Paxton, Hannan, Haines, & Story, 2006; Ohring et al., 2002). Most studies (7 of 12), however, failed to

TABLE 3.1
Longitudinal Studies Which Examined Whether Weight and Shape Concerns and General Appearance Concerns Predict Eating Problems in Adolescent Girls

Author(s)	Sample and location	Time 1 age/ Grade (range)	Measurement occasions/ Length of study	Outcome variable (Measure)	Significant baseline predictor variables (Measure)	Nonsignificant baseline predictor variables (Measure)	Control for baseline levels of outcome variable	Interview
Attie & Brooks-Gunn (1989)	193 girls and their mothers[a, b] from U.S.	7th–10th grade	2/2 years	Eating problems (EAT-26 Total score)	Higher general appearance concerns (SIQYA-BI)		Yes	No
Byely, Archibald, Graber, & Brooks-Gunn (2000)	77 White girls and their mothers[b] from U.S.	10–14 years	2/1 years	Dieting (EAT-26 Diet subscale)		General appearance concerns (SIQYA-BI)	Yes	No
Cattarin & Thompson (1994)	87 girls[a, c] from U.S.	10–15 years	2/3 years	Drive for thinness (EDI-DFT)	Higher weight and shape concerns (EDI-BD)	General appearance concerns (SIQYA-BI)	Yes	No
				Bulimia (EDI-BU)		General appearance concerns (SIQYA-BI), weight and shape concerns (EDI-BD)		

(continues)

TABLE 3.1 (Continued)

Author(s)	Sample and location	Time 1 age/ Grade (range)	Measurement occasions/ Length of study	Outcome variable (Measure)	Significant baseline predictor variables (Measure)	Nonsignificant baseline predictor variables (Measure)	Control for baseline levels of outcome variable	Interview
Field et al. (2002)	6460 girls and 4898 boys[a] from U.S.	9–14 years	2/1 year	Binge eating (YRBS)	Higher weight and shape concerns (MRFS)		Yes	Yes
				Purging (YRBS)	Higher weight concerns (MRFS)			No
Field et al. (1999)	6928 girls and 5,287 boys[e] from U.S.	9–14 years	2/1 year	Purging (YRBS)	Higher weight and shape concerns (MRFS)		Yes	No
Field et al. (2001)	6,770 girls and 5,287 boys[e] from U.S.	9–14 years	2/1 year	Dieting (YRBS)	Higher weight and shape concerns (MRFS)		Yes	No
Friestad & Rise (2004)	924 girls[e] from Norway	15 years	3/6 years	Dieting at age 18 years (single item defined by authors)	Higher general appearance concerns at age 15 years (single items defined by authors)		No	No
				Dieting at age 21 years (single item defined by authors)	Higher general appearance concerns at age 15 years, higher general appearance concerns at age 18 years (single items defined by authors)			

Graber, Brooks-Gunn, Paikoff, & Warren (1994)	116 girls[a,b] from U.S.	7th–9th grade	3/8 years	Onset of eating problems at Time 3 (EAT-26)	Higher general appearance concerns (SIQYA-BI)	Yes	No
Keel, Fulkerson, & Leon (1997)	80 girls and 80 boys[a,b] from U.S.	5th–6th grade	2/2 years	Eating problems (9 items from EAT-26)	General appearance concerns (SIQYA-BI)	Yes	No
Killen et al. (1994)	887 girls[a, d] from U.S.	6th–7th grade	2/3 years	Partial syndrome and full syndrome bulimia nervosa (criteria defined by authors)	Higher weight and shape concerns (items defined by authors); also predictive in multivariate analyses	Yes	No
					Higher weight and shape concerns (EDI-DFT and EDI-BD); not predictive in multivariate analyses		

(continues)

TABLE 3.1 (Continued)

Author(s)	Sample and location	Time 1 age/ Grade (range)	Measurement occasions/ Length of study	Outcome variable (Measure)	Significant baseline predictor variables (Measure)	Nonsignificant baseline predictor variables (Measure)	Control for baseline levels of outcome variable	Interview
Leon, Fulkerson, Perry, & Early-Zald (1995)	843 girls and 797 boys[a,c] from U.S.	7th–10th grade	3/3 years	Eating disorder risk status at Time 3 (Eating Disorders Checklist, Leon et al., 1993), and abnormal scores on EDI-DT, EDI-BU, and BMI less <17 or >30)		Weight and shape concerns at Time 1 and 2 (EDI-BD)	Yes	No
Neumark-Sztainer, Butler, & Palti (1997)	143 girls[a,c] from Israel	10th grade	2/2½ years	Number of weight loss behaviors in last month (the use of 14 weight loss methods)	Higher weight and shape concerns (EDI-BD)		Yes	No

Study	Sample	Age	Time interval	Measure		Yes	No
Neumark-Sztainer, Paxton, Hannan, Haines, & Story (2006)	1,386 girls and 1,130 boys [a,c] from U.S.	12–16 years	1/5 years	Dieting (single item designed by authors)	Higher general appearance concerns at Time 1 (BSSS) when BMI was and was not controlled		
				Unhealthy weight control (single items designed by authors)	Higher general appearance concerns at Time 1 (BSSS) when BMI was not controlled	Higher general appearance concerns at Time 1 (BSSS) when BMI was controlled	
				Very unhealthy weight control (single items designed by authors)	Higher general appearance concerns at Time 1 (BSSS) when BMI was and was not controlled		
				Binge eating (single items designed by authors)	Higher general appearance concerns at Time 1 (BSSS) when BMI was not controlled	Higher general appearance concerns at Time 1 (BSSS) when BMI was controlled	

(continues)

TABLE 3.1 (Continued)

Author(s)	Sample and location	Time 1 age/ Grade (range)	Measurement occasions/ Length of study	Outcome variable (Measure)	Significant baseline predictor variables (Measure)	Nonsignificant baseline predictor variables (Measure)	Control for baseline levels of outcome variable	Interview
Patton, Johnson-Sabine, Wood, Mann, & Wakeling (1990)	735 girls[a,e] from U.K.	14–16 years	2/1 year	Attempts at weight control (questions on food restriction for weight control)	Higher weight and shape concerns (discrepancy between current and ideal weight)		Yes	Yes
					Eating disorder diagnosis (semi-structured interview designed by authors)	Weight and shape concerns (discrepancy between current and ideal weight)		
Santonastaso, Friederici, & Favaro (1999)	394 girls[a,c] from Italy	15–20 years	2/1 year	Bulimia nervosa and partial syndrome (DSM-IV)		General appearance concerns (single items designed by authors)	Yes	Yes
				Eating disorder risk (5 items from EAT-40)		General appearance concerns (single items designed by authors)		
Shaw, Stice, & Springer (2004)	496 girls[a,d] from U.S.	11–15 years	4/4 years	Bulimia nervosa symptoms at Time 4 (EDE)	Higher weight and shape concerns at Time 3 (SDBPS)		Yes	Yes

Study	Sample	Age	Follow-up	Outcome	Predictor	Notes		
Stice (2001)	231 girls[a,d] from U.S.	13–17 years	3/20 months	Dieting frequency (DRES)	Higher weight and shape concerns (SDBPS)		Yes	No
				Bulimic symptoms (EDE-Q)	Higher weight and shape concerns (SDBPS)	Weight and shape concern was not a predictor when dieting or negative affect was considered (SDBPS)		
Stice & Agras (1998)	218 girls[a,d] from U.S.	16–19 years	2/9 months	Binge onset (BULIT-R and EAT-26 BU)	Higher weight and shape concerns (SDBPS)		Yes	No
				Compensatory behaviors (BULIT-R and EAT-26 BU)	Higher weight and shape concerns (SDBPS)			
Stice, Mazotti, Krebs, & Martin (1998)	216 girls[a,d] from U.S.	16–18 years	2/9 months	Dieting (DRES)	Higher weight and shape concerns (SDBPS)		Yes	No
				Dieting intention (DIS)	Higher weight and shape concerns (SDBPS)			

(continues)

TABLE 3.1 (Continued)

Author(s)	Sample and location	Time 1 age/ Grade (range)	Measurement occasions/ Length of study	Outcome variable (Measure)	Significant baseline predictor variables (Measure)	Nonsignificant baseline predictor variables (Measure)	Control for baseline levels of outcome variable	Interview
Stice, Shaw, & Nemeroff (1998)	218 girls[a,d] from U.S.	16–19 years	2/9 months	Bulimic symptomatology (BULIT-R and EAT-26 BU subscale)	Higher weight and shape concerns and general appearance concerns (when dieting or negative affect was considered) (SDBPS and BASS)	Weight and shape concerns and general appearance concerns (SDBPS and BASS)	No	No
Wertheim, Koerner, & Paxton (2001)	435 girls[e] from Australia	7th, 8th, and 10th grade	2/8 months	Drive for thinness (EDI-DFT)	Higher weight and shape concerns in Grade 7 girls (EDI-BD)	Weight and shape concerns in Grade 8 and 10 girls (EDI-BD)	Yes	No
				Bulimic tendencies (EDI-BU)		Weight and shape concerns in Grade 7, 8, and 10 girls (EDI-BD)		
Wichstrom (2000)	7,751 girls and boys[e] from Norway	12–19 years	2/2 years	Eating problems (12 items from EAT-26)		General appearance concerns (BASS)	Yes	No

Note. [a]Mostly White; [b]Mostly middle to upper class; [c]Mostly working to middle class; [d]SES information not presented; [e]Race or SES information not presented.

BASS, Body Areas Satisfaction Scale (Brown, Cash, & Lewis, 1989; Cash, 1991); BMI, b mass index; BSSS, Body Shape Satisfaction Scale (Pingitore, Spring, & Garfield, 1997); BULIT-R, Bulimia Test-Revised (Thelen Farmer, Wonderlich, & Smith, 1991); DIS, Dietary Intent Scale (Stice, 1998); DRES, Dutch Restrained Eating Scale (van Strien, Frijters, van Staveren, Defares, & Deurenberg, 1986); *DSM-IV, Diagnostic and Statistical Manual of Mental Disorders* (APA, 1994); EAT-26, Eating Attitudes Test (Garner, Olmsted, Bohr, & Garfinkel, 1982); EAT-40, Eating Attitudes Test (Garner & Garfinkel, 1979); EDE, Eating Disorder Examination (Fairburn & Cooper, 1993); EDE-Q, Eating Disorder Examination Questionnaire (Fairburn & Beglin, 1994); EDI-BD, Eating Disorder Inventory-Body Dissatisfaction subscale (Garner, Olmsted, & Polivy, 1983); EDI-BU, Eating Disorder Inventory-Bulimia subscale (Garner, 1991; Garner et al., 1983); EDI-DFT, Eating Disorder Inventory-Drive For Thinness subscale (Garner, 1991; Garner et al., 1983); MRFS, McKnight Risk Factor Survey (Shisslak et al., 1999); SDBPS, Satisfaction & Dissatisfaction with Body Parts Scale (Berscheid, Walster, & Bohrnstedt, 1973); SES, socioeconomic status; SIQYA-BI, Self-Image Questionnaire for Young Adults-Body Image subscale (Petersen, Schulenberg, Abramowitz, Offer, & Jarcho, 1984); YRBS, Youth Risk Behaviour Surveillance System questionnaire (Kann et al., 1996).

find such a relationship (e.g., Byely, Archibald, Graber, & Brooks-Gunn, 2000; Keel, Fulkerson, & Leon, 1997; Ohring et al., 2002; Santonastaso, Friederici, & Favaro, 1999).

Overall, the longitudinal studies suggest that weight and shape concerns in adolescent, and possibly preadolescent, girls predict the development of later eating problems. However, evidence for a predictive role of general appearance concerns is less robust. A previous review of longitudinal studies conducted by Jacobi and colleagues (2004) similarly concluded that weight concerns, negative body image, and dieting are well-supported risk factors for disordered eating. Jacobi et al. (2004) noted, however, that the longitudinal studies reviewed had not clarified the specificity of this link, in that body concerns could also be risk factors for more general psychopathology.

Body Image as a Prospective Predictor of General Well-Being

Until relatively recently, the broader psychological ramifications of poor body image in terms of general well-being or psychopathology had not been explored, with the assumption being made that body dissatisfaction may be the product of low self-esteem or depressive mood, rather than the cause of these problems. However, all studies that we are aware of that have examined whether weight and shape concerns and general appearance concerns predicted depressive symptoms over the course of adolescence have found positive effects (Cole, Martin, Peeke, Seroczynski, & Hoffman, 1998; Holsen, Kraft, & Roysamb, 2001; Lau, 2000; Paxton, Neumark-Sztainer et al., 2006; Rierdan, Koff, & Stubbs, 1989; Siegel, 2002; Stice & Bearman, 2001; Stice, Hayward, Cameron, Killen, & Taylor, 2000). Similarly, two studies have found body dissatisfaction predicted the development of low self-esteem (Friestad & Rise, 2004), although a further study by Lau (2000) did not find weight concerns predicted self-esteem (more than 6 months). Therefore, body image concerns in girls appear to not only be risk factors for disordered eating, but also for more general psychopathology and decreased well-being.

CONCLUSIONS

Body image disturbance occurs frequently in preadolescent and adolescent girls. Increasingly, it is being recognized that in a proportion of girls, body image disturbance may have serious and far-reaching negative consequences and cannot be assumed merely to be benign aspects of growing up. It is also clear that the responsibility for body image disturbance does not rest solely with the individual girl—environmental appearance pressures play a large part. The challenge for future research is to identify effective means to address both individual and environmental pressures that contribute to the widespread body image disturbance we observe in girls today.

REFERENCES

Albertini, R. S., & Phillips, K. A. (1999). Thirty-three cases of body dysmorphic disorder in children and adolescents. *Journal of the American Academy of Child and Adolescent Psychiatry, 38*, 453–459.

American Psychiatric Association. (2000). *Diagnostic and statistical manual of mental disorders* (4th ed., text rev.). Washington, DC: Author.

Ata, R. N., Ludden, A. B., & Lally, M. M. (2007). The effects of gender and family, friend and media influences on eating behaviors and body image during adolescence. *Journal of Youth and Adolescence, 36*, 1024–1037.

Attie, I., & Brooks-Gunn, J. (1989). Development of eating problems in adolescent girls: A longitudinal study. *Developmental Psychology, 25*, 70–79.

Benedikt, R., Wertheim, E. H., & Love, A. (1998). Eating attitudes and weight-loss attempts in female adolescents and their mothers. *Journal of Youth and Adolescence, 27*, 43–57.

Brylinsky, J. A., & Moore, J. C. (1994). The identification of body build stereotypes in young children. *Journal of Research in Personality, 28*, 170–181.

Button, E. J., Sonuga Barke, E. J. S., Davies, J., & Thompson, M. (1996). A prospective study of self-esteem in the prediction of eating problems in adolescent schoolgirls: Questionnaire findings. *British Journal of Clinical Psychology, 35*, 193–203.

Byely, L., Archibald, A. B., Graber, J., & Brooks-Gunn, J. (2000). A prospective study of familial and social influences on girls' body image and dieting. *International Journal of Eating Disorders, 28*, 155–164.

Cash, T. F., & Labarge, A. S. (1996). Development of the Appearance Schemas Inventory: A new cognitive body-image assessment. *Cognitive Therapy and Research, 20*, 37–50.

Cash, T. F., & Pruzinsky, T. (2002). Future challenges for body image theory, research and clinical practice. In T. F. Cash & T. Pruzinsky (Eds.), *Body image: A handbook of theory, research and clinical practice* (pp. 509–516). New York: Guilford Press.

Cattarin, J. A., & Thompson, J. K. (1994). A three-year longitudinal study of body image, eating disturbance, and general psychological functioning in adolescent females. *Eating Disorders: The Journal of Treatment and Prevention, 2*, 114–115.

Clark, L. S., & Tiggemann, M. (2006). Appearance culture in 9 to 12 year old girls: Media and peer influences on body dissatisfaction. *Social Development, 15*, 628–643.

Clark, L., & Tiggemann, M. (2007). Sociocultural influences and body image in 9 to 12 year old girls: The role of appearance schemas. *Journal of Clinical Child and Adolescent Psychology, 36*, 76–86.

Cole, D. A., Martin, J. M., Peeke, L., Seroczynski, A. D., & Hoffman, K. (1998). Are negative cognitive errors predictive or reflective of depressive symptoms in children: A longitudinal study. *Journal of Abnormal Psychology, 107*, 481–496.

Cramer, P., & Steinwert, T. (1998). Thin is good, fat is bad: How early does it begin? *Journal of Applied Developmental Psychology, 19*, 429–451.

Davison, K. K., Markey, C. N., & Birch, L. L. (2003). A longitudinal examination of patterns in girls' weight concerns and body dissatisfaction from ages 5 to 9 years. *International Journal of Eating Disorders, 33*, 320–332.

Dittmar, H., Halliwell, E., & Ive, S. (2006). Does Barbie make girls want to be thin? The effect of experimental exposure to images of dolls on the body image of 5- to 8-year-old girls. *Developmental Psychology, 42*, 283–292.

Dohnt, H., & Tiggemann, M. (2006). The contribution of peer and media influences to the development of body satisfaction and self-esteem in young girls: A prospective study. *Developmental Psychology, 42*, 929–936.

Duncan, M. J., Al-Nakeeb, Y., & Nevill, A. M. (2004). Body esteem and body fat in British school children. *Body Image, 1*, 311–315.

Dunkley, T. L., Wertheim, E. H., & Paxton, S. J. (2001). Examination of a model of multiple sociocultural influences on adolescent girls' body dissatisfaction and dietary restraint. *Adolescence, 36*, 265–279.

Durkin, S. J., & Paxton, S. J. (2002). Predictors of vulnerability to reduced body image satisfaction and psychological wellbeing in response to exposure to idealized female media images in adolescent girls. *Journal of Psychosomatic Research, 53*, 995–1005.

Durkin, S. J., Paxton, S. J., & Sorbello, M. (2007). Mediators of the impact of exposure to idealized female images on adolescent girls' body satisfaction: An integrative model. *Journal of Applied Social Psychology, 37*, 1092–1117.

Eisenberg, M. E., Neumark-Sztainer, D., & Paxton, S. J. (2006). Five year change in body satisfaction among adolescents. *Journal of Psychosomatic Research, 61*, 521–527.

Eisenberg, M. E., Neumark-Sztainer, D., & Story, M. (2003). Associations of weight-based teasing and emotional well-being among adolescents. *Archives of Pediatric and Adolescent Medicine, 157*, 733–738.

Fear, J. L., Bulik, C. M., & Sullivan, P. (1996). The prevalence of disordered eating behaviours and attitudes in adolescent girls. *New Zealand Journal of Psychology, 26*, 7–12.

Field, A. E., Austin, S. B., Frazier, A. L., Gillman, M. W., Camargo, C. A., Jr., & Colditz, G. A. (2002). Smoking, getting drunk, and engaging in bulimic behaviors: In which order are the behaviors adopted? *Journal of the Academy of Child and Adolescent Psychiatry, 41*, 846–853.

Field, A. E., Austin, S. B., Taylor, C. B., Malspeis, S., Rosner, B., Rockett, H. R., et al. (2003). Relation between dieting and weight change among preadolescents and adolescents. *Pediatrics, 112*, 900–906.

Field, A. E., Camargo, C. A., Jr., Taylor, C. B., Berkey, C. S., Frazier, A. L., Gillman, M. W., et al. (1999). Overweight, weight concerns and bulimic behaviours among girls and boys. *Journal of American Academy of Child and Adolescent Psychiatry, 38*, 754–760.

Field, A. E., Camargo, C. A., Jr., Taylor, C. B., Berkey, C. S., Roberts, S. B., & Colditz, G. A. (2001). Peer, parent, and media influences on the development of weight concerns and frequent dieting among preadolescent and adolescent girls and boys. *Pediatrics, 107*, 54–60.

Friestad, C., & Rise, J. (2004). A longitudinal study of the relationship between body image, self-esteem and dieting among 15–21 year olds in Norway. *European Eating Disorders Review, 12*, 247–255.

Garner, D. M., Garfinkel, P. E., Schwartz, D., & Thompson, M. (1980). Cultural expectations of thinness in women. *Psychological Reports, 47*, 483–491.

Goldstein, N. (2006). *GirlForce You*. Sydney: Australian Broadcasting Corporation.

Graber, J. A., Brooks-Gunn, J., Paikoff, R. L., & Warren, M. (1994). Prediction of eating problems: An 8-year study of adolescent girls. *Developmental Psychology, 30*, 823–834.

Grigg, M., Bowman, J., & Redman, S. (1996). Disordered eating and unhealthy weight reduction practices among adolescent females. *Preventive Medicine, 25*, 748–756.

Groesz, L. M., Levine, M. P., & Murnen, S. K. (2002). The effect of experimental presentation of thin media images on body dissatisfaction: A meta-analytic review. *International Journal of Eating Disorders, 31*, 1–16.

Hargreaves, D., & Tiggemann, M. (2002a). The effect of television commercials on mood and body dissatisfaction: The role of appearance-schema activation. *Journal of Social and Clinical Psychology, 21*, 287–308.

Hargreaves, D., & Tiggemann, M. (2002b). The role of appearance schematicity in the development of adolescent body dissatisfaction. *Cognitive Therapy and Research, 26*, 691–700.

Holsen, I., Kraft, P., & Roysamb, E. (2001). The relationship between body image and depressed mood in adolescence: A 5-year longitudinal panel study. *Journal of Health Psychology, 6*, 613–627.

Huon, G. F., Mingyi, Q., Oliver, K., & Xiao, G. (2002). A large-scale survey of eating disorder symptomatology among female adolescents in the People's Republic of China. *International Journal of Eating Disorders, 32*, 192–205.

Jacobi, C., Hayward, C., de Zwaan, M., Kraemer, H. C., & Agras, W. S. (2004). Coming to terms with risk factors for eating disorders: Application of risk terminology and suggestions for a general taxonomy. *Psychological Bulletin, 130*, 19–65.

Jones, D. C. (2004). Body image among adolescent girls and boys: A longitudinal study. *Developmental Psychology, 40*, 823–835.

Jones, D. C., Vigfusdottir, T. H., & Lee, Y. (2004). Body image and the appearance culture among adolescent girls and boys: An examination of friend conversations, peer criticism, appearance magazines, and internalization of appearance ideals. *Journal of Adolescent Research, 19*, 323–339.

Keel, P. K., Fulkerson, J. A., & Leon, G. R. (1997). Disordered eating precursors in pre and early adolescent girls and boys. *Journal of Youth and Adolescence, 26*, 203–216.

Keery, H., Boutelle, K., van den Berg, P., & Thompson, J. K. (2005). The impact of appearance-related teasing by family members. *Journal of Adolescent Health, 37*, 120–127.

Kelly, A. M., Wall, M., Eisenberg, M. E., Story, M., & Neumark-Sztainer, D. (2005). Adolescent girls with high body satisfaction: Who are they and what can they teach us? *Journal of Adolescent Health, 37*, 391–396.

Killen, J. D., Taylor, C. B., Hayward, C., Haydel, K. F., Wilson, D. M., Hammer, L., et al. (1996). Weight concerns influence the development of eating disorders: A 4-year prospective analysis. *Journal of Consulting and Clinincal Psychcology, 64*, 936–940.

Killen, J. D., Taylor, C. B., Hayward, C., Wilson, D. M., Haydel, K. F., Hammer, L. D., et al. (1994). Pursuit of thinness and onset of eating disorder symptoms in a community sample of adolescent girls: A three-year propsective analysis. *International Journal of Eating Disorders, 16*, 227–238.

Kimm, S. Y., Barton, B. A., Obarzanek, E., & Crawford, P. (1997). Changes in adiposity in a biracial cohort during puberty: NHLBI Growth and Health Study (NGHS). *Canadian Journal of Cardiology, 13*, 218B.

Knauss, C., Paxton, S. J., & Alsaker, F. D. (2007). Relationships amongst body dissatisfaction, internalization of the media body ideal and perceived pressure from media in adolescent girls and boys. *Body Image, 4*, 353–360.

Latner, J. D., & Schwartz, M. B. (2005). Weight bias in a child's world. In K. D. Brownell, R. M. Puhl, M. B. Schwartz, & L. Rudd (Eds.), *Weight bias: Nature, consequences and remedies* (pp. 54–67). New York: Guilford Press.

Latner, J. D., & Stunkard, A. J. (2003). Getting worse: The stigmatization of obese children. *Obesity Research, 11*, 452–456.

Latner, J. D., Stunkard, A. J., & Wilson, G. T. (2005). Stigmatized students: Age, sex, and ethnicity effects in the stigmatization of obesity. *Obesity Research, 13*, 1226–1231.

Lau, B. (2000). Global negative self-evaluations, weight and eating concerns and depressive symptoms: A prospective study of adolescents. *Eating and Weight Disorders, 5*, 7–15.

Leon, G. R., Fulkerson, J. A., Perry, C. L., & Early-Zald, M. B. (1995). Prospective analysis of personality and behavioral vulnerabilities and gender influences in the later development of disordered eating. *Journal of Abnormal Psychology, 104*, 140–149.

Levine, M. P., Smolak, L., & Hayden, H. (1994). The relation of sociocultural factors to eating attitudes and behaviors among middle school girls. *Journal of Early Adolescence, 14*, 471–490.

Li, Y., Hu, K., Ma, W., Wu, J., & Ma, G. (2005). Body image perceptions among Chinese children and adolescents. *Body Image, 2*, 91–103.

Lowes, J., & Tiggemann, M. (2003). Body dissatisfaction, dieting awareness and the impact of parental influence in young children. *British Journal of Health Psychology, 8*, 135–147.

Lunner, K., Wertheim, E. H., Thompson, J. K., Paxton, S. J., McDonald, F., & Halvarsson, R. (2000). A cross-cultural investigation of the role of teasing and weight and dieting concerns in adolescent girls from Sweden and Australia. *International Journal of Eating Disorders, 48*, 430–435.

Markovic, J., Votava-Raic, A., & Nikolic, S. (1998). Study of eating attitudes and body image perception in the preadolescent age. *Collegium Antropologicum, 22*, 221–232.

Maude, D., Wertheim, E. H., Paxton, S. J., Gibbons, K., & Szmukler, G. I. (1993). Body dissatisfaction, weight loss behaviours and bulimic tendencies in Australian adolescents with an estimate of female data representativeness. *Australian Psychologist, 28*, 128–132.

McCabe, M. P., & Ricciardelli, L. A. (2003). Body image and strategies to lose weight and increase muscle among boys and girls. *Health Psychology, 22*, 39–46.

Neumark-Sztainer, D., Butler, R., & Palti, H. (1997). Persistence of weight loss behaviors among adolescent girls in Jerusalem. *International Journal of Adolescent Medicine and Health, 9*, 19–35.

Neumark-Sztainer, D., Croll, J., Story, M., Hannan, P. J., French, S. A., & Perry, C. (2002). Ethnic/racial differences in weight-related concerns and behaviors among adolescent girls and boys: Findings from Project EAT. *Journal of Psycho-somatic Research, 53*, 963–974.

Neumark-Sztainer, D., Paxton, S. J., Hannan, P. J., Haines, J., & Story, M. (2006). Does body satisfaction matter? Five-year longitudinal associations between body satisfaction and health behaviors in adolescent females and males. *Journal of Adolescent Health, 39*, 244–251.

Nichter, M. (2000). *Fat talk: What girls and their parents say about dieting.* Cambridge, MA: Harvard University Press.

Nobakht, M., & Dezhkam, M. (2000). An epidemiological study of eating disorders in Iran. *International Journal of Eating Disorders, 28*, 265–271.

Ohring, R., Graber, J. A., & Brooks-Gunn, J. (2002). Girls' recurrent and concurrent body dissatisfaction: Correlates and consequences over 8 years. *International Journal of Eating Disorders, 31*, 404–415.

Patton, G. C., Johnson-Sabine, E., Wood, K., Mann, A. H., & Wakeling, A. (1990). Abnormal eating attitudes in London schoolgirls—A prospective epidemio-logical study: Outcome at twelve month follow-up. *Psychological Medicine, 20*, 383–394.

Paxton, S. J., Eisenberg, M. E., & Neumark-Sztainer, D. (2006). Prospective pre-dictors of body dissatisfaction in adolescent girls and boys: A five year longitu-dinal study. *Developmental Psychology, 42*, 888–899.

Paxton, S. J., Neumark-Sztainer, D., Hannan, P. J., & Eisenberg, M. E. (2006). Body dissatisfaction prospectively predicts depressive mood and low self-esteem in adolescent girls and boys. *Journal of Clinical Child and Adolescent Psychology, 35*, 539–549.

Paxton, S. J., Norris, M., Wertheim, E. H., Durkin, S. J., & Anderson, J. (2005). Body dissatisfaction, dating and importance of thinness to attractiveness in adolescent girls. *Sex Roles, 53*, 663–675.

Paxton, S. J., Schutz, H. K., Wertheim, E. H., & Muir, S. L. (1999). Friendship clique and peer influences on body image concerns, dietary restraint, extreme weight-loss behaviors, and binge eating in adolescent girls. *Journal of Abnormal Psychology, 108*, 255–266.

Paxton, S. J., Wertheim, E. H., Gibbons, K., Szmukler, G. I., Hillier, L., & Petrovich, J. L. (1991). Body image satisfaction, dieting beliefs and weight loss behaviors in adolescent girls and boys. *Journal of Youth and Adolescence, 20*, 361–379.

Phillips, K. A., & Diaz, S. F. (1997). Gender differences in body dysmorphic dis-order. *Journal of Nervous and Mental Disease, 185*, 570–577.

Phillips, K. A., Menard, W., & Fay, C. (2006). Gender similarities and differences in 200 individuals with body dysmorphic disorder. *Comprehensive Psychiatry, 47*, 77–87.

Ricciardelli, L. A., & McCabe, M. P. (2001a). Children's body image concerns and eating disturbance: A review of the literature. *Clinical Psychology Review, 21*, 325–344.

Ricciardelli, L. A., & McCabe, M. P. (2001b). Dietary restraint and negative affect as mediators of body dissatisfaction and bulimic behavior in adolescent girls and boys. *Behaviour Research and Therapy, 39*, 1317–1328.

Rierdan, J., Koff, E., & Stubbs, M. L. (1989). A longitudinal analysis of body image as a predictor of the onset and persistence of adolescent girls' depression. *Journal of Early Adolescence, 9*, 454–466.

Rolland, K., Farnill, D., & Griffiths, R. A. (1997). Body figure perceptions and eating attitudes among Australian schoolchildren aged 8 to 12 years. *International Journal of Eating Disorders, 21,* 273–278.

Sanftner, J. L., Crowther, J. H., Crawford, P. A., & Watts, D. D. (1996). Maternal influences (or lack thereof) on daughters' eating attitudes and behaviors. *Eating Disorders: The Journal of Treatment & Prevention, 4,* 147–159.

Santonastaso, P., Favaro, A., Ferrara, S., Sala, A., & Zanetti, T. (1995). Prevalence of body image disturbance in a female adolescent sample: A longitudinal study. *Eating Disorders, 3,* 342–350.

Santonastaso, P., Friederici, S., & Favaro, A. (1999). Full and partial syndromes in eating disorders: A 1-year prospective study of risk factors among female students. *Psychopathology, 32,* 50–56.

Sarwer, D. B. (2001). Plastic surgery in children and adolescents. In J. K. Thompson & L. Smolak (Eds.), *Body image, eating disorders, and obesity in youth: Assessment, prevention, and treatment* (pp. 341–366). Washington, DC: American Psychological Association.

Schutz, H. K., Paxton, S. J., & Wertheim, E. H. (2002). Investigation of body comparison among adolescent girls. *Journal of Applied Social Psychology, 32,* 1906–1937.

Shaw, H. E., Stice, E., & Springer, D. W. (2004). Perfectionism, body dissatisfaction, and self-esteem in predicting bulimic symptomatology: Lack of replication. *International Journal of Eating Disorders, 36,* 41–47.

Siegel, J. M. (2002). Body image change and adolescent depressive symptoms. *Journal of Adolescent Research, 17,* 27–41.

Smolak, L., & Levine, M. P. (2001). Body image in children. In J. K. Thompson & L. Smolak (Eds.), *Body image, eating disorders, and obesity in youth: Assessment, prevention, and treatment* (pp. 41–66). Washington, DC: American Psychological Association.

Smolak, L., Levine, M. P., & Gralen, S. (1993). The impact of puberty and dating on eating problems among middle school girls. *Journal of Youth and Adolescence, 22,* 355–368.

Stice, E. (1994). Review of the evidence for a socio-cultural model of bulimia nervosa and an exploration of the mechanisms of action. *Clinical Psychology Review, 14,* 633–661.

Stice, E. (2001). A prospective test of the dual-pathway model of bulimic pathology: Mediating effects of dieting and negative affect. *Journal of Abnormal Psychology, 110,* 124–135.

Stice, E., & Agras, W. S. (1998). Predicting onset and cessation of bulimic behaviors during adolescence: A longitudinal grouping analysis. *Behavior Therapy, 29,* 257–276.

Stice, E., & Bearman, S. K. (2001). Body-image and eating disturbances prospectively predict increases in depressive symptoms in adolescent girls: A growth curve analysis. *Developmental Psychology, 37,* 597–607.

Stice, E., Hayward, C., Cameron, R. P., Killen, J. D., & Taylor, C. B. (2000). Body-image and eating related factors predict onset of depression among female adolescents: A longitudinal study. *Journal of Abnormal Psychology, 109,* 438–444.

Stice, E., Mazotti, L. Krebs, M., & Martin, S. (1998). Predictors of adolescent dieting behaviors: A longitudinal study. *Psychology of Addictive Behaviors, 12,* 195–205.

Stice, E., Presnell, K., & Spangler, D. (2002). Risk factors for binge eating onset: A prospective investigation. *Health Psychology, 21,* 131–138.

Stice, E., Shaw, H., & Nemeroff, C. (1998). Dual pathway model of bulima nervosa: Longitudinal support of dietary restraint and affect-regulation mechanisms. *Journal of Social and Clinical Psychology, 17,* 129–149.

Striegel-Moore, R. H., Schreiber, G. B., Lo, A., Crawford, P., Obarzanek, E., & Rodin, J. (2000). Eating disorder symptoms in a cohort of 11 to 16-year-old Black and White girls: The NHLBI Growth and Health Study. *International Journal of Eating Disorders, 27,* 49–66.

Taylor, C. B., Sharpe, T., Shisslak, C., Bryson, S., Estes, L. S., Gray, N., et al. (1998). Factors associated with weight concerns in adolescent girls. *International Journal of Eating Disorders, 24,* 31–42.

Thompson, J. K., Heinberg, L. J., Altabe, M. N., & Tantleff-Dunn, S. (1999). *Exacting beauty: Theory, assessment, and treatment of body image disturbance.* Washington, DC: American Psychological Association.

Thompson, J. K., & Stice, E. (2001). Thin-ideal internalization: Mounting evidence for a new risk factor for body-image disturbance and eating pathology. *Current Directions in Psychological Science, 10,* 181–183.

Tiggemann, M. (2005). Television and adolescent body image: The role of program content and viewing motivation. *Journal of Social and Clinical Psychology, 24,* 361–381.

Tiggemann, M., & Pennington, B. (1990). The development of gender differences in body-size satisfaction. *Australian Psychologist, 25,* 306–311.

Truby, H., & Paxton, S. J. (2002). Development of the Children's Body Image Scale. *British Journal of Clinical Psychiatry, 41,* 185–203.

Usmiani, S., & Daniluk, J. (1997). Mothers and their adolescent daughters: Relationship between self-esteem, gender role identity, and body image. *Journal of Youth and Adolescence, 26,* 45–62.

van den Berg, P., Thompson, J. K., Obremski-Brandon, K., & Coovert, M. (2002). The Tripartite Influence model of body image and eating disturbance: A covariance structure modelling investigation testing the mediational role of appearance comparison. *Journal of Psychosomatic Research, 53,* 1007–1020.

Wade, T. D., & Lowes, J. (2002). Variables associated with disturbed eating habits and the overvaluation of ideas about the personal implications of body shape and weight in a female adolescent population. *International Journal of Eating Disorders, 32,* 39–45.

Wardle, J., Voltz, C., & Golding, C. (1995). Social variation in attitudes to obesity in children. *International Journal of Obesity, 19,* 562–569.

Wertheim, E. H., Koerner, J., & Paxton, S. J. (2001). Longitudinal predictors of restrictive eating and bulimic tendencies in three different age groups of adolescent girls. *Journal of Youth and Adolescence, 30,* 69–81.

Wertheim, E. H., Martin, G., Prior, M., Sanson, A., & Smart, D. (2002). Parent influences in the transmission of eating and weight related values and behaviors. *Eating Disorders: The Journal of Treatment and Prevention, 10,* 321–334.

Wertheim, E. H., Mee, V., & Paxton, S. J. (1999). Relationships among adolescent girls' eating behaviors and their parents' weight-related attitudes and behaviors. *Sex Roles, 41,* 169–187.

Wertheim, E. H., Paxton, S. J., & Blaney, S. (2004). Risk factors for body image dissatisfaction. In J. K. Thompson (Ed.), *Handbook of eating disorders and obesity* (pp. 463–494). New York: Wiley.

Wertheim, E. H., Paxton, S. J., Schutz, H. K., & Muir, S. L. (1997). Why do adolescent girls watch their weight? An interview study examining sociocultural pressures to be thin. *Journal of Psychosomatic Research, 42,* 345–355.

Wertheim, E. H., Paxton, S. J., & Tilgner, L. (2004). Test–retest reliability and construct validity of Contour Drawing Rating Scale scores in a sample of early adolescent girls. *Body Image, 1,* 199–205.

Wichstrom, L. (2000). Psychological and behavioral factors unpredicitive of disordered eating: A prospective study of the general adolescent population in Norway. *International Journal of Eating Disorders, 28,* 33–42.

Wiseman, C. V., Gray, J. J., Mosimann, J. E., & Athens, A. H. (1992). Cultural expectations of thinness in women: An update. *International Journal of Eating Disorders, 11,* 85–89.

4

BODY IMAGE IN PREADOLESCENT BOYS

LINA A. RICCIARDELLI, MARITA P. MCCABE, ALEXANDER J. MUSSAP,
AND KATE E. HOLT

An increasing number of studies have examined body image attitudes
and concerns among children. In this chapter we review studies that have
included preadolescent boys, with the main focus on boys between ages 6
and 11 years. There is very little research on body image among boys younger
than 6 years of age. Adolescents were not included as they have been
examined in a recent and comprehensive review (Ricciardelli & McCabe,
2007). This review is limited to studies that have been conducted since 2001
or work that was not included in two previous comprehensive reviews of
research with both girls and boys (Ricciardelli & McCabe, 2001a; Smolak
& Levine, 2001).

Since the late 1990s, there has been a growing interest in males' body-
image concerns and their pursuit of muscularity (e.g., Cafri et al., 2005;
Grogan & Richards, 2002; McCabe & Ricciardelli, 2004; McCreary & Sasse,
2000; Pope, Phillips, & Olivardia, 2000; Ricciardelli & McCabe, 2004).
Several health problems and other deleterious psychological behaviors are
associated with these concerns, including low self-esteem, depression, eating
disorders, muscle dysmorphia, and the use of steroids and other bodybuilding

supplements such as ephedrine (see Cafri et al., 2005, for a review). Although researchers have primarily studied adolescent and young adult males, an increasing number of studies are showing that preadolescent boys are already manifesting many of the same concerns (Grogan & Richards, 2002; Hopkins, 2006; McCabe & Ricciardelli, 2003; Smolak, Levine, & Thompson, 2001). Many young boys develop problems that have a negative impact on their health because of their attempts to achieve a more muscular body (Cafri et al., 2005; Pope et al., 2000). Additionally, many males develop patterns of disordered eating (Ricciardelli & McCabe, 2004). Studies that track the development of boys' body-image concerns from a young age through adolescence are needed to help us gain a better understanding of how these problems develop. Such work will assist us in designing prevention programs to address the development of problem behaviors before adolescence.

MEASUREMENT OF BODY IMAGE

In this section we provide an updated review of the measures that have been used to assess body-image concerns among children with a particular focus on the major developments since our 2001 paper (Ricciardelli & McCabe, 2001a). The main measures include figure preference tasks, and other measures that have been adapted from instruments originally designed with adolescents and adults (e.g., Body-Esteem Scale, Body Dissatisfaction subscale, and the Drive for Muscularity).

Figure preference tasks continue to be used frequently with children (e.g., Kostanski & Gullone, 1999; Ricciardelli, McCabe, Holt, & Finemore, 2003; Ricciardelli, McCabe, Lillis, & Thomas, 2006; Williamson & Delin, 2000). These require children to indicate their perceived and ideal body size, and usually consist of five or seven drawings of bodies that range in size from very thin to obese silhouettes. Typically, a measure of body dissatisfaction is obtained by subtracting one's ideal body size from one's perceived size. This measure has been shown to have good test–retest reliability and corresponds well with children's actual body size (Ricciardelli & McCabe, 2001a). Additionally, evidence shows that boys' body dissatisfaction as assessed by figure preference tasks is stable over a 16-month period (Ricciardelli et al., 2006).

A new body figure preference task, Children's Body Image Scale, has been devised. This uses photographic images in order to increase the lifelike qualities of the figure and to help make these easier for children to identify with (Truby & Paxton, 2002). Construct validity for this new scale has been demonstrated in that it was found to correlate highly with the Body-Esteem Scale and the Dutch Eating Behavior Questionnaire-Restraint Scale (Truby & Paxton, 2002).

Body figure preference tasks have also been used with children as young as 3 (Hendy, Gustitus, & Leitzel-Schwalm, 2001) and 4 years of age

(Musher-Eizenman, Holub, Edwards-Leeper, Persson, & Goldstein, 2003). However, no data is available on the reliability of this measure with such young children. Other researchers have further adapted the body figure preference tasks for more specific cultural groups that include Native American children (Rinderknecht & Smith, 2002; Stevens et al., 1999), Chinese children (Li, Hu, Ma, Wu, & Ma, 2005), and Mexican-American children (Olvera, Suminski, & Power, 2005). Finally, one researcher has also adapted the figure preference task for boys to emphasize muscular definition more in the arms, legs, and chest (Holt, 2005). However, the dimension of muscularity needs to be made more specific, as has been done with adult male figure preference tasks, as these now consist of silhouettes that vary concurrently in both their degree of muscularity and adiposity (Cafri, Strauss, & Thompson 2002).

The Body-Esteem Scale and the Body Dissatisfaction subscale from the Eating Disorders Inventory also reviewed in Ricciardelli and McCabe (2001a), are two other measures that continue to be used with young boys (e.g., Gehrman, Hovell, Sallis, & Keating, 2006; Lunde, Frisen, & Hwang, 2006; Smolak et al., 2001). The Body-Esteem Scale was designed by Mendelson, White, and Mendelson (1996) to assess children's attitudes and feelings about their bodies and appearance. Mendelson et al. found that the scale has good psychometric properties for children as young as 8 years. This includes internal consistency, test–retest, factorial validity, and concurrent validity with the body figure preference task.

The Body Dissatisfaction subscale, based on the adult version, assesses beliefs that various parts of the body are too large or are associated with fatness. The scale has been found to demonstrate good psychometric properties with boys as young as 8 years old (Ricciardelli & McCabe, 2001a). However, one of its major limitations is that it focuses exclusively on weight-loss behaviors and concerns about being too fat. The scale has been adapted for use with adolescent boys to include a focus on muscles and building upper body strength (e.g., Ricciardelli & McCabe, 2001b). These modifications also need to be made when the scale is used with preadolescent boys, so that it can more fully capture their range of body-image concerns.

Harter's (1985) Physical Appearance subscale is one of the five subscales from the Self-Perception Profile for Children (McVey, Tweed, & Blackmore, 2005). It assesses children's views about their looks, height, and weight, body, and face and hair (e.g., "Are happy with they way they look"; "Wish their body was different"; "Wish something about their face and hair was different"). It is a standardized and well-validated measure designed for children in Grades 3 to 9. In particular, it has good factorial validity and a high level of internal consistency.

The four-item Body Size Acceptance scale (McVey et al., 2005) is a self-report measure that assesses children's acceptance of varying body shapes and sizes ("I don't care if my if my friends are fat or thin"). It was adapted by

McVey et al. from the Sociocultural Attitudes Towards Appearance Questionnaire (Smolak et al., 2001) for children between ages 10 and 14 years. The available psychometric data on the Body Size Acceptance scale relate only to its internal consistency and this has been found to be in the modest range.

The Drive for Muscularity Scale (Smolak & Stein, 2006), which includes both a behavioral (e.g., "I wish I were more muscular" and an attitudinal (e.g., "I wish that I were more muscular") assessment of one's preoccupation with muscle size, has been primarily validated in adolescents and adults (Cafri & Thompson, 2004; McCreary & Sasse, 2000; McCreary, Sasse, Saucier, & Dorsch, 2004). However, Smolak and colleagues (Smolak, Murnen, & Thompson, 2005; Smolak & Stein, 2006) have used the scale with boys between ages 11 and 15 years; and Harrison and Bond (2007) have adapted the scale for boys as young as 8 years of age. Both Harrison and Bond (2007), and Smolak and Stein (2006) conducted a factor analysis of Drive for Muscularity items with this younger age group but failed to replicate the original factor structure. This may be because some of the items (e.g., weight-lifting equipment and use of food supplements) are less accessible to younger boys, thus suggesting that more work is needed to ensure that the scale is suitable for preadolescent boys.

The Physical Self Description Questionnaire (Marsh, Hau, Sung, & Yu, 2007), originally designed for children of 12 years or older (Byrne, 1996), has been used to study physical self-concepts in children from Hong Kong between ages 8 and 15 years (Marsh et al., 2007). The instrument contains 11 subscales, including one that specifically focuses on appearance (i.e., being good looking, having a nice face) and body fat (i.e. not being overweight, not being too fat). The overall factor structure with the children from Hong Kong 8 to 12 years of age is consistent with the original factor with children 12 years and older. Additionally, all scales demonstrated satisfactory levels of internal consistency with children between ages 8 and 11 years, but these were on the whole, lower, than those found with children aged 12 to 15.

The use of computerized video projection techniques to assess body size estimations among children was also reviewed in Ricciardelli and McCabe (2001a). A distorted image is projected on a video screen, and children are asked to adjust the image until it matches their perceived body size (Gardner, Sorter, & Friedman, 1997). Recordings of children's over- and underestimation of their actual body size are made. However, this method continues to be used infrequently with children. In fact, we found only one other study that has examined video projection methods to assess body size estimates among children (Gardner, Friedman, Stark, & Jackson, 1999).

Finally, we have used single-item questions to assess weight dissatisfaction ("How happy are you with your weight?"), muscle dissatisfaction ("How happy are you with your muscle size?"), weight importance ("How important is your weight?"), and muscle importance among preadolescent boys ("How important is your muscle size?"; McCabe & Ricciardelli, 2003). However, we do not have any reliability or validity data on these single-item scales. We also need to extend these scales to include multiple items that address size, weight, and muscle concerns, in order to more comprehensively assess the nature of body-image concerns in young boys.

PREVALENCE OF BODY IMAGE CONCERNS

In Ricciardelli and McCabe (2001a) we reviewed studies that had been conducted in Australia, Croatia, Great Britain, Israel, Japan, Mexico, Sweden, and the United States. Other studies have been conducted in China (Li et al., 2005), Finland (Angle et al., 2005), Germany (Berger, Schilkel, & Strauss, 2005; Vogele & Woodward, 2005), Ireland (Griffin, Younger, & Flynn, 2004), and Korea (Lee, Sohn, Lee, & Lee, 2004), and with other cultural groups, which include Native Americans (Rinderknecht & Smith, 2002; Stevens et al., 1999), and Mexican Americans (Olvera, Suminski, & Power, 2005).

Based on our review of nine different studies using the figure preference task, we found that estimates of the number of boys who desire a thinner body size range between 27% and 47%. Similarly, estimates of the number of boys who desire a larger body size range between 15% and 44% (Berger et al., 2005; Kostanski & Gullone, 1999; Olvera et al., 2005; Ricciardelli et al., 2003; Rinderknecht & Smith, 2002; Schur, Sanders, & Steiner, 2000; Stevens et al., 1999; Truby & Paxton, 2002; Vogele & Woodward, 2005). The estimates for the number of boys who desire a larger body size are similar to what we found in Ricciardelli and McCabe (13%–48%). However, since the 2001 review, we found a higher number of boys desiring a thinner body size. In 2001 this estimate only ranged between 17% and 30%.

Based on the problems inherent in fully understanding how young children interpret the figure preference task, it is also important that we assess the prevalence of children's body-image concerns using other measures. In a recent cross-sectional study with children between ages 8 and 11, we found that there were no overall sex differences on the desire for a thinner body size, importance placed on weight, strategies to lose weight, or the perceived pressure associated with losing weight (Ricciardelli et al., 2003). However, boys were more likely than girls to desire a larger body size, place a greater importance on muscles, utilize muscle gain strategies, and perceive a greater pressure to increase their muscles. More specifically, we found that close to half the boys desired a thinner body size (47.4%), whereas only 20.7% desired a larger body size as indicated on the Children's Figure Drawings (Collins, 1991). The majority of boys rated both their weight (58.5%) and muscles (59.5%) as important. Additionally, close to one third of boys frequently engaged in weight-loss strategies (responses to individual items ranged from

21.5%–39.6%), whereas almost half of the boys frequently engaged in muscle gain strategies (responses to individual items ranged from 31.7%–51.4%).

AGE

Although body dissatisfaction has been shown to become more pronounced with increasing age (Ricciardelli & McCabe, 2001a), this trend is not as apparent for boys as it is for girls (Gardner et al., 1999; Sands, Tricker, Sherman, Armatas, & Maschette, 1997). However, there has been limited research that has examined body-image concerns that are more relevant to young males, such as the pursuit or the preference for muscularity. In one early study, the preference for a mesomorph body build was found to increase among boys between the ages of 6 to 16 years (Lerner, 1972). Clearly, additional studies are needed to further evaluate the relationship between age and a range of body-image concerns that are relevant for young boys.

BODY MASS INDEX

As found in Ricciardelli & McCabe (2001a), body mass index (BMI) has been shown to be a consistently strong correlate of body dissatisfaction among young boys (Griffin et al., 2004; Holt & Ricciardelli, 2002; Lunde et al., 2006; McCabe & Ricciardelli, 2003; Ricciardelli et al., 2003; Thomas, Ricciardelli, & Williams, 2000; Vogele & Woodward, 2005). BMI is defined as a relationship between weight and height that is associated with body fat and health risk. In McCabe and Ricciardelli (2005), we found that boys classified as overweight or underweight reported the greatest body dissatisfaction, whereas normal-weight boys reported minimal body dissatisfaction. Similarly, another recent study has shown that body dissatisfaction at age 8 was related to increases in BMI during the previous 5 years (Angle et al., 2005).

The relationship between BMI and muscle concerns has been less consistent as two studies have shown no relationship between muscle concerns and BMI (e.g., Holt & Ricciardelli, 2002; Ricciardelli et al., 2006). On the other hand, findings from one cross-sectional study found that lower BMI was correlated with muscle importance (Ricciardelli et al., 2003). Similarly, in a recent longitudinal study we found that lower BMI predicted muscle dissatisfaction 8 months later (McCabe & Ricciardelli, 2005). Additional studies are needed to replicate these findings with more sensitive and comprehensive measures that assess muscle concerns in boys.

Overall, these results would suggest that boys may demonstrate a different pattern from girls. Whereas girls with a high BMI show greater levels of body dissatisfaction (Stice, 2002), boys with a high and low BMI show higher levels of body dissatisfaction. It seems as if boys with a low BMI want to increase their muscles, whereas boys with a high BMI want to lose weight. Additional studies with preadolescent boys are needed to clarify these views.

It is also important to determine whether or not the relationship between BMI and body dissatisfaction is consistent across boys from different cultural groups. However, only one study was located which has addressed this issue. Among Mexican Americans, young boys' perceptions of their actual body size were not found to be related to their BMI nor were they related to their mothers' perceptions of their child's actual body size (Olvera et al., 2005). These findings suggest that some cultural groups may place more importance on a larger body size and this acts as a protective factor in preventing body-image concerns; however, it may place young boys at a greater risk of developing obesity. Research has shown a strong relationship between ethnicity and obesity (Johnson et al., 2007; Skelton, Busey, & Havens, 2006). Clearly, these relationships need to be further explored with boys from other cultural groups.

SOCIOCULTURAL INFLUENCES

Culture

One way of studying the role of sociocultural influences is to examine body-image concerns in different cultures. Since our 2001 review (Ricciardelli & McCabe, 2001a) we have located additional studies that have examined body-image concerns among preadolescents from different cultural groups. However, as this literature is still so sparse, we also include the previous reviewed studies. These include studies that have targeted young Blacks, Hispanics, and Asians. Five located studies that have examined body-size preferences among preadolescent Black boys (Adams et al., 2000; Collins, 1991; Lawrence & Thelen, 1995; Thompson, Corwin, & Sargent, 1997; Welch, Gross, Bronner, Dewberry-Moore, & Paige, 2004) showed that Blacks had a greater preference for a larger body size than Whites.

One factor that may explain why Black boys have a greater preference for a larger body size is their family environment. Black mothers, and even fathers, are likely to transmit positive attitudes about large body sizes to their children through their own acceptance and tolerance of larger body sizes, via direct messages, and indirectly via modeling their own behaviors and attitudes. Although no study was located that has examined the direct or indirect transmission of body image values and messages between parents and children among Black families, one study was found that showed that Black adult males in comparison with Whites reported less emphasis on food and weight concerns in their immediate families (Gray, Ford, & Kelly, 1987).

This has been identified as a potential protective factor for the prevention of body image disturbance and eating disorders (Shisslak & Crago, 2001). However, it may be a risk factor for obesity. Research is needed to address this possibility.

Only one study was located that compared preadolescent Hispanic boys with Whites on body dissatisfaction, but this study showed no differences (Ericksen, Markey, & Tinsley, 2003). A further study included Chinese and Vietnamese preadolescents and adolescents living in Australia (Wang, Byrne, Kenardy, & Hills, 2005). No differences were found between the Chinese/Vietnamese and the White boys.

Other studies have examined body-image concerns among young boys in other non-Western cultural groups although these have not included direct comparisons with Whites. However, these studies have provided evidence that levels of body-image concerns among young males from various cultures are similar to those found among Western cultures. These include the Chinese living in China (Li et al., 2005), American Indians (Story et al., 2001; Rinderknecht & Smith, 2002), Koreans living in Korea (Lee et al., 2004), and Mexican Americans (Olvera et al., 2005).

In future research it will be important to better understand the messages being received from boys in these different cultural groups, how these messages shape boys' body-image concerns, and/or how these may be risk factors for obesity. The major sources of messages for both boys and girls are the media, parents, and peers.

Media

The role of the media has been shown to be an important factor in determining body-image concerns among adolescent girls and to some extent among same-age boys (Ricciardelli & McCabe, 2004). There is less research that has examined the impact of the media on children's body-image concerns; however, this research shows that the media is an important sociocultural force among this younger age group (Cusumano & Thompson, 2001; Smolak et al., 2001).

One measure developed for children is the Multidimensional Media Influence Scale (Cusumano & Thompson, 2001). An analysis identified three factors for both boys and girls. These were the internalization of the thin ideal, awareness of the thin ideal, and perceived pressure from the media to achieve thinness. The three subscales were found to be only weakly correlated with body dissatisfaction among boys, but this is probably due to the fact the scales did not assess internalization, awareness, and perceived media pressure to achieve muscularity, which are likely to be more relevant to boys of all ages.

Another scale that taps into the impact of the media is the preadolescent male version of the Sociocultural Attitudes Towards Appearance concerns many not be adequately assessing relevant body-image concerns among young boys.

INDIVIDUAL FACTORS

Self-Esteem

The relationship between self-esteem and body-image concerns has been increasingly investigated since 2001. However, the evidence for a relationship between these variables remains inconsistent. Some studies have continued to find support for this relationship cross-sectionally (McCabe & Ricciardelli, 2003; Phares et al., 2004; Ricciardelli et al., 2003) and longitudinally (McCabe, Ricciardelli, & Holt, 2005); whereas others have found no support (Ricciardelli et al., 2006; Thomas, Ricciardelli, & Williams, 2000). One possibility for some of these inconsistent findings, as found by McCabe et al. (2005), is that the relationship between self-esteem and body-image concerns is moderated by children's BMI.

Another factor, which may be more closely related to boys' self-esteem and their weight and muscle concerns, is involvement in sports. Sports plays an important socializing role in promoting physical, mental, and social development during childhood and adolescence, particularly for boys (Cooper, 1969; Eppright, Sanfacon, Beck, & Bradley, 1997; Weiss & Duncan, 1992; Weiss, Smith, & Theeboom, 1996). Moreover, sporting activity has been found to be associated with a more positive self-image among adolescent boys (Ferron, Narring, Cauderay, & Michuad, 1999). The importance of sports as a socializing force and as a way of defining body has also been highlighted in a recent qualitative study with preadolescent boys (Hopkins, 2006). Studies that track boys' sporting competency and self-efficacy in this domain from preadolescence to early adulthood may highlight factors related to young boys' body-image concerns.

Negative Affect

No studies were found that examined the relationship between negative affect and body-image concerns among preadolescent boys. Additionally, although there is increasing evidence of an association between negative affect and aspects of disordered eating among both young girls and boys (Saling, Ricciardelli, & McCabe, 2005), only one of four studies has provided evidence to support this association in young boys (Phares et al., 2004; cf. Holt & Ricciardelli, 2002; Ricciardelli et al., 2003, 2006). The failure to consistently detect this relationship may be the result of the low

Questionnaire (Smolak et al., 2001). More specifically, this scale was designed to assess three factors: internalization of the muscular ideal, awareness of the muscular ideal, and the muscular look. Two of these scales were found to correlate with young boys' body esteem scores: internalization of the muscular ideal and the muscular look.

The Media Influence Scale for Adolescent Boys (MISAB; Haselhuhn et al., 2001) has also been used with boys as young as 11 years of age and has been found to predict their muscle-building techniques (Smolak et al., 2005; Smolak & Stein, 2006). The MISAB specifically assesses the perceived influence of muscular images in the media. Included are questions that examine one's interest in looking like the muscular ideal in magazines, on TV, and in movies (e.g., "Reading magazines makes me want to have bigger muscles"). The MISAB has been validated in two samples of boys between 11 and 13 years of age (Haselhuhn et al., 2001).

Another measure adapted from work completed in McCabe and Ricciardelli (2001) with adolescents is the Sociocultural Influences on Body Image and Body Change Questionnaire. We have used this scale with children 8 to 11 years of age to also assess the perceived pressure from mother, father, best friend, and the media to lose weight, and perceived messages from the same sources to increase muscles (Ricciardelli et al., 2003, 2006). Moderate to high intercorrelations were found among the different measures of sociocultural pressures (Ricciardelli et al., 2003). These findings suggest that perceived pressure to lose weight and increase muscles is better conceptualized as two overall scales, rather than as eight individual subscales. Furthermore, it appears that children may not be differentiating well among the different sources of the perceived pressure, but may be responding more to a global internalization of sociocultural ideals about thinness and muscularity. An alternative explanation is that children may be consistently receiving the same type of messages from families, friends, and the media (Flannery-Schroeder & Chrisler, 1996). This pattern of results differs from findings with adolescents, where perceived pressure from parents and peers has been found to be distinct from perceived media pressure. However, further studies are now required to verify these differences between children and adolescents.

In McCabe and Ricciardelli (2005), we found that perceived media pressure to lose weight predicted weight dissatisfaction among young boys over a 16-month period, whereas perceived media pressure to increase muscles predicted weight importance over an 8-month period. Unexpectedly, perceived media pressure was not found to predict muscle dissatisfaction or importance. However, it may be that there was too little variance in boys' scores to detect the influence of the media. Clearly, additional studies are needed with more comprehensive and sensitive measures to assess the range of body-image concerns displayed by young boys. Additionally, studies are needed to examine the actual impact of media exposure on young boys' body-image concerns. All the studies conducted to date have examined perceived media messages.

It has also been suggested that preadolescent boys may be less affected by media influences than young girls. In one study, Murnen, Smolak, Mills, and Good (2003) found that young boys were aware of sociocultural messages about the ideal body, but they were affected less than girls. For example, boys were found to be as aware of the muscular ideal as girls were of the thin and sexy ideal, but this awareness did not predict boys' body-image concerns. Overall, these findings suggest that during preadolescence, boys may be better equipped to ignore media messages about their bodies and do not fully internalize sociocultural messages about ideal weight and muscles. Additionally, although there has been an increase in the number of media images highlighting muscular male bodies (Pope et al., 2000), it is likely that males are still subjected to a wider range of acceptable body shapes and sizes in the media and relatively fewer media messages in comparison to females (Andersen & DiDomenico, 1992). However, further research on the nature and prevalence of media images about body size and shape targeted at both males and females is needed to verify these earlier findings.

Another possibility is that researchers have yet to fully tap into the media sources that may be influencing young boys. One such understudied source is gaming magazines (Harrison & Bond, 2007). Harrison and Bond targeted these magazines, as their review of the literature indicated that boys were reading gaming magazines more than any other form of literature, and content analyses showed that video game characters were extremely muscular. Moreover, the researchers concluded that exposure to video game magazines predicted an increase in drive for muscularity, after 1 year, among White boys between ages 8 and 10.

Two other potential influences on boys' body-image concerns are action figure toys and animated cartoons. Action figure toys have become more muscular, with physiques comparable to advanced bodybuilders, and some exceeding the muscularity of even the largest human bodybuilders (Pope, Olivardia, Gruber, & Borowiecki, 1999). The possible effects of playing with action figures on body-image concerns and related behaviors have not been examined among preadolescent children (Barlett, Harris, Smith, & Bonds-Raacke, 2005). However, one controlled experimental study revealed that young adult males who touched and manipulated unrealistically muscular action figures showed lowered body esteem (Barlett et al., 2005). Clearly, this same type of study needs to be conducted with preadolescent and adolescent boys.

Animated cartoons are also likely to be influential as children are exposed to these from an early age and on a regular basis (Klein & Shiffman, 2006). Although there has been no study examining the impact of messages portrayed by animated cartoons on children's body image and/or appearance concerns, the findings from a recent study suggest that they are likely to be very influential. Klein and Shiffman (2006) found that cartoons provided positive messages about being attractive and negative messages about being unattractive. Studies are now needed that specifically examine exposure and the internalization of cartoon messages on children's body-image concerns.

Parental Influences

As with adolescent and preadolescent girls, mothers are one of the main influences that shape young boys' body-image concerns. Consistently, mothers' messages and own body dissatisfaction have been found to be correlated with body dissatisfaction in their sons (Hendy et al., 2001; Lowes & Tiggemann, 2003). In one study, perceived pressure from mothers to increase muscles (mean age = 9.26 years) predicted weight dissatisfaction 8 months later (mean age = 10.12 years), and muscle dissatisfaction 16 months later (mean age = 10.66 years; McCabe & Ricciardelli, 2005). The role of fathers, although studied less frequently, has not been found to be as influential (Lowes & Tiggemann, 2003; McCabe & Ricciardelli, 2005). Finally, another study also showed that a family history of eating problems was correlated with body dissatisfaction among young boys (Phares, Steinberg, & Thompson, 2004).

Peer Influences

Peer influence is another important sociocultural force that impacts children's body-image concerns. In particular, teasing by peers has been shown to be related to boys' level of body dissatisfaction (Phares et al., 2004) and their body esteem (Lunde et al., 2006).

Peers also can exert their influence indirectly via social comparisons, which have been shown to be important in determining body-image concerns among adolescent girls (Jones, 2001; Jones & Crawford, 2005). Social comparisons also are likely to be important during preadolescence. This is the time when these comparisons first appear and they appear to play a role in other developmental domains such as in overall self-evaluation and academic performance (Holt, 2005). Only one study was located that has examined the relationship between social comparisons and body-image concerns among preadolescent boys (Holt & Ricciardelli, 2002). Boys were found to engage in more social comparisons with adults, whereas girls engaged in more social comparisons with their peers. However, social comparisons among boys were not associated with body dissatisfaction. On the other hand, social comparisons among boys were found to be associated with dieting, food preoccupation, and strategies to increase muscles. These findings raise the possibility that social comparisons may impact on body change strategies but not on body dissatisfaction. Alternatively, the measures used to assess body-image

variance in boys' negative affect scores. For example, it has been shown that the majority of boys attained low scores on negative affect. Clearly, additional studies with more sensitive measures are needed to further assess the relationship between negative affect and body image in young boys.

Perfectionism

Perfectionism is related to preadolescent boys' dieting and muscle preoccupation (both attitudes and strategies to increase muscles; Saling et al., 2005). However, perfectionism has yet to be examined in relation to any aspects of boys' body-image concerns. This is an aspect of individual functioning that may impact on body dissatisfaction, as perfectionists are thought to strive to meet their own high appearance-related standards or those of significant others, such as parents, peers or society more generally (Heatherton & Baumeister, 1991; Hewitt, Flett, & Ediger, 1995).

EATING ATTITUDES AND BEHAVIORS, AND BODY CHANGE STRATEGIES

In line with the findings from Ricciardelli and McCabe (2001a) extensive evidence exists that body-image concerns are linked to eating attitudes and behaviors associated with disordered eating and body change strategies. Body dissatisfaction and other indicators of poor body image have been found to be related to dieting and other weight-loss strategies (Lee et al., 2004; McVey et al., 2005; Ricciardelli et al., 2003; Vogele & Woodward, 2005), the Eating Disorder Inventory (Gardner, Stark, Friedman, & Jackson, 2000; Phares et al., 2004), the Eating Attitudes Test (Keel, Fulkerson, & Leon, 1997) and the Dieting subscale of the Children's Eating Attitude Test (Gardner et al., 2000; Kostanski & Gullone, 1999), and strategies to increase muscles (McVey et al., 2005; Ricciardelli et al., 2003).

One of the limitations with the research just cited is that it has been conducted using cross-sectional research designs. When body-image concerns are examined longitudinally, there is no evidence to show that they predict any eating attitudes and behaviors associated with disordered eating and/or strategies to increase muscles (Gardner et al., 2000; Ricciardelli et al., 2006). Clearly, more research is needed to more fully examine these relationships using more sensitive and comprehensive measures to assess body image. However, these findings are consistent with the overall results found with adolescent boys (Ricciardelli & McCabe, 2004). Thus, it may be that there are other mediating and/or moderating factors that can account for the lack of an overall relationship between body dissatisfaction and disordered eating/strategies to increase muscles among boys.

CONCLUSIONS

Given a limited understanding of the development of body-image concerns among preadolescent boys and the lack of comprehensive and sensitive measures to assess their body image, in-depth and less-structured interview studies, which allow for greater qualitative data analysis, may assist in furthering research in this field. The use of qualitative research designs, such as those used by Grogan and Richards (2002), will allow for issues that are specifically relevant for young boys to emerge from the data and be incorporated into future theoretical models. It is important that measures that are more relevant to boys' body image be developed so that there can be a better understanding of the variables that predict the development of body dissatisfaction among preadolescent boys. More longitudinal and longer term studies are needed so that the antecedents versus the consequences of one's poor body image can be distinguished, and so the various relationships that have been demonstrated cross-sectionally can be more fully assessed. The majority of studies have only examined direct relationships among a set of variables. However, many variables such as BMI and negative affect may act as moderators or even mediators of the relationship between other individual factors and sociocultural influences and body-image concerns (Ricciardelli & McCabe, 2004).

In order to more fully understand the development of body-image concerns, it is important to investigate whether or not the risk factors associated with body-image concerns among children are the same as those found for adolescents. A greater understanding of the development of these concerns will lead to more appropriate and effective educational programs. More research on this topic is also needed, so that better educational and intervention programs that target protective and risk factors in children can be implemented before their body-image concerns, body change strategies, and eating problems increase in frequency and severity.

REFERENCES

Adams, K., Sargent, R. G., Thompson, S. H., Richter, D., Corwin, S. J., & Rogan, T. J. (2000). A study of body weight concerns and weight control practices of 4th and 7th grade adolescents. *Ethnicity and Health, 5,* 79–94.

Andersen, A. E., & DiDomenico, L. (1992). Diet vs. shape contents of popular male and female magazines: A dose–response relationship to the incidence of eating disorders? *International Journal of Eating Disorders, 11,* 283–287.

Angle, S., Keskinen, S., Lapinleimu, H., Helenius, H., Raittinen, P., Ronnemaa, T., & Simell, O. (2005). Weight gain since infancy and prepubertal body dissatisfaction. *Archives of Pediatric and Adolescent Medicine, 159,* 567–571.

Barlett, C., Harris, R., Smith, S., & Bonds-Raacke, J. (2005). Action figures and men. *Sex Roles, 53*, 877–885.

Berger, U., Schilkel, C., & Strauss, B. (2005). Weight concerns and dieting among 8- to 12-year-old children. *Psychotherapie Psychomatik Medizinische Psychologie, 55*, 331–338.

Byrne, B. (1996). *Measuring self-concept across the life span: Issues and instrumentation.* Washington, DC: American Psychological Association.

Cafri, G., Strauss, J., & Thompson, J. K. (2002). Male body image: Satisfaction and its relationship to well-being using the somatomorphic matrix. *International Journal of Men's Health, 1*, 215–231.

Cafri, G., & Thompson, J. K. (2004). Evaluating the convergence of muscle appearance attitude measures. *Assessment, 11*, 224–229.

Cafri, G., Thompson, J. K., Ricciardelli, L. A., McCabe, M. P., Smolak, L., & Yesalis, C. (2005). Pursuit of the muscular ideal: Physical and psychological consequences and putative risk factors. *Clinical Psychology Review, 25*, 215–239.

Collins, M. E. (1991). Body figure perceptions and preferences among preadolescent children. *International Journal of Eating Disorders, 10*, 199–208.

Cooper, L. (1969). Athletics, activity, and personality: A review of the literature. *Research Quarterly, 40*, 17–22.

Cusumano, D. L., & Thompson, J. K. (2001). Media influence and body image in 8- to 11-year-old boys and girls: A preliminary report on the Multidimensional Media Influence Scale. *International Journal of Eating Disorders, 29*, 37–44.

Ericksen, A. J., Markey, C. N., & Tinsley, B. J. (2003). Familial influences on Mexican American and Euro-American preadolescent boys' and girls' body dissatisfaction. *Eating Behaviors, 4*, 245–255.

Eppright, T. D., Sanfacon, J. A., Beck, N. C., & Bradley, J. S. (1997). Sport psychiatry in childhood and adolescence: An overview. *Child Psychiatry and Human Development, 28*, 71–88.

Ferron, C., Narring, F., Cauderay, M., & Michuad, P. A. (1999). Sport activity in adolescence: Associations with health perceptions and experimental behaviours. *Health Education Research, 14*, 225–233.

Flannery-Schroeder, E. C., & Chrisler, J. C. (1996). Body esteem, eating attitudes, and gender-role orientation in three age groups of children. *Current Psychology, 15*, 235–248.

Gardner, R. M., Friedman, B. N., Stark, K., & Jackson, N. A. (1999). Body-size estimations in children six through fourteen: A longitudinal study. *Perceptual and Motor Skills, 88*, 541–555.

Gardner, R. M., Sorter, R. G., & Friedman, B. N. (1997). Development of changes in children's body images. *Journal of Social Behavior and Personality, 12*, 1019–1036.

Gardner, R. M., Stark, K., Friedman, B. N., & Jackson, N. A. (2000). Predictors of eating disorder scores in children ages 6 to 14: A longitudinal study. *Journal of Psychosomatic Research, 49*, 199–205.

Gehrman, G. A., Hovell, M. F., Sallis, J. F., & Keating, K. (2006). The effects of a physical activity and nutrition intervention on body dissatisfaction, drive for thinness, and weight concerns in pre-adolescents. *Body Image, 3*, 345–351.

Gray, J. J., Ford, K., & Kelly, L. (1987). The prevalence of bulimia in a black college population. *International Journal of Eating Disorders, 6*, 733–740.

Griffin, A. C., Younger, K. M., & Flynn, M. A. T. (2004). Assessment of obesity and fear of fatness among inner-city Dublin schoolchildren in a one-year follow-up study. *The Nutrition Society, 7*, 729–735.

Grogan, S., & Richards, H. (2002). Body image: Focus groups with boys and men. *Men and Masculinities, 4*, 219–232.

Harrison, K., & Bond, B. J. (2007). Gaming magazines and the drive for muscularity in preadolescent boys: A longitudinal examination. *Body Image, 4*, 269–277.

Harter, S. (1985). *Manual for the self-perception profile for children.* Denver, CO: University of Denver.

Haselhuhn, G., Thompson, J. K., Roehrig, M., Shroff, H., van den Berg, P., Keery, H., et al. (2001, November). *Development of the media influence scale for adolescent boys.* Paper presented at the Association of the Advancement of Behavior Therapy, Philadelphia.

Heatherton, T. F., & Baumeister, R. F. (1991). Binge eating as escape from self-awareness. *Psychological Bulletin, 110*, 86–108.

Hendy, H. M., Gustitus, C., & Leitzel-Schwalm, J. (2001). Social cognitive predictors of body image in preschool children. *Sex Roles, 44*, 557–569.

Hewitt, P. L., Flett, G. L., & Ediger, E. (1995). Perfectionism traits and perfectionistic self-presentation in eating disorder attitudes, characteristics, and symptoms. *International Journal of Eating Disorders, 18*, 317–326.

Holt, K., & Ricciardelli, L. A. (2002). Social comparisons and negative affect as indicators of problem eating and muscle preoccupation among children. *Journal of Applied Developmental Psychology, 23*, 285–304.

Holt, K. E. (2005). *Preventing weight and muscle concerns among preadolescents.* Unpublished doctoral thesis, Deakin University, Melbourne, Australia.

Hopkins, V. (2006). *Understanding pre-pubescent and post-pubescent boys' body image: An interpretative phenomenological analysis.* Unpublished thesis, Staffordshire University, Stoke-on-Trent, United Kingdom.

Johnson, S. B., Pilkington, L. L., Deeb, L. C., Jeffers, S., He, J., & Lamp, C. (2007). Prevalence of overweight in north Florida elementary and middle school children: Effects of age, sex, ethnicity, and socioeconomic status. *Journal of School Health, 77*, 630–636.

Jones, D. C. (2001). Social comparison and body image: Attractiveness comparison to models and peers among adolescent girls and boys. *Sex Roles, 45*, 645–664.

Jones, D. C., & Crawford, J. K. (2005). Adolescent boys and body image: Weight and muscularity concerns as dual pathways to body dissatisfaction. *Journal of Youth and Adolescence, 34*, 629–636.

Keel, P. K., Fulkerson, J. A., & Leon, G. R. (1997). Disordered eating precursors in pre- and early adolescent girls and boys. *Journal of Youth and Adolescence, 26*, 203–216.

Klein, H., & Shiffman, K. S. (2006). Messages about physical attractiveness in animated cartoons. *Body Image, 3*, 353–363.

Kostanski, M., & Gullone, E. (1999). Dieting and body image in the child's world: Conceptualization and behavior. *The Journal of Genetic Psychology, 160*, 488–499.

Lawrence, C. M., & Thelen, M. H. (1995). Body image, dieting, and self-concept: Their relation in African-American and Caucasian children. *Journal of Clinical Child Psychology, 24,* 41–48.

Lee, K., Sohn, H., Lee, S., & Lee, J. (2004). Weight and BMI over 6 years in Korean children: Relationships to body image and weight loss efforts. *Obesity, 12,* 1959–1966.

Lerner, R. M. (1972). "Richness" analyses of body build stereotype development. *Developmental Psychology, 7,* 219.

Li, Y., Hu, X., Ma, W., Wu, J., & Ma, G. (2005). Body image perceptions among Chinese children and adolescents. *Body Image, 2,* 91–104.

Lowes, J., & Tiggemann, M. (2003). Body dissatisfaction, dieting awareness and the impact of parental influences in young children. *British Journal of Health Psychology, 8,* 135–147.

Lunde, C., Frisen, A., & Hwang, C. P. (2006). Is peer victimization related to body esteem in 10-year old girls and boys? *Body Image, 3,* 25–33.

Marsh, H. W., Hau, K. T., Sung, R. Y. T., & Yu, C. W. (2007). Childhood obesity, gender, actual-ideal body image discrepancies, and physical self-concept in Hong Kong children: Cultural differences in the value of moderation. *Developmental Psychology, 43,* 647–662.

McCabe, M. P., & Ricciardelli, L. A. (2001). Body image and body change techniques among young adolescent boys. *European Eating Disorders Review, 9,* 335–347.

McCabe, M. P., & Ricciardelli, L. A. (2003). Body image and strategies to lose weight and increase muscle among boys and girls. *Health Psychology, 22,* 39–44.

McCabe, M. P., & Ricciardelli, L. A. (2004). Body image dissatisfaction among males across the lifespan: A review of past literature. *Journal of Psychosomatic Research, 56,* 675–685.

McCabe, M. P., & Ricciardelli, L. A. (2005). A longitudinal study of body image and strategies to lose weight and increase muscles among children. *Journal of Applied Developmental Psychology, 26,* 559–577.

McCabe, M. P., Ricciardelli, L. A., & Holt, K. (2005). A longitudinal study to explain strategies to change weight and muscles among normal weight and overweight children. *Appetite, 45,* 225–234.

McCreary, D. R., & Sasse, D. K. (2000). An exploration of the drive for muscularity in adolescent boys and girls. *Journal of American College Health, 48,* 297–304.

McCreary, D. R., Sasse, D. K., Saucier, D. M., & Dorsch, K. (2004). Measuring the drive for muscularity: Factorial validity for the Drive for Muscularity Scale in men and women. *Psychology of Men and Masculinity, 6,* 83–94.

McVey, G. L., Tweed, S., & Blackmore, E. (2005). Correlates of weight loss and muscle-gaining behavior in 10- to 14-year-old males and females. *Preventive Medicine, 40,* 1–9.

Mendelson, B. K., White, D. R., & Mendelson, M. J. (1996). Self-esteem and body esteem: Effects of gender, age, and weight. *Journal of Applied Developmental Psychology, 17,* 321–346.

Murnen, S. K., Smolak, L., Mills, A. J., & Good, L. (2003). Thin, sexy women and strong muscular men: Grade-school children's responses to objectified images of women and men. *Sex Roles, 49,* 427– 437.

Musher-Eizenman, D. R., Holub, S. C., Edwards-Leeper, L., Persson, A. V., & Goldstein, S. E. (2003). The narrow range of acceptable body types of preschoolers and their mothers. *Journal of Applied Developmental Psychology, 24,* 259–272.

Olvera, N., Suminski, R., & Power, T. G. (2005). Intergenerational perceptions of body image in Hispanics: The role of BMI, gender, and acculturation. *Obesity Research, 13,* 1970–1979.

Phares, V., Steinberg, A. R., & Thompson, J. K. (2004). Gender differences in peer and parental influences: Body image disturbance, self-worth, and psychological functioning in preadolescent children. *Journal of Youth and Adolescence, 33,* 421–429.

Pope, H. G., Olivardia, R., Gruber, A., & Borowiecki, J. (1999). Evolving ideals of male body image as seen through action toys. *International Journal of Eating Disorders, 26,* 65–72.

Pope, H. G., Phillips, K. A., & Olivardia, R. (2000). *The Adonis complex: The secret crisis of male body obsession.* New York: The Free Press.

Ricciardelli, L. A., & McCabe, M. P. (2001a). Children's body image concerns and eating disturbances. *Clinical Psychology Review, 21,* 325–344.

Ricciardelli, L. A., & McCabe, M. P. (2001b). Dietary restraint and negative affect as mediators of body dissatisfaction and bulimic behavior in adolescent girls and boys. *Behaviour Research and Therapy, 39,* 1317–1328.

Ricciardelli, L. A., & McCabe, M. P. (2004). A biopsychosocial model of disordered eating and the pursuit of muscularity in adolescent boys. *Psychological Bulletin, 130,* 179–205.

Ricciardelli, L. A., & McCabe, M. P. (2007). Pursuit of muscularity among adolescents. In J. K. Thompson & G. Cafri (Eds.), *The muscular ideal: Psychological, social, and medical perspectives* (pp. 199–216). Washington, DC: American Psychological Association.

Ricciardelli, L. A., McCabe, M. P., Holt, K. E., & Finemore, J. (2003). A biopsychosocial model for understanding body image and body change strategies among children. *Journal of Applied Developmental Psychology, 24,* 475–495.

Ricciardelli, L. A., McCabe, M. P., Lillis, J., & Thomas, K. (2006). A longitudinal investigation of the development of weight and muscle concerns among preadolescent boys. *Journal of Youth and Adolescence, 35,* 177–187.

Rinderknecht, K., & Smith, C. (2002). Body-image perceptions among urban Native-American youth. *Obesity Research, 10,* 315–327.

Saling, M., Ricciardelli, L. A., & McCabe, M. P. (2005). A prospective study of individual factors in the development of weight and muscle concerns among preadolescent children. *Journal of Youth and Adolescence, 34,* 651–661.

Sands, R., Tricker, J., Sherman, C., Armatas, C., & Maschette, W. (1997). Disordered eating patterns, body image, self-esteem, and physical activity in preadolescent school children. *International Journal of Eating Disorders, 21,* 159–166.

Schur, E. A., Sanders, M., & Steiner, H. (2000). Body dissatisfaction and dieting in young children. *International Journal of Eating Disorders, 27,* 74–82.

Shisslak, C. M., & Crago, M. (2001). Risk and protective factors in the development of eating disorders. In J. K. Thompson & L. Smolak (Eds.), *Body image, eating disorders, and obesity in youth: Assessment, prevention, and treatment* (pp. 103–125). Washington, DC: American Psychological Association.

Skelton, J. A., Busey, S. L., & Havens, P. L. (2006). Weight and health status of inner city African American children: Perceptions of children and their parents. *Body Image, 3,* 289–293.

Smolak, L., & Levine, M. P. (2001). Body image in children. In J. K. Thompson & L. Smolak (Eds), *Body image, eating disorders, and obesity in youth: Assessment, prevention, and treatment* (pp. 41–66). Washington, DC: American Psychological Association.

Smolak, L., Levine, M. P., & Thompson, J. K. (2001). The use of the Sociocultural Attitudes Towards Appearance Questionnaire with middle school boys and girls. *International Journal of Eating Disorders, 29,* 216–223.

Smolak, L., Murnen, S. K., & Thompson, J. K. (2005). Sociocultural influences and muscle building in adolescent boys. *Psychology of Men and Masculinity, 6,* 227–239.

Smolak, L., & Stein, J. A. (2006). The relationship of drive for muscularity to sociocultural factors, self-esteem, physical attributes, gender role, and social comparison in middle school boys. *Body Image, 3,* 121–129.

Stevens, J., Story, M., Becenti, A., French, S. A., Gittelsohn, J., & Going, S. B. (1999). Weight-related attitudes and behaviors in fourth grade American Indian children. *Obesity Research, 7,* 34–42.

Stice, E. (2002). Risk and maintenance factors for eating pathology: A meta-analytic review. *Psychological Bulletin, 128,* 825–848.

Story, M., Stevens, J., Evans, M., Cornell, C. E., Juhaeri, Gittelsohn, J. J., et al. (2001). Weight loss attempts and attitudes toward body size, eating, and physical activity in American Indian children: Relationship to weight status and gender. *Obesity Research, 9,* 356–363.

Thomas, K., Ricciardelli, L. A., & Williams, R. J. (2000). Gender traits and self-concept as indicators of problem eating and body dissatisfaction among children. *Sex Roles, 43,* 441–458.

Thompson, S. H., Corwin, S. J., & Sargent, R. G. (1997). Ideal body size beliefs and weight concerns of fourth-grade children. *International Journal of Eating Disorders, 21,* 279–284.

Truby, H., & Paxton, S. J. (2002). Development of the Children's Body Image Scale. *British Journal of Clinical Psychology, 41,* 185–203.

Vogele, C., & Woodward, H. (2005). Body image, dietary restraint, and physical activity in 9-10-year-old children. *Kindheit Und Entwicklung, 14,* 229–236.

Wang, Z., Byrne, N. M., Kenardy, J. A., & Hills, A. P. (2005). Influences of ethnicity and socioeconomic status on the body dissatisfaction and eating behaviour of Australian children and adolescents. *Eating Behaviors, 6,* 23–33.

Weiss, M. R., & Duncan, S. C. (1992). The relationship between physical competence and peer acceptance in the context of children's sports participation. *Journal of Sport Exercise Psychology, 14,* 177–191.

Weiss, M. R., Smith, A. L., & Theeboom, M. (1996). "That's what friends are for": Children's and teenager' perceptions of peer relationships in the sport domain. *Journal of Sport Exercise Psychology, 18,* 347–379.

Welch, C., Gross, S. M., Bronner, Y., Dewberry-Moore, N., & Paige, D. M. (2004). Discrepancies in body image perception among fourth-grade public school children from urban, suburban, and rural Maryland. *Journal of the American Dietetic Association, 104,* 1080–1085.

Williamson, S., & Delin, C. (2000). Young children's figural selections: Accuracy of reporting and body size dissatisfaction. *International Journal of Eating Disorders, 29,* 80–84.

5

OVERWEIGHT, EATING BEHAVIORS, AND BODY IMAGE IN ETHNICALLY DIVERSE YOUTH

DEBRA L. FRANKO AND JESSICA B. EDWARDS GEORGE

The prevalence of overweight is rapidly increasing among children and adolescents and rates are especially elevated among ethnic minority youth (Ogden, Flegal, Carroll, & Johnson, 2002). At the same time, the occurrence of eating disorders, body image disturbance, and problematic eating behaviors in youth is also alarmingly high (McDermott & Jaffa, 2005). Although once thought to be solely the purview of White children and adolescents, eating disorders and related body image concerns are now known to affect all racial and ethnic groups (Franko, Becker, Thomas, & Herzog, 2007; Ruiz, Pepper, & Wilfley, 2004). Examining eating disorders, body image issues, and weight-related problems such as obesity in ethnic groups is important for several reasons. First, rates of occurrence differ across ethnic groups, with some more affected than others. Second, health disparities in recognition, access to care, and treatments have been documented. Third, risk factors for these problems vary because of social, cultural, and economic factors. Finally, because of these differences, the need for treatments that are culturally, racially, and ethnically relevant is great. This chapter examines these topics in five groups in the United States: African American youth; Latinos/Latinas; youth of Asian descent, Native Hawaiians, and Pacific Islanders; Native American/Alaskan Natives; and non-Hispanic White youth. We begin with a review of overweight and conclude with a summary of eating disorders, body image, and problematic eating behaviors among these five groups.

OVERWEIGHT IN ETHNICALLY DIVERSE CHILDREN AND ADOLESCENTS

Prevalence studies provide estimates of the frequency of overweight, allowing for comparisons among groups and identification of trends over time. This section will also highlight possible etiologic factors and health implications of overweight in youth.

Prevalence

The prevalence of overweight in children and adolescents has increased dramatically over the last several decades. Among children and adolescents ages 6 to 19 years, the prevalence of overweight has risen from 4% to 5% in the late 1960s to 16% in 2002 (Centers for Disease Control and Prevention [CDC], 2004a), causing great concern among health-care professionals and the general public (Ogden et al., 2002). These rates have remained the same between 2002 and 2006 (Ogden, Carroll, & Flejal, 2008). High rates of overweight in children and adolescents are particularly worrisome because overweight is likely to persist and exert its health effects into adulthood (Guo & Chumlea, 1999; Must, 2003). In fact, Dietz and Gortmaker (2001) specified that "obesity during adolescence is the single best predictor of adult obesity" (p. 338). Currently, health experts caution that today's children may be among the first to have a shorter life span than their parents as a result of overweight-related deaths.

Although the overweight epidemic affects all ethnic, racial, and socio-economic groups, and both sexes, some ethnically diverse groups are dispropor-tionately affected. It is important to note when discussing rates of overweight in children and adolescents from diverse ethnic groups that although many prevalence studies have been conducted, no one data source has been able to estimate prevalence among all the major minority subgroups.

Native American, African American, and Mexican American children and adolescents are more likely to be overweight than their White peers and youth from poorer families (CDC, 2004b; Freedman, Khan, Serdula, Ogden, & Dietz, 2006; Ogden et al., 2008; Sorof, Lai, Turner, Poffenbarger, & Portman, 2004; U.S. Department of Health and Human Services, 2001). A recent study of 3-year-old children found that the prevalence of obesity (defined as a body mass index [BMI] at the 95th percentile or higher for age and sex) was 25.8% among Hispanics (of any race), 16.2% among Blacks, and 14.8% for White children (Whitaker & Orzol, 2006). BMI is defined as the relationship between weight and height that is associated with body fat and health risk. BMI of 30 to 39 is considered obese; 40 or greater is considered morbid obesity. By adolescence, the prevalence of overweight in African American girls is twice as high as White girls, and prevalence rates are rising most in Hispanic adolescents (Troiano & Flegal, 1998). Based on representative data from the National Longitudinal Study of Adolescent Health (AdHealth) of 7th- to 12th-grade students, overweight prevalence was highest among non-Hispanic Black girls, non-Hispanic White boys, and Hispanic boys and girls, with mean BMI values ranging from 31.6 at 12 years to 35.2 at 18 years in the overweight group (Gordon-Larsen, Adair, & Popkin, 2003). A study by Patrick et al. (2004) showed that girls had a greater risk of being overweight if they were Hispanic or from another minority background. More than one fourth of Samoan preschool children were found to be overweight in a study of Hawaii's Supplemental Nutrition Program for Women, Infants, and Children (Baruffi, Hardy, Waslien, Uyehara, & Krupitsky, 2004). This rate was more than double than that of any other ethnic subgroup represented in the study's sample.

Asian American children and adolescents, on the other hand, appear to be the exception among ethnically diverse groups. The AdHealth study found that Asian American adolescents had relatively low rates of overweight when compared with their White, African American, and Latino/Latina peers (Gordon-Larsen et al., 2003). Specifically, 23% of Asian American boys and only 10% of Asian American girls were overweight, whereas 26% of African American, 27% of White, and 28% of Latino boys and 38% of African American, 22% of White, and 30% of Latina girls were found to be overweight. It is important to note that a lower prevalence of overweight in Asian American children may not necessarily reflect an equivalent lower level of health risk in adulthood, because BMIs below the usual cutoff for overweight are associated with higher health risks in people of Asian decent when compared with other White and non-White populations (World Health Organization Expert Consultation, 2004). The rate of overweight among immigrant Asian/Pacific Islanders has been found to increase with a greater number of years in the United States (Popkin & Udry, 1998). Lifestyle, acculturation, and cultural beliefs and practices may contribute to the comparatively lower rate of overweight in Asian American youth.

Although the prevalence of overweight in youth from diverse ethnic groups is of great concern, the prevalence of overweight in non-Hispanic White youth is also increasingly problematic. Ogden and colleagues (2002) found that 20.5% of non-Hispanic White children between the ages of 2 and 5 years, 26.2% of non-Hispanic White children between the ages of 6 and 11 years, and 26.5% of non-Hispanic White adolescents between the ages of 12 and 19 years were overweight or at risk for becoming overweight. In summary, African American, Latino/Latina, and Native American youth have generally been found to have higher rates of overweight than their White peers. Rates are particularly high for African American girls and Latino boys and for Native American children. Although Samoan children appear to be at high risk, Asian American children in general seem to be insulated from the trend of increased overweight in ethnic minority children and adolescents. Additionally, children and adolescents from poorer families are more likely to be obese. Understanding why children and adolescents from diverse ethnic groups are more liable to become and remain overweight, in conjunction with developing and implementing culturally specific and effective prevention and treatment strategies, is an important public health priority.

Health Implications

Overweight can be a direct or an indirect contributor to the occurrence of several major health problems and chronic diseases. It is clear that children experience negative effects of overweight in ways similar to adults (Daniels et al., 2005). Diabetes, hypertension, coronary heart disease, high cholesterol, asthma, arthritis, stroke, psychological disorders/psychosocial difficulties, and sleep apnea are just a few of the comorbidities that can develop as a result of being overweight (Daniels, 2006; Wadden & Stunkard, 2002). As BMI increases so does the risk for these health problems (Mokdad et al., 2001), which are appearing in many overweight children and adolescents much earlier than in the past (Daniels, 2006). The greater risk of developing health problems affects all groups, regardless of race and ethnicity (Must et al., 1999). However, because children who are ethnically diverse are more likely to be overweight than White children, they are at higher risk to experience weight-related health problems, a trend that will become increasingly problematic as they age.

Why the Disproportionate Prevalence of Overweight in Diverse Ethnic Groups of Children?

There is no doubt that childhood overweight is the result of the interaction of multiple factors, including genetics, the environment, and behavior. Increased portion sizes, greater availability and consumption of soft drinks and fast foods, more time spent engaging in sedentary activities (e.g., computer use, television viewing, and video games), and higher stress levels are just a few of the many identified environmental culprits that contribute to an energy imbalance (more energy consumed than burned) in children and adolescents (Ebbeling, Pawlak, & Ludwig, 2002). The evolution of a "toxic environment" (Wadden, Brownell, & Foster, 2002) provides ideal conditions for the development of childhood overweight and this is especially the case for youth from diverse groups.

The intersection of socioeconomic status (SES), race, and ethnicity is important to examine in order to better understand the differential rates of overweight in minority youth. Low-income levels are substantially more prevalent among minority communities and families (CDC, 2004b). Links between SES, ethnicity, and overweight in children and adolescents have been found to vary, although it is clear that the relationships exist and are quite complex (Gordon-Larsen et al., 2003). Access to and availability of healthy foods are related to SES and, thus, often race and ethnicity. For example, fresh fruits and vegetables, relative to processed foods, cost significantly more (Egger & Swinburn, 1997). Processed foods are not only less expensive and often more caloric than fresh foods, but they are also much more accessible to urban communities, where many ethnically and racially diverse individuals reside (Smith, 2004). Fresh food can be difficult to obtain in urban areas where large grocery stores are few and families rely on a small number of neighborhood markets with little fresh food choices. Poorer neighborhoods also have a disproportionately higher number of fast food restaurants (Nayga & Weinberg, 1999; Zenk et al., 2005). Additionally, the preparation of fresh meals can be time consuming because they require planning, shopping, and preparing/cooking. It can be difficult for many minority working families to find the additional time necessary to prepare fresh meals each day and a low income may preclude buying healthy prepre-pared foods for consumption.

Culturally influenced food preferences and means of preparing foods may also be contributing to the overweight problem in minority children and adolescents (Airhihenbuwa, Kumanyika, Agurs, & Lowe, 1995; Vazquez, Millen, Bissett, Levelnson, & Chipkin, 1998). In many minority groups, food is particularly important as currency in familial and social relationships. Eating large quantities of food is considered not only acceptable, but is sometimes encouraged. Additionally, certain traditional ethnic cuisine is prepared with higher caloric ingredients and by using food preparation techniques high in fat. When this type of food is preferred and eaten frequently, it may cause an increase in weight that starts early in childhood and continues throughout development.

Ethnic minority children and adolescents have been found to spend disproportionately more time engaging in sedentary behaviors (e.g., television watching and computer use) as well as less time spent engaging in physical activities. One consequence is greater exposure to media and marketing activities than other children (Roberts, Foehr, & Rideout, 1999; Rose & Bodor, 2006). Television viewing has been found to be especially common in African American and low-income households. One report found that African American and Latino/a youth spend significantly more time watching television and movies and playing video games then their White counterparts (Roberts et al., 1999). In general, children who watch less than 2 hours of television per day have significantly lower BMIs than children who watch 4 or more hours per day (Andersen, Crespo, Bartlett, Cheskin, & Pratt, 1998). Getting enough physical activity is a particularly difficult problem for ethnically diverse youth. Communities in which these children often live have barriers to physical activity participation, such as unsafe neighborhoods and minimal recreational facilities (Barlow & Dietz, 1998; King et al., 2000). Additionally, a lack of adult supervision for children after school due to parents' work schedules limits the opportunity to engage in physical activity.

With the disproportionate prevalence of overweight in ethnic minority children and adolescents (i.e., Native Americans, African Americans, and Hispanic Americans, all groups whose numbers are increasing in the United States), it is important to address the complex interplay of factors responsible for this public health crisis. Fully understanding why minority children and adolescents are more prone to become overweight, in combination with developing and implementing effective overweight prevention and intervention strategies, needs to be a priority for researchers and clinicians. Further quantification of prevalence, contributing factors, and what cultural adaptations, if any, are effective in preventing and treating overweight in minority children and adolescents is necessary for the health of ethnic minority families.

PROBLEMATIC EATING BEHAVIORS AND BODY IMAGE

Although obesity has taken center stage as a major health problem in children and adolescents, the prevalence of problematic eating behaviors and body dissatisfaction also ranks high as an area of significant concern for youth. The potential links between obesity and eating disorders are important to understand for a number of reasons: (a) each of these issues affects a large number of children and adolescents; (b) both are associated with significant health and psychosocial problems; and (c) efforts to date indicate that these are preventable conditions, although prevention efforts have not been altogether successful (Flodmark, Marcus, & Britton, 2006; chap. 11, this volume; Stice, Shaw, & Marti, 2007).

With the media focus on high rates of obesity, continued attention to celebrity weight fluctuations (either getting too thin or gaining too much weight), and proliferation of teenage fashion and sports magazines, children and adolescents are exposed repeatedly to messages that "fat is bad and thin is good." At the same time, advertisements for high-calorie foods, the abundance of fast food restaurants, and the explosion of video and computer games have been associated with less healthy eating and more sedentary behaviors. The interplay between the environmental factors that increase risk for obesity and messages that being overweight is to be avoided at all costs conspire to make overweight and eating disorders (and the related body dissatisfaction and problematic eating behaviors) significant issues for youth. The societal directive to "not be fat" may in fact increase the potential for body dissatisfaction, dieting, use of extreme weight-loss behaviors, and potentially, clinical eating disorders (Neumark-Sztainer, 2005). We now turn our focus to review what is currently known about body image and problematic eating behaviors in the four major ethnic groups and non-Hispanic White youth in the United States, noting that there are no studies of the prevalence of clinical eating disorders (anorexia nervosa and bulimia nervosa) in ethnically diverse children and adolescents.

Definitions

Body image has been defined in a number of ways (Cash, 1991), but most simply it is the perception of one's body shape and size. Body dissatisfaction is the difference between that perception and one's preferred body shape and size. The larger the discrepancy between perception and preference, the greater the body dissatisfaction. Eating disturbances refer to a variety of problematic eating behaviors, including extreme dieting, binge eating, vomiting or laxative use, diet pill use, fasting, and excessive exercise. Data from an early study (French et al., 1997) of more than 17,000 adolescent girls concluded that ethnic group "did not protect against the broader sociocultural factors that foster body dissatisfaction among adolescent females" (p. 315). As seen in Table 5.1, problematic eating behaviors affected girls from all five groups to varying degrees.

Body Image and Eating Disturbances in African American Children and Adolescents

Body dissatisfaction and eating disturbances have been studied in African Americans and overall, studies indicate that African American youth generally prefer a larger body size than other groups and are less likely to endorse a thin body ideal (Ruiz et al., 2004). African American adolescent girls choose a larger figure as ideal and are less likely to view themselves as overweight even when they have high BMIs (Flynn & Fitzgibbon, 1998). And, in contrast to White adolescent females, African American adolescents have higher self-esteem even when at a higher weight (Biro, Striegel-Moore, Franko, Padgett, & Bean, 2006). Vander Wal and Thomas (2004) reported that young African American girls had significantly lower body dissatisfaction than their Hispanic counterparts. However, one small study comparing African American, Latina, and White youth found that although African American adolescents chose a larger body figure as their

TABLE 5.1
Frequency of Dieting, Binge Eating, and Purging in Adolescent Girls

	White	Black	Hispanic	American Indian	Asian
Dieting[a]	21.5%	13.6%	23.6%	20.6%	17.4%
Binge eating[b]	20.6%	23.0%	25.2%	29.0%	33.6%
Purging[c]	14.3%	19.4%	25%	22.3%	17.9%

Note. "Ethnic Differences in Psychosocial and Health Behavior Correlates of Dieting, Purging, and Binge Eating in a Population-Based Sample of Adolescent Females," by S. A. French, M. Story, D. Neumark-Sztainer, B. Downes, M. Resnick, and R. Blum, 1997, *International Journal of Eating Disorders, 22,* pp. 315–322. Copyright 1997 by John Wiley Sons, Inc. Adapted with permission of John Wiley & Sons, Inc.
[a]"How often have you gone on a diet in the last year? By dieting we mean changing the way you eat so you can lose weight."
[b]"Have you ever eaten so much in a short period of time that you felt out of control and would be embarrassed if others saw you?"
[c]"How often do you vomit on purpose after eating? Do you use laxatives, diuretics, or Ipecac to lose weight?"

preferred body type, there were no significant differences in the discrepancy between current and ideal body size across the three groups (Perry, Rosenblatt, & Wang, 2004). Overall, however, the majority of studies indicate that African American youth tend to have higher body ideals and generally less body dissatisfaction relative to other groups (Franko & Striegel-Moore, 2002; Grabe & Hyde, 2006).

Explanations for the differences between African American and White girls come from data suggesting that Black women tend to underestimate their body weight and do not view themselves accurately when they actually are overweight (Flynn & Fitzgibbon, 1998). It is possible that African American mothers communicate their weight-related attitudes to their daughters (Brown, Schreiber, McMahon, Crawford, & Ghee, 1995). Maternal and family influences may translate into positive body image attitudes; Black adolescent girls may share these views with their peers. Parker and her colleagues concluded that rather than using thinness as a standard for beauty, African American girls emphasized making what they had work for themselves, and reported receiving more positive than negative feedback about their looks from their friends and family (Parker, Nichter, Vuckovic, Sims, & Ritenbaugh, 1995). Furthermore, Black girls described themselves as being very supportive of each other, as compared with White girls who expressed competitiveness and envy regarding body-related issues. African American girls appear to take pride in their bodies in a manner that sets them apart from White adolescent girls, suggesting they hold a different and heavier body ideal and feel better about a larger body size.

Some have suggested that this phenomenon may have implications for obesity rates in African American adolescents (Flynn & Fitzgibbon, 1998). If a larger body size is preferred, and body dissatisfaction is not apparent, the increased tolerance for higher weight and lower motivation to decrease weight may sustain high rates of obesity. As pointed out by Ruiz and colleagues (2004), researchers are left to "disentangle" two competing cultural issues in the African American community: (a) the extent to which higher body satisfaction is protective against the development of body image and eating disorder problems, and (b) the possibility that the preference for a larger body size might lead to problematic eating behaviors and potentially, higher weight and overweight.

It should be noted, however, that the relatively more positive body image found in African Americans does not mean that problematic eating behaviors do not occur in this group. In fact, binge eating occurs with some frequency in African American youth. Johnson, Rohan, and Kirk (2002) reported that binge-eating prevalence was highest among African American boys relative to the other demographic groups, with 26% of African American boys, 17% of African American girls, 19% of White boys, and 18% of White girls reporting binge eating. Other behaviors (e.g., dieting, food restriction, vomiting) have been found to be less common in African American youth relative to other groups (Bisaga et al., 2005; French et al., 1997). However, in a large study of third-grade students, Robinson, Chang, Haydel, and Killen (2001) found that Latina and African American girls manifested equivalent or higher levels of disordered eating attitudes and behaviors as White and Asian American girls. And, in a study of high school athletes, a group thought to be at risk for eating disturbances, Pernick et al. (2006) reported the prevalence for disordered eating to be 19.2%, 18.4%, and 23.3% for African Americans, Whites, and Latinas, respectively.

In summary, the literature on eating disorders, body image, and problematic eating behaviors indicates that generally dieting and body dissatisfaction are less likely to occur in African American youth relative to other groups, although binge eating occurs to a similar or even greater extent.

Body Image and Eating Disturbances in Latino/Latina, Asian, and Native American Youth

Surprisingly, much less research has been conducted with Latino/a, Asian, and Native American youth, relative to African American and White children and adolescents. Robinson et al. (1996) assessed desired body shape among 939 White, Latina, and Asian sixth- and seventh-grade girls and reported no differences among these groups, a finding replicated with younger girls (Robinson et al., 2001). In an early study of high school students in New Mexico, Smith and Krejci (1991) concluded that the rate of binge eating among Hispanic youth (13.1%) was comparable to White adolescents (10.1%). Although they did not measure body image *per se*, 13.8% of Hispanics, as compared with 19.1% of Whites, responded with "never" to the statement "I feel satisfied with my body." Snow and Harris

(1989) found an 11% rate of disturbed eating behaviors and weight concerns among a sample of Hispanic adolescents, and Lachenmeyer and Muni-Brander (1988) reported comparable rates of bingeing and purging between 209 Hispanic (6.5%) and 410 White (7.3%) high school students. Gardner, Friedman, and Jackson (1999a, 1999b) compared perceived and ideal body sizes between White and Latino children (ages 6–13) and reported no differences between these two groups. Mirza, Davis, and Yanovski (2005) found significant associations between BMI, self-esteem, and body dissatisfaction in a sample of El-Salvadoran American children and adolescents. Finally, Neumark-Sztainer et al. (2002) documented that in comparison to White adolescent girls, Hispanic, Asian American, and Native American girls tended to report similar or more concerns or behaviors.

Granillo, Jones-Rodriguez, and Carvajal (2005) utilized data from the AdHealth study to estimate the occurrence of eating disorders and body image disturbance in a sample of Latina adolescents (e.g., Mexican American, Cuban American, Puerto Rican, and mixed Latina groups). For all Latinas, 2.5% reported BMI of 17 or less, 5.5% had stopped menarche, 53.3% reported current dieting, and 1.9% had bulimic symptomatology. Relative to the non-Latina AdHealth participants, Latinas were less likely to be of low weight, had higher dietary restraint, and were similar in rates of amenorrhea and bulimic symptomatology. The body image measure in this study was participants' response to the question "How do you think of yourself in terms of weight?" In the Latina group, 43.5% reported feeling overweight, and they were more likely to be dieting and to exhibit bulimic symptoms. However, it should be noted that this question is not a typical measure of body dissatisfaction and is also problematic because the response "overweight" may in fact be an accurate estimate of body weight rather than a measure of body image concerns. Acculturation has been found to be an important consideration in Hispanic groups (Nieri, Kullis, Keith, & Hurdle, 2005) and will be discussed in chapter 6.

For Asian youth, the literature is mixed, with some reports finding high rates of body dissatisfaction, and other studies reporting lower levels, relative to other groups. For example, in the Robinson et al. (1996) study, among the leanest 25% of the sample of more than 900 sixth and seventh graders, Asian girls described more body dissatisfaction than White girls. However, more recent studies find the lowest rates of abnormal eating and weight control behaviors in Asian adolescents (Forman-Hoffman, 2004). Bisaga and colleagues (2005) reported that rates of eating disorder symptoms in Asian girls fell in between Hispanic and non-Hispanic White girls, who had the highest, and African American and Caribbean girls, who had the lowest rates of eating disorder symptoms. Interestingly, African American and Asian American boys were at greater risk for potentially harmful weight-related concerns and behaviors than White boys (Neumark-Sztainer et al.,

2002), suggesting there may be sex differences within Asian youth in regard to body image and eating disturbances.

In a study focused solely on 155 Native American youth (ages 5–18) living in an urban setting, younger children selected thinner ideal body figures than adolescents, and overweight youth chose ideal figures similar to those of normal-weight youth (Rinderknecht & Smith, 2002). Body dissatisfaction measures revealed that 41% of the boys and 61% of the girls expressed a desire to be thinner and those with the highest dissatisfaction were the overweight girls. Although based on a small sample size, this study suggests that Native American children and adolescents experience significant body dissatisfaction and particularly do so when they are overweight. In contrast, Story, French, Resnick, and Blum (1995) in a study of Grade 7 through 12 students reported that African American and Native American girls were more likely to be satisfied with their body than White or Hispanic students. In a larger study, Story and colleagues (2001) studied 1,441 second and third graders living in the southwest from seven tribes and found that 42% were overweight or obese. The heavier children were more likely to have tried to lose weight or were currently trying to lose weight than normal-weight children. This study suggests that very young Native American children are dissatisfied with a large body size and engage in weight-loss efforts. Consistent with these findings, Croll, Neumark-Sztainer, Story, and Ireland (2002) found that Native American youth (and also Hispanic youth) reported the highest prevalence of disordered eating in a large study of 9th and 12th graders. Native American ethnicity was found to be associated with significantly higher dieting and restricting/purging scores, relative to White girls aged 14.2 years (Lynch, Eppers, & Sherrodd, 2004). In this study, both Native American ethnicity and low BMI were associated with higher restricting/purging scores and social pressure/oral control scores on the Eating Attitudes Test. Overall, the literature is somewhat mixed regarding the degree of body dissatisfaction and disturbed eating behaviors in Native American youth; however, studies converge in the finding that overweight Native Americans prefer a smaller body size and engage in problematic eating behaviors.

SUMMARY AND CONCLUSIONS

In conclusion, both overweight and problematic eating behaviors and body image issues affect many youth, and may be particularly problematic in children and adolescents from diverse ethnic groups. The social, cultural, and economic risk factors for youth from diverse ethnic groups play an important role in the development of overweight, problematic eating behaviors, and body image issues. Although the health disparities and differences in access to care and treatment among racially and ethnically diverse groups have been well documented (Park, Mulye, Adams, Brindis, & Irwin, 2006), few culturally specific interventions have been developed for any of these health concerns. The need for treatments that are culturally, racially, and ethnically relevant to address overweight, problematic eating behaviors, and body image concerns continues to be great. Future research will need to focus on designing both prevention and treatment programs for ethnic minority youth in order to address these disparities.

REFERENCES

Airhihenbuwa, C. O., Kumanyika, S., Agurs, T. D., & Lowe, A. (1995). Perceptions and beliefs about exercise, rest, and health among African Americans. *American Journal of Health Promotion, 9*, 426–429.

Andersen, R. E., Crespo, C. J., Bartlett, S. J., Cheskin, L. J., & Pratt, M. (1998). Relationship of physical activity and television watching with body weight and level of fatness among children: Results from the Third National Health and Nutrition Examination Survey. *JAMA, 279*, 938–942.

Barlow, S. E., & Dietz, W. H. (1998). Obesity evaluation and treatment: Expert committee recommendations. *Pediatrics, 102*, E29–E37.

Baruffi, G., Hardy, C. J., Waslien, C. I., Uyehara, S. J., & Krupitsky, D. (2004). Ethnic differences in the prevalence of overweight among young children in Hawaii. *Journal of the American Dietetic Association, 104*, 1701–1707.

Biro, F. M., Striegel-Moore, R. H., Franko, D. L., Padgett, J., & Bean, J. A. (2006). Self-esteem in adolescent females. *Journal of Adolescent Health, 39*, 501–507.

Bisaga, K., Whitaker, A., Davies, M., Chuang, S., Feldman, J., & Walsh, B. T. (2005). Eating disorder and depressive symptoms in urban high school girls from different ethnic backgrounds. *Journal of Developmental and Behavioral Pediatrics, 26*, 257–266.

Brown, K. M., Schreiber, G. B., McMahon, R. P., Crawford, P., & Ghee, K. L. (1995). Maternal influences on body satisfaction in black and white girls aged 9 and 10: The NHLBI growth and health study. *Annals of Behavioral Medicine, 17*, 213–220.

Cash, T. F. (1991). *Body-image therapy: A program for self-directed change*. New York: Guilford.

Centers for Disease Control and Prevention. (2004a). *Prevalence of overweight among children and adolescents: United States 1999–2002*. Retrieved July 16, 2006 from http://www.cdc.gov/nchs/products/pubs/pubd/hestats/overwght99.htm

Centers for Disease Control and Prevention. (2004b). *REACH 2010 Surveillance for Health Status in Minority Communities: United States 2001–2002*. Retrieved July 16, 2006 from http://www.cdc.gov/mmwr/preview/mmwrhtml/ss5306a1.htm#tab5

Croll, J., Neumark-Sztainer, D., Story, M., & Ireland, M. (2002). Prevalence and risk and protective factors related to disordered eating behaviors among adolescents: Relationship to gender and ethnicity. *Journal of Adolescent Health, 31*, 166–175.

Daniels, S. R., Arnett, D., Eckel, R., Gidding, S., Hayman, L., & Kumanyika, S. (2005). Overweight in children and adolescents: Pathophysiology, consequences, prevention, and treatment. *Circulation, 111,* 1999–2012.

Daniels, S. R. (2006). The consequences of childhood overweight and obesity. *Childhood Obesity, 16,* 18–45.

Dietz, W. H., & Gortmaker, S. L. (2001). Preventing obesity in children and adolescents. *Annual Review of Public Health, 22,* 337–353.

Ebbeling, C. B., Pawlak, D. B., & Ludwig, D. S. (2002). Childhood obesity: Public health crisis, common sense cure. *Lancet, 360,* 473–482.

Egger, G., & Swinburn, B. (1997). An "ecological" approach to the obesity pandemic. *British Medical Journal, 315,* 477–480.

Flodmark, C. E., Marcus, C., & Britton, M. (2006). Interventions to prevent obesity in children and adolescents: A systematic literature review. *International Journal of Obesity, 30,* 579–589.

Flynn, K. J., & Fitzgibbon, M. (1998). Body images and obesity risk among Black females: A review of the literature. *Annals of Behavioral Medicine, 20,* 13–24.

Forman-Hoffman, V. (2004). High prevalence of abnormal eating and weight control practices among U.S. high-school students. *Eating Behaviors, 5,* 325–336.

Franko, D. L., Becker, A. E., Thomas, J. J., & Herzog, D. B. (2007). Cross-ethnic differences in eating disorder symptoms and related distress. *International Journal of Eating Disorders, 40,* 156–164.

Franko, D. L., & Striegel-Moore, R. H. (2002). The role of body dissatisfaction as a risk factor for depression in adolescent girls: Are the differences black and white? *Journal of Psychosomatic Research, 53,* 1–9.

Freedman, D. S., Khan, L., Serdula, M. K., Ogden, C. L., & Dietz, W. (2006). Racial and ethnic difference in secular trends for childhood BMI, weight, and height. *Obesity, 14,* 301–308.

French, S. A., Story, M., Neumark-Sztainer, D., Downes, B., Resnick, M., & Blum, R. (1997). Ethnic differences in psychosocial and health behavior correlates of dieting, purging, and binge eating in a population-based sample of adolescent females. *International Journal of Eating Disorders, 22,* 315–322.

Gardner, R. M., Friedman, B. N., & Jackson, N. A. (1999a). Body size estimations, body dissatisfaction, and ideal size preferences in children six through thirteen. *Journal of Youth and Adolescence, 28,* 603–618.

Gardner, R. M., Friedman, B. N., & Jackson, N. A. (1999b). Hispanic and White children's judgments of perceived and ideal body size and others. *Psychological Record, 49,* 555–564.

Gordon-Larsen, P., Adair, L., & Popkin, B. M. (2003). The relationship of ethnicity, socioeconomic factors, and overweight in U.S. adolescents. *Obesity Research, 11,* 121–129.

Grabe, S., & Hyde, J. S. (2006). Ethnicity and body dissatisfaction among women in the United States: A meta-analysis. *Psychological Bulletin, 132,* 622–640.

Granillo, T., Jones-Rodriguez, G., & Carvajal, S. C. (2005). Prevalence of eating disorders in Latina adolescents: Associations with substance use and other correlates. *Journal of Adolescent Health, 36,* 214–220.

Guo, S. S., & Chumlea, W. C. (1999). Tracking of body mass index in children in relation to overweight in adulthood. *American Journal of Clinical Nutrition, 70*(1), 145S–148S.

Johnson, W. G., Rohan, K. J., & Kirk, A. A. (2002). Prevalence and correlates of binge eating in white and African American adolescents. *Eating Behaviors, 3*, 179–189.

King, A. C., Castro, C., Eyler, A. A., Wilcox, S., Sallis, J. F., & Brownson, R. C. (2000). Personal and environmental factors associated with physical activity among different racial-ethnic groups of U.S. middle-aged and older-aged women. *Health Psychology, 19*, 354–364.

Lachenmeyer, J. R., & Muni-Brander, P. (1988). Eating disorders in a nonclincial adolescent population. *Adolescence, 23*, 303–312.

Lynch, W. C., Eppers, K., & Sherrodd, J. (2004). Eating attitudes of Native American and white female adolescents: A comparison of BMI- and age-matched groups. *Ethnic Health, 9*, 253–266.

McDermott, B. M., & Jaffa, T. (2005). Eating disorders in children and adolescents: An update. *Current Opinion in Psychiatry, 18*, 407–410.

Mirza, N. M., Davis, D., & Yanovski, J. A. (2005). Body dissatisfaction, self-esteem, and overweight among inner-city Hispanic children and adolescents. *Journal of Adolescent Health, 36*(3), 267.e16–267.e20. doi:10.1016/j.jadohealth.2004.02.033

Mokdad, A. H., Ford, E. S., Bowman, B. A., Dietz, W. H., Vinicor, F., Bales, V. S., & Marks, J. (2001). Prevalence of obesity, diabetes, and obesity related health risk factors. *JAMA, 289*, 76–79.

Must, A. (2003). Does overweight in childhood have an impact on adult health? *Nutrition Review, 61*, 139–142.

Must, A., Spadano, J., Coakley, E. H., Field, A. E., Colditz, G., & Dietz, W. H. (1999). The disease burden associated with overweight and obesity. *JAMA, 282*, 1523–1529.

Nayga, R., Jr., & Weinberg, Z. (1999). Supermarket access in the inner cities. *Journal of Retailing and Consumer Services, 6*, 141–145.

Neumark-Sztainer, D. (2005). Can we simultaneously work toward the prevention of obesity and eating disorders in children and adolescents? *International Journal of Eating Disorders, 38*, 220–227.

Neumark-Sztainer, D., Croll, J., Story, M., Hannan, P. J., French, S. A., & Perry, C. (2002). Ethnic/racial differences in weight-related concerns and behaviors among adolescent girls and boys: Findings from Project EAT. *Journal of Psychosomatic Research, 53*, 963–974.

Nieri, T., Kulis, S., Keith, V. M., & Hurdle, D. (2005). Body image, acculturation, and substance abuse among boys and girls in the southwest. *American Journal of Drug and Alcohol Abuse, 31*, 617–639.

Ogden, C. L., Carroll, M. D., & Flegal, K. M. (2008). High body mass index for age among US children and adolescents, 2003–2006. *JAMA, 299*, 2401–2405.

Ogden, C. L., Flegal, K. M., Carroll, M. D., & Johnson, C. L. (2002). Prevalence and trends in overweight among U.S. children and adolescents, 1999–2000. *JAMA, 288*, 1772–1773.

Park, M. J., Mulye, T. P., Adams, S. H., Brindis, C. D., & Irwin, C. E. (2006). The health status of young adults in the United States. *Journal of Adolescent Health, 39*, 305–317.

Parker, S., Nichter, M., Vuckovic, N., Sims, C., & Ritenbaugh, C. (1995). Body image and weight concerns among African American and White adolescent females: Differences which make a difference. *Human Organization, 54,* 103–114.

Patrick, K., Norman, G. J., Calfas, K. J., Sallis, J. F., Zabinski, M. F., Rupp, J., & Cella, J. (2004). Diet, physical activity, and sedentary behaviors as risk factors for overweight in adolescence. *Archives of Pediatrics & Adolescent Medicine, 158,* 385–390.

Pernick, Y., Nichols, J. F., Rauh, M. J., Kern, M., Ji, M., Lawson, M. J., & Wilfley, D. (2006). Disordered eating among a multi-racial/ethnic sample of female high-school athletes. *Journal of Adolescent Health, 38,* 689–695.

Perry, A. C., Rosenblatt, E. B., & Wang, X. (2004). Physical, behavioral, and body image characteristics in a tri-racial group of adolescent girls. *Obesity Research, 12,* 1670–1679.

Popkin, B. M., & Udry, J. R. (1998). Adolescent obesity increases significantly in second and third generation US immigrants: The National Longitudinal Study of Adolescent Health. *Journal of Nutrition, 128,* 701–706.

Rinderknecht, K., & Smith, C. (2002). Body-image perceptions among urban Native American youth. *Obesity Research, 10,* 315–327.

Roberts, D., Foehr, V., & Rideout, V. (1999). *Kids and media at the new millennium.* Menlo Park, CA: Kaiser Family Foundation.

Robinson, T. N., Chang, J. Y., Haydel, K. F., & Killen, J. D. (2001). Overweight concerns and body dissatisfaction among third-grade children: The impacts of ethnicity and socioeconomic status. *Journal of Pediatrics, 138,* 181–187.

Robinson, T. N., Killen, J. D., Litt, I. F., Hammer, L. D., Wilson, D. M., Haydel, K. F., et al. (1996). Ethnicity and body dissatisfaction: Are Hispanic and Asian girls at increased risk for eating disorders? *Journal of Adolescent Health, 19,* 384–393.

Rose, D., & Bodor, J. (2006). Household food insecurity and overweight status in young school children: Results from the Early Childhood Longitudinal Study. *Pediatrics, 117,* 464–473.

Ruiz, S. Y., Pepper, A., & Wilfley, D. E. (2004). Obesity and body image among ethnically diverse children and adolescents. In J. K. Thompson (Ed.), *Handbook of eating disorders and obesity* (pp. 656–678). Hoboken, NJ: Wiley.

Smith, S. (2004, November 30). The cost of good nutrition: Why the poor eat so poorly. *The Boston Globe,* p. B7.

Smith J. E., & Krejci, J. (1991). Minorities join the majority: Eating disturbances among Hispanic and Native American youth. *International Journal of Eating Disorders, 10,* 179–186.

Snow, J. T., & Harris, M. B. (1989). Disordered eating in southwestern Pueblo Indians and Hispanics. *Journal of Adolescence, 12,* 329–336.

Sorof, J. M., Lai, D., Turner, J., Poffenbarger, T., & Portman, R. J. (2004). Overweight, ethnicity, and the prevalence of hypertension in school-aged children. *Pediatrics, 113,* 475–482.

Stice, E., Shaw, H., & Marti, C. N. (2007). A meta-analytic review of eating disorder prevention programs: Encouraging findings. *Annual Review of Clinical Psychology, 3,* 207–231.

Story, M., French, S. A., Resnick, M. D., & Blum, R. W. (1995). Ethnic/racial and socioeconomic differences in dieting behaviors and body image perceptions in adolescents. *International Journal of Eating Disorders, 18,* 173–179.

Story, M., Stevens, J., Evans, M., Cornell, C. E., Juhaeri, Gittelsohn, J., et al. (2001). Weight loss attempts and attitudes toward body size, eating, and physical activity in American Indian children: Relationship to weight status and gender. *Obesity Research, 9,* 356–363.

Troiano, R. P., & Flegal, K. M. (1998). Overweight children and adolescents: Description, epidemiology, and demographics. *Pediatrics, 101,* 497–504.

U.S. Department of Health and Human Services. (2001). *The Surgeon General's call to action to prevent and decrease overweight and obesity.* Rockville, MD: Author.

Vander Wal, J. S., & Thomas, N. (2004). Predictors of body image dissatisfaction and disturbed eating atttitudes and behaviors in African American and Hispanic girls. *Eating Behaviors, 5,* 291–301.

Vazquez, I. M., Millen, B., Bissett, L., Levelnson, S. M., & Chipkin, S. R. (1998). A preventative nutrition intervention in Caribbean Latinos with Type 2 diabetes. *American Journal of Health Promotion, 13,* 116–119.

Wadden, T. A., Brownell, K. D., & Foster, G. D. (2002). Obesity: Responding to the global epidemic. *Journal of Consulting and Clinical Psychology, 70,* 510–525.

Wadden, T. A., & Stunkard, A. J. (2002). *Handbook of obesity treatment.* New York: Guilford.

Whitaker, R. C., & Orzol, S. M. (2006). Obesity among US urban preschool children. *Archives of Pediatric and Adolescent Medicine, 160,* 578–584.

World Health Organization Expert Consultation. (2004). Appropriate body-mass index for Asian populations and its implications for policy and intervention strategies. *Lancet, 363,* 157–163.

Zenk, S., Schulz, A., Hollis-Neely, T., Campbell, R., Holmes, N., Watkins, G., et al. (2005). Fruit and vegetable intake in African Americans: Income and store characteristics. *American Journal of Preventative Medicine, 29,* 1–9.

6

CROSS-CULTURAL ISSUES IN BODY IMAGE AMONG CHILDREN AND ADOLESCENTS

EILEEN ANDERSON-FYE

Body image and eating concerns have become increasingly common among children and adolescents cross-culturally. In fact, in its 2003 report, "Caring for Children and Adolescents With Mental Disorders: Setting WHO Directions," the World Health Organization (WHO) lists eating disorders as a priority based on their increasing prevalence and impact in both developed and developing nations (WHO, 2003, p. 11). Although the burden of these disorders is well established particularly among adolescents, understanding the specific mechanisms and routes by which they are becoming more widespread is much less well understood. This chapter prioritizes looking across nations, regions, and locally salient groups that share certain experiences, beliefs, practices, and statuses within nations and regions. Additionally, movement from one cultural area to another is privileged because cultural change is a well-established risk factor for the development of disordered eating (Anderson-Fye & Becker, 2003).

Sociocultural factors, as well as genetics, are implicated in the prevalence, etiology, and phenomenology of eating disorders (Becker, Keel,

Anderson-Fye, & Thomas, 2004). Although the cross-cultural spread of eating disorders such as anorexia nervosa (AN) and bulimia nervosa (BN) was initially associated with increasing "westernization," this theory has been called into question (e.g., Pike & Borovoy, 2004). The processes of Westernization, modernization, industrialization, urbanization, and social transition have been offered as reasons for the cross-cultural spread of eating disorders, but none of these processes fully explain emerging patterns (Anderson-Fye & Becker, 2003). Researchers are currently debating why the disorders have become more common among diverse populations, how the changing prevalence can inform understandings of the etiology of eating disorders, and how this increase impacts on prevention and clinical practice with those affected.

The cross-cultural knowledge of body image and eating concerns among children and adolescents comes from several sources. Individual school-based surveys are most common. Increasingly, larger multisite and community-based epidemiological studies are being conducted to try to catalogue prevalence and incidence rates around the world. Clinical samples and case studies are particularly useful in attempting to understand culturally specific symptomatology of eating disorders. A current example of the usefulness of such studies can be found in the examination of "non-fat phobic" AN in Asian clinical samples (e.g., Ngai, Lee, & Lee, 2000). In this case, AN is diagnosed, yet the patients lack thediagnostic criterion of "fear of fatness" from the fourth edition of the *Diagnostic and Statistical Manual of Mental Health* (*DSM–IV*; American Psychiatric Association, 1994), which calls into question core features and current psychiatric nosology of AN. A few studies take a more ethnographic approach in investigating body image and eating concerns. These studies tend to include detailed qualitative data that foreground the participants' meanings of their symptoms and concerns. Such studies aim to understand the cultural and psychological microprocesses involved in the onset of previously undiagnosed disorders into a new community or population, the symptom phenomenology, or both. Even with the combination of these diverse sorts of data, the cultural and transcultural components of body image and eating concerns are incompletely understood and widely debated (Littlewood, 2004).

This chapter first summarizes the data on body image and eating-disordered attitudes and behaviors among youth in various regions of the world with a particular focus on anorexic and bulimic symptomatology. Most of the extant data in these areas regards adolescents, although information on children is mentioned when relevant. Next, the chapter discusses key cross-cultural patterns and issues raised in the data. Finally, the chapter concludes with the implications of the cross-cultural data for globalization and immigration that are likely to impact diagnosis and treatment of body image and eating disorders in increasingly transnational and multicultural societies such as the United States.

BODY IMAGE AND EATING DISORDERS CROSS-CULTURALLY

Disordered eating and body image concerns have been found in most regions of the world where they have been studied. Although the majority of cross-cultural samples include university students, a growing number include school-age children and adolescents. These latter studies have found disordered eating attitudes and behaviors in southeast and east Asia (Shroff & Thompson, 2004; Tsai, Curbow, & Heinberg, 2003), Africa (Caradas, Lambert, & Charlton, 2001), the Middle East (Eapen, Mabrouk, & Bin-Othman, 2006), Latin America (Moya, Fleitlich-Bilyk, & Goodman, 2006), the Caribbean (Marlowe, 2005), Pacific Island societies (Becker, Burwell, Gilman, Herzog, & Hamburg, 2002), Eastern Europe (Rukavina & Pokrajac-Bulian, 2006), and aboriginal populations (McCabe, Ricciardelli, Mellor, & Ball, 2005), in addition to the United States, western Europe, Canada, and Australia. Only a few studies (Anderson-Fye, 2004; Bennett, Sharpe, Freeman, & Carson, 2004; de Azevedo & Ferreira, 1992) have found little evidence of disordered eating among adolescent populations in various world regions. Understanding the cross-cultural prevalence and presentation of eating disorders is not only important as a global health concern, but may improve the understanding of the nature and variation of eating disorders. Moreover, because children and adolescents comprise between 33% and 50% the population in developing nations, ensuring their health is crucial to the well-being of the next generation.

North America, Australia, and Europe

Rates of body image and eating concerns among children and adolescents are thought to be approximately equal in the United States, Canada, Australia, and nations in western Europe such as England, Spain, France, and Italy (Guarino et al., 2005). Additionally, studies from eastern Europe have increasingly reported high rates of these concerns as well as similar clinical characteristics to those in Western nations in a number of countries such as in Croatia (Rukavina & Pokrajac-Bulian, 2006) and Poland (Iniewicz, 2005). In several of the contexts, the age of onset of body image concern appears to be decreasing (Vega Alonso, Rasillo Rodriguez, Lozano Alonso, Rodriguez Carretero, & Martin, 2005), although the modal ages of onset continue to occur around the transitions into and out of adolescence, with some exceptions that place onset in mid-adolescence (Lahortiga-Ramos et al., 2005). Girls and young women account for the vast majority of eating disorder cases in these contexts, although several of the studies note that males report considerable rates of body dissatisfaction and eating-disordered behavior. In fact, some disorders such as body dysmorphic disorder are at least as commonly diagnosed in males as females (see chap. 4, this volume).

In the United States, type, prevalence, and severity of body image and eating concerns can vary by ethnic and racial background (see chap. 5, this volume). Similarly, in Britain, eating-disordered symptoms have been found to be more common among Asian schoolgirls when compared with their White and African-descended counterparts (Furnham & Adam-Saib, 2001). In contrast, White British girls report higher rates of body image dissatisfaction (Furnham & Adam-Saib, 2001) and weight preoccupation (Tareen, Hodes, & Rangel, 2005) than their peers from other ethnic groups in both clinical and nonclinical settings. In Australia, a sample of 14- to 17-year-old girls also found Asian adolescents to have higher rates of eating pathology than their White peers (Jennings, Forbes, McDermott, Hulse, & Juniper, 2005). This finding contrasts with another study by the same authors that found a slightly older sample of Asian and White Australian students to report no differences on Eating Attitudes Test (EAT) scores (Jennings, Forbes, McDermott, Hulse, & Juniper, 2006). Australian aboriginal adolescents were found to engage in more strategies to lose weight, increase weight, and increase muscles than were nonindigenous adolescents, with more females than males dissatisfied with their weight and engaging in strategies to lose weight (McCabe et al., 2005). Data from Native American adolescents also indicate relatively high rates of disordered eating and body image among these groups (see chap. 8, this volume). In contrast, Sami adolescents, who are indigenous in Norway and mostly live in Artic areas, were found to have greater body satisfaction and fewer eating problems than their majority peers (Kvernmo, 2004). These data indicate that risk for disordered eating and body image may vary by ethnicity cross-culturally, although factors such as local context, age, and immigration status impact risk profiles.

Asia

Body image and eating disorders have been well established among adolescents in many parts of Asia including Japan (Pike & Mizushima, 2005), China (Lee & Lee, 2000), Singapore (Ung, 2003), Hong Kong (Ngai et al., 2000), Korea (Ko & Cohen, 1998), Thailand (Tsai et al., 2003), the Phillipines (Lorenzo, Lavori, & Lock, 2002), and India (Shroff & Thompson, 2004). A number of studies have reported rates of eating disorders in Asian adolescents as high as those in Western nations (Gupta, Chaturvedi, Chandarana, & Johnson, 2001). Few studies have found rates of eating disorders to be lower among east-Asian adolescents than those in the west (Nakamura et al., 2000). Two intriguing studies found disordered eating to be more prevalent among young women in Korea (Ko & Cohen, 1998) and Taiwan (Tsai et al., 2003) than in their Korean American or Taiwanese American counterparts. Similarly, a study of adolescent girls in Thailand found them to report more eating-disordered attitudes and psychopathology than either Asian Australian or White Australian girls (Jennings et al., 2006). The authors suggested that cultural pressures for thinness were more intense for young women in Thailand than in Australia. Findings such as these have called into question theories of "westernization" as the cause of the global spread of eating disorders (Pike & Borovoy, 2004). Based on the data from Asia, some have argued for "modernization" as a critical factor in the emergence of eating disorders (Littlewood, 2004), yet other data refute that argument as well (Becker et al., 2002), indicating that there are probably multiple systemic routes by which eating disorders emerge in a society (Anderson-Fye & Becker, 2003).

Studies among adolescents in Asia have also been important in classifying eating disorder phenomenology that appears different from initial descriptions in the West. In particular, Lee described "non-fat phobic" AN among adolescent girls in Hong Kong (Lee, Ho, & Hsu, 1993). Non-fat phobic AN has also now been found among British south Asian adolescent girls (Tareen et al., 2005) as well as replicated in east Asia (Ngai et al., 2000). Based on these findings, the core diagnostic and clinical features of AN may have to be reconsidered in light of the cross-cultural data. Lai (2000), however, pointed out that more than 80% of younger Chinese patients with AN in a study in Hong Kong did indeed endorse fear of fatness. This study concluded that the impact of westernization may vary by generation and that fat phobia should not be overlooked in Asian populations. Relatedly, a comparison study between Indian and Canadian adolescent girls found a different underlying body image construct between the two groups, even though their eating pathology scores were not significantly different (Gupta et al., 2001). On the other hand, a recent study of middle school and young adult women in Bombay indicated that similar pathways of teasing and internalization mediated the effects of body mass index (BMI; the measure of body fat based on height and weight) on body dissatisfaction as have been found in Western samples from several nations (Shroff & Thompson, 2004). Both the variations in body image construct and eating disorder phenomenology as well as similarities in intrapopulation risk factors should be considered in preventing and addressing eating disorders cross-culturally.

Although most Asian studies have been conducted with young women, several case-based studies have found clinical eating disorders among young men. In central China, Tong and colleagues (2005) reported on five cases of eating disorders with fat phobia among young men. The authors linked both cultural change and Westernization to the unexpected increase of disordered eating in this area. Similarly, in Sri Lanka, where eating disorders were previously thought to be rare, Perera, Wickramasinghe, Wanigasinghe, and Perera (2002) reported four cases of typical AN among 13- to 15-year-olds. Two of the cases were male and all were severe, leading the authors to conclude that incidence of AN in Sri Lanka could be higher than is commonly thought and that males, as well as females, should be evaluated, particularly in early adolescence.

Sub-Saharan Africa

Eating disorders among children and adolescents are thought to be rare in sub-Saharan Africa, with the exception of South Africa. In South Africa, eating-disordered attitudes and behaviors have been found among both Black and White adolescent girls in urban settings at prevalence rates similar to those found in the United States and western Europe (le Grange, Telch, & Tibbs, 1998). Black girls in rural Zulu-speaking areas have also been found to report disordered-eating attitudes, albeit at lower rates than in urban areas (Szabo & Allwood, 2004). Some studies (le Grange et al., 1998; Marais, Wassenaar, & Kramers, 2003) have found eating-disordered attitudes among adolescent boys in South Africa to be as high as their female counterparts, with young Black men scoring even higher than young White men. A study of Black Nigerian secondary school and university women also using the EAT-26 found a similar rate of scores above the cutoff (Oyewumi & Kazarian, 1992), indicating that groups of adolescents in other sub-Sarahan locations may also struggle with eating concerns. Similarly, Hooper and Garner (1986) administered the Eating Disorder Inventory (EDI) to Black, White, and mixed-race school-age girls in Zimbabwe, and reported high sub-scale scores among the Black female respondents.

However, in an intriguing piece, le Grange and colleagues pointed out the dangers of a single-wave survey study that does not include interview follow-up and called into question previous work in sub-Saharan Africa in general and in South Africa in particular (le Grange, Louw, Breen, & Katzman, 2004). Drawing on a two-stage study conducted with 13- to 20-year-olds in Tanzania that found very low endorsement of any eating-disordered features (Eddy & Hennessey, 2003), the authors conducted a structured interview follow-up to a self-report study among secondary students scoring above the EAT-26 cutoff. Consistent with a prior study involving 1,435 South African college students (le Grange et al., 1998), the authors found that the Black secondary students scored higher than their White and mixed-race peers on the EAT-26. However, when interviews were conducted, the meanings of these students' responses were found to be significantly different than the intended question. For example, one student who reported "always" being preoccupied with food on the EAT-26 said this was because of living in poverty where there was not enough food to eat. The interviewees also reported having trouble understanding the questions on the survey. In addition to the implications of the study for future regional work, the authors discussed the importance of instrument validity when studying eating disorders cross-culturally as well as the complexity yet importance of cross-cultural work.

Consistent with this line of critique, a study of 668 secondary school students that included both survey and interview components in Ghana found that of the 10 students who had a BMI below 17.5 kg/m^2 (18.5–24.9

is considered healthy; 30–39 obese; and ≥40 morbidly obese) solely due to self-starvation, all of them viewed their food restriction positively and in religious terms without the focus on weight or shape characteristic of contemporary AN (Bennett et al., 2004). Commenting on the le Grange et al. (2004) South Africa article, Lee (2004) underscored the importance of combining meaning-centered approaches with epidemiology in order to maximize validity and reliability.

The Middle East

Disordered eating and body image concerns have been well established among adolescents in the Middle East. Disordered eating, disordered body image attitudes, or both have been found to be as common among several populations of Middle Eastern young women as in western Europe or the United States (e.g., Al-Adawi et al., 2002; Bas, Asci, Karabudak, & Kiziltan, 2004; Eapen et al., 2006; Halevy & Halevy, 2000). Several authors also commented on the high rates of self-reported eating-disordered attitudes among adolescent boys in the region. In one study, 36.4% of Omani teenage boys and 29.4% of Omani teenage girls reported a propensity for anorexic-like behaviors compared with 9% of their non-Omani peers (Al-Adawi et al., 2002). In contrast, in the same study, more non-Omani teens reported bulimic-like behaviors (18.4%) than did Omani teens (12.4%). Both partial and full-syndrome BN among high school girls in Egypt were found with about the same prevalence rates as among girls in Western nations (Nasser, 1994). In Bahrain, a study of 447 adolescents found their weight-related beliefs and attitudes to be bimodal (Al-Sendi, Shetty, & Musaiger, 2004). On the one hand, there was a tolerance of obesity, and on the other, there was exaggerated concern about its occurrence.

Eating-disordered attitudes and behaviors are reported among young Israeli women across the spectrum of adolescence. Both partial-syndrome AN and BN were found to be very common among a sample of 534 high school girls, with those struggling with bulimic symptoms reporting more psychological distress (Stein et al., 1997). Halevy and Halevy (2000) focused on "social age" rather than chronological age and report a significant increase in self-reported eating-disordered symptoms between the sixth and seventh grades. In a study of 1,316 girls (aged 12–18 years) from five Israeli school subtypes and five residential neighborhoods, Latzer and Tzischinsky (2003) found 16.6- to 18-year-old girls reported the highest scores on the EDI-2 as compared with the other age groups.

Latin America and the Caribbean

Until recently, rates of disordered eating and body image attitudes and practices were relatively unknown throughout Latin America and the

Caribbean. In several Latin American countries, such as Argentina, where slender figures seem to be preferred and heavier women may be socially and economically disadvantaged (Meehan & Katzman, 2001), intense social pressure for thinness has been suspected to be related to disordered eating. Indeed, weight dissatisfaction and bulimic behaviors were found to be frequent among female adolescents from five schools in Buenos Aires City, with 43% of students reporting having been on a diet for solely aesthetic reasons (Leiderman & Triskier, 2004). Similarly, in Venezuela, a relatively high prevalence of BN was found among 1,363 adolescents in the city of Maracaibo, Zulia State, whereas no AN was found (Quintero-Parraga et al., 2003). Prevalence of binge-eating disorder (BED) was found to be moderate. In southeast Brazil, a sample of 1,251 children aged 7 to 14 years old found prevalence of those "at risk" for eating disorders to be 1.4% based on child and parent interviews, higher among females and rising with age (Moya et al., 2006). Moreover, at-risk status was related to higher socioeconomic status (SES), which the authors linked with increased westernization and preferences for thinness.

Continuing the empirical evidence for high regional rates of eating and body image concerns, a cross-national study of eighth and ninth graders in Buenos Aires, Guatemala City, Havana, Lima, Panama City, and Santiago found students in all six locations to have a preference to become thinner, even though few perceived themselves as overweight (McArthur, Holbert, & Pena, 2005). In 1982, Pumarino and Vivanco first reported 30 cases of eating disorders in Chile. In 1987, again based on case data, the same authors concluded that the disorders were probably becoming increasingly common, although that conclusion was not validated in epidemiologic studies.

Although eating concerns have been established among young Mexican American women (see chap. 8, this volume), little has been known about the disorders in Mexico until recently. One study in Mexico found high frequencies of dangerous eating behaviors among teenage girls in the nonurban area of the state of Michoacan (Bojorquez & Unikel, 2004). What was surprising about that study is that the rates of disordered eating attitudes and behaviors were even higher than those previously found among adolescent girls in Mexico City, causing the authors to suggest a more precise definition of "culture" in trying to understand its effects on eating disorders.

In the Caribbean, where more full-figured body shapes are thought to be preferred, obesity is considered a significant problem among women rather than eating disorders such as AN and BN. However, recent data suggest that eating disorders may be increasingly common among certain subgroups of young women. For example, Hoek and colleagues (2005) found the incidence of AN among 15- to 24-year-old women in Curaçao to be lower than rates in the United States and western Europe on the whole; however, the rates were equivalent to those in these countries among the minority mixed-race and White Curaçao subgroups. In Bermuda, a survey of 836 adolescents found no differences by sex or ethnicity on self-reports of disordered eating attitudes, however, in contrast to some of the Latin American data, lower SES was correlated with more reported eating pathology (Marlowe, 2005). Tendency toward anorexic behavior was also more common than toward bulimic behavior in this sample.

In a longitudinal ethnographic study, adolescent girls from all ethnicities in Belize were found to have very low reports of eating-disordered behavior over a 5-year period, despite the presence of societal risk factors of social transition and increasing Americanization (Anderson-Fye, 2004). In Trinidad, although obesity rates were not high among an adolescent sample of 1,090 students, the majority of students associated overweight and obese body silhouettes with wealth, although 40% associated the male overweight and obese silhouettes with happiness (Simeon et al., 2003), causing the authors concern about the acceptability and even desirability of obese body shapes among adolescents. In contrast to this concern, another study of 362 schoolgirls in Trinidad and Barbados reported that 68% of the girls endorsed being terrified of becoming fat, although none were found to have a diagnosis of BN (Bhugra, Mastrogianni, Maharajh, & Harvey, 2003). African-descended adolescents in this study were found to have more unusual eating patterns and more eating concerns than other girls. The authors of both the Belize and Trinidad and Barbados studies expressed concern about the emergence or expansion of disordered eating in the region with continued development and Westernization, although local protective factors such as the importance of body shape over body size have also been identified (Anderson-Fye, 2004).

Pacific Island Societies

Eating disorders in Pacific Island societies have been thought to be rare because of a variety of reasons, including preferences for large body sizes (Becker, 1995). Recent concern has been predominantly directed at adult obesity in the Federated States of Micronesia and other nations in this region as modernization and global food trade interrupt traditional balances of physical activity and nutritional intake. In one of the first studies to assess this problem among children, Tongan adolescent girls in particular were found to have alarming rates of obesity, especially for the levels of modernization found (Fukuyama et al., 2005). Given these regional concerns, Becker and colleagues' studies in a small-scale indigenous Melanesian population are especially surprising. These researchers found significant anorexic and bulimic symptomatology (Becker et al., 2002) as well as high prevalence of binge eating and BED (Becker, Burwell, Navara, & Gilman, 2003) among ethnic Fijian young women following the introduction of Western television programming to this previously media-naïve community. Consistent with concerns about the insidious nature of eating-disordered attitudes and behaviors, a comparison of Samoan, Australian, and Malay young women found evidence that traditional protective factors among Samoan and Malay females may change in the face of Western ideals of weight and shape (McDowell & Bond, 2006).

TRENDS IN THE GLOBAL DATA

Taken as a whole, the world data on child and adolescent eating disorders reveals six principle trends, although there are almost always exceptions to these trends.

1. Generally, the eating disorders described here do not emerge in a society or subset of a society until there is more than subsistence food intake.
2. Sex differences are found in eating-disordered attitudes and behaviors, with females reporting more disordered attitudes and behaviors than males.
3. Eating-disordered behavior seems to be particularly salient among adolescents and appears to often emerge first in a society among this group.
4. Upward mobility seems to place young women at risk for eating disorders across contexts, although the disorders occur among those from across the range of socioeconomic backgrounds.
5. Urban contexts appear to place children and adolescents at increased risk of both obesity and eating disorders when compared with rural.
6. Cultural change appears to be associated with eating pathology, although the pathways between these phenomena appear to be multiple, complex, and hold key exceptions.

A less well-studied trend established in some contexts includes the relationship of individual and group trauma or violence with disturbed eating. Given that the first two of these trends are already well established in the cross-cultural literature, the following discussion focuses on the others.

Adolescence

Although not every society in the world has a life period considered adolescence, this time often seen as a transition between childhood and adulthood is becoming more widespread and is lasting longer (WHO, 2003). Adolescence, a period of enormous neurological change in places where it has been studied (Spear, 2000), is an important time for mental health issues generally (WHO, 2003), with many disorders emerging, intensifying, and becoming predictive of adult outcomes at that time. In developed Western nations, eating disorders have been found to be most prevalent during adolescence with both physiological and psychological factors appearing to be involved in this pattern. Puberty and its significant gain of body fat for adolescent girls are thought to be a possible trigger factor for eating disorders in places where a thin body ideal reigns. In twin studies, puberty has been found to be related to significant increases in genetic influence on disordered eating (Klump, Perkins, Alexandra Burt, McGue, & Iacono, 2007). These findings are in addition to the neural plasticity implicated generally in adolescent psychopathology (Spear, 2000). Concurrently, the normative developmental changes of Western adolescence such as becoming more capable of abstract thought, more dependent on peers, more attuned to the social world and social comparison, and having increasing independence can contribute to body image dissatisfaction and disordered eating. Moreover, adolescents are often the first in a developing society to adopt new technologies and transnational media that may impact disordered eating (Anderson-Fye, 2004). It is perhaps then no surprise that the global expansion of adolescence coincides with the cross-cultural expansion of eating disorders. However, the empirical data on the explanatory models of this relationship are limited.

Social developmental goals of adolescence may also vary significantly cross-culturally. For example, individuation and identity formation are considered key goals among U.S. adolescents, and weakness in these areas has been linked with disordered eating (Strong & Huon, 1998). In societies that are more collectivistic and communally focused, assumption of full adult roles may lead to different sorts of adolescent achievements. It is not known how such variable developmental goals would relate to the development of body image and eating disorders. Nascent correlational data indicate that culturally specific developmental goals are relevant to intracultural variation on disordered eating. For example, among adolescent females, it was the upwardly mobile girls who had lived outside of the country and had personal goals conflicting with those considered "traditional" who reported eating-disordered symptoms in Curaçao (Katzman, Hermans, Van Hoeken, & Hoek, 2004). In contrast, immigrant Asian girls who were less acculturated (Jennings et al., 2005) and classified as more traditional (Mumford, Whitehouse, & Platts, 1991) in Australia and Britain, respectively, reported more disordered eating attitudes. In the United Arab Emirates, it was girls who watched more Western television programming and reported significant family conflict who scored higher on measures of eating pathology (Eapen et al., 2006). Even subcultural context can affect eating disorder risk as was found by type of school in Israel, with those on a kibbutz reporting the least amount of eating pathology and those in a secular boarding school the most (Latzer & Tzischinsky, 2003). The actual mechanisms and pathways by which such variables take effect are still relatively unknown around the world and would benefit from more in-depth ethnographic and ethnopsychological study.

An additional problem with the apparent finding that eating concerns are most salient among adolescents cross-culturally is the typical cross-cultural sampling technique. Secondary schools and colleges/universities are most often targeted for nonclinical sampling in developing and non-Western nations. Sampling younger children is more difficult for a nonclinical sample, and therefore less is known about this group. Moreover, the tension between reliability and validity of measures is a constant problem for any cross-cultural psychiatric work as discussed above regarding the South African data, and the impact of these problems on the current body of data drawn heavily from adolescents is unknown.

Upward Mobility

Contrary to initial reports of eating disorders as a pathology of the elite, AN, BN, and BED have been found among those from all class backgrounds (Anderson-Fye & Becker, 2003), although in some areas such as southeast Brazil higher SES is still associated with increased risk for symptoms of eating disorders (Moya et al., 2006). Although the diversity of class backgrounds is also represented in the cross-cultural data, the pattern of upward mobility in the data is striking. Upward mobility—regardless of socioeconomic status—has been associated with disordered eating among ethnic minority groups in the United States (Yates, 1989) and Afro-Caribbeans in Britain (Soomro, Crisp, Lynch, Tran, & Joughin, 1995). Nascent cases of eating-disordered symptomatology were associated with processes involved in upward mobility among young women in Belize (Anderson-Fye, 2004), Fiji (Becker, 2004), and Zimbabwe (Buchan & Gregory, 1984). Social comparison theory has been offered as one process by which the thin body becomes idealized in cases of upward mobility (Anderson-Fye & Becker, 2003). The thin female body has been written about as a carrier of multiple social meanings, and cross-culturally, it may be considered a possible route into transnational systems and values.

Urban Contexts

On the whole, eating disorders have been found among children and adolescents in urban contexts with greater frequency than among those in rural contexts. Additionally, processes of urbanization via social change or migration appear to be linked to higher rates of at least some types of eating-disordered behavior such as bulimic symptoms (Hoek et al., 1995). Urban settings cross-culturally are thought to foster more exposure to Western media and technologies that are implicated in eating disorders. In Western nations, adolescents exposed to higher levels of mainstream media report worse body image and eating attitudes compared with those with less exposure (Stice, Maxfield, & Wells, 2003). Studies in non-Western nations have also linked

Western media exposure with more pathological body image and eating attitudes (Becker et al., 2002; Eapen et al., 2006; Shroff & Thompson, 2004). Children in urban settings have been found to be more sedentary than those in rural settings such as in Mexico (Yamamoto-Kimura et al., 2006) and the South Pacific (Fukuyama et al., 2005), leading to greater concerns about obesity and weight management among urban school-age children. The paradox of simultaneous continued malnutrition and increasing rates of overweight and obesity among children and adolescents in urban areas is of increasing concern in many developing nations.

In contrast, some studies have found rates of disordered eating attitudes to be similar between rural and urban high school students, particularly in Western developed nations (Jonat & Birmingham, 2004). One recent study found higher rates of disordered eating among adolescents in rural Mexico than among their peers in Mexico City (Bojorquez & Unikel, 2004). Another found higher EAT-26 scores among female Indian university students in rural areas compared with those in urban (Sjostedt, Schumaker, & Nathawat, 1998). Noncomparative studies in rural communities have established that eating concerns can be present in these areas as well (Becker, 2004). These discrepant data may be pointing to a new trend or to the need to more closely study *type* of eating and body image pathology prevalent in the different settings as well as differential pathways to the development of the disorders. Regardless, they are evidence that even adolescents in rural areas in developing nations are not immune to developing eating concerns and disorders, particularly as globalization continues to expand its reach.

Cultural Change and Acculturation

Two key routes of cultural change are immigration and globalization. Both processes have been associated with an increase in body image and eating concerns among adolescents. Studies with children in these situations have focused predominantly on obesity. A few interesting studies have compared young women in a country of origin with their counterparts who immigrate to a new, usually Western and more developed nation. These studies have reported mixed results. Some of these studies have found the émigrés to report greater rates of eating-disordered attitudes and behaviors. For example, Arab female undergraduates living in London were found to exhibit more bulimic tendencies compared with a matched sample in Cairo (Nasser, 1986). Similarly Greek adolescents in Germany were found to have more anorexic syndromes compared with those in Greece, though other symptomatology was higher among those in their native country (Fichter, Weyerer, Sourdi, & Sourdi, 1983). However, over a 20-year period, the differences between the latter samples were found to be greatly reduced, with both samples reporting bulimic syndromes (Fichter, Quadflieg, Georgopoulou, Xepapadakos, & Fthenakis, 2005). Another subset of these comparative studies has found equivalent rates of eating-disordered attitudes between the immigrants and those who remained in the country of origin. An example of this type of study includes Iranian late adolescents and Iranian immigrants in Los Angeles, where exposure to Westernization and acculturation did not appear to place young women at greater risk for disordered eating (Abdollahi & Mann, 2001).

Finally, a few studies have reported higher rates of eating pathology among young women in their native contexts compared with émigrés. Ko and Cohen (1998) found higher EAT-26 scores among Korean college students in Seoul than among Korean American students from a variety of colleges in the United States. In a similar study that also tested effect of generation, Korean and first-generation Korean American female students were found to have higher EAT-26 scores than second-generation Korean Americans (Jackson, Keel, & Lee, 2006) pointing to the importance of native factors and not just westernization in disordered eating. Similarly, Taiwanese young women were found to have higher rates of body dissatisfaction and disordered eating than their Taiwanese American peers (Tsai et al., 2003), and late adolescent Thai women reported higher rates of eating-disordered attitudes and behaviors than their Asian Australian or White Australian counterparts (Jennings et al., 2006). These studies reporting higher rates of disordered eating among young women in Asian cultures when compared with those who immigrate to Western societies indicate the need for closer ethnographic investigation into the cultural or globalization factors involved in these results.

A related set of studies compares immigrant schoolgirls to native-born girls in Western nations. Many of these studies find higher rates of disordered eating symptoms among the immigrant girls including Asian schoolgirls in England (Mumford et al., 1991). Studies with Latina girls in the United States where immigration status was not necessarily tracked also indicate that they have increased risk for some types of eating-disordered behaviors (see chap. 8, this volume). A study with older women (mean age = 29.1) indicated that second-generation Mexican American women have increased risk of eating-disordered behaviors compared with newer immigrants, and that risk was associated with increased acculturation (Chamorro & Flores-Ortiz, 2000).

Regarding globalization, mixed results have also been reported. In addition to mentioning the effects of globalization in some of the survey studies in which native young women have higher rates of disordered eating than émigrés, a handful of detailed ethnographic studies have been conducted examining the effects of globalization among adolescent girls including those conducted in Fiji (Becker, 2004) and Belize (Anderson-Fye, 2004). These contrasting studies, where, with respect to disordered eating, adolescents were relatively quickly influenced by Western television programming in the former study and surprisingly immune to a host of globalization effects including Western television in the latter, point to the importance of meaning-centered work in trying to understand patterns and processes of influence of globalization on eating disordered attitudes and behaviors.

Taken as a whole, these cross-cultural and intracultural comparative studies raise interesting questions about the processes by which cultural contexts and cultural change affect eating disorders risk, particularly among mid- to late-adolescents. Many studies implicate westernization *per se* as a risk factor for the development of eating disorders, yet other studies do not support this hypothesis. Some scholars suggest more broad social risk factors such as the cultural conflict created in postindustrial societies (Appels, 1986), although recent empirical work in nonindustrial societies calls that theory into question as well. Although some cultural factors related to globalization that contribute to eating disorders such as thin body ideals, exposure to transnational media, social transition, and modernization have been found to be compelling in the cross-cultural data, additional work is needed to understand exactly which factors become salient and interact in local contexts to explain divergent data. A promising approach to the study of cultural emergence of eating disorders, particularly among adolescents who are acutely attuned to changing social contexts, may be to parse out more specific social dynamics. For example, in examining risk for eating disorders in east Asia, Lee (1996) described the social factors of food abundance, changing weight norms, affluence, and transitioning social roles for women as contributing to risk for eating disorders in young women. Specific stressors involved in cultural change—whether that change is a result of globalization or migration—are another promising area in which to continue more meaning-centered analysis.

CONCLUSION

The cross-cultural data regarding eating disorders in children and adolescents are not only important for understanding global mental health issues, but also raise many interesting questions about the nature, etiology, variation, and measurement of eating disorders. Because sociocultural factors are well-established contributors to the individual development and societal expansion of eating disorders (Anderson-Fye & Becker, 2003), the cross-cultural data provide a unique lens through which to examine these factors in particular, although genetic, psychological, and other factors may also eventually benefit by cross-cultural comparisons. In the increasingly multicultural receiving contexts of immigration such as the United States, understanding the factors involved in the etiology of eating disorders for those experiencing migration is important to diagnosis, successful treatment, and ultimately prevention of eating disorders. Moreover, because preliminary data indicate that varying phenomenology, body image constructs, and routes to disordered eating may be culturally or subculturally specific, knowledge about particular populations may aid clinicians. Similarly, culturally appropriate models of healing are important to eating disorders recovery, especially when working with children, adolescents, and their families (Dancyger et al., 2002). Although the global data are not comprehensive, and the trends that are established almost always have notable exceptions, there are some strong models for how to proceed in this research. Namely, the combination of epidemiological and qualitative or ethnographic materials appears to be particularly promising to ensure both reliable and valid studies.

REFERENCES

Abdollahi, P., & Mann, T. (2001). Eating disorder symptoms and body image concerns in Iran: Comparisons between Iranian women in Iran and in America. *International Journal of Eating Disorders, 30*(3), 259–268.

Al-Adawi, S., Dorvlo, A., Burke, D., Al-Bahlani, S., Martin, R., & Al-Ismaily, S. (2002). Presence and severity of anorexia and bulimia among male and female Omani and non-Omani adolescents. *Journal of the American Academy of Child and Adolescent Psychiatry, 41*(9), 1124–1130.

Al-Sendi, A., Shetty, P., & Musaiger, A. (2004). Body weight perception among Bahraini adolescents. *Child: Care, Health, and Development, 30*(4), 369–376.

American Psychiatric Association. (1994). *Diagnostic and statistical manual of mental disorders* (4th ed.). Washington, DC: Author.

Anderson-Fye, E. (2004). A "Coca-Cola" shape: Cultural change, body image, and eating disorders in San Andres, Belize. *Culture, Medicine, and Psychiatry, 28*(4), 561–595.

Anderson-Fye, E., & Becker, A. (2003). Sociocultural aspects of eating disorders. In J. K. Thomson (Ed.), *The handbook of eating disorders and obesity* (pp. 565–589). Hoboken, NJ: Wiley.

Appels, A. (1986). Culture and disease. *Social Science and Medicine, 23*(5), 477–483.

Bas, M., Asci, F. H., Karabudak, E., & Kiziltan, G. (2004). Eating attitudes and their psychological correlates among Turkish adolescents. *Adolescence, 39*(155), 593–599.

Becker, A. (1995). *Body, self, and society: The view from Fiji*. Philadelphia: University of Pennsylvania.

Becker, A. (2004). Television, disordered eating, and young women in Fiji: Negotiating body image and identity during rapid social change. *Culture, Medicine, and Psychiatry, 28*(4), 533–559.

Becker, A., Burwell, R., Gilman, S., Herzog, D. B., & Hamburg, P. (2002). Eating behaviours and attitudes following prolonged exposure to television among ethnic Fijian adolescent girls. *British Journal of Psychiatry, 180*, 509–514.

Becker, A., Burwell, R., Navara, K., & Gilman, S. (2003). Binge eating and binge eating disorder in a small-scale, indigenous society: The view from Fiji. *International Journal of Eating Disorders, 34*(4), 423–431.

Becker, A., Keel, P., Anderson-Fye, E., & Thomas, J. (2004). Genes and/or jeans?: Genetic and socio-cultural contributions to risk for eating disorders. *Journal of Addictive Disorders*, *23*(3), 81–103.

Bennett, D., Sharpe, M., Freeman, C., & Carson, A. (2004). Anorexia nervosa among female secondary school students in Ghana. *British Journal of Psychiatry*, *185*, 312–317.

Bhugra, D., Mastrogianni, A., Maharajh, H., & Harvey, S. (2003). Prevalence of bulimic behaviours and eating attitudes in schoolgirls from Trinidad and Barbados. *Transcultural Psychiatry*, *40*(3), 409–428.

Bojorquez, I., & Unikel, C. (2004). Presence of disordered eating among Mexican teenage women from a semi-urban area: Its relation to the cultural hypothesis. *European Eating Disorders Review*, *12*(3), 197–202.

Buchan, T., & Gregory, L. D. (1984). Anorexia nervosa in a black Zimbabwean. *British Journal of Psychiatry*, *145*, 326–330.

Caradas, A., Lambert, E., & Charlton, K. (2001). An ethnic comparison of eating attitudes and associated body image concerns in adolescent South African schoolgirls. *Journal of Human Nutrition and Dietetics*, *14*(2), 111–120.

Chamorro, R., & Flores-Ortiz, Y. (2000). Acculturation and disordered eating patterns among Mexican American women. *International Journal of Eating Disorders*, *28*(1), 125–129.

Dancyger, I., Fornari, V., Fisher, M., Schneider, M., Frank, S., Wisotsky, W., et al. (2002). Cultural factors in orthodox Jewish adolescents treated in a day program for eating disorders. *International Journal of Adolescent Medicine and Health*, *14*(4), 317–328.

de Azevedo, M., & Ferreira, C. (1992). Anorexia nervosa and bulimia: A prevalence study. *Acta Psychiatrica Scandinavica*, *86*(6), 432–436.

Eapen, V., Mabrouk, A., & Bin-Othman, S. (2006). Disordered eating attitudes and symptomatology among adolescent girls in the United Arab Emirates. *Eating Behaviors*, *7*(1), 53–60.

Eddy, K., & Hennessey, M. (2003). Eating disorder attitudes and behaviors and media exposure in East African women. *International Journal of Eating Disorders*, *34*, 25.

Fichter, M. M., Quadflieg, N., Georgopoulou, E., Xepapadakos, F., & Fthenakis, E. (2005). Time trends in eating disturbances in young Greek migrants. *International Journal of Eating Disorders*, *38*(4), 310–322.

Fichter, M. M., Weyerer, S., Sourdi, L., & Sourdi, Z. (1983). The epidemiology of anorexia nervosa: A comparison of Greek adolescents living in Germany and Greek adolescents living in Greece. In P. L. Darby, P. E. Garfinkel, D. M. Garner, & D. V. Coscina (Eds.), *Anorexia nervosa: Recent developments in research* (pp. 95–105). New York: Alan R. Liss.

Fukuyama, S., Inaoka, T., Matsumura, Y., Yamauchi, T., Natsuhara, K., Kimura, R., et al. (2005). Anthropometry of 5-19-year-old Tongan children with special interest in the high prevalence of obesity among adolescent girls. *Annals of Human Biology*, *32*(6), 714–723.

Furnham, A., & Adam-Saib, S. (2001). Abnormal eating attitudes and behaviours and perceived parental control: A study of white British and British-Asian school girls. *Social Psychiatry and Psychiatric Epidemiology*, *36*(9), 462–470.

Guarino, R., Pellai, A., Bassoli, L., Cozzi, M., Di Sanzo, M. A., Campra, D., et al. (2005). Overweight, thinness, body self-image and eating strategies of 2,121 Italian teenagers. *The Scientific World Journal, 5,* 812–819.

Gupta, M. A., Chaturvedi, S., Chandarana, P., & Johnson, A. (2001). Weight-related body image concerns among 18-24-year-old women in Canada and India: An empirical comparative study. *Journal of Psychosomatic Research, 50*(4), 193–198.

Halevy, N., & Halevy, A. (2000). Eating disorders in early adolescence—study from the section on young adolescent nutrition in Jerusalem. *Harefuah, 138*(7), 523–531, 616.

Hoek, H., Bartelds, A., Bosveld, J., van der Graaf, Y., Limpens, V., Maiwald, M., et al. (1995). Impact of urbanization on detection rates of eating disorders. *American Journal of Psychiatry, 152*(9), 1272–1278.

Hoek, H., van Harten, P., Hermans, K., Katzman, M., Matroos, G., & Susser, E. (2005). The incidence of anorexia nervosa on Curaçao. *American Journal of Psychiatry, 162*(4), 748–752.

Hooper, M., & Garner, D. M. (1986). Application of the Eating Disorder Inventory to a sample of black, white, and mixed race schoolgirls in Zimbabwe. *International Journal of Eating Disorders, 5,* 161–168.

Iniewicz, G. (2005). Samoocena i jej zwiazki z obrazem siebie dziewczat chorujacych na anoreksje psychiczna. [Self-esteem and its relations with self-image in female adolescents suffering from anorexia nervosa]. *Psychiatria Polska, 39*(4), 719–729.

Jackson, S. C., Keel, P., & Lee, Y. H. (2006). Trans-cultural comparison of disordered eating in Korean women. *International Journal of Eating Disorders, 39*(6), 498–502.

Jennings, P., Forbes, D., McDermott, B., & Hulse, G. (2005). Acculturation and eating disorders in Asian and Caucasian Australian university students. *Eating Behaviors, 7*(3), 214–219.

Jennings, P., Forbes, D., McDermott, B., Hulse, G., & Juniper, S. (2006). Eating disorder attitudes and psychopathology in Caucasian Australian, Asian Australian and Thai university students. *The Australian and New Zealand Journal of Psychiatry, 40*(2), 143–149.

Jonat, L., & Birmingham, C. (2004). Disordered eating attitudes and behaviours in the high-school students of a rural Canadian community. *Eating and Weight Disorders, 9*(4), 285–289.

Katzman, M. A., Hermans, K., Van Hoeken, D., & Hoek, H. (2004). Not your "typical island woman": Anorexia nervosa is reported only in subcultures in Curaçao. *Culture, Medicine, and Psychiatry, 28*(4), 463–492.

Klump, K. L., Perkins, P., Alexandra Burt, S., McGue, M., & Iacono, W. G. (2007). Puberty moderates genetic influences on disordered eating. *Psychological Medicine, 37*(5), 627–634.

Ko, C., & Cohen, H. (1998). Intraethnic comparison of eating attitudes in native Koreans and Korean Americans using a Korean translation of the eating attitudes test. *Journal of Nervous and Mental Disorders, 186*(10), 631–636.

Kvernmo, S. (2004). Mental health of Sami youth. *International Journal of Circumpolar Health, 63*(3), 221–234.

Lahortiga-Ramos, F., De Irala-Estevez, J., Cano-Prous, A., Gual-Garcia, P., Martinez-Gonzalez, M. A., & Cervera-Enguix, S. (2005). Incidence of eating disorders in Navarra (Spain). *European Psychiatry, 20*(2), 179–185.

Lai, K. Y. C. (2000). Anorexia nervosa in Chinese adolescents—Does culture make a difference? *Journal of Adolescence, 23*(5), 561–568.

Latzer, Y., & Tzischinsky, O. (2003). Weight concern, dieting and eating behaviors. A survey of Israeli high school girls. *International Journal of Adolescent Medicine and Health, 15*(4), 295–305.

le Grange, D., Louw, J., Breen, A., & Katzman, M. A. (2004). The meaning of "self-starvation" in impoverished black adolescents in South Africa. *Culture, Medicine, and Psychiatry, 28*(4), 439–461.

le Grange, D., Telch, C., & Tibbs, J. (1998). Eating attitudes and behaviors in 1,435 South African Caucasian and non-Caucasian college students. *American Journal of Psychiatry, 155*(2), 250–254.

Lee, S. (1996). Reconsidering the status of anorexia nervosa as a western culture-bound syndrome. *Social Science and Medicine, 42*(1), 21–34.

Lee, S. (2004). Engaging culture: An overdue task for eating disorders research. *Culture, Medicine, and Psychiatry, 28*(4), 617–621.

Lee, S., Ho, T., & Hsu, L. (1993). Fat-phobic and non-fat phobic anorexia nervosa: A comparative study of 70 Chinese patients in Hong Kong, *Psychological Medicine, 23*, 999–1017.

Lee, S., & Lee, A. (2000). Disordered eating in three communities of China: A comparative study of female high school students in Hong Kong, Shenzhen, and rural Hunan. *International Journal of Eating Disorders, 27*(3), 317–327.

Leiderman, E., & Triskier, F. (2004). Actitudes, conducta alimentarias y rasgos obsevio-compulsios en adolescentes de la ciudad de Buenos Aires. [Eating behaviors, attitudes and obsessive-compulsive traits in adolescents of Buenos Aires City] . *Vertex, 15*(57), 175–179.

Littlewood, R. (2004). Globalization, culture, body image, and eating disorders. *Culture, Medicine, and Psychiatry, 28*(4): 597–602.

Lorenzo, C., Lavori, P., & Lock, J. (2002). Eating attitudes in high school students in the Philippines: A preliminary study. *Eating and Weight Disorders, 7*(3), 202–209.

Marais, D., Wassenaar, D., & Kramers, A. (2003). Acculturation and eating disorder symptomatology in Black men and women. *Eating and Weight Disorders, 8*(1), 44–54.

Marlowe, K. (2005). A preliminary study of EAT and BITE scores for one school year in Bermuda: Increased early anorexic measures related to socio-economic factors. *The International Journal of Social Psychiatry, 51*(1), 5–12.

McArthur, L., Holbert, D., & Pena, M. (2005). An exploration of the attitudinal and perceptual dimensions of body image among male and female adolescents from six Latin American cities. *Adolescence, 40*(160), 801–816.

McCabe, M. P., Ricciardelli, L. A., Mellor, D., & Ball, K. (2005). Media influences on body image and disordered eating among indigenous adolescent Australians. *Adolescence, 40*(157), 115–127.

McDowell, A. J., & Bond, M. (2006). Body image differences among Malay, Samoan, and Australian women. *Asia Pacific Journal of Clinical Nutrition, 15*(2), 201–207.

Meehan, O., & Katzman, M. A. (2001). Argentina: The social body at risk. In M. Nasser, M. Katzman, & R. Gordon (Eds.), *Eating disorders and cultures in transition* (pp. 148–170). New York: Taylor & Francis.

Moya, T., Fleitlich-Bilyk, B., & Goodman, R. (2006). Brief report: Young people at risk for eating disorders in Southeast Brazil. *Journal of Adolescence, 29*(2), 313–317.

Mumford, D., Whitehouse, A., & Platts, M. (1991). Sociocultural correlates of eating disorders among Asian schoolgirls in Bradford. *British Journal of Psychiatry, 158*, 222–228.

Nakamura, K., Yamamoto, M., Yamazaki, O., Kawashima, Y., Muto, K., Someya, T., et al. (2000). Prevalence of anorexia nervosa and bulimia nervosa in a geographically defined area in Japan. *International Journal of Eating Disorders, 28*(2), 173–180.

Nasser, M. (1986). Comparative study of the prevalence of abnormal eating attitudes among Arab female students of both London and Cairo universities. *Psychological Medicine, 16*(3), 621–625.

Nasser, M. (1994). Screening for abnormal eating attitudes in a population of Egyptian secondary school girls. *Social Psychiatry and Psychiatric Epidemiology, 29*(1), 25–30.

Ngai, E., Lee, S., & Lee, A. (2000). The variability of phenomenology in anorexia nervosa. *Acta Psychiatrica Scandinavica, 102*(4), 314–317.

Oyewumi, L., & Kazarian, S. (1992). Abnormal eating attitudes among a group of Nigerian youths: II. Anorexic behaviour. *East African Medical Journal, 69*(12), 667–669.

Perera, H., Wickramasinghe, V., Wanigasinghe, K., & Perera, G. (2002). Anorexia nervosa in early adolescence in Sri Lanka. *Annals of Tropical Paediatrics, 22*(2), 173–177.

Pike, K. M., & Borovoy, A. (2004). The rise of eating disorders in Japan: Issues of culture and limitations of the model of "westernization." *Culture, Medicine, and Psychiatry, 28*(4), 493–531.

Pike, K. M., & Mizushima, H. (2005). The clinical presentation of Japanese women with anorexia nervosa and bulimia nervosa: A study of the Eating Disorders Inventory–2. *International Journal of Eating Disorders, 37*(1), 26–31.

Pumarino, H., & Vivanco, N. (1982). Anorexia nerviosa: Caracteristicas medicas y psiquiatricas en 30 casos. [Anorexia nervosa: Medical and psychiatric characteristics of 30 cases]. *Revista Medica de Chile, 110*(11), 1081–1092.

Pumarino, H., & Vivanco, N. (1987). Trastornos del apetito y del comer: Una patologia en aumento? [Appetite and eating disorders: An increasing pathology?]. *Revista Medica de Chile, 115*(8), 785–787.

Quintero-Parraga, E., Perez-Montiel, A. C., Montiel-Nava, C., Pirela, D., Acosta, M., & Pineda, N. (2003). Trastornos de la conducta alimentaria. Prevalencia y caracteristicas clincásen adolescentes de la ciudad de Maracaibo, Estado Zulia, Venezuela. [Eating behavior disorders. Prevalence and clinical features in adolescents in the city of Maracaibo, Zulia State, Venezuela]. *Investigacion Clinica, 44*(3), 179–193.

Rukavina, T., & Pokrajac-Bulian, A. (2006). Thin-ideal internalization, body dissatisfaction and symptoms of eating disorders in Croatian adolescent girls. *Eating and Weight Disorders 11*(1), 31–37.

Shroff, H., & Thompson, J. K. (2004). Body image and eating disturbance in India: Media and interpersonal influences. *International Journal of Eating Disorders, 35*(2), 198–203.

Simeon, D., Rattan, R., Panchoo, K., Kungeesingh, K., Ali, A., & Abdool, P. (2003). Body image of adolescents in a multi-ethnic Caribbean population. *European Journal of Clinical Nutrition, 57*(1), 157–162.

Sjostedt, J., Schumaker, J., & Nathawat, S. (1998). Eating disorders among Indian and Australian university students. *The Journal of Social Psychology, 138*(3), 351–357.

Soomro, G., Crisp, A. H., Lynch, D., Tran, D., & Joughin, N. (1995). Anorexia nervosa in "non-white" populations. *British Journal of Psychiatry, 167*(3), 385–389.

Spear, L. (2000). The adolescent brain and age-related behavioral manifestations. *Neuroscience and Biobehavioral Reviews, 24*(4), 417–463.

Stein, D., Meged, S., Bar-Hanin, T., Blank, S., Elizur, A., & Weizman, A. (1997). Partial eating disorders in a community sample of female adolescents. *Journal of the American Academy of Child and Adolescent Psychiatry, 36*(8), 1116–1123.

Stice, E., Maxfield, J., & Wells, T. (2003). Adverse effects of social pressure to be thin on young women: an experimental investigation of the effects of "fat talk." *International Journal of Eating Disorders, 34*(1), 108–117.

Strong, K., & Huon, G. F. (1998). An evaluation of a structural model for studies of the initiation of dieting among adolescent girls. *Journal of Psychosomatic Research, 44*(3–4), 315–326.

Szabo, C., & Allwood, C. (2004). Application of the Eating Attitudes Test (EAT-26) in a rural, Zulu speaking, adolescent population in South Africa. *World Psychiatry, 3*(3), 169–171.

Tareen, A., Hodes, M., & Rangel, L. (2005). Non-fat-phobic anorexia nervosa in British South Asian adolescents. *International Journal of Eating Disorders, 37*(2), 161–165.

Tong, J., Miao, S., Wang, J., Zhang, J, Wu, H., Li, T., et al. (2005). Five cases of male eating disorders in Central China. *International Journal of Eating Disorders, 37*(1), 72–75.

Tsai, G., Curbow, B., & Heinberg, L. (2003). Sociocultural and developmental influences on body dissatisfaction and disordered eating attitudes and behaviors of Asian women. *Journal of Nervous and Mental Disorder, 191*(5), 309–318.

Ung, E. (2003). Eating disorders in Singapore: A review. *Annals of the Academy of Medicine of Singapore, 32*(1), 19–24.

Vega Alonso, A. T., Rasillo Rodriguez, M. A., Lozano Alonso, J. E., Rodriguez Carretero, G., & Martin, M. F. (2005). Eating disorders: Prevalenve and risk profile among secondary school students. *Social Psychiatry and Psychiatric Epidemiology, 40*(12), 980–987.

World Health Organization. (2003). *Caring for children and adolescents with mental disorders: Setting WHO directions.* Geneva, Switzerland: Author.

Yamamoto-Kimura, L., Posadas-Romero, C., Posadas-Sanchez, R., Zamora-Gonzalez, J., Cardoso-Saldana, G., & Mendez Ramirez, I. (2006). Prevalence and interrelations of cardiovascular risk factors in urban and rural Mexican adolescents. *Journal of Adolescent Health, 38*(5), 591–598.

Yates, A. (1989). Current perspectives on the eating disorders: I. History, psychological and biological aspects. *Journal of the American Academy of Child and Adolescent Psychiatry, 28*(6), 813–828.

7

RISK FACTORS IN THE DEVELOPMENT OF BODY IMAGE, EATING PROBLEMS, AND OBESITY

LINDA SMOLAK

Body image, eating disorders, and obesity could each have their own chapters on risk and protective factors. Yet, there are at least two compelling reasons to consider all three topics in the same chapter. First, body image, eating disorders, and obesity share some risk factors. This is evident from examining Tables 7.1 to 7.4. For example, media images may contribute to body image in both boys and girls as well as eating problems in girls (see, e.g., Groesz, Levine, & Murnen, 2002; McKnight Investigators, 2003; Smolak & Stein, 2006). Participation in sports has been implicated in the development of later body shame as well as the prevention of obesity in women (Alfano, Klesges, Murray, Beech, & McClanahan, 2002; Parsons & Betz, 2001). Sports also provide a context in which boys can discuss, and perhaps understand, their body image concerns (Ricciardelli, McCabe, & Ridge, 2006).

Second, body image, disordered eating, eating disorders, and obesity are linked to each other in interesting ways. Although broad measures of body image may not predict disordered eating in girls, weight concerns, a specific form of body image problems focused on fears about being or becoming

TABLE 7.1
Risk Factors for the Development of Body Image Problems in Girls

Variable	Experimental support[a]	Prospective support	Correlational support
Internalization of thin ideal		XXX	XXX
Social comparison		XXX	XXX
Media influences	XXX	XXX	XXX
Self-esteem		XXX	XXX
Peer teasing		XXX	XXX
Peer modeling		XXX	XXX
Peer conversations		XXX	XXX
Paternal comments			
Maternal comments			XXX
Paternal modeling		XXX	
Maternal modeling			XXX
Child sexual abuse			
Sexual harassment			XXX
Serotonin, dopamine, norepinephrine levels			
Genetics			
Body mass index		XXX	XXX
Ethnicity		XXX	XXX

Note. [a]Experimental support includes data from prevention studies.

overweight, is one of the most robust early adolescent predictors of the onset of late adolescent disordered eating (see chap. 3, this volume). Naturalistic dieting in adolescence may contribute to obesity (e.g., Field et al., 2003; Neumark-Sztainer et al., 2006; Stice, Cameron, Killen, Hayward, & Taylor, 1999; Stice, Presnell, Shaw, & Rohde, 2005) in both boys and girls. Dieting may be a step in the development of eating disorders (e.g., Neumark-Sztainer et al., 2006; Steiger, 2004; Stice, 2002). The body mass index (BMI) is commonly found to affect body satisfaction, a component of body image. These links are important in developing prevention programs that consider both eating disorders and obesity (Haines & Neumark-Sztainer, 2006; chap. 11, this volume). Thus, it is reasonable to give some consideration to risk factors for body image, eating disorders, and obesity within a single chapter.

Researchers and theorists have long considered eating disorders, obesity, and body image to be multidetermined (see, e.g., Smolak & Levine,

TABLE 7.2
Risk Factors for the Development of Eating Disorders
and Eating Disorders' Symptoms in Girls

Variable	Experimental support[a]	Prospective support	Correlational support
Weight concerns		XXX	
Internalization of thin ideal		XXX	XXX
Body dissatisfaction		XXX	XXX
Social comparison		XXX	XXX
Neuroticism		XXX	
Negative affect		XXX	
Poor interoceptive awareness		XXX	
Media influences	XXX	XXX	XXX
Early feeding and eating patterns		XXX	
Parental restriction of child's eating		XXX	XXX
Peer teasing			XXX
Peer modeling			XXX
Peer conversations			
Paternal comments			XXX
Maternal comments			XXX
Paternal modeling			
Maternal modeling		XXX	XXX
Child sexual abuse			XXX
Dating violence			XXX
Self weighing		XXX	
Naturalistic dieting		XXX	
Serotonin, dopamine, norepinephrine levels			
Genetics			XXX
BMI		XXX	XXX
Childhood overweight		XXX	
Ethnicity			XXX

Note. *Experimental support includes data from prevention studies.

TABLE 7.3
Risk Factors for the Development of Body Image Problems in Boys

Variable	Experimental support[a]	Prospective support	Correlational support
Internalization of muscular ideal		XXX	XXX
Social comparison		XXX	XXX
Gender role			XXX
Depression		XXX	XXX
Self-esteem		XXX	XXX
Media influences	XXX	XXX	XXX
Peer teasing		XXX	XXX
Peer modeling			XXX
Peer conversations			
Paternal comments			XXX
Maternal comments			XXX
Paternal modeling			
Maternal modeling			XXX
Child sexual abuse			
Sexual harassment			XXX
Serotonin, dopamine, norepinephrine levels			
Genetics			
BMI		XXX	XXX
Ethnicity		XXX	XXX

Note. [a]Experimental support includes data from prevention studies.

1996; J. Thompson, Heinberg, Altabe, & Tantleff-Dunn, 1999). Thus, roles were assigned to biological, psychological, and social factors. It would seem, however, that social factors have received much of the research attention, especially in terms of body image and eating disorders, until recently when biological factors, particularly genetics, began to receive substantial attention. Chapters in this edition focus on ethnicity (chap. 5) and cultural differences (chap. 6). There are also chapters that examine early parental influences on eating (chap. 1) and the development of body image and eating problems in girls (chap. 3) and boys (chap. 4). The development of obesity also has its own chapter (chap. 8). Although the present chapter may briefly summarize some of the risk and protective factor information

TABLE 7.4
Risk Factors for the Development of Obesity in Children and Adolescents

Variable	Experimental support[a]	Prospective support	Correlational support
Bottle feeding			XXX
Parental restriction of child's eating		XXX	XXX
Naturalistic dieting		XXX	
High infant weight		XXX	
Rapid growth in infancy		XXX	
Extreme weight control behaviors		XXX	
Depression		XXX	
Child sexual abuse			
Television viewing	XXX	XXX	XXX
Genetics			XXX
BMI		XXX	XXX
Ethnicity			XXX
Parental overweight		XXX	
Child temperament (high emotions)		XXX	
Tantrums re: food in childhood		XXX	
Less sleep in childhood		XXX	

Note. *Experimental support includes data from prevention studies.

that appears in these chapters, the primary focus is on factors not covered in the other chapters. Thus, a substantial amount of attention will be given to four areas—genetics, neurobiology, gender, and trauma—as they apply to children and adolescents. The chapter also focuses more pointedly on body image and eating disorders, especially in girls, largely because of the available psychological literature.

DEFINING RISK FACTORS

A risk factor is an individual or environmental characteristic that significantly increases the likelihood of a pathological outcome. Kraemer et al.'s (1997) definitions of risk factors are widely used in the field (see, e.g., Jacobi, Hayward, de Zwaan, Kraemer, & Agras, 2004; Shisslak & Crago, 2001; Stice,

2002). Kraemer et al. made two major contributions in defining risk factors. First, they distinguished between "fixed" and "variable" risk factors. As the names imply, fixed risk factors may mark risk and may even be causative, but they cannot be changed and are, therefore, often of limited interest to psychologists. Gender is often treated as fixed risk factor (e.g., Jacobi et al., 2004), a position that will be challenged shortly. The variable risk factors, whose levels or influence can be altered, such as media images or teasing by peers, tend to receive greater attention.

Kraemer et al. (1997) delineated the requirements for establishing a risk factor as causal. First, it has to show temporal precedence to the outcome variable. This requires prospective, longitudinal data. This is the minimal requirement for establishing a causal relationship. Second, following in the traditional of empiricism, one has to demonstrate, preferably through experimental manipulation, that altering the levels of the risk factor changes the levels of the outcome variable in some predictable fashion. This might be accomplished in studies that look directly at a particular putative risk factor (e.g., Calogero, 2004) or as part of a prevention study (see, e.g., Levine & Smolak, 2006, for a review).

It is difficult for certain variables to meet Kraemer et al.'s (1997) criteria because they cannot be subjected to experimental techniques. Indeed, prospective data may even be difficult to obtain for ethical reasons. Specifically, those variables concerned with sexual violence, including sexual harassment, rape, and child sexual abuse, do not easily lend themselves to the types of data collection and analysis outlined by Kraemer et al. Indeed, Stice (2002) did not include any of these variables in his meta-analysis despite the substantial data available on child sexual abuse and body image and eating problems (e.g., Smolak & Murnen, 2002; K. Thompson & Wonderlich, 2004). Given the potential importance of these variables, I have opted not to restrict the discussion in this chapter to the Kraemer et al. criteria for risk factors.

GENETICS

There has been considerable enthusiasm recently for genetic explanations of the eating disorders—anorexia nervosa (AN), bulimia nervosa (BN), binge-eating disorders (BED)—and their symptoms, including body dissatisfaction. There have been several reviews of the recent explosion of research in this area (e.g., Bulik & Tozzi, 2004; Mazzeo, Landt, van Furth, & Bulik, 2006). In general, these reviews suggest family aggregation of eating disorders and moderate to high heritability estimates. Although there are some clues about specific chromosomal or autosomal loci for the disorders or the symptoms, there have not been consistent findings.

There are a variety of general critiques of the behavioral genetics approach that also apply to eating disorders studies (e.g., Gottlieb, 1995; Lerner, 2002). For example, the model used in most of the eating disorders research reflects three components: genetics, unique environment, and shared environment. There is no component explicitly representing the interactions between genes and the environment. These genetic models tend to assume that genetics influence environment more than vice versa and so implicitly include genetic—environment interactions under the genetic components of the model. These models also do not recognize what Gottlieb referred to as the probabilistic effect of genes, which will depend heavily on the timing and availability of environmental factors.

Most of the genetic studies have been performed with adult samples. It is not clear that these studies are applicable to children and adolescents because there are important differences between eating disorders in children and in adults (see chap. 2, this volume). For example, BN is more common than AN in adults but the reverse is true in children. The gender difference in eating disorders is more pronounced in adults than in children. Indeed, the limited research suggests different levels of heritability in prepubertal adolescents compared with pubertal or older adolescents (Klump, McGue, & Iacono, 2000, 2003). In prepubertal twins, genetic influences seem to be negligible, whereas shared environment is a significant contributor to Minnesota Eating Disorders Inventory scores. The correlations for monozygotic and dizygotic twins were virtually identical for this age group. In pubertal and 17-year-old twins, however, genetic influences were significant, whereas shared environment effects were negligible. This study certainly requires replication.

Much more research is needed to understand the genetic contribution to the risk for body image or eating problems in children and adolescents. It would be helpful to have prospective studies of genetic risk as well as more studies like Klump et al.'s (2003) actually employing child samples. These studies should closely examine different types of eating problems as well as specific symptoms.

It is also noteworthy that obesity is widely held to have a substantial genetic component, with heritability estimates often in the range of .50 to .80 (see chap. 8, this volume). This argument seems to be bolstered by a recent systematic review demonstrating that infant weight and growth patterns reliably predict later obesity (Baird et al., 2005). However, researchers also have argued that the rapid and substantial increase in obesity, including in children and adolescents, suggests that psychological and behavioral, rather than biological, factors are primarily responsible (e.g., Wadden, Brownell, & Foster, 2002). This, again, underscores Gottlieb's argument about the probabilistic effects of genes. As the environment and behavior have changed, the effect of genes related to obesity has apparently changed.

NEUROBIOLOGY

There is substantial evidence of neurochemical abnormalities during episodes of AN and BN (see, e.g., Jimerson & Wolfe, 2006; Kaye, Frank, Bailer, & Henry, 2005). Given the starvation and purging involved in eating disorders, this is not surprising. These findings almost certainly have implications for the pharmacological treatment of eating disorders. The larger question involves the role of neurobiology as a risk factor for the development of AN and BN. Reviewers frequently suggest that serotonin is a likely risk factor for the development of AN (e.g., Kaye et al., 2005). Steiger (2004) hypothesized that genetics might create a serotonin system that is vulnerable to trauma, hence increasing the likelihood of developing BN.

However, there are no prospective studies establishing serotonin disturbances as a causal factor in the development of AN or BN. Instead, the arguments that serotonin dysfunction or imbalances may be a risk factor are based on studies of people who have recovered from AN or BN. Beyond the difficulties in agreeing on what constitutes "recovery," basing arguments on these populations is problematic because the disorders themselves may have long-term, and perhaps permanent, effects on brain functioning (Streigel-Moore & Smolak, 2004). Such lingering marks of eating disorders are sometimes called "scar effects" (Lilenfeld, Wonderlich, Riso, Crosby, & Mitchell, 2006). Neuroscience has clearly established that even the adult brain is susceptible to environmental influences. Environmental events of various sorts may result in reorganizations of the brain's anatomic, chemical, or metabolic systems (see Cicchetti & Curtis, 2006, for a review). Furthermore, some of the serotonin system changes that have been observed in women who have recovered from eating disorders, including increased levels of some forms of serotonin and hypersensitivity to acute tryptophan depletion (Jimerson & Wolfe, 2006), are consistent with the effects of early malnutrition seen in animal experiments (Schmidt & Georgieff, 2006).

On the other hand, perhaps early nutrition deficits, associated with maternal dieting or even maternal AN during pregnancy or childhood dieting (see chap. 1, this volume), actually create a vulnerable serotonin system that "overreacts" to later tryptophan reductions associated with dieting thereby creating an increased risk for eating disorders (Cowen, Clifford, Walsh, Williams, & Fairburn, 1996). Interestingly, animal research has shown that early malnutrition is also linked to reductions in the γ-aminobutyric acid (GABA) transmitter (Schmidt & Georgieff, 2006). Topiramate, a drug that has recently shown some effectiveness in treating BN (Nickel et al., 2005), appears to work in part by increasing GABA levels (e.g., White, 2005).

Early malnutrition is not the only environmental event that might alter neurobiology. Animal studies have clearly demonstrated, and human studies have suggested, that stress alters serotonin levels (Cichetti & Curtis, 2006; Steiger, 2004). The prospective animal data indicate that the effects of social stress may be permanent. Behavioral research with Romanian orphans indicates that the permanence of the effects of social stress depends on timing of interventions (Rutter & the English and Romanian Adoptees Study Team, 1998). The point here is that the brain is a self-organizing system (Cicchetti & Curtis, 2006) that is constantly reorganizing itself in response to the environment. Genes may help to probabilistically determine how an individual's brain will react to the environment (Gottlieb, 1995).

Unfortunately, we do not yet have the data necessary to explain how these processes work during childhood and adolescence to contribute to the development of body image and eating problems. Such research, although time consuming and expensive, is desperately needed to illuminate whether and how neurochemical systems increase the risk for eating disorders.

GENDER

The term *gender* refers to the culturally constructed roles associated with being male or female (i.e., the qualities we frequently refer to as "masculinity" and "femininity"). In theory, gender can be distinguished from "biological sex" which refers to the physiological differences between males and females. Although biological sex is typically (although not invariably) considered immutable, gender can and does change over time and across cultures.

Feminists consider gender to be acquired, something we learn to perform or "do." Although there are many elements to the process of acquiring gender, part of that process is the "lived experience" of being female or male. Lived experiences are events or characteristics of events that are more common for one gender than the other. These experiences carry with them certain cultural meanings. For boys, lived experiences might include playing football or drinking beer or engaging in high-risk behavior in order to be "one of the guys". For girls, lived experiences might include sexual harassment or commiserating about appearance (see Smolak & Murnen, 2004, for a discussion). Lived experiences might well contribute to the development of body image and eating problems. Insomuch as they do, they represent ways in which gender contributes to body image and eating problems. Sexual harassment and child sexual abuse are examples of gendered lived experiences that might contribute to body image and eating problems.

Objectification

Objectification theory (Fredrickson & Roberts, 1997) emphasizes the role of power in gender differences in body image. Objectification theory begins with the premise that society imbues the male and female body with different meanings. Men's bodies, particularly White men's bodies, are viewed as active and functional. They are meant to do things, to accomplish things. Men are actors. Women's—and girls'—bodies, on the other hand, are meant to be looked at, like objects. Furthermore, the gaze is a sexual one; according to Fredrickson and Roberts (1997), the main social purpose of women's bodies is to provide men with a pleasurable, sensual experience. Women who fail to do this are fair game to be subjected to jokes, teasing, comments (even from boys), or to be ostracized.

This process of treating women's bodies as sexual objects is termed *objectification*. What is truly insidious is that women internalize the gaze of the other and self-objectify. This means women will judge and monitor their own bodies to make sure that they are sufficiently attractive, that they meet societal standards. Even elementary school-age girls are aware of and have internalized these standards. A substantial minority of elementary school-age girls—studies commonly report 40% by Grade 4 or 5—report concerns about being or becoming too fat (see, e.g., Smolak & Levine, 2001, for a review). In fact, in a recent longitudinal study, approximately 40% of 5- to 9-year-old girls wished to be thinner and this desire was influenced by peer pressures (Dohnt & Tiggemann, 2006).

McKinley and Hyde (1996) suggested that women who see themselves as objects to be looked at and evaluated by other people are experiencing *objectified body consciousness* (OBC). OBC, a construct similar to self-objec- tification, consists of three components. The first is body surveillance in which women experience their bodies as an outside observer might. They are neither in touch with what their bodies can do nor with what they feel. This is consistent with feminist arguments that adolescent girls and women have lost their "voices" (e.g., Brown & Gilligan, 1992; Tolman, Impett, Tracy, & Michael, 2006) or that they engage in "self-silencing" (Jack, 1991).

The second component of OBC is body shame (McKinley & Hyde, 1996). As part of objectification, women internalize societal standards of beauty, including the ideal of an unrealistically thin body. There is much evidence that many women and adolescent girls internalize the thin ideal and that the internalization of the thin ideal is an important component of eating problems (see, e.g., J. Thompson & Stice, 2001, for a review). Indeed, weight concerns are a well-established predictor of the development of eating disorders in adolescent girls (see chap. 3, this volume). Substantial empirical data indicate that the internalization of the thin ideal is rooted in cultural messages. For example, a meta-analysis of experimental research (Groesz et al., 2002) found a moderate effect size for fashion magazine exposure and internalization of the thin ideal ($d = .42$). This forms the basis of body shame according to objectification theory.

The third component of OBC is control beliefs. This refers to the set of beliefs that women can control their weight, shape, and appearance sufficiently to actually achieve the cultural standard. Research indicates that even elementary school-age girls are aware of and engage in various techniques for achieving the thin ideal (e.g., Murnen, Smolak, Mills, & Good, 2003; Smolak & Levine, 1994).

OBC may develop during puberty (Lindberg, Hyde, & McKinley, 2006). Lindberg et al. (2006) developed a measure of OBC for preadolescent youth that they distributed to girls and boys ages 10 to 12. Lindberg et al. reported that girls' OBC surveillance scores were significantly higher than boys' ($d = -.49$), even at this young age. In this sample, there was no gender difference in body shame or body esteem. Lindberg et al. hypothesized that aspects of OBC develop during puberty as girls start to become objectified. They found that girls' pubertal development was associated with self-surveillance and body shame scores, but this was not true for boys. Finally, they found that sexual harassment was related to OBC surveillance and body shame scores for both boys and girls, although it should be noted that sexual harassment was defined so as not to be limited to cross-gender harassment. Thus, this is not the type of sexual harassment that feminist theorists frequently suggest differentiates boys' and girls' experiences (e.g., Larkin & Rice, 2005). This new OBC measure will enable prospective studies examining the role of self-objectification in adolescence, and perhaps earlier, in the development of body image and eating problems.

Sexual Harassment

Sexual harassment is one type of experience that might teach girls that their bodies are commodities. Although a number of studies show that boys and girls report similar rates of sexual harassment, research also indicates that girls react more strongly to cross-gender sexual harassment than boys (e.g., American Association of University Women, 2001; Murnen & Smolak, 2000). This may be because girls associate sexual harassment with the possibility of rape and so are more intimidated (Sheffield, 1995). Sexual harassment appears to focus girls on their bodies, perhaps because it reinforces other forms of sexual objectification (Fredrickson & Roberts, 1997). Thus, sexual harassment has been associated with increased body dissatisfaction in elementary school (Murnen & Smolak, 2000), middle school (Lindberg et al., 2006), and high school (Larkin & Rice, 2005; Piran, 2001) girls. These data are overwhelmingly cross-sectional and occasionally retrospective. Prospective data are needed to clarify these relationships although they will be difficult to collect because of the ethical necessity of intervening if victims of harassment are identified. Prevention programs aimed at reducing harassment (see, e.g., Larkin & Rice, 2005) may offer a way to collect experimental data to assess the role of sexual harassment as a risk factor.

Child Sexual Abuse

Child sexual abuse (CSA) has been heavily researched as a possible risk factor for the development of body image and eating problems, including obesity. There is increasingly widespread agreement that CSA is statistically associated with and may be a risk factor for eating disorders, especially for BN (e.g., Jacobi et al., 2004; Smolak & Levine, 2007; K. Thompson & Wonderlich, 2004). A limited number of studies have also examined the link between CSA and obesity in adulthood, generally reporting a modest relationship between the two (Gustafson & Sarwer, 2004). Whether the relationship between obesity and CSA is mediated by binge eating is unknown. It is also not clear when symptoms of eating disorders or when obesity associated with CSA might onset (i.e., whether CSA actually increases the risk of childhood or adolescent BN, binge eating, or obesity). A recent review by K. Thompson and Wonderlich (2004) suggested that retrospective reports indicate that eating disorder symptoms tend to onset fairly quickly after the abuse has occurred, typically 1 to 5 years.

CSA does not, however, appear to be a specific risk factor for eating disorders, but rather increases risk for a variety of forms of psychopathology (K. Thompson & Wonderlich, 2004). This should not undermine the importance of continuing to investigate CSA as a potential causal risk factor for eating disorders, however. Other putative risk factors, including serotonin imbalances and even genetic vulnerabilities, may be linked to other psychiatric disorders. Indeed, even body dissatisfaction, a commonly cited risk factor for eating problems (e.g., Stice, 2002; chap. 3, this volume), is also a risk factor for negative affect and depression (Stice & Bearman, 2001; Wichstrom, 1999.

It is crucial to assess temporal precedence of CSA to establish it as a risk factor because experimental studies are not ethically possible. However, temporal precedence of CSA has been difficult to definitively establish. Prospective studies, following CSA victims from childhood or adolescence until they develop an eating problem or obesity, do not currently exist and are difficult to perform, partly because of ethical concerns (see, e.g., Smolak & Levine, 2007, for a discussion). A review of seven studies using retrospective reports found that CSA consistently preceded the onset of eating problems (K. Thompson & Wonderlich, 2004).

Other Sexual Violence

Sometime in adolescence, girls may start to date. At that point, they are at risk for dating violence. Some research (e.g., Silverman, Raj, Mucci, & Hathaway, 2001) indicates that up to 20% of high school girls (Grades 9–12) experience physical or sexual abuse at the hands of their dating partners. Correlational data suggest that these girls have higher rates of unhealthy weight control behaviors, including purge behaviors such as laxative abuse or vomiting. Although other studies have found considerably lower (<10%) rates of dating violence, they again report that those adolescents, boys and girls, who have experienced violence and rape while on dates were more likely to demonstrate a variety of eating problems including laxative and diet pill use and vomiting (Ackard & Neumark-Sztainer, 2002).

The possibility that dating violence, including date rape, occurs in a sizeable minority of adolescent girls is of concern for several reasons. First, it may be a risk factor for eating problems. Very limited research with adults suggests that rape, more so than some other traumas, is related to eating problems (Faravelli, Giugni, Salvatori, & Ricca, 2004). Second, adolescents who report dating violence are more likely than other adolescents to report that they were abused by adults (Ackard & Neumark-Sztainer, 2002) and thus carry the risks associated with CSA. Finally, adolescent girls who are victims of dating violence are more likely to be sexually victimized in college (Smith, White, & Holland, 2003). Multiple sexual victimizations among adolescents are associated with higher rates of disordered eating than single victimizations (Ackard & Neumark-Sztainer, 2003).

Explanations of the Associations

In their objectification theory, Fredrickson and Roberts (1997) argued that self-objectification can lead directly to eating problems and disorders. The obsessive self-monitoring and sense of failing to meet cultural standards of feminine beauty, and hence worth, lay the groundwork for both depression and eating disorders. Objectification has been associated with depression among adolescent girls (Grabe, Hyde, & Lindberg, 2007; Tolman et al., 2006) and depression predicts an increase in eating pathology during adolescence (Measelle, Stice, & Hogansen, 2006). Furthermore, objectification and OBC have been associated with a variety of body image and eating problems in correlational and experimental studies with adults (e.g., Calogero, 2004; Calogero, Davis, & Thompson, 2005; Frederickson, Roberts, Noll, Quinn, & Twenge, 1998; Hebl, King, & Lin, 2004). We now need experimental studies, as well as prospective research, with children and adolescents of the direct and indirect (e.g., mediated by depression) links among objectification, body image, and eating disorders.

It is also possible that the "lived experiences" just discussed, particularly the traumatic experiences such as CSA or date rape, create neurochemical or neurobiological changes that increase the risk of eating problems or disorders (Steiger, 2004). The serotonin system may be particularly affected by such stressors, perhaps especially in those with a genetically vulnerable system (i.e., one that is more easily affected by external forces). Then if the girl begins to diet (Cowen et al., 1996), for example, or encounters an additional stressor (perhaps a second sexual abuse), she may begin to develop eating symptoms. This model, which combines behavioral, genetic, and neurobiological elements, deserves much more research attention, particularly with adolescents.

OTHER RISK FACTORS

Tables 7.1 to 7.4 provide a broad summary of the research on risk factors for body image in girls, disordered eating in girls, body image in boys, and obesity in boys and girls. The tables summarize risk factors for problems that onset during childhood or adolescence rather than risk factors in childhood or adolescence that predict adult problems. The tables are organized to note when there are cross-sectional, prospective/longitudinal, or experimental data available on several risk factors commonly identified in etiological theories. These tables, then, include a wider range of data than those that meet the criteria for identifying risk factors set forth by Kraemer et al. (1997). In taking this approach, I highlight some interesting variables that have received limited empirical attention and hence to spur more research in those areas rather than provide definitive information on what is truly a risk factor. For example, there are mixed results for some of the listed variables. Furthermore, predictors may vary with developmental level (Paxton, Eisenberg, & Neumark-Sztainer, 2006). In fact, in many instances the prospective and experimental data are available for adolescent but not elementary school aged girls and boys.

PROTECTIVE FACTORS

Not all children and adolescents struggle with body image problems, much less eating disorders. And despite the media's attention to the "epidemic" of childhood obesity, most children are not obese or even overweight. Yet, most children encounter at least some of the risk factors for at least one of these problems. Exposure to the thin ideal for females in the media, for example, borders on being ubiquitous. In the face of exposure to risk factors, something "protects" some children from developing problematic body image or eating behaviors. What are those protective factors?

Some researchers would first and foremost answer "genetics." It is commonly argued that up to 80% of the variance in BMI is attributable to genetics, even in childhood (chap. 8, this volume). This is not to say that diet and exercise bear no relationship to an individual's weight. However, it is clear that not all thin people eat balanced, nutritious diets and exercise in healthy, consistent ways. The recent evidence that thinner (<50th percentile) 4.5-year-olds have less than a .20 probability of being overweight by age 12 (Nader et al., 2006) probably at least partly reflects this genetic tendency to maintain a particular body shape.

In a recent study of middle and high school-age girls, Kelly, Wall, Eisenberg, Story, and Neumark-Sztainer (2005) reported that girls with high body satisfaction were more likely to be Black. This finding is consistent with others that the Black culture's acceptance of a wider range of body types might be protective against the development of certain (but not all) body image and eating problems (Grabe & Hyde, 2006; Smolak & Striegel-Moore, 2001). Girls who were underweight and had lower weight concerns also had higher body satisfaction. Interestingly, girls who reported that their parents and peers encouraged healthy eating and exercise for fitness rather than dieting had higher body satisfaction. These data suggest that girls can live in a healthy culture that does not focus on the thinness and dieting although the fact that the satisfied girls were disproportionately (although not universally) thin means that many of them already met the ideal.

Prevention studies also provide some clues concerning protective factors. Only a few prevention programs have been aimed at elementary school-age children (see Levine & Smolak, 2006 for a review). The very limited research suggests that arming children with knowledge about exercise and nutrition as well as the skills to resist sociocultural messages about thinness and weight management may improve body image and eating practices (e.g., Kater, Rohwer, & Londre, 2002; Smolak & Levine, 2001). Substantially more programs have been attempted with adolescents, particularly middle school-age students, especially girls (Levine & Smolak, 2006, chap. 11, this volume). Again, increased knowledge and resistance skills, sometimes coupled with feminist assertiveness training or consciousness raising, have positively impacted body image and eating problems (e.g., Elliot et al., 2006; McVey, Davis, Tweed, & Shaw, 2004; Steiner-Adair et al., 2002; Stewart, Carter, Drinkwater, Hainsworth, & Fairburn, 2001). The potential value of feminism as a protective factor deserves more investigation given that feminist identity appears to be negatively related to body dissatisfaction, internalization of the thin ideal, and disordered eating among adult women (Murnen & Smolak, in press).

Effects of a prevention program are often short-lived but they do suggest that children might be able to develop skills that would protect them from cultural messages about ideal body shapes. Furthermore, these programs might be even more successful (i.e., the protection might be greater) if the environment conveying the negative body messages about body and body shaping techniques was altered (Levine & Smolak, 2006, chap. 11, this volume). The potential value of such an approach is underscored by prevention research in other fields. For example, drug prevention programs aimed at families as well as adolescents have enjoyed particular success (e.g., Spoth, Clair, Shin, & Redmond, 2006). This is also consistent with Kelly et al.'s (2005) findings concerning the importance of a healthy peer and parent environment in distinguishing high body satisfaction girls from other adolescents.

CONCLUSIONS

As the other chapters in this book demonstrate, a great deal of information has accumulated about body image, eating problems, and obesity in childhood and adolescence since the 2001 publication of the first edition of this volume. Yet, particularly in terms of children, we still have much to learn in terms of risk and protective factors. Given the cost in terms of time and money, it is not surprising that we are lacking longitudinal research for many risk factors. Even when we do have longitudinal research, it is often less than a year-long follow-up. We desperately need longer term studies, especially studies that start before children have developed body image concerns. Given that worries about being fat are evident in girls by about age 6 (Dohnt & Tiggemann, 2006) and that current measures of body image attitudes may be unreliable with children of that age much less younger (Smolak, 2004), this is a challenging area indeed.

Current evidence continues to point to the importance of sociocultural variables as risk factors for the development of body image and eating problems in girls and boys. Much more research is needed before the role of genetics and neurobiology can be delineated. Research examining how sociocultural and biological factors work together, as in Steiger's (2004) model, would appear to be a particularly fruitful path.

We also continue to need studies on protective factors. Identifying girls who reject media images (e.g., Murnen et al., 2003) or are high on body esteem (Kelly et al., 2005) and their distinguishing characteristics may provide clues as to how to design better prevention programs.

REFERENCES

Ackard, D., & Neumark-Sztainer, D. (2002). Date violence and date rape among adolescents: Associations with disordered eating behaviors and psychological health. *Child Abuse & Neglect, 26*, 455–473.

Ackard, D., & Neumark-Sztainer, D. (2003). Multiple sexual victimizations among adolescent boys and girls: Prevalence and associations with eating behaviors and psychological health. *Journal of Child Sexual Abuse, 12*, 17–37.

Alfano, C., Klesges, R., Murray, D., Beech, B. M., & McClanahan, B. (2002). History of sport participation in relation to obesity and related health behaviors in women. *Preventive Medicine, 34*, 82–89.

American Association of University Women. (2001). *Hostile hallways: Bullying, teasing, and sexual harassment in school.* Washington, DC: Author.

Baird, J., Fisher, D., Lucas, P., Kleijnen, J., Roberts, H., & Law, C. (2005). Being big or growing fast: Systematic review of size and growth in infancy and later obesity. *BMJ*, 331: 929. doi:10.1136/bmj.38586.411273.E0 (published 14 October 2005).

Brown, L., & Gilligan, C. (1992). *Meeting at the crossroads*. Cambridge, MA: Harvard University Press.

Bulik, C. M., & Tozzi, F. (2004). Genetics in eating disorders: State of the science. *CNS Spectrums, 9*, 511–515.

Calogero, R. M. (2004). A test of Objectification Theory: The effect of the male gaze on appearance concerns in college women. *Psychology of Women Quarterly, 28*, 16–21.

Calogero, R. M., Davis, W. N., & Thompson, J. K. (2005). The role of self-objectification in the experience of women with eating disorders. *Sex Roles, 52*, 43–50.

Cicchetti, D., & Curtis, W. J. (2006). The developing brain and neural plasticity: Implications for normality, psychopathology, and resilience. In D. Cicchetti & D. Cohen (Eds.), *Developmental psychopathology, Vol. 2: Developmental Neuroscience* (2nd ed., pp. 1–64). New York: Wiley.

Cowen, P., Clifford, E., Walsh, A., Williams, C., & Fairburn, C. G. (1996). Moderate dieting causes 5-HT2C receptor supersensitivity. *Psychological Medicine, 26*, 1155–1159.

Dohnt, H., & Tiggemann, M. (2006). The contribution of peer and media influences to the development of body satisfaction and self-esteem in young girls: A prospective study. *Developmental Psychology, 42*, 929–936.

Elliot, D. L., Moe, E. L., Goldberg, L., DeFrancesco, C. A., Durham, M. B., & Hix-Small, H. (2006). Definition and outcome of a curriculum to prevent disordered eating and body-shaping drug use. *Journal of School Health, 76*, 67–73.

Faravelli, C., Giugni, A., Salvatori S., & Ricca, V. (2004). Psychopathology after rape. *American Journal of Psychiatry, 161*, 1483–1485.

Field, A. E., Austin, S. B., Taylor, C. B., Malspeis, S. Rosner, B., Rockett, H. R., et al. (2003). Relation between dieting and weight change among preadolescents and adolescents. *Pediatrics, 112*, 900–906.

Fredrickson, B. L., & Roberts, T. A. (1997). Objectification theory: Toward understanding women's lived experiences and mental health risks. *Psychology of Women Quarterly, 21*, 173–206.

Fredrickson, B. L., Roberts, T. A., Noll, S. M., Quinn, D. M., & Twenge, J. M. (1998). That swimsuit becomes you: Sex differences in self-objectification, restrained eating, and math performance. *Journal of Personality and Social Psychology, 75*, 269–284.

Gottlieb, G. (1995). Some conceptual deficiencies in "developmental" behavioral genetics. *Human Development, 38*, 131–141.

Grabe, S., & Hyde, J. S. (2006). Ethnicity and body dissatisfaction among women in the United States: A meta-analysis. *Psychological Bulletin, 132*, 622–640.

Grabe, S., Hyde, J. S., & Lindberg, S. (2007). Body objectification and depression in adolescents: The role of gender, shame, and rumination. *Psychology of Women Quarterly, 31*, 164–175.

Groesz, L. M., Levine, M. P., & Murnen, S. K. (2002). The effect of experimental presentation of thin media images on body satisfaction: A meta-analytic review. *International Journal of Eating Disorders, 31*, 1–16.

Gustason, T., & Sarwer, D. B. (2004). Childhood sexual abuse and obesity. *Obesity Reviews, 5,* 129–136.

Haines, J., & Neumark-Sztainer, D. (2006). Prevention of obesity and eating disorders: A consideration of shared risk factors. *Health Education Research, 21,* 770–782.

Hebl, M., King, E., & Lin, J. (2004). The swimsuit becomes us all: Ethnicity, gender, and vulnerability to self-objectification. *Personality and Social Psychology Bulletin, 30,* 1322–1331.

Jack, D. C. (1991). *Silencing the self: Women and depression.* Cambridge, MA: Harvard University Press.

Jacobi, C., Hayward, C., de Zwaan, M., Kraemer, H. C., & Agras, W. S. (2004). Coming to terms with risk factors for eating disorders: Application of risk terminology and suggestions for a general taxonomy. *Psychological Bulletin, 130,* 19–65.

Jimerson, D., & Wolfe, B. (2006). Psychobiology of eating disorders. In S. Wonderlich, J. Mitchell, M. de Zwaan, & H. Steiger (Eds.), *Annual review of eating disorders part 2–2006* (pp. 1–15). Oxford, England: Radcliffe.

Kater, K. J., Rohwer, J., & Londre, K. (2002). Evaluation of an upper elementary school program to prevent body image and weight concerns. *Journal of School Health, 72,* 199–204.

Kaye, W., Frank, G., Bailer, U., & Henry, S. (2005). Neurobiology of anorexia nervosa: Clinical implications of alterations of the function of serotonin and other neuronal systems. *International Journal of Eating Disorders, 37,* S15–S19.

Kelly, A. M., Wall, M., Eisenberg, M. E., Story, M., & Neumark-Sztainer, D. (2005). Adolescent girls with high body satisfaction: Who are they and what can they teach us? *Journal of Adolescent Health, 37,* 391–396.

Klump, K., McGue, M., & Iacono, W. G. (2000). Age differences in genetic and environmental influences on eating attitudes and behaviors in preadolescent and adolescent female twins. *Journal of Abnormal Psychology, 109,* 239–251.

Klump, K., McGue, M., & Iacono, W. G. (2003). Differential heritability of eating attitudes and behaviors in prepubertal versus pubertal twins. *International Journal of Eating Disorders, 33,* 287–292.

Kraemer, H., Kazdin, A., Offord, D., Kessler R., Jensen, P., & Kupler, D. (1997). Coming to terms with the terms of risk. *Archives of General Psychiatry, 54,* 337–343.

Larkin, J., & Rice, C. (2005). Beyond "health eating" and "healthy weights": Harassment and the health curriculum in middle schools. *Body Image, 2,* 219–232.

Lerner, R. (2002). *Concepts and theories of human development* (3rd ed.). Mahwah, NJ: Erlbaum.

Levine, M. P., & Smolak, L. (2006). *The prevention of eating problems and eating disorders: Theory, research, and practice.* Mahwah, NJ: Erlbaum.

Lilenfeld, L., Wonderlich, S., Riso, L., Crosby, R., & Mitchell, J. (2006). Eating disorders and personality: A methodological and empirical review. *Clinical Psychology Review, 26,* 299–320.

Lindberg, S., Hyde, J. S., & McKinley, N. M. (2006). A measure of objectified body consciousness for preadolescent and adolescent youth. *Psychology of Women Quarterly, 30,* 65–76.

Mazzeo, S., Landt, M., van Furth, E., & Bulik, C. (2006). Genetics of eating disorders. In S. Wonderlich, J. Mitchell, M. de Zwaan, & H. Steiger (Eds.), *Annual review of eating disorders part 2–2006* (pp. 17–33). Oxford, England: Radcliffe.

McKinley, N. M., & Hyde, J. S. (1996). The objectified body consciousness scale: Self-objectification, body shame, and disordered eating. *Psychology of Women Quarterly, 22*, 623–636.

McKnight Investigators. (2003). Risk factors for the onset of eating disorders in adolescent girls: Results of the McKnight Longitudinal Risk Factor Study. *American Journal of Psychiatry, 160*, 248–254.

McVey, G. L., Davis, R., Tweed, S., & Shaw, B. P. (2004). Evaluation of a school-based program designed to improve body image satisfaction, global self-esteem, and eating attitudes and behaviors: A replication study. *International Journal of Eating Disorders, 36*, 1–11.

Measelle, J., Stice, E., & Hogansen, J. (2006). Developmental trajectories of co-occurring depressive, eating, antisocial, and substance abuse problems in female adolescents. *Journal of Abnormal Psychology, 115*, 524–538.

Murnen, S. K., & Smolak, L. (2000). The experience of sexual harassment among grade-school students: Early socialization of female subordination? *Sex Roles, 43*, 1–17.

Murnen, S. K., & Smolak, L. (in press). Are feminist women protected from body image problems? A meta-analytic review of relevant research. *Sex Roles.*

Murnen, S. K., Smolak, L., Mills, J. A., & Good, L. (2003). Thin, sexy women and strong, muscular men: Grade-school children's responses to objectified images of women and men. *Sex Roles, 49*, 427–437.

Nader, P. R., O'Brien, M., Houts, R., Bradley, R., Belsky, J., Crosnoe, R., et al. (2006). Identifying risk for obesity in early childhood. *Pediatrics, 118*, e594–601. Retrieved from http://www.pediatrics.org

Neumark-Sztainer, D., Wall, M., Guo, J., Story, M., Haines, J., & Eisenberg, M. (2006). Obesity, disordered eating, and eating disorders in a longitudinal study of adolescents: How do dieters fare 5 years later? *Journal of the American Dietetic Association, 106*, 559–568.

Nickel, C., Tritt, K., Muehlbacher, M., Pedrosa Gil, F., Mitterlehner, F. O., Kaplan, P., et al. (2005). Topiramate treatment in bulimia nervosa patients: A randomized, double-blind, placebo-controlled trial. *International Journal of Eating Disorders, 38*, 295–300.

Parsons, E., & Betz, N. E. (2001). The relationship of participation in sports and physical activity to body objectification, instrumentality, and locus of control among young women. *Psychology of Women Quarterly, 25*, 209–222.

Paxton, S. J., Eisenberg, M. E., & Neumark-Sztainer, D. (2006). Prospective predictors of body dissatisfaction in adolescent girls and boys: A five-year longitudinal study. *Developmental Psychology, 42*, 888–899.

Piran, N. (2001). Re-inhabiting the body from the inside out: Girls transform their school environment. In D. Tolman & M. Brydon-Miller (Eds.), *From subjects to subjectivities: A handbook of interpretative and participatory methods* (pp. 218–238). New York: New York University Press.

Ricciardelli, L. A., McCabe, M. P., & Ridge, D. (2006). The construction of the adolescent male body through sport. *Journal of Health Psychology, 11*, 577–587.

Rutter, M., & the English and Romanian Adoptees Study Team. (1998). Developmental catch-up and deficit, following adoption after severe global early privation. *Journal of Child Psychology and Psychiatry, 39,* 465–476.

Sheffield, C. (1995). Sexual terrorism. In J. Freeman (Ed.), *Women: A feminist perspective* (pp. 1–21). Mountain View, CA: Mayfield.

Schmidt, A., & Georgieff, M. (2006). Early nutritional deficiencies in brain development: Implications for psychopathology. In D. Cicchetti & D. Cohen (Eds.), *Developmental psychopathology, Vol. 2: Developmental neuroscience* (2nd ed., pp. 1–64). New York: Wiley.

Shisslak, C., & Crago, M. (2001). Risk and protective factors in the development of eating disorders. In J. K. Thompson & L. Smolak (Eds.), *Body image, eating disorders, and obesity in youth: Assessment, prevention, and treatment* (pp. 103–126). Washington, DC: American Psychological Association.

Silverman, J., Raj, A., Mucci, L., & Hathaway, J. (2001). Dating violence against adolescent girls and associated substance use, unhealthy weight control, sexual risk behavior, pregnancy, and suicidality. *JAMA, 286,* 572–579.

Smith, P., White, J., & Holland, L. (2003). A longitudinal perspective on dating violence among adolescent and college-age women. *American Journal of Public Health, 93,* 1104–1109.

Smolak, L. (2004). Body image in children and adolescents: Where do we go from here? *Body Image, 1,* 15–28.

Smolak, L., & Levine, M. P. (1994). Toward an empirical basis for primary prevention of eating problems with elementary school children. *Eating Disorders: The Journal of Treatment and Prevention, 2,* 293–307.

Smolak, L., & Levine, M. P. (1996). Adolescents' transitions and the development of eating problems. In L. Smolak, M. P. Levine, & R. Striegel-Moore (Eds.), *The psychopathology of eating disorders: Implications for research, prevention, and treatment* (pp. 207–234). Mahwah, NJ: Erlbaum.

Smolak, L., & Levine, M. P. (2001). Two-year follow-up of a primary prevention program for negative body image and unhealthy weight regulation. *Eating Disorders: The Journal of Treatment and Prevention, 9,* 313–326.

Smolak, L., & Levine, M. P. (2007). Trauma, eating problems, and eating disorders. In S. Wonderlich, J. Mitchell, H. Steiger, & M. deZwaan (Eds.), *Annual review of eating disorders Part I–2007* (pp. 113–124). New York: Radcliffe/Oxford.

Smolak, L., & Murnen, S. K. (2002). A meta-analytic examination of the relationship between child sexual abuse and eating disorders. *International Journal of Eating Disorders, 31,* 136–150.

Smolak, L., & Murnen, S. K. (2004). A feminist approach to eating disorders. In J. K. Thompson (Ed.), *Handbook of eating disorders and obesity* (pp. 590–605). New York: Wiley.

Smolak, L., & Stein, J. A. (2006). The relationship of drive for muscularity to sociocultural factors, self-esteem, physical attributes gender role, and social comparison in middle school boys. *Body Image, 3,* 121–129.

Smolak, L., & Striegel-Moore, R. (2001). The myth of the golden girl: Ethnicity and eating disorders. In R. Striegel-Moore & L. Smolak (Eds.), *Eating disorders: New directions for research and practice* (pp. 111–132). Washington, DC: American Psychological Association.

Spoth, R., Clair, S., Shin, C., & Redmond, C. (2006). Long-term effects of universal preventive interventions on methamphetamine use among adolescents. *Archives of Pediatric & Adolescent Medicine, 160*, 876–882.

Steiger, H. (2004). Eating disorders and the serotonin connection: State, trait and developmental effects. *Journal Psychiatry Neuroscience, 29*, 20–29.

Steiner-Adair, C., Sjostrom, L., Franko, D. L., Pai, S., Tucker, R., Becker, A. E., & Herzog, D. B. (2002). Primary prevention of eating disorders in adolescent girls: Learning from practice. *International Journal of Eating Disorders, 32*, 401–411.

Stewart, D., Carter, J., Drinkwater, J., Hainsworth, J., & Fairburn, C. G. (2001). Modification of eating attitudes and behavior in adolescent girls: A controlled study. *International Journal of Eating Disorders, 29*, 107–118.

Stice, E. (2002). Risk and maintenance factors for eating pathology: A meta-analytic review. *Psychological Bulletin, 128*, 825–848.

Stice, E., & Bearman, S. K. (2001). Body image and eating disturbances prospectively predict increases in depressive symptoms in adolescent girls: A growth curve analysis. *Developmental Psychology, 37*, 597–607.

Stice, E., Cameron, R. P., Killen, J. D., Hayward, C., & Taylor, C. B. (1999). Naturalistic weight-reduction efforts prospectively predict growth in relative weight and onset among female adolescents. *Journal of Consulting and Clinical Psychology, 67*, 967–974.

Stice, E., Presnell, K., Shaw, H., & Rohde, P. (2005). Psychological and behavioral risk factors for obesity onset in adolescent girls: A prospective study. *Journal of Consulting and Clinical Psychology, 71*, 195–202.

Striegel-Moore, R., & Smolak, L. (2004). Future directions in eating disorders research. In J. K. Thompson (Ed.), *Handbook of eating disorders and obesity* (pp. 738–754). New York: Wiley.

Thompson, J. K., Heinberg, L. J., Altabe, M. N., & Tantleff-Dunn, S. (1999). *Exacting beauty: Theory, assessment, and treatment of body image disturbance.* Washington, DC: American Psychological Association.

Thompson, J. K., & Stice, E. (2001). Internalization of the thin-ideal: Mounting evidence for a new risk factor for body image disturbance and eating pathology. *Current Directions in Psychological Science, 10*, 181–183.

Thompson, K. M., & Wonderlich, S. (2004). Child sexual abuse and eating disorders. In J. K. Thompson (Ed.), *Handbook of eating disorders and obesity* (pp. 679–694). New York: Wiley.

Tolman, D., Impett, E., Tracy, A., & Michael, A. (2006). Looking good, sounding good: Femininity ideology and adolescent girls' mental health. *Psychology of Women Quarterly, 30*, 85–95.

Wadden, T., Brownell, K. D., & Foster, G. D. (2002). Obesity: Responding to the global epidemic. *Journal of Consulting and Clinical Psychology, 70*, 510–525.

White, H. S. (2005). Molecular pharmacology of topiramate: Managing seizures and preventing migraine. *Headache, 45*(Suppl. 1), S48–S56.

Wichstrom, L. (1999). The emergence of gender differences in depressed mood during adolescence: The role of intensified gender socialization. *Developmental Psychology, 35*, 232–245.

8

PROXIMAL CAUSES AND BEHAVIORS ASSOCIATED WITH PEDIATRIC OBESITY

EVE KUTCHMAN, SARAH LAWHUN, JENN LAHETA,
AND LESLIE J. HEINBERG

The increasing prevalence in pediatric obesity since the 1970s is a public health crisis. Prevalence rates are far greater when including children who are at risk for overweight (body mass index-[BMI]-for-age is ≥ 85th percentile) rather than just those who are overweight or obese (BMI-for-age is 95th percentile, 97th percentile, or higher, respectively). One third of 6- to 11-year-old boys and 30.5% of 12- to 19-year-old boys are at risk for overweight, overweight or obese and 27.8% of 6- to 11-year-old girls and 30.2% of 12- to 19-year-old girls are at risk for overweight, overweight or obese. These statistics represent more than a 700% increase for both age groups since the 1960s and an increase of 250% during the 1990s (Ogden, Flegal, Carroll & Johnson, 2002). Data are more striking when examining childhood obesity by sex, ethnicity and socioeconomic status (SES; Mei et al., 1998). Epidemiological data suggest that minority children from lower SES have an almost one in two chance of being overweight or obese (Mei et al., 1998; National Center for Health Statistics, 2001).

Research demonstrates a strong link between pediatric and adult obesity. The odds of being obese as an adult (BMI>30) were 1.3 for obesity at 1 to 2 years and increase to 17.5 for obesity at 15 to 17 years compared with non-obese BMI's (Whitaker, Wright, Pepe, Seidel, & Dietz, 1997). Evidence also demonstrates that patterns of diet and physical activity are established in childhood (Telama, Yang, Laakso, & Viikari, 1997), likely leading to the strong link between early obesity and overweight and subsequent obesity in adulthood.

Addressing causes and behaviors associated with pediatric obesity has become a major focus for professionals concerned with this growing epidemic. Although multifactorial in its etiology, obesity is ultimately the result of energy imbalance—when energy intake is greater than energy expenditure. In the majority of cases, when medical reasons cannot be found to explain the energy imbalance, the focus shifts to lifestyle factors that may contribute to this energy imbalance. In this chapter, we discuss three global types of proximal causes and behaviors associated with pediatric obesity: activity, dietary, and psychosocial factors. Although genetic and biological risk factors, as well as the gene–environment interaction, are receiving significant research attention, these lifestyle aspects are consistently shown to be highly predictive and also may be more amenable to treatment interventions. (See chap. 7, this volume, for a broader discussion of pediatric obesity risk factors including genetic influences).

ENERGY EXPENDITURE

Any increase in weight results from a basic imbalance between energy intake and energy expenditure. We will first discuss the physical activity end of the energy balance equation.

Physical Activity

Physical activity is any bodily movement produced by the contractions of skeletal muscles that substantially increases energy expenditure (Kaminsky et al., 2006). Engaging in regular physical activity has many benefits including building and maintaining healthy bones and muscles, controlling weight, building lean muscle, reducing fat, reducing blood pressure, and improving blood glucose control. It also decreases the risk of obesity and chronic diseases, such as cardiovascular disease; reduces feelings of depression and anxiety while promoting psychological well-being; and improves the quality of life for people of all ages (Centers for Disease Control and Prevention [CDC], 2004).

There are two types of physical activity: moderate and vigorous. Standard recommendations for children include 60 minutes of moderate physical activity most days of the week, preferably daily, and 30 minutes of vigorous physical activity three to five times per week (CDC, 2006c; Whaley, Brubaker, & Otto, 2006). However, questions remain regarding the recommended amount and type of physical activity needed to improve health status and prevent obesity (Sallis, Prochaska, & Taylor, 2000) and the causal link between hypoactivity and obesity in children (Gillis, Kennedy, & Bar-Or, 2006). This is compounded by many studies only examining frequency of sedentary behavior in comparison to time spent in vigorous activity.

For example, Colleran et al. (2006) found "no difference in reported physical activity levels" between overweight children and nonoverweight 10- to 14-year-old children. In this study, 89.5% of the overweight group correctly classified themselves as being overweight, whereas 47.7% of the nonoverweight children incorrectly classified themselves as overweight (Colleran et al., 2006). Nearly 91% of the overweight group and 72% of the nonoverweight group reported trying to lose weight, and of those, only 36.8% of the overweight group was using exercise as a means for weight loss in contrast to 75% of the nonoverweight group (Colleran et al., 2006). This may be an important distinctive factor as physical activity plays an essential role in improving energy balance. Gillis and colleagues (2006) hypothesized that lower physical activity levels in overweight children could be due to a lack of motor skills and self-confidence needed to perform activities. It has been observed that children who are more athletically inclined within a group often receive the most attention from teachers and overweight children tend to spend more time inactive, even when supervised and during short time periods (Gillis et al., 2006). Additionally, many overweight youth experienced physical discomfort during even light activity, making the experience a negative one to be avoided (Gillis et al., 2006). As a result, many studies are now focusing on increasing daily lifestyle activities rather than structured moderate or vigorous physical activity. Such interventions have been met with more compliance and may, therefore, to go further toward instilling a healthier lifestyle (Bar-Or et al., 1998; Gillis et al., 2006). Such work also has concluded that reducing sedentary behavior can lead to greater success and be more sustainable as a weight-loss or weight maintenance program than a structured exercise prescription (Bar-Or et al., 1998).

Sedentary Behavior

Children have developed a more sedentary lifestyle (CDC, 2006b). There are many factors contributing to and reinforcing a sedentary lifestyle including, but not limited to (a) the increase in nonacademic computer-use time (e.g., Internet use, instant messaging); (b) reduction in physical activity during the school day; (c) shift in family activity patterns; and (d) perceptions of environmental barriers to activity.

The Framingham Children's Study showed that children who watched less than 1.75 hours per day of television had BMIs that were significantly lower than those who watched 3 hours or more, and the children who watched the most television during childhood had the greatest increase in body fat over time (Proctor et al., 2003). In a cross-sectional and longitudinal study of TV viewing and BMI in 7- to 11-year-old girls, girls who exceeded a 2-hour limit, at ages 7, 9, and 11 were 13.2 times more likely to be overweight at age 11 (Krahnsoever-Davison, Marshall, & Birch, 2006). Decreasing global screen time not only frees up time for increased daily physical activity but it also may decrease the tendency for mindless snacking (Matheson, Killen, Wang, Varady, & Robinson, 2004).

Barriers to Energy Expenditure

The clear link between physical activity, weight maintenance, sedentary activity, and higher BMI has led researchers to turn their attention to barriers to adequate energy expenditure. In this section, we provide an overview for community, family, and individual causes that lead to this important risk for overweight in children.

The CDC explained the following:

> the school setting offers multiple opportunities for all students, not just those athletically inclined, to enjoy physical activity outside of physical education classes: walking to and from school, enjoying recess, physical activity clubs, intramural sports, and having classroom lessons that incorporate physical activities . . . helping students learn how to weave physical activity into their daily routine. (CDC, 2004, p. 2)

Unfortunately, these opportunities have been largely unrealized although recently more states are implementing school wellness policies to address the problems of pediatric obesity. The implementation of such policies require schools to make necessary changes to encourage healthier lifestyle behaviors that include increased physical activity by re-evaluating the traditional school day. By offering more activity options, greater caloric expenditure can be achieved.

Another barrier to physical activity is a shift in family activity patterns. Families, in general, spend less time being active with each other and more time engaged in sedentary behaviors (Covington et al., 2001). Many physical activities are not feasible for those who are in fear of neighborhood safety or for parents who must work long hours (Covington et al., 2006). Instead, many family gatherings focus around food and sedentary activities instead of family sports or games. There are other safety concerns in neighborhoods that constrain outdoor physical activity. Many streets do not have sidewalks to walk or jog on or bike lanes for safe travel (CDC, 2006b). The enforcement of speed limits in residential areas also regulates the play areas of children

(CDC, 2006b). Forming neighborhood watches and becoming a participating member on community boards and committees can help with some of these concerns. Planning indoor activities is another encouraged alternative. Other specific barriers addressed in our work with children and families include misconceptions about outside activity in inclement weather, false impressions about the need for equipment to be accessible for activity, and outdoor safety concerns (American Academy of Pediatrics, 2003).

Perceived lack of time is a common reason for inactivity. Healthy Kids–Healthy Weight, as well as many other pediatric obesity programs (Sothern, von Almen, & Schumacher, 2001), recommends scheduling activity into daily plans and keeping it as if it were a doctor's appointment or a meeting. Often, rearranging time currently spent in sedentary behaviors will free up time for activity. For example, a 100-lb. individual will expend a mere 144 calories while watching 4 hours of television. But if that same person took those same 4 hours and split it up into 2 hours of television, 1 hour of computer homework, a 30-minute walk, and 30 minutes of chores, 306 calories would be expended.

Physical activity is necessary for energy balance in any weight-loss or weight maintenance phase of life, and it should not be viewed as optional. Recognizing and addressing the barriers to physical activity is one of the first steps toward leading a healthier lifestyle.

DIETARY FACTORS

Dietary factors have been consistently shown to play a major role in the global causes of childhood obesity. As previously stated, obesity is ultimately the result of energy imbalance (i.e., when energy intake is greater than energy expenditure). Excessive caloric intake can be linked to many eating habits/eating behaviors, including the use of food for non-nutritive purposes (e.g., using food as a reward or punishment and using food for comfort; Baughcum, Burklow, Deeks, Powers, & Whitaker, 1998). Furthermore, poor eating habits are exacerbated by a lack of nutrition education, which in turn may worsen excessive weight gain in children. This lack of nutritional knowledge affects food choices and eating behavior in the home and can play a vital role in a child's nutrition status and intake (Maffeis, 2000). Next, dietary factors associated with childhood obesity are discussed with a focus on five major components with significant empirical evidence: beverage choice, meal patterns/meal frequency, television viewing while eating, fast food intake, and portion sizes.

Beverage Consumption

There has been a major increase in beverage consumption by children and adolescents since the 1980s (Rampersaud, Bailey, & Kauwell, 2003) and consumption of sugar-sweetened beverages has become a major dietary predictor of pediatric obesity. Currently, energy intake coming from beverages represents 21% of total caloric intake for Americans older than 2 years of age (Nielson & Popkin, 2004). The number of calories from beverages, which happen to be sugar-sweetened, generally increases total caloric intake for the day as food consumption does not change (Dimeglio & Mattes, 2000). Many studies show that children and adolescents who consume sugar-sweetened beverages are at risk for becoming overweight or more likely to remain overweight (Ebbeling et al., 2006; Ludwig, Peterson, & Gortmaker, 2001) and there has been a link between sweetened fruit juice intake of more 12 oz per day and obesity in children (Dennison, Rockwell, & Baker, 1997). Beverage choice can also have a negative impact on nutrient intake. Soft drinks are the main source of added sugar in the diets of children and teens (Guthrie & Morton, 2000). Studies also demonstrate that as children get older their consumption of soft drinks increases considerably (Lytle, Seifert, Greenstein, & McGovern, 2000).

Meal Patterns/Meal Frequency

Children's meal patterns and frequency have changed, leading to a negative impact on caloric intake. Breakfast consumption among children has dramatically declined since the 1970s, with 10% to 30 % of today's children and adolescents not eating breakfast on a regular basis (Rampersaud, Pereira, Girard, Adams, & Metzl, 2005). Reports have shown that those who do not eat breakfast have a greater overall daily caloric intake (Stanton & Keast, 1989). Studies have also shown that skipping breakfast is associated with being overweight or obese (Berkey, Rockett, Gillman, Field, & Colditz, 2003), whereas children who eat breakfast are less likely to be overweight or obese (Rampersaud et al., 2005).

Snacking behaviors of children have also changed significantly. One study reported that the number of snacks consumed by 2- to 18-year-old children increased by 24% to 32% from 1977 to 1996 (Jahns, Siega-Riz, & Popkin, 2001). This resulted in a 30% increase in the amount of calories provided by snacks (Jahns et al., 2001). The type of snack consumed also influences the caloric intake. Empty calorie foods are commonly eaten at snack time with trends in snack behavior showing an increase in the consumption of snacks that are high in fat and sugar (Nielson, Siega-Riz, & Popkin, 2002). On average, individuals should consume low-fat snacks containing no more than 300 calories (American Academy of Pediatrics, 2003; Sothern et al., 2001). Furthermore, individuals should be encouraged to consume more fruits and vegetables at snack time to increase nutrient intake (American Academy of Pediatrics, 2003; Wilson et al., 2002).

Television Viewing

As previously noted, there is a positive correlation between increased global TV-viewing time and obesity (Robinson, 2001). Most studies correlate increased TV viewing with increased sedentary time, however, it should also be noted that eating while watching television can contribute to increased calorie intake in children. One study showed that children who watch television while eating consume more calories than children who had the television off while eating (Matheson et al., 2004). Feelings of fullness or satiety can be ignored and large portions can be consumed when viewing television while eating, contributing to excess calorie intake. Furthermore, advertisements during children's programming are saturated with enticements for high-sugar beverages and calorie-dense snack items (Story & Faulkner, 1990). We have seen this pattern in our own practices, and we believe more research needs to be conducted in this area.

Fast Food Consumption

The traditional pattern of families eating meals at home has shifted dramatically in the United States. Fast food consumption increased among children from 2% of total energy intake in the 1970s to 19.3% of total energy intake in the mid-1990s. According to a one national survey, 30% of children between 4 and 19 years of age consume fast food on a typical day (Bowman, Gortmaker, Ebbeling, Pereira, & Ludwig, 2004). Children consuming fast food meals two or more times per week are consuming larger portion sizes, more calories, more fat, more sodium, more sugar, less fiber, and less fruits and vegetables than children who consumei fast food less often. Increased intake of fast food meals can put a child at risk for becoming overweight or obese due to the negative impact on energy intake. Longitudinal studies on children and fast food intake demonstrating a causal link to weight change have not been conducted, but increased fast food intake and increased body weight are potentially related.

Portion Sizes

Since the 1970s, increases in portion sizes have occurred in foods served in the home, in restaurants, and in grocery stores (Young & Nestle, 2002). Obviously, larger portion sizes lead to a higher intake of calories. Children will tend to consume the larger portions when presented with them (Fisher, Rolls, & Birch, 2003). It appears that some children ignore or do not respond to feelings of fullness or satiety signals (Barkeling, Elkman, & Rossner, 1992; Birch & Fisher, 1998). No studies have been conducted on this topic in youth, but the adult literature establishes that consuming large portion sizes directly leads to increased caloric intake (Rolls, Roe, & Meengs, 2006). Thus, it is likely that increased portion size plays a role in increased weight gain among children.

SOCIAL, FAMILY, AND PSYCHOLOGICAL FACTORS

Much of the literature on the etiology of pediatric obesity has focused on the previously discussed dietary and activity behaviors of youth and families. Although the psychosocial effects of pediatric obesity have been examined (Schwimmer, Burwinkle, & Varni, 2003; Strauss, 2000), far less work has reviewed putative psychosocial predictors of future pediatric obesity. We briefly review the etiological factors most frequently presented in the pediatric obesity literature. These include demographic, parenting. and psychological factors.

Ethnicity/Demographic/Socioeconomic Factors

Although a number of genetic and biological factors have been postulated to explain racial epidemiological differences in obesity, data demonstrating the existence of such factors is lacking (Foster, Wadden, Swain, Anderson, & Vogt, 1999). Thus, there is substantial interest in examining differential exposure to the obesogenic factors of the physical, economic,and sociocultural environments for minority and low-income children who are at highest risk. Eating and activity practices are rooted in cultural traditions and attitudes. Additionally, many of the previously described activity and dietary factors may vary substantially based on cultural, ethnic, and racial factors. Community context is an important variable in obesity prevention, to the extent that it influences the type of foods that can be purchased and access to safe and affordable means to increase physical activity (Kumanyika, 2002).

In children, racial/cultural differences have been found on other etiological/maintaining factors such as parental feeding patterns (Faith et al., 2003); television viewing (Ariza, Chen, Binns, & Christoffel, 2004); content of bag lunches (Jones, Sallis, Conway, Marshall, & Pelletier, 1999); consumption of sugar-sweetened beverages (Ariza et al., 2004); consumption of fast food (Bowman et al., 2004); breastfeeding rates (Grummer-Strawn & Mei, 2004); consumption of fruits and vegetables (Neuhouser, Thompson, Coronado, & Solomon, 2004), and physical activity (Kimm et al., 2002).

These factors have been shown to interact with other variables of interest in minority populations such as living in a single-parent household (Lindquist, Reynolds, & Goran, 1999) and acculturation (Mazur, Marquis, & Jensen, 2003). Socioeconomic status both alone (CDC, 2001) and in its inter-

action with ethnicity (O'Loughlin, Gray-Donald, Paradis, & Meshefedjian, 2000) significantly increases children's risk for developing obesity.

Parenting Factors

Although the genetic link between parent and child obesity has long been known, researchers have also examined parenting factors that may have predictive utility independent of biology. A prominent area of studied influence on children's eating behavior is parental control. Parents provide a food environment for their children, model eating behavior and exert varying levels of control over of their children's dietary intake. A number of laboratory studies have demonstrated that a high level of parental control over child eating is associated with poorer eating regulation and that parental restriction is associated with increased food intake by children (Fisher & Birch, 1999). However, laboratory and cross-sectional studies have been unable to determine whether parental control is a result, rather than a cause, of child overweight. A recent study tracked children at 3, 5, and 7 years of age and measured parental feeding attitudes and styles (Faith et al., 2004) and indeed found that the relationship between parental feeding styles and child BMI depends on baseline obesity predisposition. That is, among children predisposed to obesity (as defined by mother's BMI), elevated child BMI seems to lead to restrictive feeding practices, which in turn may lead to greater weight gain (Faith et al., 2004).

Parental modeling of over control as well as under control may also play an important role. For example, maternal dietary disinhibition predicts daughter's overweight status even when controlling for the child's dietary disinhibition in a laboratory environment (Cutting, Fisher, Grimm-Thomas, & Birch, 1999). Longitudinal work also demonstrates that over a 6-year span children's body fat increases linearly with increasing levels of parental disinhibition (Hood et al., 2000). Similarly, a positive relationship was shown between parental dietary restraint scores and increased body fatness compared to children of parents with the lowest levels of dietary restraint. Furthermore, dietary restraint only adversely affected children's overweight when it was also associated with high levels of parental disinhibition (Hood et al., 2000). Other researchers have looked directly at modeling of appropriate healthy eating behaviors. For example, there may be important interactions between ambivalence about modeling healthy eating and children's active resistance, which puts youth at higher risk for overweight (Breis & Gartin, 2006). The essential role of the parent, whether via modeling, parental control, or because parents largely control the home environment and promote (or impede) the child's healthy lifestyle change has led to family-based interventions for pediatric obesity. Although generally efficacious, the most effective treatments do not work for all families, successful responders often relapse and drop-out numbers are high

(Kitzmann & Beech, 2006). Future research should empirically examine strategies and interventions that could improve on family-based programs or that can utilize family-based approaches for preventing obesity. However, Neumark-Sztainer's (2005) parental recommendations for preventing the broad spectrum of weight-related problems (e.g., obesity, eating disorders) should be strongly considered: (a) role model healthful behaviors; (b) provide an environment that makes it easy for children to make healthful choices; (c) focus less on weight and more on healthy lifestyle behaviors; and (d) provide a supportive environment for children in order to augment parent–child communication.

Psychological Factors

Much of the etiological research in pediatric obesity has focused on factors associated with energy balance, with far fewer examining a larger range of personal, behavioral, and psychological variables (Haines, Neumark-Sztainer, Wall, & Story, 2007). Some of these studies have found important clues by relating psychological factors to problematic eating (e.g., greater body image dissatisfaction related to greater extreme dieting) or by its relationship with physical activity (e.g., greater body image dissatisfaction related to decreased physical activity; Neumark-Sztainer, Paxton, Hannan, Haines, & Story, 2006).

Although a large literature exists documenting the prevalence and risk factors associated with eating disorders in children and adolescents, binge eating and its relationship to obesity in youth has largely been ignored (Marcus & Kalarchian, 2003). Binge-eating disorder (BED) is characterized by recurrent episodes (at least 2 days a week) of binge eating. Binge eating is defined as (a) eating, in a discrete period of time, an amount of food that is definitely larger than most people would eat in a similar period of time under similar circumstances; and (b) a lack of control over eating during the episode (American Psychiatric Association, 1994), although research suggests that loss of control may be a more important factor in children than eating an objectively large amount (Marcus & Kalarchian, 2003). Studies of binge-eating prevalence in obese adults suggest that approximately 25% of those presenting to university-based weight-loss programs meet criteria for BEDs and that binge-eating behavior among obese individuals generally begins during adolescence (Mussell et al., 1995). Recent studies using strict diagnostic criteria suggest that 5% to 6% of overweight adolescents have BED whereas subthreshold binge eating (i.e., less frequent episodes) is far more common, occurring in 36.5% of obese adolescents (Decaluwe, Braet, & Fairburn, 2002). Although a number of studies have examined the extent of BED in children and adolescents, there are no longitudinal studies examining the effect of binge-eating behavior on the development of overweight in childhood. Much more needs to be done to better understand the link between binge-eating behaviors and the development and maintenance of overweight in children.

Interestingly, dieting—or more specifically extreme and/or unhealthy dieting behaviors—may be associated with greater likelihood of future obesity. Stice, Cameron, Killen, Hayward, and Taylor (1999) demonstrated that elevated dieting and radical weight-loss efforts predicted subsequent weight gain and obesity risk over a 4-year period. One population-based, longitudinal study followed socioeconomically and ethnically diverse adolescents over a 5-year period (Neumark-Sztainer, Wall, et al., 2006). Results demonstrated that BMI increased by about 1 unit in adolescents using unhealthful weight-control behaviors at baseline as compared with adolescents not using any weight-control behaviors and this group was three times as likely to be overweight. Thus, preventative and treatment strategies should shift from a drastic dieting focus to long-term, lifestyle-based behavior change.

Another longitudinal study by this research group found that body dissatisfaction and weight concerns at baselines predicted overweight 5 years later for both adolescent boys and girls (Haines et al., 2007). Additionally, dieting and unhealthy weight-control behaviors (e.g., fasting, purging, smoking cigarettes) at Time 1 predicted overweight at Time 2. Finally, weight-related teasing and greater weight-related behaviors and focus by parents were predictive of overweight over time (Haines et al., 2007).

FUTURE DIRECTIONS

As research on these three global areas has grown, how to better address these issues becomes paramount. Lifestyle changes need to occur in the home, however, support needs to be given when children are outside of the home as well. As a result, many organizations are coming together to address these problems in an effective manner.

School Wellness Policies

As part of the Child Nutrition and WIC Reauthorization Act of 2004, the U.S. Congress established new requirements to address childhood obesity. This act stated that all school districts with federally funded school meal programs had to develop and implement wellness policies that address nutrition and physical activity by the start of the 2006–2007 school year. This legislation placed the responsibility of developing the policy on the local school districts but, unfortunately for many struggling school districts, this legislation is an unfunded mandate resulting in only minimal efforts with likely minimal benefit.

Another positive example includes the recent actions of the Alliance for a Healthier Generation. This organization's recent work with the representatives of Cadbury Schweppes, Coca Cola, PepsiCo and the American Beverage Association was key in establishing new beverage guidelines in schools (Alliance for a Healthier Generation, 2006). These guidelines were established to limit portion sizes and reduce the number of beverage-related calories available to children in the school day. According to the new guidelines, only lower calorie and nutritious beverages are sold to schools. Similarly, in October 2006, five large snack food manufacturers (Kraft Foods, Inc.; Mars, Inc.; Campbell Soup Co.; Dannon; and PepsiCo, Inc.) agreed to a plan brokered by former President Bill Clinton to discourage schools from stocking vending machines with treats that are high in calories, fat, sugar, and salt and agreed instead to promote snacks that meet new nutrition guidelines backed by the American Heart Association. These positive steps indicate that pressure may be growing to address pediatric obesity, at least within the school environment.

Prevention

A number of excellent, innovative, and successful interventions have been developed and evaluated for the prevention of obesity in pediatric populations. Chapter 12 (this volume) reviews how the proximal causes and behaviors reviewed here may be targeted within larger populations.

Behavior Change

The foundation for the vast majority of prevention and intervention programs remains modification of eating and activity—although simple to describe, this is rarely simple to implement. Future research should continue to incorporate principles of health behavior change, self-efficacy, motivational principles, and relapse-prevention strategies to help develop optimally effective strategies.

CONCLUSIONS

As awareness of the childhood obesity epidemic increases and more organizations are participating in combating this growing problem, efforts must ultimately promote healthy lifestyle changes. Lifestyle change is the key ingredient for all programs from global topics to individual families. Making these lifestyle changes reasonable and achievable for communities, schools, families, and individuals is the key component in their success and in changes for a healthier population. Although many theories and opinions exist on how to best address this problem, there are no easy answers or quick fixes to optimal energy balance.

REFERENCES

Alliance for a Healthier Generation. (2006, May). *Alliance for a Healthier Generation and industry leaders set healthy school beverage guidelines for US schools*. New York: Author.

American Academy of Pediatrics. (2003). Policy statement: Prevention of pediatric overweight and obesity. *Pediatrics, 112*, 424–430.

American Psychiatric Association. (1994). *Diagnostic and statistical manual of mental disorders* (4th ed.). Washington, DC: Author.

Ariza, A. J., Chen, E. H., Binns, H. J., & Christoffel, K. K. (2004). Risk factors for overweight in five- to six-year-old Hispanic-American children: A pilot study. *Journal of Urban Health, 81*, 150–161.

Barkeling, B., Elkman, S., & Rossner, S. (1992). Eating behavior in obese and normal weight 11-year-old children. *International Journal of Obesity and Related Metabolic Disorders, 16*, 355–60.

Bar-Or, O., Foreyt, J., Bouchard, C., Brownell, K. D., Dietz, W. H., Ravussin, E., et al. (1998). Physical activity, genetic, and nutritional considerations in childhood weight management. *Medicine & Science in Sports & Exercise, 30*, 2–10.

Baughcum, A. E., Burklow, K. A., Deeks, C. M., Powers, S. W., & Whitaker, R. C. (1998). Maternal feeding practices and childhood obesity: A focus group study of low-income mothers. *Archives of Pediatrics and Adolescent Medicine, 152*(10), 1010–1014.

Berkey, C. S., Rockett, H. R., Gillman, M. W., Field, A. E., & Colditz, G. A. (2003). Longitudinal study of skipping breakfast and weight change in adolescents. *International Journal of Obesity Related Metabolic Disorders, 27*, 1258–1266.

Birch, L. L., & Fisher, J. O. (1998). Development of eating behaviors among children and adolescents. *Pediatrics, 101*, 539–549.

Bowman, S. A., Gortmaker, S. L., Ebbeling, C. B., Pereira, M. A., & Ludwig, D. S. (2004). Effects of fast-food consumption on energy intake and diet quality among children in a national household survey. *Pediatrics, 113*, 112–118.

Breis, A., & Gartin, M. (2006). Biocultural construction of obesogenic econologies of childhood: Parent-feeding versus child-eating strategies. *Americal Journal of Human Biology, 18*, 203–213.

Centers for Disease Control and Prevention. (2001). *Prevalence of overweight among children and adolescents: United States, 1999–2002*. Retrieved December 11, 2006, from http://www.cdc.gov/nchs/products/pubs/pubd/hestats/overwght99.htm

Centers for Disease Control and Prevention. (2004). *Physical activity for everyone: Physical activity and health*. Retrieved August 2, 2006, from http://www.cdc.gov/nccdphp/dnpa/physical/everyone/health/index.htm

Centers for Disease Control and Prevention. (2006a). *Physical activity for everyone: Are there speical recommendations for young children?* Retrieved August 2, 2006, from http://www.cdc.gov/nccdphp/dnpa/physical/everyone/recommendations/children.htm

Centers for Disease Control and Prevention. (2006b). *Physical activity for everyone: Making physical activity part of your life—Overcoming barriers to physical activity.* Retrieved August 2, 2006, from http://www.cdc.gov/nccdphp/dnpa/physical/life/overcome.htm

Centers for Disease Control and Prevention. (2006c). *Physical activity recommendations for children.* Retrieved August 8, 2006, from http://www.cdc.gov/nccdphp/dnpa/physical/recommendations/young.htm

Colleran, E. G., Wyson, A. C., Wyson, C., Wroten, C., Milliken, L., McInnis, K., McInnis, K. (2006). Physical activity, nutritional intake, and sedentary behaviors in overweight versus normal weight children. *Medicine & Science in Sports & Exercise, 38*(5) (Suppl:S115).

Covington, C. Y., Cybulski, M. J., Davis, T., L., Duca, G. E, Farrell, E. B., Kasgorgis, M. L., et al. (2001). Kids on the move: Preventing obesity among urban children. *American Journal of Nursing, 101(3), 73–82.*

Cutting, T. M., Fisher, J. O., Grimm-Thomas, K., & Birch, L. L. (1999). Like mother, like daughter: Familial patterns of overweight are mediated by mothers' dietary disinhibition. *American Journal of Clinical Nutrition, 69,* 608–613.

Decaluwe, V., Braet, C., & Fairburn, C. G. (2002). Binge eating in obese children and adolescents. *International Journal of Eating Disorders, 33,* 78–84.

Dennison, B. A., Rockwell, H. L., & Baker, S. L. (1997). Excess fruit juice consumption by preschool-aged children is associated with short stature and obesity. *Pediatrics, 99,* 15–22.

Dimeglio, D. P., & Mattes, R. D. (2000). Liquid versus solid carbohydrate: Effects on food intake and body weight. *International Journal of Obesity Related Metabolic Disorders, 24*(6), 794–800.

Ebbeling, C. B., Feldman, H. A., Osganian, S. K., Chomitz, V. R., Ellenbogen, S. J., & Ludwig, D. S. (2006). Effects of decreasing sugar-sweetened beverage consumption on body weight in adolescents: A randomized, controlled pilot study. *Pediatrics, 117,* 673–680.

Faith, M. S., Berkowitz, R. I., Stallings, V. A., Kerns, J., Storey, M., & Stunkard, A. J. (2004). Parental feeding attitudes and styles and child body mass index: Prospective analysis of a gene–environment interaction. *Pediatrics, 114,* e429–e436.

Faith, M. S., Heshka, S., Keller, K. L., Sherry, B., Matz, P. E., Pietrobelli, A., et al. (2003). Maternal–child feeding patterns and child body weight: Findings from a population-based sample. *Archives of Pediatric and Adolescent Medicine, 157,* 926–932.

Fisher, J. O., & Birch, L. L. (1999). Restriction access to palatable foods affects children's behavioral response, food selection, and intake. *American Journal of Clinical Nutrition, 76,* 226–231.

Fisher, J. O., Rolls, B. J., & Birch, L. L. (2003). Children's bite size and intake of an entrée are greater with large portions than with age-appropriate or self-selected portions. *American Journal of Clinical Nutrition, 77,* 1164–70.

Foster, G. D., Wadden, T. A., Swain, R. M., Anderson, D. A., & Vogt, R. A. (1999). Changes in resting energy expenditure after weight loss in obese

African American and White women. *American Journal of Clinical Nutrition, 69,* 13–17.

Gillis, L., Kennedy, L. C., & Bar-Or, O. (2006). Overweight children reduce their activity levels earlier in life than healthy weight children. *Clinical Journal of Sport Medicine, 16,* 51–55.

Grummer-Strawn, L. M., & Mei, Z. (2004). Does breastfeeding protect against pediatric overweight? Analysis of a longitudinal data from the Centers for Disease Control and Prevention pediatric nutrition surveillance system. *Pediatrics, 113,* 81–86.

Guthrie, J. F., & Morton, J. F. (2000). Food sources of added sweeteners in the diets of Americans. *Journal of the American Dietetic Association, 100,* 43–48.

Haines, J., Neumark-Sztainer, D., Wall, M., & Story, M. (2007). Personal, behavioral, and environmental risk and protective factors for adolescent overweight. *Obesity, 15,* 2748–2760.

Hood, M. Y., Moore, L. L., Sundarajan-Ramamurti, A., Singer, M., Cupples, L. A., & Ellison, R. C. (2000). Parental eating attitudes and the development of obesity in children: The Framingham Children's Study. *International Journal of Obesity and Related Metabolic Disorders, 24,* 1319–1325.

Jahns, L., Siega-Riz, A. M., & Popkin, & B. M. (2001). The increasing prevalence of snacking among US children from 1977–1996. *Journal of Pediatrics, 138,* 493–498.

Jones, L. R., Sallis, J. F., Conway, T. L., Marshall, S. J., & Pelletier, R. L. (1999). Ethnic and gender differences in request of and use of low/non-fat foods in bag lunches. *The Journal of School Health, 69,* 332–336.

Kaminsky, L. A., Bonzheim, K. A., Garber, C. E., Glass, S. C., Hamm, L. F., Kohl, H. W., Mikesky, A. (Eds.). (2006). *ACSM's Guidelines for exercise testing and prescription.* Baltimore: Lippincott Williams & Wilkins.

Kimm, S. Y. S., Glynn, N. W., Kriska, A. M., Barton, B. A., Kronsberg, S. S., Daniels, S. R., et al. (2002). Decline in physical activity in black girls and white girls during adolescence. *New England Journal of Medicine, 347,* 709–715.

Kitzmann, K. M., & Beech, B. M. (2006). Family-based interventions for pediatric obesity: Methodological and conceptual challenges from family psychology. *Journal of Family Psychology, 20,* 175–189.

Krahnsoever-Davison, K., Marshall, S. J., & Birch, L. L. (2006). Cross-sectional and longitudinal associations between TV viewing and girls' body mass index, overweight status, and percentage of body fat. *Journal of Pediatrics, 149,* 32–37.

Kumanyika, S. K. (2002). Obesity treatment in minorities. In T. A. Wadden & A. J. Stunkard (Eds.), *Handbook of obesity treatment.* New York: Guilford Press.

Lindquist, C. H., Reynolds, K. D., & Goran, M. I. (1999). Sociocultural determinants of physical activity among children. *Preventive Medicine, 29,* 305–312.

Ludwig, D. S., Peterson, K. E., & Gortmaker, S. L. (2001). Relation between consumption of sugar-sweetened drinks and childhood obesity: A prospective, observational analysis. *Lancet, 357,* 505–508.

Lytle, L. A., Seifert, S., Greenstein, J., & McGovern, P. (2000) How do children's eating patterns and food choices change over time? Results from a cohort study. *American Journal of Health Promotion, 14,* 222–228.

Maffeis, C. (2000). Etiology of overweight and obesity in children and adolescents. *European Journal of Pediatrics, 159,* S35–S44.

Marcus, M. D., & Kalarchian, M. A. (2003). Binge eating in children and adolescents. *International Journal of Eating Disorders, 34,* S47–S57.

Matheson, D. M., Killen, J. D., Wang, Y., Varady, A., & Robinson, T. N. (2004). Children's food consumption during television viewing. *American Journal of Clinical Nutrition, 79,* 1088–1094.

Mazur, R. E., Marquis, G. S., & Jensen, H. H. (2003). Diet and food insufficiency among Hispanic youths: Acculturation and socioeconomic factors in the third National Health and Nutrition Examination Survey. *American Journal of Clinical Nutrition, 78,* 1120–1127.

Mei, Z., Scanlon, K. S., Grummer-Strawn, L. M., Freedman, D. S., Yip, R., & Trowbridge, F. L. (1998). Increasing prevalence of overweight among US low-income preschool children: The Centers for Disease Control and Prevention pediatric nutrition surveillance, 1983 to 1995. *Pediatrics, 101,* E12.

Mussell, M. P., Mitchell, J. E., Weller, C. L., Raymond, N. C., Crow, S. J., & Crosby, R. D. (1995). Onset of binge eating, dieting, obesity, and mood disorders among subjects seeking treatment for binge eating disorder. *International Journal of Eating Disorders, 17,* 395–401.

Neuhouser, M. L., Thompson, B., Coronado, G. D., & Solomon, C. C. (2004). Higher fat intake and lower fruit and vegetables intakes are associated with greater acculturation among Mexicans living in Washington State. *Journal of the American Dietetic Association, 104,* 51–57.

Neumark-Sztainer, D. (2005). Preventing the broad spectrum of weight-related problems: Working with parents to help teens achieve a healthy weight and a positive body image. *Journal of Nutrition Education and Behavior, 37,* S133–S140.

Neumark-Sztainer, D., Paxton, S. J., Hannan, P. J., Haines, J., & Story, M. (2006). Does body satisfaction matter? Five-year longitudinal associations between body satisfaction and health behaviors in adolescent females and males. *Journal of Adolescent Health, 39* (2), 244–251.

Neumark-Sztainer, D., Wall, M., Guo, J., Story, M. Haines, J., & Eisenberg, M. (2006). Obesity, disordered eating, and eating disorders in a longitudinal study of adolescents: How do dieters fare 5 years later? *Journal of the American Dietetic Association, 106,* 559–568.

Nielson, S. J., & Popkin, B. M. (2004). Changes in beverage intake between 1977 and 2001. *American Journal of Preventative Medicine, 27,* 205–210.

Nielson, S. J., Siega-Riz, A. M., & Popkin, B. M. (2002). Trends in food locations and sources among adolescents and young adults. *Preventative Medicine, 35,* 107–113.

Ogden, C. L., Flegal, K. M., Carroll, M. D., Johnson, C. L. (2002). Prevalence and trends in overweight among US children and adolescents, 1999–2000. *JAMA, 288,* 1728–1732.

O'Loughlin J., Gray-Donald, K., Paradis, G., & Meshefedjian, G. (2000). One- and two-year predictors of excess weight gain among elementary schoolchildren in multiethnic, low-income, inner-city neighborhoods. *American Journal of Epidemiology, 152,* 739–746.

Proctor, M. H., Moore, L. L., Gao, D., Cupples, L. A., Bradlee, M. L., Hood, M. Y., & Ellison, R. C. (2003). Television viewing and change in body fat from preschool to early adolescence: The Framingham children's study. *International Journal of Obesity, 27*, 827–833.

Rampersaud, G. C., Bailey, L. B., & Kauwell, G. P. (2003). National survey beverage consumption data for children and adolescents indicate the need to encourage a shift toward more nutritive beverages. *Journal of the American Dietetic Association, 103*, 97–100.

Rampersaud, G. C., Pereira, M. A., Girard, B., Adams, J., & Metzl, J. D. (2005). Breakfast habits, nutritional status, body weight, and academic performance in children and adolescents. *Journal of the American Dietetic Association, 105*, 743–760.

Robinson, T. N. (2001). Television viewing and childhood obesity. *Pediatric Clinics of North America, 48*, 1017–1025.

Rolls, B. J., Roe, L. S., & Meengs, J. S. (2006). Larger portion sizes lead to a sustained increase in energy intake over 2 days. *Journal of the American Dietetic Association, 106*(4), 543–549.

Sallis, J. F., Prochaska, J. J., & Taylor, W. C. (2000). A review of correlates of physical activity of children and adolescents. *Medicine & Science in Sports & Exercise, 32*, 963–975.

Schwimmer, J. B., Burwinkle, T. M., & Varni, J. W. (2003). Health-related quality of life of severely obese children and adolescents. *JAMA, 289*, 1813–1819.

Sothern, M. S., von Almen, T. K., & Schumacher, H. (2001). *Trim kids*. New York: HarperCollins.

Stanton, J. L., & Keast, D. R. (1989). Serum cholesterol, fat intake, and breakfast consumption in the United States adult population. *Journal of American College of Nutrition, 8*, 567–572.

Stice, E., Cameron, R. P., Killen, J. D., Hayward, C., & Taylor, C. B. (1999). Naturalistic weight-reduction efforts prospectively predict growth in relative weight and onset of obesity among female adolescents. *Journal of Consulting and Clinical Psychology, 67*, 967–974.

Story, M., & Faulkner, P. (1990). The prime time diet: A content analysis of eating behavior and food messages in television program content and commercials. *American Journal of Public Health, 80*, 738–740.

Strauss, R. S. (2000). Childhood obesity and self-esteem. *Pediatrics, 105*, e1–e5.

Telama, R., Yang, X., Laakso, L., & Viikari, J. (1997). Physical activity in childhood and adolescence as predictor of physical activity in young adulthood. *American Journal of Preventative Medicine, 13*, 317–323.

Whaley, M. H, Brubaker, P. H., & Otto, R. M. (Eds.). (2006). *ACSM's Guidelines for exercise testing and prescription*. Baltimore: Lippincott Williams & Wilkins.

Whitaker, R. C., Wright, J. A., Pepe, M. S., Seidel, K. D., & Dietz, W. H. (1997). Predicting obesity in young adulthood from childhood and parental obesity. *New England Journal of Medicine, 337*, 869–873.

Wilson, D. K., Friend, R., Teasley, N., Green, S., Reaves, I. L., & Sica, D. A. (2002). Motivational versus social cognitive interventions for promoting fruit and vegetable intake and physical activity in African American adolescents. *Annals of Behavioral Medicine, 24*, 310–319.

Young, L. R., & Nestle, M. (2002). The contribution of expanding portion sizes to the U.S. obesity epidemic. *American Journal of Public Health, 92*, 246–249.

III

ASSESSMENT, PREVENTION, AND TREATMENT

9

ASSESSMENT OF BODY IMAGE IN CHILDREN AND ADOLESCENTS

TOVAH YANOVER AND J. KEVIN THOMPSON

A wide variety of body image measures are available for the assessment of many facets of the construct (Thompson & van den Berg, 2002). In the early part of the 21st century many new measurement instruments are being developed specifically for younger individuals. The primary advances in body image assessment in recent years have been in the development of scales focused on body image concerns related to muscularity, translations of existing measures for use in cross-cultural research, and development of software programs. This chapter reviews many of the commonly used and newer measures of body image for children and adolescents. We focus on self-report measures generally designed to index the subjective and/or attitudinal components of body image, but also briefly examine behavioral and perceptual assessment strategies. A list and description of these and other measures is provided in Table 9.1 along with reliability information if such data were available. We conclude with an examination of methodological issues and particular assessment issues related to clinical management of body image disturbances.

TABLE 9.1
Frequently Used Body Image Measures

Type and name of instrument	Author(s)	Description	Reliability	Standardization sample
Figural ratings				
Figure Rating Scale	Stunkard, Sorenson, & Schlusinger (1983); Fallon & Rosen (1985)	Two rows of female body drawings ranging from emaciated to obese	TR (4–5 weeks): current figure = .87; ideal figure = .83	393 Grade 9 females, mean age = 14.5 (Banasiak, Wertheim, Koerner, & Voudouris, 2001) 34 females and 37 boys, aged 9–10; 40 girls and 38 boys, aged 15–16 (Tiggeman & Pennington, 1990)
None Given	Brennan & Kevany (1985)	Six female figure drawings	No data	218 girls, aged 14–17
None Given	Carroll, Gleeson, Risby, & Dugdale (1986)	Six male and 6 female figure drawings	No data	296 girls, aged 11–19 and 252 boys, aged 11–18
None Given	Collins (1991)	Figure drawings of 7 boys and 7 girls ranging from thin to obese	TR (3 days): self = .71; ideal/ self =.59; ideal/other child = .38	1,118 preadolescents, mean age = 7.97
Kid's Eating Disorder Survey	Childress, Brewerton, Hodges, & Jarrell (1993)	Figure drawings of 8 boys and 8 girls	TR (4 months): .83 for entire survey; not given for figures only	3,129 children, Grades 5–8
Body Rating Scale (BRS)	Sherman, Iacono, & Donnelly (1995)	Two scales; 9 figures representing preadolescent (BRS 11) and adolescent (BRS 17) girls	Interrater	108 girls, age 11 and 102 girls, age 17
Contour Drawing Rating Scale	M. Thompson & Gray (1995)	Nine male and 9 female figures	TR (2–14 weeks): current = .77–.84; ideal = .65–.78	1,056 girls, aged 11–14 (Wertheim, Paxton, & Tilgner, 2004)
Body Image Assessment – Children	Veron-Guidry & Williamson (1996)	Two scales; 9 silhouettes of male and females, children and preadolescents	TR (immediate): current = .94, ideal = .93; (1 week): current = .79, current/ideal = .67	22 boys and girls aged 8–10 100 boys and girls, aged 8–10
Body Image Scale	Sands, Tricker, Sherman, Armatas, & Maschette (1997)	Seven side profiles of pre-pubescent boys and girls	TR (3 months): current = .56; (6 months): current = .40	26 girls and 35 boys, aged 10–12

Measure	Citation	Description	Reliability	Sample
Children's Body Image Scale	Truby & Paxton (2002)	Seven pictures of females and 7 pictures of males ranging from thin to obese	No data	163 girls and 149 boys, aged 7–12
Body Mass Index Silhouette Matching Test	Peterson, Ellenberg, & Crossan (2003)	27-item interval scale with 4 gender-specific figures to anchor	TR: males current = .79, females current = .85; males ideal = .83, females ideal = .82	75 girls and 140 boys, Grades 9–12

Subjective and attitudinal measures

Measure	Citation	Description	Reliability	Sample
Body Esteem Scale	(1) Mendelson & White (1982)	24 yes/no items related to how participants feel about their bodies	(1) IC: split-half reliability = .85	(1) 15 boys and 21 girls, aged 7.5–12
Eating Disorder Inventory (EDI, EDI–2, and EDI–3) Body Dissatisfaction Scale	Garner (1991b); Garner (2004)	Nine-item subscale assesses feeling about satisfaction with body size; items are 6-point, forced-choice; reading level is fifth grade	IC: Adolescents (11–18) Girls: .91 Boys: .86 Children (8–10) Girls: .84 Boys: .72	196 boys and 414 girls, aged 11–18 (Shore & Porter, 1990) 95 boys and 109 girls, aged 8–10 (Wood, Becker, & Thompson, 1996)
Body Concept Scale	Merbaum, Marwit, & Hermann (1986)	Participants evaluate 27 external body parts using a five-color code system, with ratings from extremely favorable to extremely unfavorable	No data	148 children, aged 8–14
Body-Cathexis Scale	Mintz & Betz (1986)	Participants rate satisfaction with 15 body characteristics or parts, using response scale ranging from 1 (extremely satisfied) to 7 (extremely dissatisfied)	No data	170 girls, aged 8.1–15.5 (Hill, Oliver, & Rogers, 1992)

TABLE 9.1
(Continued)

Type and name of instrument	Author(s)	Description	Reliability	Standardization sample
Body Shape Questionnaire (BSQ)	Cooper, Taylor, Cooper, & Fairburn (1987)	34-item self-report questionnaire about the phenomenal experience of "feeling fat"; scored on a Likert scale ranging from 1 (never) to 6 (always)	No data	81 eating disordered patients age 18 and under (Bunnell, Cooper, Hertz, & Shenker, 1992)
Multidimensional Body Self-Relations Questionnaire (MBSRQ) Appearance Evaluation Subscale	Cash (2008)	Global measure of satisfaction with your looks	IC = .76 TR (4–5 weeks): .89	393 Grade 9 girls, mean age = 14.5 (Banasiak, Wertheim, Koerner, & Voudouris, 2001)
Eating Disorders Inventory for Children (EDI-C); Body Dissatisfaction Sale	(1) Garner (1991a) (2) Thurfjell, Edlund, Arinell, Hägglöf, & Engstöm (2003)	Same 9-item subscale as EDI. Wording was rephrased for Grade 1–2 reading level	(1) No data	(1) None (2) 211 girls and 9 boys diagnosed with eating disorders, aged 13–17; 2,073 girls, Grades 7–12
Body Image and Eating Questionnaire	Thelen, Powell, Lawrence, & Kuhnert (1992)	14 items focusing on overweight concerns, dieting, and restraint. Items assessed by a 4- or 5-point Likert scale or yes/no format	IC: all values ≥.68	191 children, aged 7.8–13.6
Body Image Questionnaire	Huddy, Nieman, & Johnson (1993)	20 items on a Likert scale ranging from 1 (agree) to 3 (disagree)	TR (6 weeks): .97	69 boys, 43 girls, aged 12–14 (Duncan, Woodfield, O'Neill, & Al-Nakeeb, 2002)
Objectified Body Conciousness—Youth	McKinley & Hyde (1996)	14-tems assessing body surveillance, shame, and control beliefs	TR (1 week): surveillance = .91; body shame = .62; control beliefs = .70	17 girls and 14 boys, aged 9–12 (Lindberg, Hyde & McKinley, 2006)
McKnight Risk Factor Survey (MFRS-III)	Shisslak et al. (1999)	Five-item subscale assesses concern with weight and shape	IC: Elementary = .82; Middle school = .86; High school = .87; TR: Elementary = .79; Middle school = .84; High school = .90	134 girls, Grades 4–5; 243 girls Grades 6–8; 274 girls, Grades, 9–12

Measure	Authors	Description	Reliability	Sample
Body Satisfaction Scale	Siegel, Yancey, Aneshensel, & Schuler, (1999)	Participants rate satisfaction with four aspects of pubertal development using response scale ranging from 1 (*very dissatisfied*) to 4 (*very satisfied*)	IC: .73 to .80	469 boys and 407 girls, aged 12–17
Body Esteem Scale for Adolescents and Adults	Mendelson, Mendelson, & White (2001)	Three-factor scale assessing weight, appearance, and attribution	IC: weight = .94; appearance = .92; attribution = .81	763 girls and 571 boys, aged 12–25
Body Attitude Test (BAT)—Japanese Version	Kashima et al. (2003)	20-item self-report measure of body dissatisfaction	IC = .90	46 girls with eating disorder, mean age 16.6; 599 university controls, mean age 20.2
Body Uneasiness Test (BUT)	Cuzzolaro, Vetrone, Marano, & Garfinkel (2006)	34 items assessing body shape and/or weight dissatisfaction, compulsive control behaviors, feelings of detachment and another 37 items assessing concern about specific body parts or functions	IC = .79–.90 for BUT-A; .69–.90 for BUT-B TR (1 week) = BUT-A .71–.91 (nonclinical); .80–.94 (clinical): BUT-B .78–.94 (nonclinical); .68–.92 (clinical)	IC: 491 females and 40 males (clinical); 2,017 females and 1,257 males (nonclinical), aged 13–80 TR: subset from initial sample of 32 girls and 6 boys (clinical); 56 girls and 24 boys (nonclinical)
Eating Disorder Belief Questionnaire—Self Acceptance Subscale	Rose, Cooper, & Turner (in press)	Six-item scale assessing how attractive one will feel if one is slim	IC = .85	367 girls, aged 17–18
Eating Disorder Belief Questionnaire—Acceptance by Others subscale	Rose, Cooper, & Turner (in press)	Nine-item subscale assessing how others will feel if the body is slim and toned	IC = .94	367 girls, aged 17–18
Body Image Disturbance—Software				
None Given	Benson, Emery, Cohen-Tovée, & Tovée (1999)	Computer program allows participants to adjust body shape and size using sliders	No data	No data
Body Image	Shibata (2002)	Computer program using image distortion technique to assess body image disturbance	No data	No data

TABLE 9.1
(Continued)

Type and name of instrument	Author(s)	Description	Reliability	Standardization sample
None Given	Tovée, Benson, Emery, Mason, & Cohen-Tovée (2003)	Computer program using body part alteration to assess body perception	TR (difference between first 2 settings): anorexics = .92; bulimics = .89; controls = .78	30 girl anorexics, 30 girl bulimics, and 137 girl controls, aged not given
Body Size Distortion Program	Gardner & Boice (2004)	Computer program allowing adjustment of imaged to match perceived body size	No data	No data
Muscularity Measures				
Drive for Bulk	Furham & Calnan (1998)	Participants rate their desire to be bigger and to gain weight	IC (α): .70	143 boys, aged 16–18
Drive for Muscularity—Body Image subscale	(1) McCreary & Sasse (2000) (2) Cafri, van den Berg, & Thompson (2006)	Seven-item subscale assessing satisfaction with appearance related to a muscular physique	(1) IC = .84 (whole scale) (2) IC = .90	(1) 101 girls and 96 boys, aged 16–24 (2) 269 boys aged 13–18
Muscle Appearance Satisfaction Scale	Mayville, Williamson, White, Netemeyer, & Drab (2002)	Five-subscale measure assessing symptoms of muscle dysmorphia	Adolescents (13–18) all ICs >.70	269 boys aged 13–18 (Cafri, van den Berg, & Thompson, 2006)

Subjective and attitudinal measures ask participants to report on various components of their body dissatisfaction and body image disturbance. There are two broad categories of subjective and attitudinal measures. Figural stimuli consist of a range of images (usually schematic line drawings or silhouettes) that vary in terms of body size, weight, and/or muscularity. Individuals are asked to choose the image most representative of their current and ideal selves. The discrepancy between the two ratings is used as an index of dissatisfaction. A second broad category consists of self-report questionnaires that assess the cognitive, attitudinal, and affective aspects of body image.

A variety of figural stimuli have been developed; several of these are outlined in Table 9.1. Some of these scales are potentially problematic when used in children because they were initially developed as adult scales (this methodological issue is discussed in detail later in the chapter). One commonly used measure that was developed specifically for children is the Body Image Assessment—Children (Veron-Guidry & Williamson, 1996). A strength of this scale is that there are separate figures for children and for preadolescents so that the participants are basing their ratings on figures similar to themselves in body composition and pubertal status.

A wide variety of questionnaire measures are available for the assessment of the subjective and/or attitudinal component of body image. Some of these measures provide a global or generic estimate of size, weight, muscularity, or overall dissatisfaction. For example, the Appearance Evaluation subscale of the Multidimensional Body Self-Relations Questionnaire (Cash, 2008) asks participants to respond to such items as "I like my looks just the way they are." The Body Shape Questionnaire (Cooper, Taylor, Cooper, & Fairburn, 1987) assesses the phenomenological experience of "feeling fat" with items such as "Have you worried about your flesh not being firm enough?" Other measures are more site specific such as the Body Dissatisfaction subscale of the Eating Disorder Inventory (EDI)–3 (Garner, 2004). This subscale asks participants to rate satisfaction with nine weight-relevant body sites including the stomach, hips, thighs, and so on.

Some measures also assess affective reactions toward one's body. The Body Shape Questionnaire (Cooper et al., 1987) asks respondents whether they have cried because they feel fat. The Body Esteem Scale (Mendelson & White, 1982) also assesses how respondents feel about their bodies. The Body Esteem Scale was originally developed for children but a newer version also has been developed for adolescents and adults (Mendelson, Mendelson, & White, 2001).

Some questionnaire assessments attempt to measure aspects of body dissatisfaction beyond the realm of global or site-specific satisfaction. The Body Image Questionnaire (Thelen, Powell, Lawrence, & Kuhnert, 1992) assesses overweight concerns, along with two eating-related variables (dieting and restraint). The Objectified Body Consciousness—Youth (McKinley & Hyde, 1996) scale assesses body surveillance, shame, and control beliefs. The Body Uneasiness Test (Cuzzolaro, Vetrone, Marano, & Garfinkel, 2006) assesses avoidance, compulsive control behaviors, and feelings of detachment in addition to assessing global and site specific dissatisfaction.

In addition to self-report questionnaire and figural methods of assessment, interview strategies have been used with children and adolescents. The Eating Disorder Examination (EDE; Fairburn & Cooper, 1993) is a semi-structured interview of eating pathology currently in its 12th edition. This interview contains two subscales relevant to body image: shape and weight concern. This interview consists of symptom ratings by two interviewers. It was originally designed for adults, however Bryant-Waugh, Cooper, Taylor, and Lask (1996) performed a small pilot study with 16 children between 7 and 14 years of age who were attending an eating disorders clinic. The researchers administered a modified version of the EDE and found that the measure works well in children. Subscale and global scores obtained in children were found to be consistent with those seen in adult female patients.

BEHAVIORAL ASSESSMENT

A literature search did not reveal any behavioral assessments for use in children and adolescents. Behavioral assessment of body image is difficult and is seldom attempted even with adults. Rosen, Srebnik, Saltzberg, and Wendt (1991) developed the Body Image Avoidance Questionnaire for adults, a self-report measure of behavioral avoidance. Behavioral avoidance refers to the avoidance of specific activities that provoke body-related anxiety. For example, some individuals avoid looking in mirrors or social situations because these activities remind them of aspects of their bodies that make them uncomfortable. Because this is a self-report measure, however, it cannot be considered a true behavioral assessment. Likewise, Cuzzolaro et al. (2006) created the Body Uneasiness Test, which contains several items assessing avoidance behaviors such as not looking in mirrors or avoiding being seen by others. Some of the newer measures that address body change strategies also have items that assess self-reported behaviors (discussed in more detail later), however, again, these are not true behavioral measures. J. Thompson, Heinberg, and Marshall (1994) attempted to create a behavioral avoidance test for adults in which participants use an escape button. Participants were able to escape from anxiety-provoking situations by pressing an "escape button" that ended the exposure to body-related stimuli. They found, however, that participants responded to the demands of the situation and opted not to use the button to terminate exposure to images of increasing size. Researchers are still seeking a valid behavioral body image measure for all age groups.

MEASUREMENT OF SIZE PERCEPTION

Measurement of size perception in children and adolescents may be site-specific or whole body-size estimations may be collected. A variety of procedures exist for obtaining these estimates, although there are several methodological limitations of using these procedures with children (Gardner, 2001). Methods for assessing site-specific perceptions include the manipulation of light beams (e.g., J. Thompson & Spana, 1988), cardboard sleeves on a wooden rod, or even the child's hands and fingers (Gardner, 2001). Whole body-size estimates can be obtained using photographic distortion or video images. One video distortion technique used in children is the staircase method (Cornsweet, 1962; Gardner & Boice, 2004) in which children are presented with an initially distorted photograph of themselves that proceeds to get either wider or thinner at a constant rate of change. Children are asked to stop the change when the image resembles their actual body size.

Perceptual measures are seldom used with children, adolescents, or adults when the purpose of the measurement is clinical or applied because of the many methodological limitations documented with the procedures (e.g., Thompson, Heinberg, Altabe, & Tantleff-Dunn, 1999) and the lack of correspondence between perceptual and subjective scores.

RECENT INNOVATIONS IN ASSESSMENT

One of the newest developments in the area of body image assessment is in the development of measures dealing specifically with muscularity and muscular dissatisfaction (see J. Thompson & Cafri, 2007). Researchers have recently begun to realize the importance of body image disturbance in males and have begun to develop measures that assess drive for muscularity and satisfaction with musculature including the Drive for Muscularity Scale (McCreary & Sasse, 2000) and the Muscle Appearance Satisfaction Scale (Mayvill, Williamson, White, Netemeyer, & Drab, 2002). These measures are designed to tap into the idea that males (and some females) tend to be dissatisfied with their bodies not because they are too big, but because they are too small and lacking in sufficient muscle tone and definition. Some of these measures also assess the use of strategies to change the body, such as steroids, weightlifting, and extreme dietary practices (see J. Thompson &

Cafri, 2007). The Body Change Inventory (Ricciardelli & McCabe, 2002) is one such measure focusing on weight-change strategies. This measure was not included in Table 9.1 because of its focus on behavior change rather than body image.

Researchers are also beginning to realize the importance of the cross-cultural study of body image. To that end, Kashima et al. (2003) translated the Body Attitude Test into Japanese and Thurfjell, Edlund, Arinell, Hägglöf, and Engstöm (2003) created a Swedish translation of the Body Dissatisfaction subscale of the EDI for Children (Garner, 1991a). Both of these scales show good internal consistency in the samples in which they were studied. These new measures will allow researchers to assess the same construct across cultures and to perform comparative studies. Such studies may shed some light on factors leading to body image disturbance in various cultures around the world.

Another innovation in the assessment of body image is the use of computer software. The software programs listed in Table 9.1 can be used to assess the degree of perceptual disturbance experienced by the participant. These scales do not yield themselves easily to psychometric evaluation nor have they been so evaluated in most cases. One should be cautious in choosing to use such a measure; however, they do offer an exciting opportunity for researchers to assess perceptual disturbances in body image.

ASSESSMENT OF BODY DYSMORPHIC DISORDER

Body dysmorphic disorder (BDD) is a *DSM–IV* disorder, housed in the Somatoform Disorder section. BDD involves an extreme disturbance in body image, often to the point that the individual's disparagement of a particular body site is of delusional proportions (American Psychiatric Association, 2000). BDD has received a great deal of attention in adults (e.g., Olivardia, 2004), but has yet to receive substantial attention in youth. However, there is good evidence that BDD does occur in children and adolescents, therefore it is important to assess for this extreme form of body image disturbance. Mayville, Katz, Gipson, and Cabral (1999) developed the Body Image Rating Scale and evaluated the presence of BDD in an ethnically diverse sample of 566 adolescents. The Body Image Rating Scale is a brief, 15-item self-report measure that assesses cognitive, affective, and behavioral features of BDD. It also contains items to help rule out similar diagnoses such as eating disorders and gender identity disorder (Mayville et al., 1999). They found a prevalence rate of BDD of 2.2%. This prevalence rate is comparable to that seen in adults where between 1% and 2% of the population is thought to have BDD (Olivardia, 2004).

Several of the measures listed in Table 9.1 were designed for use with adults. Certain measures are included in the table because psychometric evaluations were conducted indicating, minimally, that the measures were reliable. In some cases, notably with the EDI Body Dissatisfaction subscale, there is a good database suggesting that use of the measure is appropriate with youth. However, given the wide array of measures developed specifically for children, we encourage the evaluation of these measures for research and clinical purposes before defaulting to a measure geared primarily toward adults. A further limitation of the measures reviewed in this chapter is that no reliable measures for very young children (i.e., younger than 6 years) could be identified. Measure selection also has implications for longitudinal studies of children. Body shape and size changes with development and a figure scale appropriate for an 8-year-old child is likely no longer suitable when that child is 12. Questionnaire measures with broader age-range applicability may be more appropriate for use in longitudinal studies with long follow-up periods.

There are several other issues that should be considered when selecting a measure (see also Gardner, 2001; J. Thompson & van den Berg, 2002). For instance, researchers should make an effort to use measures that have a minimum reliability (test–retest, internal consistency, split-half, etc.) of .70. The measure should also evidence good convergent validity with other measures of body image. Additionally, many scales are also age-specific and one must be careful to choose a scale that is appropriate for the age of the sample one wishes to assess. Figural scales are easier to use with adults because their body shape is more stable over time. The bodies of children and adolescents, however, are constantly changing so it is important to select a scale that is at the appropriate level of maturity for the sample under study. Investigators and clinicians should also be aware of the standardization sample on which the scale was developed (age, sex, ethnicity).

It is also important to be precise when labeling the specific type of body image disturbance one is interested in measuring, so that an appropriate measure can be selected (J. Thompson, 2004). Although most of the measures discussed in this chapter (and those used in research thus far with adolescents and children) assess some aspect of the subjective or affective component of body image, there are a variety of other measures validated on adults that assess cognitive dimensions (such as schema). Additionally, it is important to differentiate between a measure that assesses dissatisfaction and one that assesses concern or investment in appearance. The Multidimensional Body Self-Relations Questionnaire (Cash, 2008) has subscales that tap into each component, and the factors are orthogonal. The Appearance

Evaluation subscale taps into appearance evaluation (dissatisfaction) and the Appearance Orientation subscale measures an investment in appearance dimension, reflecting that appearance is an important component of one's self-evaluation. Simply put, it is important to clearly specify the assessment of body dissatisfaction vis-à-vis the assessment of whether appearance is important to the individual.

CONCLUSIONS AND RECOMMENDATIONS

A great deal of research attention has been directed toward the assessment of body image disturbance (J. Thompson, 2004; J. Thompson et al., 1999). Increasingly, researchers are creating and evaluating measures specifically for use with younger populations. However, much work remains to be undertaken in this area. In particular, researchers often adapt adult measures for use with younger groups, rather than develop such instruments from the ground up, using qualitative methods and focus groups to inform the creation of quantitative, questionnaire measures. It is encouraging that researchers have begun to focus on a broader array of measures, such as those designed to index muscularity concerns and BDD symptoms. Overall, however, the field of assessment of body image disturbance in youth lags behind the accomplishments that researchers have obtained in adults.

It is encouraging that there are a range of measures (see Table 9.1) that have been used and evaluated in younger ages that are available for selection when considering clinical assessment of body image. Our recommendations, based largely on our discussion of methodological limitations, are for the assessor to carefully consider the merits of the measures available for the specific individual who is to be assessed. A measure developed and validated on a largely White sample may not be appropriate for a patient of a different ethnicity. It may also be important to assess for a range of dimensions of disturbance (weight, shape, muscularity) given the specific case (e.g., if the individual is an adolescent boy or a girl engaged in athletic activities). Finally, if an extreme level of disturbance exists, it may be important to assess for components of BDD. Overall, a careful body image assessment may not only inform the particular type of body image disturbance present, but is essential for the selection of an appropriate treatment.

REFERENCES

American Psychiatric Association. (2000). *Diagnostic and statistical manual of mental disorders* (4th ed., text rev.). Washington, DC: Author.

Banasiak, S. J., Wertheim, E. H., Koerner, J., & Voudouris, N. J. (2001). Test–retest reliability and internal consistency of a variety of measures of dietary restraint and body concerns in a sample of adolescent girls. *International Journal of Eating Disorders, 29,* 85–89.

Benson, P. J., Emery, J. L., Cohen-Tovée, E. M., & Tovée, M. J. (1999). A computer-graphic technique for the study of body size perception and body types. *Behavior Research Methods, Instruments, & Computers, 31,* 446–454.

Brennan, N., & Kevany, J. (1985). Anthropometry and body image in a selected sample of adolescent girls. *Irish Journal of Medical Science, 154,* 220–227.

Bryant-Waugh, R. J., Cooper, P. J., Taylor, C. L., & Lask, B. D. (1996). The use of the Eating Disorder Examination with children: A pilot study. *International Journal of Eating Disorders, 19,* 391–397.

Bunnell, D., Cooper, P., Hertz, S., & Shenker, I. (1992). Body shape concerns among adolescents. *International Journal of Eating Disorders, 11,* 79–83.

Cafri, G., van den Berg, P., & Thompson, J. K. (2006). Pursuit of muscularity in adolescent boys: Relations among biopsychosocial variables and clinical outcomes. *Journal of Clinical Child and Adolescent Psychology, 35,* 283–291.

Carroll, D., Gleeson, C., Risby, B., & Dugdale, A. E. (1986). Body build and the desire for slenderness in young people. *Australian Pediatric Journal, 22,* 121–125.

Cash, T. F. (2008). *Manual for the Multidimensional Body-Self Relations Scale.* Retrieved September 10, 2008, from http://www.body-images.com

Childress, A. C., Brewerton, T. D., Hodges, E. L., & Jarrell, M. P. (1993). The Kids' Eating Disorders Survey (KEDS): A study of middle school students. *Journal of the American Academy of Child and Adolescent Psychiatry, 32,* 843–850.

Collins, M. E. (1991). Body figure perceptions and preferences among preadolescent children. *International Journal of Eating Disorders, 10,* 199–208.

Cooper, P. J., Taylor, M. J., Cooper, Z., & Fairburn, C. G. (1987). The development and validation of the Body Shape Questionnaire. *International Journal of Eating Disorders, 6,* 485–494.

Cornsweet, T. N. (1962). The staircase method in psychophysics. *American Journal of Psychology, 75,* 485–568.

Cuzzolaro, M., Vetrone, G., Marano, G., & Garfinkel, P. E. (2006). The Body Uneasiness Test (BUT): Development and validation of a new body image assessment scale. *Eating and Weight Disorders, 11,* 1–13.

Duncan, M. J., Woodfield, L. A., O'Neill, S. J., & Al-Nakeeb, Y., Nevill, A. M., & Lane, A. M. (2002). Test–retest stability of body image scores in a sample of 12- to 14-yr.-olds. *Perceptual and Motor Skills, 95,* 1007–1012.

Fairburn, C. G., & Cooper, Z. (1993). The Eating Disorder Examination (12th ed.). In C. G. Fairburn & G. T. Wilson (Eds.), *Binge eating: Nature, assessment and treatment* (pp. 317–360). New York: Guilford Press.

Fallon, A. E., & Rozin, P. (1985). Sex differences in the perceptions of body shape. *Journal of Abnormal Psychology, 94,* 102–105.

Furham, A., & Calnan, A. (1998). Eating disturbance, self-esteem, reasons for exercising and body weight dissatisfaction in adolescent makes. *European Eating Disorders Review, 6*(1), 58–72.

Gardner, R. M. (2001). Assessment of body image disturbance in children and adolescents. In J. K. Thompson & L. Smolak (Eds.), *Body image, eating disorders, and obesity in youth: Assessment, prevention, and treatment* (pp. 193–213). Washington, DC: American Psychological Association.

Gardner, R. M., & Boice, R. (2004). A computer program for measuring body size distortion and body dissatisfaction. *Behavior Research Methods, Instruments, and Computers, 36,* 89–95.

Garner, D. M. (1991a). *Eating Disorder Inventory for Children (EDI-C).* Odessa, FL: Psychological Assessment Resources.

Garner, D. M. (1991b). *Manual for the Eating Disorder Inventory–2 (EDI-2).* Odessa, FL: Psychological Assessment Resources.

Garner, D. M. (2004). *Manual for the Eating Disorder Inventory–3 (EDI-3).* Odessa, FL: Psychological Assessment Resources.

Garner, D. M. (1984). *Manual for the Eating Disorder Inventory (EDI).* Odessa, FL: Psychological Assessment Resources.

Hill, A. J., Oliver, S., & Rogers, P. (1992). Eating in the adult world: The rise of dieting in childhood and adolescence. *British Journal of Clinical Psychology, 31,* 95–105.

Huddy, D. C., Nieman, D. C., & Johnson, R. L. (1993). Relationship between body image and percent body fat among college male varsity athletes and non-athletes. *Perceptual and Motor Skills, 77,* 851–857.

Kashima, A., Yamashita, T., Okamoto, A., Nagoshi, Y., Wada, Y., Tadai, T., & Fukui, K. (2003). Japanese version of the Body Attitude Test: Its reliability and validity. *Psychiatry and Clinical Neurosciences, 57,* 511–516.

Lindberg, S. M., Hyde, J. S., & McKinley, N. M. (2006). A measure of objectified body consciousness for preadolescent and adolescent youth. *Psychology of Women Quarterly, 30,* 65–76.

Mayville, S. B., Katz, R. C., Gipson, M. T., & Cabral, K. (1999). Assessing the prevalence of body dysmorphic disorder in an ethnically diverse group of adolescents. *Journal of Child and Family Studies, 8,* 357–362.

Mayville, S. B., Williamson, D. A., White, M. A., Netemeyer, R., & Drab, D. L. (2002). Development of the Muscle Appearance Satisfaction Scale: A self-report measure for the assessment of muscle dysmorphia symptoms. *Assessment, 9,* 351–360.

McCreary, D. R., & Sasse, D. K. (2000). An exploration of the drive for muscularity in adolescent boys and girls. *Journal of American College Health, 48,* 297–304.

McKinley, N. M., & Hyde, J. S. (1996). The Objectified Body Consciousness Scale: Development and validation. *Psychology of Women Quarterly, 20,* 181–215.

Mendelson, B. K., Mendelson, M. J., & White, D. R. (2001). Body-Esteem Scale for adolescents and adults. *Journal of Personality Assessment, 76,* 90–106.

Mendelson, B. K., & White, D. R. (1982). Relation between body-esteem and self-esteem of obese and normal children. *Perceptual and Motor Skills, 54,* 899–905.

Merbaum, M., Marwit, S., & Hermann, J. (1986). *Children's and adolescent's perception of body parts: Appearance, effectiveness, and vulnerability.* Unpublished manuscript.

Mintz, L. B., & Betz, N. E. (1986). Sex differences in the nature, realism, and correlates of body image. *Sex Roles, 15,* 185–195.

Olivardia, R. (2004). Body dysmorphic disorder. In J. K. Thompson (Ed.), *Handbook of eating disorders and obesity* (pp. 542–561). Hoboken, NJ: Wiley.

Peterson, M., Ellenberg, D., & Crossan, S. (2003). Body-image perceptions: Reliability of a BMI-based silhouette-matching test. *American Journal of Health Behavior, 27,* 355–363.

Ricciardelli, L. A., & McCabe, M. P. (2002). Psychometric evaluation of the Body Change Inventory: An assessment instrument for adolescent boys and girls. *Eating Behaviors, 3,* 45–59.

Rose, K. S., Cooper, M. J., & Turner, H. (in press). The eating disorder belief questionnaire: Psychometric properties in an adolescent sample. *Eating Behaviors.*

Rosen, J. C., Srebnik, D., Saltzberf, E., & Wendt, S. (1991). Development of a body image avoidance questionnaire. *Psychological Assessment, 3,* 32–37.

Sands, R., Tricker, J., Cherman, C., Armatas, C., & Maschette, W. (1997). Disordered eating patterns, body image, self-esteem, and physical activity in preadolescent school children. *International Journal of Eating Disorders, 21,* 159–166.

Sherman, D. K., Iacono, W. G., & Donnelly, J. M. (1995). Development and validation of body rating scales for adolescent females. *International Journal of Eating Disorders, 18,* 327–333.

Shibata, S. (2002). A Macintosh and Windows program for assessing body-image disturbance using adjustable image distortion. *Behavior Research Methods, Instruments, & Computers, 34,* 90–92.

Shisslak, C. M., Renger, R., Sharpe, T., Crago, M., McKnight, K. M., Gray, N., et al. (1999). Development and evaluation of the McKnight Risk Factor Survey for assessing potential risk and protective factors for disordered eating in preadolescent and adolescent girls. *International Journal of Eating Disorders, 25,* 195–214.

Shore, R. A., & Porter, J. E. (1990). Normative and reliability data for 11 to 18 year olds on the Eating Disorder Inventory. *International Journal of Eating Disorders, 9,* 201–207.

Siegel, J. M., Yancey, A. K., Aneshensel, C. S., & Schuler, R. (1999). Body image, perceived pubertal timing, and adolescent mental health. *Journal of Adolescent Health, 25,* 255–266.

Stunkard, A., Sorenson, T., & Schlusinger, F. (1983). Use of the Danish Adoption Registry for the study of obesity and thinness. In S. Kety, L. P. Rowland, R. L. Sidman, & S. W. Matthysse (Eds.), *The genetics of neurological and psychiatric disorders* (pp. 115–120). New York: Raven.

Thelen, M., Powell, A., Lawrence, C., & Kuhnert, M. (1992). Eating and body image concerns among children. *Journal of Clinical Child Psychology, 21,* 41–46.

Thompson, J. K. (2004). The (mis)measurement of body image: Ten strategies to improve assessment for applied and research purposes. *Body Image: An International Journal of Research, 1,* 7–14.

Thompson, J. K., & Cafri, G. (2007). *The muscular ideal: Psychological, social, and medical perspectives.* Washington, DC: American Psychological Association.

Thompson, J. K., Heinberg, L. J., Altabe, M. N., & Tantleff-Dunn, S. (1999). *Exacting beauty: Theory, assessment and treatment of body image disturbance.* Washington, DC: American Psychological Association.

Thompson, J. K., Heinberg, L., & Marshall, K. (1994). The Physical Appearance Behavior Avoidance Test (PABAT): Preliminary findings. *The Behavior Therapist, 17,* 9–10.

Thompson, J. K., & Spana, R. (1988). The adjustable light beam method for the assessment of size estimation accuracy: Description, psychometrics, and normative data. *International Journal of Eating Disorders, 5,* 1061–1068.

Thompson, J. K., & van den Berg, P. (2002). Measuring body image attitudes among adolescents and adults. In T. F. Cash & T. Pruzinsky (Eds.), *Body images: A handbook of theory, research and clinical practice* (pp. 142–153). New York: Guilford.

Thompson, M. A., & Gray, J. J. (1995). Development and validation of a new body-image assessment scale. *Journal of Personality Assessment, 64,* 258–269.

Thurfjell, B., Edlund, B., Arinell, H., Hägglöf, B., & Engström, I. (2003). Psychometric properties of Eating Disorder Inventory for Children (EDI-C) in Swedish girls with and without a known eating disorder. *Eating and Weight Disorders, 8,* 296–303.

Tiggemann, M., & Pennington, B. (1990). The development of gender differences in body-size dissatisfaction. *Australian Psychologist, 25,* 306–311.

Tovée, M. J., Benson, P. J., Emery, J. L., Mason, S. M., & Cohen-Tovée, E. M. (2003). Measurement of body size and shape perception in eating-disordered and control observers using body-shape software. *British Journal of Psychology, 94,* 501–516.

Truby, H., & Paxton, S. J. (2002). Development of the Children's Body Image Scale. *British Journal of Clinical Psychology, 41,* 185–203.

Veron-Guidry, S., & Williamson, D. A. (1996). Development of a body image assessment procedure for children and preadolescents. *International Journal of Eating Disorders, 20,* 287–293.

Wertheim, E. H., Paxton, S. J., & Tilgner, L. (2004). Test–retest reliability and construct reliability of Contour Drawing Rating Scales scores in a sample of early adolescent girls. *Body Image, 1,* 199–205.

Wood, K. C., Becker, J. A., & Thompson, J. K. (1996). Body image dissatisfaction in preadolescent children. *Journal of Applied Developmental Psychology, 17,* 85–100.

10

ASSESSMENT OF EATING DISTURBANCES IN CHILDREN AND ADOLESCENTS

DREW A. ANDERSON, JASON M. LAVENDER, SUZANNE M. MILNES, AND ANGELA M. SIMMONS

ASSESSMENT OF EATING DISTURBANCES

The assessment of problematic eating and eating disorders can be complex in children and adolescents. There is a host of developmental, family, medical, nutritional, and psychological influences on eating behavior that must be thoroughly evaluated. Furthermore, it is essential to assess eating behavior in the context of normal childhood development.

This chapter provides an overview of psychological and behavioral assessment of eating disturbances in children and adolescents. We first review some common problems in the assessment of eating disturbances in these age groups. We then provide a broad overview of the assessment process and discuss different types of instruments in detail (interview, self-report, and behavioral assessment) and provide information on those that have been validated in younger populations. Finally, we provide some suggestions for future developments in the assessment of problematic eating.

PROBLEMS IN THE ASSESSMENT OF CHILDREN AND ADOLESCENTS

Researchers have identified a number of concerns and criticisms related to the assessment of children and adolescents. These issues are reviewed below.

Diagnostic Issues

A number of prominent experts and professional organizations have noted problems with the current *Diagnostic and Statiscal Manual of Mental Disorders, Fourth Edition, Text Revision* (DSM–IV–TR; American Psychiatric Association [APA], 2000) diagnostic criteria for eating disorders when applied to children and adolescents (Bryant-Waugh, 2000; Golden et al., 2003; Rome et al., 2003; Work Group on Eating Disorders, 2006). We review these criticisms here; a more thorough discussion of these issues can be found in chapter 2.

Some of these criticisms relate to specific diagnostic criteria. For example, current diagnostic criteria for anorexia nervosa (AN) require amenorrhea for at least 3 months "when menstrual cycles would be expected to occur" (APA, 2000). However, because there is variability in normal onset of menses and a number of factors not necessarily related to eating disorders can cause delays or problems with onset of menses (Keizer & Rogol, 1990; Slap, 2003), it may be difficult to determine when menstrual cycles are "expected" to occur in an adolescent.

Controversy also exists regarding the cognitive diagnostic criteria for eating disorders. Specifically, it has been suggested that many adolescents lack a level of cognitive development sufficient to understand concepts such as self-awareness and motivation to lose weight (Golden et al., 2003). However, some research suggests that the construct of dietary restraint is valid in younger children (Shunk & Birch, 2004), and studies have found that dissatisfaction with weight and shape as well as dieting behavior can occur in even young children (Davison, Markey, & Birch, 2000; Halvarsson, Lunner, & Sjoden, 2000; Schur, Sanders, & Steiner, 2000). Thus, it is not yet clear how appropriate these diagnostic criteria are for children and adolescents.

Other criticisms of the diagnostic criteria for eating disorders in children have been more general. For example, Bryant-Waugh (2000) noted that difficulties in eating and feeding are common in childhood, and some can superficially resemble eating disorders. However, although some of these problems can be serious, most appear to be developmentally normal until a child is roughly 8 years old (Bryant-Waugh, 2000). The overlap between normative eating problems and eating disorders has lead some professionals to deny that eating disorders exist in young children, whereas others claim that almost all eating-related problems represent eating disorders; the truth, however, probably lies somewhere between these extremes (Bryant-Waugh, 2000).

It has become increasingly recognized that a large proportion of individuals who seek treatment for eating disorders do not meet strict *DSM–IV–TR* (APA, 2000) diagnostic criteria for AN or bulimia nervosa (BN) and thus receive a diagnosis of eating disorder not otherwise specified (EDNOS; for a review of this issue, see Anderson & Paulosky, 2004a). However, clinically significant impairment can occur at subclinical levels of eating disorders in adolescents (Golden et al., 2003; Ricca et al., 2001; Turner & Bryant-Waugh, 2004), and intervening early can significantly improve long-term prognosis (Rome et al., 2003). Thus, assessment in children and adolescents should not be focused simply on reaching a diagnosis, but rather on the broader goals of documenting the signs and symptoms of a broad range of eating-related attitudes and behaviors as well as facilitating treatment planning.

In response to some of these concerns, alternative diagnostic categories for childhood eating disorders have been developed (Bryant-Waugh, 2000; Bryant-Waugh & Lask, 1995, 2007; Lask & Bryant-Waugh, 1992; chap. 2, this volume). Although these alternative diagnostic categories appear to have good levels of interrater reliability (Nicholls, Chater, & Lask, 2000) and provide a broader context for looking at eating-related problems, particularly among young children, they have not yet been widely adopted.

Denial and Minimization of Eating Disorder Symptoms

Denial and minimization are relatively common among individuals presenting for eating disorders (Anderson & Paulosky, 2004a). With the exception of the significant weight loss seen in AN, the symptoms of eating disorders are covert and behaviors such as binging or vomiting are usually done when the patient is alone. Also, most self-report instruments and interviews that assess for eating disorders are vulnerable to denial and minimization. There are some assessment strategies, however, that may be helpful in cases where denial or minimization are suspected. For example, obtaining collateral reports from friends and significant others can provide valuable information about eating patterns, particularly restrictive eating (Williamson, 1990). Test meals also can be a valuable tool in cases where denial or minimization are suspected (Anderson, Lundgren, Shapiro, & Paulosky, 2004; Anderson & Paulosky, 2004a; Williamson, 1990).

OVERVIEW OF THE ASSESSMENT PROCESS

Assessment of the eating disorders and problematic eating is best conceptualized as a process that occurs throughout treatment and accomplishes several purposes, including diagnosis, treatment planning, and evaluation of outcome (Crowther & Sherwood, 1997). Furthermore, a thorough assessment of eating disorders and eating-related problems in children and adolescents should be comprehensive and multidisciplinary, including a full physical examination, an examination of nutritional status, interviews with parents or guardians, an interview with the child, completion of self-report instruments of eating problems by the child, and a behavioral assessment of eating behaviors (Netemeyer & Williamson, 2001; Rome et al., 2003; Work Group on Eating Disorders, 2006). Thus, a complete assessment team should include at minimum a physician, a registered dietitian, and a mental health professional. This chapter focuses on psychological evaluation; a number of excellent reviews are available for those interested in physical/medical evaluation (Carney & Andersen, 1996; Crow & Swigart, 2005; Work Group on Eating Disorders, 2006), nutritional assessment (Rock, 2005), and family assessment (le Grange, 2005).

ASSESSMENT OF EATING DISTURBANCES

This section reviews specific interview, self-report, and behavioral assessment instruments for assessing eating disturbances in adolescence. Although a large number of instruments have been developed to assess various aspects of eating disorders and eating-related problems (e.g., Allison, 1995; Peterson & Mitchell, 2005), relatively few have been validated in child and adolescent populations. This section reviews some of the measures that do have psychometric data on their use in younger populations, with an emphasis on those that evaluate overall eating-related pathology rather than just a single aspect (e.g., restrained eating or body dissatisfaction). The constructs assessed by these instruments are summarized in Table 10.1.

Interviews

Interviews, particularly structured interviews, are widely thought to be the assessment method of choice for child and adolescent populations (Decaluwe & Braet, 2003; Tanofsky-Kraff et al., 2003; Work Group on Eating Disorders, 2006), partly because direct comparison of self-report and interview measures of eating disorders in these age groups have shown several important differences (Decaluwe & Braet, 2003; Tanofsky-Kraff et al., 2003). Although some of these differences may be related to different wordings in the measures (Tanofsky-Kraff et al., 2003), others may be related to the fact that children may have particular trouble understanding some concepts regarding eating without clarification by an interviewer (Decaluwe & Braet, 2003). Guidelines for unstructured clinical interviews are reviewed

TABLE 10.1
Constructs Assessed by Interview and Self-Report Instruments

Assessment instrument	Construct			
	Body dissatisfaction	Bulimic behaviors	Drive for thinness/ slimness	General eating disturbance
Interview				
ChEDE	X	X		X
SIAB-EX	X	X	X	X
Self-Report				
EAT/ChEAT				X
BULIT-R		X		
EDI-3	X	X	X	
KEDS	X	X	X	
MRFS-IV			X	
QEWP-A/P		X		X
SEDS		X		X

Note. Constructs were defined broadly, and the degree to which each instrument assesses the relevant constructs may differ.

here, as well as those structured interviews that have been validated for use in children and adolescents.

Unstructured Interviews

Unstructured interviews are the most common assessment tool for evaluating eating disorders in clinical practice, particularly for diagnosis and early treatment planning (Anderson & Paulosky, 2004b). Although by definition they are unstructured, guidelines have been developed to assist interviewers in ensuring their assessment is comprehensive and thorough. For example, Peterson and Mitchell (2005) suggested that a clinical interview should contain questions pertaining to binge eating, purging and other compensatory behaviors, eating patterns and dietary restriction, weight history, and body image. Similar lists are suggested by Crowther and Sherwood (1997), as well as in the latest edition of the American Psychiatric Association's practice guidelines for the treatment of patients with eating disorders (Work Group on Eating Disorders, 2006). Rome and colleagues (2003) also provide a similar list of questions in the context of primary care treatment for eating disorders. These guidelines generally parallel the content of the structured interviews reviewed next.

Structured Interviews

Structured interviews are widely used in research contexts, but do not appear to be used as often in clinical practice (Anderson & Maloney, 2001; Anderson & Paulosky, 2004b). Structured interviews have the advantages of demonstrated reliability and validity, which allows for normative comparisons, and ensures that all critical domains relevant to the eating disorders are evaluated. However, only two structured interviews to date have been developed and validated for use in children and adolescents.

Child Version of the Eating Disorder Examination. The Child version of the Eating Disorder Examination (ChEDE; Bryant-Waugh, Cooper, Taylor, & Lask, 1996) was adapted from the Eating Disorder Examination (EDE; Cooper & Fairburn, 1987; Fairburn & Cooper, 1993), which is the most widely used structured interview for the assessment of eating disorders in both research and clinical contexts (Anderson & Paulosky, 2004a, 2004b). The EDE was initially developed for the purpose of assessing the psychopathology of eating disorders, but it has also been recommended for use as a diagnostic measure and as a tool for treatment planning and evaluation of treatment progress (Anderson et al., 2004; Fairburn & Cooper, 1993). The EDE includes two behavioral indexes (overeating and methods of extreme weight control) and four subscales (eating concern, restraint, shape concern, and weight concern; Fairburn & Cooper, 1993). It has been shown to have good reliability and validity (Anderson & Paulosky, 2004a; Fairburn & Cooper, 1993).

Bryant-Waugh and colleagues (1996) adapted the EDE in a number of ways to make it more appropriate for use with children. A pilot study in a sample of children with a mean age of 9 (range: 7–14 years) found that the ChEDE yielded results consistent with those of the EDE, although they found some difficulties related to assessment of children in this age range (Bryant-Waugh et al., 1996). Watkins, Frampton, Lask, and Bryant-Waugh (2005) found the ChEDE to have good internal consistency and interrater reliability. Additionally, the ChEDE subscale scores distinguished children with AN from children with other eating disturbances, giving some evidence for discriminant validity. It should be noted that structured interviews can be time consuming and often require some training in their use, which might limit their appropriateness in clinical practice (Anderson, De Young, & Walker, in press; Anderson et al., 2004). Despite these limitations, however, the ChEDE appears to be good measure for assessment of eating disorders and eating-related problems in younger populations.

Structured Interview for Anorexia and Bulimic Disorders. The Structured Interview for Anorexia and Bulimic Disorders (SIAB) was developed by Fichter and colleagues (1990, 1991; Fichter, Herpertz, Quadflieg, & Herpertz-Dahlmann, 1998) to assess psychopathology specific to eating disorders as well as other symptoms and characteristics associated with eating disorders. The SIAB was designed as a diagnostic tool as well as a tool for following treatment progress (Fichter et al., 1991). The current version of the SIAB, the SIAB-EX, is a semistructured interview that allows for an diagnosis of an eating disorder based on *DSM–IV* (APA, 1994) or the International Classification of Diseases (ICD-10; World Health Organization, 1992) criteria (Fichter et al., 1998). However, unlike the EDE, the SIAB-EX also assesses symptoms of depression, phobias, anxieties, obsessions and compulsions related to eating, and sexual problems and sexual functioning. The SIAB-EX consists of 87 items, 61 of which are used to derive the following six subscales and a total score:

1. body image and slimness ideal;
2. general psychopathology and social integration;
3. sexual problems;
4. bulimic symptoms;
5. inappropriate compensatory behaviors to counteract weight gain, fasting, and substance abuse; and
7. atypical binges.

Scores can be calculated for both past history and present state (past 3 months). The SIAB-EX has demonstrated good psychometric properties as evidenced by good internal consistency, good interrater reliability, good convergent and discriminative validity, and a consistent factor structure across versions (Fichter & Quadflieg, 2000, 2001; Fichter et al., 1998). A detailed manual for the SIAB-EX is available, and the interview can be obtained in English, Spanish, Italian, and German versions.

Although the SIAB-EX is a promising interview, it only has been used in one study of adolescents (ages 13–19; Fichter, Quadflieg, Georgopoulou, Xepapadakos, & Fthenakis, 2005), and no normative data are available for children or younger adolescents. Thus, its use in children or younger adolescents may be premature at this point.

Self-Report Instruments

As noted previously, it has been argued that self-report methods of assessing eating disorders do not provide as much useful information as do structured interviews in younger individuals (Decaluwe & Braet, 2003; Tanofsky-Kraff et al., 2003; Work Group on Eating Disorders, 2006). Thus, it has been recommended by some researchers that self-report instruments be used primarily only as screening devices (Decaluwe & Braet, 2003; Work Group on Eating Disorders, 2006).

Eating Attitudes Test and Children's Version of the EAT. The original 40-item version of the Eating Attitudes Test (EAT) was developed by Garner and Garfinkel (1979) to assess pathological behaviors, thoughts, and attitudes associated with eating disorders. A shorter 26-item version (EAT-26) was developed following a factor analysis of the original EAT (Garner, Olmsted, Bohr, & Garfinkel, 1982).

The EAT and EAT-26 have been used extensively with adults in both clinical and research contexts (Anderson & Paulosky, 2004a, 2004b), and appear to be reliable and valid even in younger samples (Garfinkel & Newman, 2001). Nevertheless, Maloney, McGuire, and Daniels (1988) developed a children's version of the EAT-26 (ChEAT) by substituting simpler synonyms for words in the EAT-26 that were thought to be too difficult for elementary school-age children to comprehend. The ChEAT has also been shown to be reliable and valid in a number of studies (Garfinkel & Newman, 2001). As with the EAT-26, a cutoff of 20 appears to be appropriate for identifying individuals at risk for eating disorders. The factor structure of the ChEAT is unclear, however (Lynch & Eppers-Reynolds, 2005; Smolak & Levine, 1994).

In summary, the EAT, EAT-26, and ChEAT all appear to be useful for screening for overall levels of eating disturbances as well as for tracking treatment progress and change over time (Garfinkel & Newman, 2001). These measures are easy to score and have good psychometric properties, although their factor structures in younger samples presently are unclear. The ChEAT may be particularly useful in assessing younger individuals.

Bulimia Test–Revised. The Bulimia Test–Revised (BULIT-R; Thelen, Farmer, Wonderlich, & Smith, 1991), a revision of the original Bulimia Test (Smith & Thelen, 1984), is a 28-item inventory of the symptoms of BN. The BULIT-R has been shown to identify individuals with BN as defined by *DSM–IV* (APA, 1994) criteria (Thelen, Mintz, & Vander Wal, 1996). The BULIT-R has been shown to have good reliability and validity in a college-age population (Thelen et al., 1991; Williamson, Anderson, Jackman, & Jackson, 1995). Using two independent samples, Thelen and colleagues (1991) found a five-factor model best fit the data, although the individual factors differed between the two samples. Only the total score is commonly used in the literature.

The BULIT-R has shown good reliability and concurrent validity in studies of adolescents, but the percentage of participants meeting the BULIT-R cutoff score has been consistently lower in adolescent samples than older college-age samples, and there are some questions about the factor structure in younger samples (McCarthy, Simmons, Smith, Tomlinson, & Hill, 2002; Vincent, McCabe, & Ricciardelli, 1999). Nonetheless, the measure is easy to use and can be useful for screening of bulimic behaviors as well as tracking symptom change over time.

Eating Disorder Inventory—3. The Eating Disorder Inventory—3 (EDI-3; Garner, 2004), a revision of the EDI-2 (Garner, 1991), is a 91-item inventory consisting of 12 scales. There are three eating disorder-specific scales—drive for thinness, bulimia, and body dissatisfaction—as well as nine general psychological scales that are thought to be related to eating disorders: low self-esteem, personal alienation, interpersonal insecurity, interpersonal alienation, interoceptive deficits, emotional dysregulation, perfectionism, asceticism, and maturity fears. The EDI–3 also provides six composite scores, one that is eating-disorder specific (eating disorder risk) and five that are related to general psychological constructs: ineffectiveness, interpersonal problems, affective problems, overcontrol, and general psychological maladjustment.

Similar to its predecessor, clinical norms for the EDI–3 are available for adults with eating disorders. The EDI–3 also provides clinical norms for adolescents, although these norms require further empirical validation (Garner, 2004). Reliability and validity for both the scales and composite scores are good, and the scales scores appear to correlate highly with their EDI–2 counterparts (Garner, 2004).

It should be noted that a child-specific version of the EDI–2 has also been developed (Eklund, Paavonen, & Almqvist, 2005; Thurfjell, Edlund, Arinell, Hägglöf, & Engström, 2003), although it has not been used widely in the literature and it is unclear if it will be updated to compatible with the EDI–3.

In summary, although specific studies of the EDI–3 in an adolescent population are not yet available, the EDI and EDI–2 have been some of the most useful and widely used self-report measures for eating disorders (Anderson & Paulosky, 2004a, 2004b), and this trend is likely to continue for the EDI–3. Although it can be used for screening purposes, its length makes it less practical than other measures (e.g., ChEAT, BULIT-R). Researchers frequently choose to administer individual subscales (e.g., drive for thinness, body dissatisfaction) rather than the entire measure. The EDI–3 is also useful for treatment planning and tracking symptom changes over time.

Kids' Eating Disorders Survey. Childress, Brewerton, Hodges, and Jarrell (1993) developed the Kids' Eating Disorders Survey (KEDS) by simplifying and shortening the Eating Symptoms Inventory, a measure based on *DSM–III* criteria for AN and BN (Whitaker et al., 1989). The KEDS is composed of 12 items that assess weight dissatisfaction, dietary restriction, and purging, including eight child figure drawings for each sex to assist in assessing weight and body dissatisfaction. Preliminary reliability and validity data in the development sample (mean age 12 years) were promising, although further studies are needed to firmly establish the psychometric properties and usefulness of the KEDS.

McKnight Risk Factor Survey IV. The McKnight Risk Factor Survey IV (MRFS-IV; McKnight Investigators, 2003) a revised version of the MRFS-III (Shisslak et al., 1999), was developed as part of a longitudinal multisite study of risk and protective factors for eating disorders in preadolescent and adolescent girls. The MRFS-IV assesses a large number of factors thought to be related to the development of eating disorders. Two versions of the questionnaire are available; the elementary school version (Grades 4–5) is composed of 90 questions and the middle/high school version (Grades 6–12) is composed of 103 questions. MRFS-IV was specifically designed to predict the development of eating disorders, although it might also be used more broadly to track changes in symptoms and risk factors over time.

Psychometric analysis of the MRFS-III found generally good reliability and convergent validity in preadolescent and adolescent girls (Shisslak et al., 1999), but these data are not yet available for the MRFS-IV. Psychometric data for preadolescent and adolescent boys are also unavailable. The MRFS-IV was found to have a seven-factor solution:

1. thin body preoccupation and social pressure,
2. substance use,
3. parental influences,
4. general psychological influences,
5. social support,
6. number of negative life events, and
7. school performance.

Factor 1 appears to be the most reliably associated with the development of eating disorders (McKnight Investigators, 2003).

In summary, the MFRS-IV is a promising measure for the assessment of eating disorder-related risk factors, but more research is necessary to establish its psychometric properties.

Questionnaire on Eating and Weight Patterns–Adolescent Version and Parent Version. The original 13-item Questionnaire on Eating and Weight Patterns (QEWP) was designed to be a simple self-report measure to identify eating disorders, particularly binge-eating disorder, in adults (Spitzer et al., 1992; 1993; Yanovski, 1993). The 12-item adolescent and parent versions of the QEWP (QEWP-A), developed by Johnson, Grieve, Adams, and Sandy (1999) were designed to fulfill the same function in boys and girls using *DSM–IV–TR* (APA, 2000) criteria. The QEWP-A was devised by substituting simpler synonyms for the more difficult words in the original QEWP. Two questions on the QEWP were also combined to form a single, two-part question on the QEWP-A. The parents' version (QEWP-P) contains the same items as the QEWP-A, but the wording was changed to reference the children.

Johnson and colleagues (1999) found adequate evidence for concurrent validity for the QEWP-A, but found low rates of agreement between the QEWP-A and QEWP-P, with parents being much less likely to endorse problematic eating behavior in their children than they reported problematic eating themselves. A more recent study by Steinberg and colleagues (2004) also found low rates of agreement between the QEWP-A and QEWP-P. Johnson, Kirk, and Reed (2001) found that the QEWP-A had good test–retest reliability over a 3-week period for males, but the test–retest reliability of females was much less stable.

In summary, although the QEWP-A and QEWP-P hold promise, the problems identified with their reliability and validity suggest that caution should be used in their use and interpretation.

Stirling Eating Disorders Scale. The Stirling Eating Disorders Scales (SEDS; Williams et al., 1994) was developed to assess the cognitive and behavioral features of AN and BN. The measure consists of 80 true/false statements divided into eight (four "dietary" and four "nondietary") subscales. The dietary scales are anorexic dietary cognitions, anorexic dietary behaviors, bulimic dietary cognitions, and bulimic dietary behaviors. The nondietary scales are perceived external control, low assertiveness, low self-esteem, and self-directed hostility. Williams and colleagues found acceptable levels of test–retest reliability, internal consistency, and concurrent validity for the SEDS.

Although the SEDS was originally developed for use with adults, Campbell, Lawrence, Serpell, Lask, and Neiderman (2002) investigated its usefulness as a screening device for eating disorders in adolescent populations. In a sample of 53 patients (51 girls, 2 boys; mean age 15.6 years) referred for eating disorder services, the SEDS had high internal consistency, as well as good criterion and discriminant validity. The authors reported a number of problems related to the wording of the SEDS, however, including vocabulary and definitions of some items, difficulty with complex sentence structure (e.g., the use of double negatives), and difficulty with the true/false format. The authors also noted that some items were worded in such a way that adolescents might be more likely to endorse them than would adults. Although the SEDS appears to be widely used clinically in the United Kingdom, including in child and adolescent populations (Campbell et al., 2002; Openshaw & Waller, 2005), development of a child/adolescent version with simplified language may be warranted before use with younger populations is recommended. Further research to evaluate the utility of the SEDS in preadolescent and adolescent boys is also recommended.

Behavioral Assessment

Behavioral assessment procedures are designed to provide objective, idiographic measures of behaviors related to eating disorders. In some cases they can be more beneficial than more traditional assessment methods (i.e., interviews and self-report questionnaires) because they can provide for a more direct, fine-grained analysis of important eating-related behaviors and their surrounding context. Behavioral assessment procedures can be used in all phases of assessment.

Food-Monitoring Procedures. Self-monitoring of food intake and purgative behavior appears to be the most widely used procedure in the assessment of eating pathology in both clinical and research contexts (Anderson & Paulosky, 2004a, 2004b). Food records, kept by the patient, typically collect information on variables such as temporal eating patterns, type and amounts of food eaten, context in which the food was eaten, frequency and topography of binge episodes and purgative behaviors, and mood before and after the meal (Anderson et al., 2004; Williamson, 1990). Data obtained from self-monitoring records can be helpful in all aspects of eating disorders treatment, from diagnosis to treatment planning as well as evaluation of treatment outcome. There are no widely accepted standardized procedures for self-monitoring, and its exact format probably is not critical. Model forms are available, however (Schlundt, 1995; Williamson, 1990).

Although self-monitoring can provide a great deal of useful data, it requires skills such as reading, writing, ability to measure, and adequate short- and long-term memory. Sufficient motivation to keep accurate records also is required. Thus, not surprisingly, age plays an important role in the accuracy of self-monitoring. In one study, children between ages 10 and 12 kept more reliable records than younger children or adolescents (Babbitt, Elden-Nezin, Manikam, Summers, & Murphy, 1995). A more recent review of six studies examining the reliability and validity of food records in school-age children (ages 8–19 years) suggested fairly good accuracy overall for self-monitoring, although there was a tendency for participants to underestimate energy intake (McPherson, Hoelscher, Alexander, Scanlon, & Serdula, 2000). It is important to note, however, that in all but two of the studies reviewed, adult assistance was required in completing self-monitoring (McPherson et al., 2000). Thus, although self-monitoring of food or exercise can provide useful information, its reliability and validity in younger children is likely to be questionable.

Test Meals. Test meals allow an assessor to directly examine eating behaviors under controlled conditions. Test meals can be used as an assessment tool in all stages of treatment (Anderson et al., 2004; Anderson & Paulosky, 2004a; Williamson, 1990; Work Group on Eating Disorders, 2006). For example, patients who deny problems with eating at initial assessment can be asked to consume a meal containing typical feared foods in order to test for denial and treatment resistance. Also, during treatment patients can be asked to develop a hierarchy of feared foods and eat them as part of treatment. Changes in the amount of food eaten during a standardized test meal also can be used as an index of treatment progress.

Although test meals have several advantages as an assessment tool, there is little information about their reliability or validity in child and adolescent populations. Although the following protocols have been developed for the use of test meals with children, they have not been used widely in either research or clinical practice.

Behavioral Eating Test. The Behavioral Eating Test (BET) was developed as a standardized method of assessing children's eating behaviors in an experimental paradigm (Jeffrey et al., 1980). The BET primarily has been used in studies investigating the effects of television advertisements on children's subsequent intake of high- and low-nutrition foods (Bridgwater, Jeffrey, Walsh, Dawson, & Peterson, 1984; Wilson & Jeffrey, 1988). The original BET paradigm involves presenting a number of foods in cups; participants are then instructed to taste and eat as much food as they like. Following the observation period, food is weighed and converted into caloric equivalents. Despite a number of methodological refinements over the years, this procedure continues to produce large standard errors and has only moderate test–retest reliability (Bridgwater et al.,1984). Given these psychometric problems, additional research and further modifications of the BET are needed to before it can be recommended for use.

Bob and Tom's Method of Assessing Nutrition. Bob and Tom's Method of Assessing Nutrition (BATMAN) was specifically designed as an observational method to assess children's eating behaviors and parental behavior at mealtimes to identify psychosocial variables associated with childhood obesity (Klesges et al., 1983). The BATMAN uses a partial interval time-sampling system (alternating periods of 10 seconds of observation and 10 seconds of recording) to assess the child's behavior during mealtime, the parent's response to the behavior, and the child's response to the interaction. The BATMAN has been shown to have high levels of both interrater reliability (weighted Kappa coefficients from .88 to .94) and test–retest reliability (correlations from .61 to .94; Klesges et al., 1983). Although the BATMAN procedure has not been validated with children with eating disorders, it may prove helpful in establishing a functional analysis of parental behavior leading to increased or decreased eating in children.

Behaviors of Eating and Activity for Children's Health Evaluation System. Developed by McKenzie and colleagues (1991), Behaviors of Eating and Activity for Children's Health Evaluation System (BEACHES) is a comprehensive direct observational system designed to code children's physical activity and eating behaviors and related environmental events in a variety of contexts. It includes coding for 10 separate dimensions:

1. environmental conditions,
2. physical location,
3. activity level,
4. eating behavior,
5. persons who interact with the child,
6. antecedents,
7. prompted events,
8. child response to prompt,
9. consequences, and
10. events receiving consequences.

The authors found BEACHES to have good levels of interrater reliability, with the exception of the consequences dimension. They also found evidence of good concurrent validity, particularly with regard to eating and physical activity prompts. To date this method has been evaluated with White and Hispanic children aged 4 to 8 years in a variety of settings (McKenzie et al., 1991). BEACHES has not been validated with children with eating disorders, children of other ethnic backgrounds, or other age groups, however. BEACHES is a promising tool for assessing eating and physical activity as well as a wide range of social and environmental influences on these behaviors, and may prove useful in the context of assessment of eating disorders.

FUTURE DIRECTIONS IN ASSESSMENT

There are a number of promising developments in the assessment of children and adolescents, particularly in areas related to technological advancements. We review some of these developments below.

Ecological Momentary Assessment

In attempt to circumvent many of the limitations associated with traditional self-report and laboratory-based research, a relatively new and innovative means of collecting data called ecological momentary assessment (EMA; Stone & Shiffman, 1994) has been devised. EMA involves signaling participants several times per day over the course of days or weeks through an electronic device (e.g., pagers, handheld computers, personal data assistants, mobile phones, text-messaging devices), allowing for the assessment of behavior and psychological states in the natural environment. Participants may also be instructed to initiate a report when a particular event (e.g., an eating binge) occurs. This method has the advantage of enhancing both the reliability and external validity of assessment of eating-related problems. Although relatively new to the field of eating disorders, research is beginning to demonstrate that EMA is a useful tool for the assessment of eating disorders and related problems (for a review see Engel, Wonderlich, & Crosby, 2005). Although establishing the validity of EMA in the assessment of children or adolescents with eating disorders or eating-related problems will require further research, studies on related behaviors (e.g., physical activity) have shown promise for the utility of EMA in younger age groups (Dunton, Whalen, Jamner, Henker, & Floro, 2005; Gorely, Marshall, Biddle, & Cameron, 2007).

Internet-Based Assessments

Internet-based assessments represent another promising method of data collection. As Internet usage has become progressively more common in recent years, research has begun to explore the utility of online assessments and interventions (Myers, Swan-Kremeier, Wonderlich, Lancaster, & Mitchell, 2004). In general, the accessibility, convenience, and anonymity of the Internet are the primary advantages of its use in research. Particularly relevant to assessments of body image and eating disturbances is the greater anonymity that the Internet provides, potentially helping to reduce the effects of social desirability and appearance-related self-consciousness (Zabinski, Celio, Wilfley, & Taylor, 2003). Recent research with adolescents also suggests that online reports of relevant constructs (e.g., weight and shape concerns) appear to produce results that are similar to results obtained from paper-based assessments (Luce et al., 2007). Additionally, a substantial number of individuals who may have previously been inaccessible to researchers are now available electronically via the internet (Rhodes, Bowie, & Hergenrather, 2003). Although further research may be necessary to more fully establish the reliability and validity of online data collection methods, Internet-based assessments are likely to become increasingly commonplace.

CONCLUSIONS

This chapter provided an overview of psychological and behavioral assessment of eating disturbances in children and adolescents. The assessment of eating disturbances in children and adolescents is complex, and an increase in psychometrically sound instruments would benefit both research and clinical practice. Although there are measures and instruments that have been validated for use with younger individuals, more studies of these measures and additional measures are clearly needed.

REFERENCES

Allison, D. B. (1995). *Handbook of assessment methods for eating behaviors and weight-related problems: Measures, theory, and research.* Thousand Oaks, CA: Sage.

American Psychiatric Association. (1994). *Diagnostic and statistical manual of mental Disorders* (4th ed.). Washington, DC: Author

American Psychiatric Association. (2000). *Diagnostic and statistical manual of mental Disorders* (4th ed., text rev.). Washington, DC: Author

Anderson, D. A., De Young, K. P., & Walker, D. C. (in press). Assessment of eating disordered thoughts, feelings, and behaviors. In D. B. Allison (Ed.), *Handbook of assessment methods for eating behaviors and weight-related problems: Measures, theory, and research* (2nd ed.). Thousand Oaks, CA: Sage.

Anderson, D. A., Lundgren, J. D., Shapiro, J. R., & Paulosky, C. A. (2004). Assessment of eating disorders: Review and recommendations for clinical use. *Behavior Modification, 28,* 763–782.

Anderson, D. A., & Maloney, K. C. (2001). The efficacy of cognitive-behavioral therapy on the core symptoms of bulimia nervosa. *Clinical Psychology Review, 21*, 971–988.

Anderson, D. A., & Paulosky, C. A. (2004a). Psychological assessment of eating disorders and related features. In J. K. Thompson (Ed.), *Handbook of eating disorders and obesity* (pp. 112–129). New York: Wiley.

Anderson, D. A., & Paulosky, C. A. (2004b). A survey of the use of assessment instruments by eating disorder professionals in clinical practice. *Eating and Weight Disorders, 9*, 238–241.

Babbitt, R. L., Edlen-Nezin, L., Manikam, R., Summers, J. A., & Murphy, C. M. (1995). Assessment of eating and weight-related problems in children and special populations. In D. B. Allison (Ed.), *Handbook of assessment methods for eating behavioral and weight-related problems: Measures, theory, and research* (pp. 431–485). Thousand Oaks, CA: Sage.

Bridgwater, C. A., Jeffrey, D. B., Walsh, J. A., Dawson, B., & Peterson, P. (1984). Measuring children's food consumption in the laboratory: A methodological refinement of the behavioral eating test. *Behavioral Assessment, 6*, 357–364.

Bryant-Waugh, R. (2000). Overview of the eating disorders. In B. Lask & R. Bryant-Waugh (Eds.), *Anorexia nervosa and related eating disorders in childhood and adolescence* (2nd ed., pp. 27–40). Hove, England: Psychology Press.

Bryant-Waugh, R., Cooper, P. J., Taylor, C. L., & Lask, B. D. (1996). The use of the Eating Disorder Examination with children: A pilot study. *International Journal of Eating Disorders, 19*, 391–397.

Bryant-Waugh, R., & Lask, B. (1995). Annotation: Eating disorders in children. *Journal of Child Psychology and Psychiatry, 36*, 191–202.

Bryant-Waugh, R., & Lask, B. (2007). Overview. In B. Lask & R. Bryant-Waugh (Eds.), *Anorexia nervosa and related eating disorders in childhood and adolescence.* London: Routledge.

Campbell, M., Lawrence, B., Serpell, L., Lask, B., & Neiderman, M. (2002). Validating the Stirling Eating Disorders Scales (SEDS) in an adolescent population. *Eating Behaviors, 3*, 285–293.

Carney, C. P., & Andersen, A. E. (1996). Eating disorders. Guide to medical evaluation and complications. *Psychiatric Clinics of North America, 19*, 657–679.

Childress, A. C., Brewerton, T. D., Hodges, E. L., & Jarrell, M. P. (1993). The Kids' Eating Disorders Survey (KEDS): A study of middle school students. *Journal of the American Academy of Child and Adolescent Psychiatry, 32*, 843–850.

Cooper, Z., & Fairburn, C. G. (1987). The Eating Disorder Examination: A semi-structured interview for the assessment of the specific psychopathology of eating disorders. *International Journal of Eating Disorders, 6*, 1–8.

Crow, S., & Swigart, S. (2005). Medical assessment. In J. E. Mitchell & C. B. Peterson (Eds.), *Assessment of eating disorders* (pp. 120–128). New York: Guilford Press.

Crowther, J. H., & Sherwood, N. E. (1997). Assessment. In D. M. Garner & P. E. Garfinkel (Eds.), *Handbook of treatment for eating disorders* (2nd ed., pp. 34–49). New York: Guilford Press.

Davison, K. K., Markey, C. N., & Birch, L. L. (2000). Etiology of body dissatisfaction and weight concerns among 5-year-old girls. *Appetite, 35*, 143–151.

Decaluwe, V., & Braet, C. (2003). Assessment of eating disorder psychopathology in obese children and adolescents: Interview vs. self-report questionnaire. *Behaviour Research and Therapy, 42,* 799–811.

Dunton, G. F., Whalen, C. K., Jamner, L. D., Henker, B., & Floro, J. N. (2005). Using ecologic momentary assessment to measure physical activity during adolescence. *American Journal of Preventive Medicine, 29,* 281–287.

Eklund, K., Paavonen, E. J., & Almqvist, F. (2005). Factor structure of the Eating Disorder Inventory-C. *International Journal of Eating Disorders, 37,* 330–341.

Engel, S. G., Wonderlich, S. A., & Crosby, R. D. (2005). Ecological momentary assessment. In J. E. Mitchell & C. B. Peterson (Eds.), *Assessment of eating disorders* (pp. 203–220). New York: Guilford Press.

Fairburn, C. G., & Cooper, Z. (1993). The Eating Disorder Examination (12th Edition). In C. G. Fairburn & G. T. Wilson (Eds.), *Binge eating: Nature, assessment and treatment* (pp. 317–360). New York: Guilford Press.

Fichter, M. M., Elton, M., Engel, K., Meyer, A., E., Mall, H., & Poutska, F. (1991). Structured Interview for Anorexia and Bulimia Nervosa (SIAB): Development of a new instrument for the assessment of eating disorders. *International Journal of Eating Disorders, 10,* 571–592.

Fichter, M. M., Elton, M., Engel, K., Meyer, A., E., Poutska, F., & Mall, H. (1990). The Structured Interview for Anorexia and Bulimia Nervosa (SIAB): Development and characteristics of a (semi)-standardized instrument. In M. Fichter (Ed.), *Bulimia nervosa: Basic research, diagnoses, and therapy* (pp. 55–70). Chichester, England: Wiley.

Fichter, M. M., Herpertz, S., Quadflieg, N., & Herpertz-Dahlmann, B. (1998). Structured interview for anorexic and bulimic disorders for DSM–IV and ICD-10: Updated (third) revision. *International Journal of Eating Disorders, 24,* 227–249.

Fichter, M. M., & Quadflieg, N. (2000). Comparing self- and expert rating: a self-report screening version (SIAB-S) of the structured interview for anorexic and bulimic syndromes for DSM–IV and ICD-10 (SIAB-EX). *European Archives of Clinical Neuroscience, 250,* 175–185.

Fichter, M. M., & Quadflieg, N., (2001). The structured interview for anorexic and bulimic disorders for DSM–IV and ICD-10 (SIAB-EX): Reliability and validity. *European Psychiatry, 16,* 38–48.

Fichter, M. M., Quadflieg, N., Georgopoulou, E., Xepapadakos, F., & Fthenakis, E. W. (2005). Time trends in eating disturbances in young Greek migrants. *International Journal of Eating Disorders, 38,* 310–322.

Garfinkel, P. E., & Newman, A. (2001). The Eating Attitudes Test: Twenty-five years later. *Eating and Weight Disorders, 6,* 1–24.

Garner, D. M. (1991). *Eating Disorder Inventory–2 manual.* Odessa, FL: Psychological Assessment Resources.

Garner, D. M. (2004). *The Eating Disorder Inventory–3 manual.* Odessa, FL: Psychological Assessment Resources.

Garner, D. M., & Garfinkel, P. E. (1979). The Eating Attitudes Test: An index of the symptoms of anorexia nervosa. *Psychological Medicine, 9,* 273–279.

Garner, D. M., Olmsted, M. P., Bohr, Y., & Garfinkel, P. E. (1982). The Eating Attitudes Test: Psychometric features and clinical correlates. *Psychological Medicine*, *12*, 871–878.

Golden, N. H., Katzman, D. K., Kreipe, R. E., Stevens, S. L., Sawyer, S. M., Rees, J., et al. (2003). Eating disorders in adolescents: Position paper of the Society for Adolescent Medicine. *Journal of Adolescent Health*, *33*, 496–503.

Gorely, T., Marshall, S. J., Biddle, S. J. H., & Cameron, N. (2007). The prevalence of leisure time sedentary behaviour and physical activity in adolescent girls: An ecological momentary assessment approach. *International Journal of Pediatric Obesity*, *2*, 227–234.

Halvarsson, K., Lunner, K., & Sjoden, P.-O. (2000). Assessment of eating behaviours and attitudes to eating, dieting and body image in pre-adolescent Swedish girls: A one-year follow-up. *Acta Paediatrica*, *89*, 996–1000.

Jeffrey, D. G., Lemnitzer, N. B., Hickey, J. S., Hess, M. S., McLellarn, R. W., & Stroud, J. M. (1980). The development of a behavioral eating test and its relationship to a self-report food attitude scale in young children. *Behavioral Assessment*, *2*, 87–89.

Johnson, W. G., Grieve, F. G., Adams, C. D., & Sandy, J. (1999). Measuring binge eating in adolescents: Adolescent and parent versions of the Questionnaire of Eating and Weight Patterns. *International Journal of Eating Disorders*, *26*, 301–314.

Johnson, W. G., Kirk, A. A., & Reed, A. E. (2001). Adolescent version of the Questionnaire of Eating and Weight Patterns: Reliability and gender differences. *International Journal of Eating Disorders*, *29*, 94–96.

Keizer, H. A., & Rogol, A. D. (1990). Physical exercise and menstrual cycle alterations. What are the mechanisms? *Sports Medicine*, *10*, 218–235.

Klesges, R. C., Coates, T. J., Brown, G., Sturgeon-Tillisch, J., Moldenhauer-Klesges, L. M., Holzer, B., et al. (1983). Parental influences on children's eating behavior and relative weight. *Journal of Applied Behavior Analysis*, *4*, 317–378.

Lask, B., & Bryant-Waugh, R. (1992). Early-onset anorexia nervosa and related eating disorders. *Journal of Child Psychology and Psychiatry*, *33*, 281-300.

le Grange, D. (2005). Family assessment. In J. E. Mitchell & C. B. Peterson (Eds.), *Assessment of eating disorders* (pp. 148–174). New York: Guilford Press.

Luce, K. H., Winzelberg, A. J., Das, S., Osborne, M. I., Bryson, S. W., & Taylor, C. B. (2007). Reliability of self-report: Paper versus online administration. *Computers in Human Behavior*, *23*, 1384–1389.

Lynch, W. C., & Eppers-Reynolds, K. (2005). Children's Eating Attitudes Test: Revised factor structure for adolescent girls. *Eating and Weight Disorders*, *10*, 222–235.

Maloney, M. J., McGuire, J. B., & Daniels, S. R. (1988). Reliability testing of a children's version of the Eating Attitude Test. *Journal of the American Academy of Child and Adolescent Psychiatry*, *27*, 541–543.

McCarthy, D. M., Simmons, J. R., Smith, G. T., Tomlinson, K. L., & Hill, K. K. (2002). Reliability, stability, and factor structure of the Bulimia Test–Revised and Eating Disorder Inventory–2 scales in adolescence. *Assessment*, *9*, 382–389.

McKenzie, T. L., Sallis, J. F., Nader, P. R., Patterson, T. L., Elder, J. P., Berry, C. C., et al. (1991). BEACHES: An observational system for assessing children's eating and physical activity behaviors and associated events. *Journal of Applied Behavior Analysis, 24,* 141–151.

McKnight Investigators. (2003). Risk factors for the onset of eating disorders in adolescent girls: Results of the McKnight longitudinal risk factor study. *American Journal of Psychiatry, 160,* 248–254.

McPherson, R. S., Hoelscher, D. M., Alexander, M., Scanlon, K. S., & Serdula, M. K. (2000). Dietary assessment methods among school-aged children: Validity and reliability. *Preventive Medicine, 31,* S11–S33.

Myers, T. C., Swan-Kremeier, L., Wonderlich, S., Lancaster, K., & Mitchell, J. E. (2004). The use of alternative delivery systems and new technologies in the treatment of patients with eating disorders. *International Journal of Eating Disorders, 36,* 123–143.

Netemeyer, S. B., & Williamson, D. A. (2001). Assessment of eating disturbance in children and adolescents with eating disorders and obesity. In J. K. Thompson & L. Smolak (Eds.), *Body image, eating disorders, and obesity in youth: Assessment, prevention, and treatment* (pp. 215–233). Washington, DC : American Psychological Association.

Nicholls, D., Chater, R., & Lask, B. (2000). Children into DSM don't go: A comparison of classification systems for eating disorders in childhood and early adolescence. *International Journal of Eating Disorders, 28,* 317–324.

Openshaw, C., & Waller, G. (2005). Psychometric properties of the Stirling Eating Disorder Scales with bulimia nervosa patients. *Eating Behaviors, 6,* 165–168.

Peterson, C. B., & Mitchell, J. E. (2005). Self-report measures. In J. E. Mitchell & C. B. Peterson (Eds.), *Assessment of eating disorders* (pp. 98–119). New York: Guilford Press.

Rhodes, S., Bowie, D., & Hergenrather, K. (2003). Collecting behavioural data using the world wide web: Considerations for researchers. *Journal of Epidemiology and Community Health, 57,* 68–73.

Ricca, V., Mannucci, E., Mezzani, B., Di Bernardo, M., Zucchi, T., Paionni, A., et al. (2001). Psychopathological and clinical features of outpatients with an eating disorder not otherwise specified. *Eating and Weight Disorders, 6,* 157–165.

Rock, C. L. (2005). Nutritional assessment. In J. E. Mitchell & C. B. Peterson (Eds.), *Assessment of eating disorders* (pp. 129–147). New York: Guilford Press.

Rome, E. S., Ammerman, S., Rosen, D. S., Keller, R. J., Lock, J., Mammel, K. A., et al. (2003). Children and adolescents with eating disorders: The state of the art. *Pediatrics, 111,* e98–109.

Schlundt, D. G. (1995). Assessment of specific eating behaviors and eating style. In D. B. Allison (Ed.), *Methods for the assessment of eating behaviors and weight-related problems* (pp. 142–302). Thousand Oaks, CA: Sage.

Schur, E. A., Sanders, M., & Steiner, H. (2000). Body dissatisfaction and dieting in young children. *International Journal of Eating Disorders, 27,* 74–82.

Shisslak, C. M., Renger, R., Sharpe, T., Crago, M., McKnight, K. M., Gray, N., et al. (1999). Development and evaluation of the McKnight Risk Factor Survey for assessing potential risk and protective factors for disordered eating in preadolescent and adolescent girls. *International Journal of Eating Disorders, 25,* 195–214.

Shunk, J. A., & Birch, L. L. (2004). Validity of dietary restraint among 5- to 9-year old girls. *Appetite, 42,* 241–247.

Slap, G. B. (2003). Menstrual disorders in adolescence. *Best Practice and Research in Clinical Obstetrics and Gynaecology, 17,* 75–92.

Smith, M. C., & Thelen, M. H. (1984). Development and validation for a test for bulimia. *Journal of Consulting and Clinical Psychology, 52,* 863–872.

Smolak, L., & Levine, M. P. (1994). Psychometric properties of the Children's Eating Attitudes Test. *International Journal of Eating Disorders, 16,* 275–278.

Spitzer, R. L., Devlin, M. J., Walsh, B. T., Hasin, D., Wing, R., Marcus, M., et al. (1992). Binge eating disorder: A multisite field trial of the diagnostic criteria. *International Journal of Eating Disorders, 11,* 191–203.

Spitzer, R. L., Yanovski, S. Z., Wadden, T., Wing, R., Marcus, M., Stunkard, A., et al. (1993). Binge eating disorder: Its further validation in a multisite study. *International Journal of Eating Disorders, 13,* 137–153.

Steinberg, E., Tanofsky-Kraff, M., Cohen, M. L., Elberg, J., Freedman, R. J., Semega-Janneh, M., et al. (2004). Comparison of the child and parent forms of the Questionnaire on Eating and Weight Patterns in the assessment of children's eating-disordered behaviors. *International Journal of Eating Disorders, 36,* 183–194.

Stone, A., & Shiffman, S. (1994). Ecological momentary assessment (EMA) in behavioral medicine. *Annals of Behavioral Medicine, 16,* 199–202.

Tanofsky-Kraff, M., Morgan, C. M., Yanovski, S. Z., Marmarosh, C., Wilfley, D. E., & Yanovski, J. A. (2003). Comparison of assessments of children's eating-disordered behaviors by interview and questionnaire. *International Journal of Eating Disorders, 33,* 213–224.

Thelen, M. H., Farmer, J., Wonderlich, S., & Smith, M. A. (1991). A revision of the Bulimia Test: The BULIT-R. *Psychological Assessment, 3,* 119–124.

Thelen, M. H., Mintz, L. B., & Vander Wal, J. S. (1996). The Bulimia Test– Revised: Validation with DSM–IV criteria for bulimia nervosa. *Psychological Assessment, 8,* 219–221.

Thurfjell, B., Edlund, B., Arinell, H., Hägglöf, B., & Engström, I. (2003). Psychometric properties of Eating Disorder Inventory for Children (EDI-C) in Swedish girls with and without a known eating disorder. *Eating and Weight Disorders, 8,* 296–303.

Turner, H., & Bryant-Waugh, R. (2004). Eating disorder not otherwise specified (EDNOS): Profiles of clients presenting at a community eating disorder service. *European Eating Disorders Review, 12,* 18–26.

Vincent, M. A., McCabe, M. P., & Ricciardelli, L. A. (1999). Factorial validity of the Bulimia Test-Revised in adolescent boys and girls. *Behaviour Research and Therapy, 37,* 1129–1140.

Watkins, B., Frampton, I., Lask, B., & Bryant-Waugh, R. (2005). Reliability and validity of the child version of the Eating Disorder Examination: A preliminary investigation. *International Journal of Eating Disorders, 38,* 183–187.

Whitaker, A., Davies, M., Shaffer, D., Johnson, J., Abrams, S., Walsh, B. T., & Kalikow, K. (1989). The struggle to be thin: A survey of anorexic and bulimic symptoms in a non-referred adolescent population. *Psychological Medicine, 19,* 143–163.

Williams, G. J., Power, K. G., Miller, H. R., Freeman, C. P., Yellowlees, A., Dowds, T., et al. (1994). Development and validation of the Stirling Eating Disorder Scales. *International Journal of Eating Disorders, 16,* 35–43.

Williamson, D. A. (1990). *Assessment of eating disorders: Obesity, anorexia, and bulimia nervosa.* Elmsford, NY: Pergamon Press.

Williamson, D. A., Anderson, D. A., Jackman, L. P., & Jackson, S. R. (1995). Assessment of eating disordered thoughts, feelings, and behaviors. In D. B. Allison (Ed.), *Handbook of assessment methods for eating behaviors and weight-related problems* (pp. 347–386). Thousand Oaks, CA: Sage.

Wilson, G. L., & Jeffrey, D. B. (1988). Behavioral eating test. In M. Hersen & A. S. Bellack (Eds.), *Dictionary of behavioral assessment techniques* (pp. 64–66). Elmsford, NY: Pergamon Press.

Work Group on Eating Disorders. (2006). *Practice guidelines for the treatment of patients with eating disorders* (3rd ed.). Arlington, VA: American Psychiatric Press.

World Health Organization. (1992). *The ICD-10 classification of mental and behavioral disorders: Clinical descriptions and diagnostic guidelines.* Geneva, Switzerland: Author.

Yanovski, S. J. (1993). Binge eating disorder: Current knowledge and future directions. *Obesity Research, 1,* 306–324.

Zabinski, M. F., Celio, A. A., Wilfley, D. E., & Taylor, C. B. (2003). Prevention of eating disorders and obesity via the internet. *Cognitive Behaviour Therapy, 32,* 137–150.

11

RECENT DEVELOPMENTS AND PROMISING DIRECTIONS IN THE PREVENTION OF NEGATIVE BODY IMAGE AND DISORDERED EATING IN CHILDREN AND ADOLESCENTS

MICHAEL P. LEVINE AND LINDA SMOLAK

Prevention programs attempt to avoid or delay development of subclinical and full-blown eating disorders by reducing risk factors and increasing protective factors. Since the publication of our chapter in the first edition of this volume (Levine & Smolak, 2001), numerous reviews of the prevention outcome literature have been published (Levine & Piran, 2004; Levine & Smolak, 2006, 2007; O'Dea, 2005; Piran, 2005; Stewart, 2004; Taylor, 2005). To emphasize recent developments and promising directions, in the present chapter we first summarize briefly the collective implications of three recent meta-analyses. We then focus on prevention research published after 2000, using four organizing themes: (a) universal-selective prevention programs can work; (b) targeted prevention programs can work; (c) prevention programs incorporating elements of the feminist empowerment model show considerable promise; and (d) ecological approaches to eating disorders prevention also show substantial promise.

TYPES OF PREVENTION

Prevention programs attempt to avoid or delay development of subclinical and full-blown eating disorders by reducing risk factors and increasing the protective factors that provide resilience and promote health. The Institute of Medicine (IOM; Mrazek & Haggerty, 1994) proposes a prevention continuum from universal → selective → targeted → treatment. *Universal prevention* programs seek to change and reinforce government policies, social institutions, and common cultural practices in order to improve the "public health" of extremely large groups of citizens. *Selective prevention* also has a public policy component, but the primary audience consists of people who are nonsymptomatic but are considered at risk (Levine & Smolak, 2006; Mrazek & Haggerty, 1994). Risk status is determined by factors that are biological (e.g., female + family history of obsessive-compulsive disorder), psychological (e.g., parents and child are determined—"willing to make any sacrifice"—to help the child become a ballet dancer), or sociocultural (e.g., female + entering puberty + society defines women in terms of looks, and especially thinness).

In the case of eating disorders, confusion has resulted from insufficient attention to the definitions of universal, selective, and targeted interventions, and to their relationship to traditional distinctions in prevention. We assume that the universal and selective forms of prevention constitute "primary prevention" (Caplan, 1964), whereas targeted or indicated prevention corresponds to "secondary prevention" (Levine & Smolak, 2006). The potential participants "targeted" for these programs may not have clinically significant eating disorders, but they have been identified or selected (vs. selective), that is, "screened" as being "at high risk" because of the presence of clear precursors (e.g., negative body image), mild symptoms, or warning signs.

Selective prevention differs from targeted prevention in two fundamental ways. First, in accordance with the IOM's approach (Mrazek & Haggerty, 1994; Muñoz, Mrazek, & Haggerty, 1996), selective prevention is designed to help participants who are at risk, but are not yet at high risk. That is, participants in selective prevention programs are not suffering from problems such as a high level of negative body image and weight concerns that are arguably a "precursor" or even a "warning sign" (chap. 3, this volume). Thus, selective, as well as universal, programs have a closer connection to a fundamental goal of prevention: reducing the incidence of a disorder, that is, the number or rate of new cases in a year or longer time period, divided by the total population potentially at risk for that period. Note that, with respect to the ways that targeted prevention shades into treatment and away from prevention (Mrazek & Haggerty, 1994), prevention as a reduction in the incidence of a disorder is not affected one way or the other by changes in the status of those who already have, or have had, either the problem or a version of it (Jablensky, 2002).

Second, as is the case for targeted prevention, determination of at-risk status for selective prevention is, technically, based on research findings. For example, selective prevention could be guided by data showing that 9- to 11-year-old girls who have a thin ideal for themselves as older adolescents or adults are at greater risk (Harrison & Hefner, 2006), as well as multi-faceted and convergent evidence that the pubertal transition is a period of risk for development of eating disorders and mood disorders (Smolak & Levine, 1996). However, in practical terms the designation of a potentially large group for selective prevention efforts (e.g., a school-based ecological approach involving teachers, students, parents, and staff; McVey, Tweed, & Blackmore, 2007) is based essentially on broad, research-based markers of risk such as sex and age rather than actual testing (screening) to identify individuals for inclusion in a high-risk sample.

Many prevention interventions are curricula designed for general use by, for example, teachers of health classes for 11- to 13-year-olds. The lessons or units comprising such programs are delivered en masse and without significant tailoring to individual risk status. Theoretically, with government support, this type of program could be administered to all Grade 6 and 7 boys and girls in a large school district. Using the IOM's prevention continuum, we categorize those classroom-based eating disorders prevention programs as universal-selective prevention (Levine & Smolak, 2006, 2007).

PREVENTION OUTCOME RESEARCH

The efficacy of a prevention program (i.e., a "prevention effect") is demonstrated by a carefully designed study in which (a) the program is implemented as planned (i.e., fidelity was high); (b) as a group, program participants who are healthy or, at least, who do not have an eating disorder at baseline, show a low(er) onset, that is, incidence, of disordered eating over time as compared to the population incidence; (c) comparison conditions demonstrate that the effect is probably due to the processes hypothesized to be influential components of the program; (d) the reduced incidence of disordered eating is mediated by decreases in the risk factors—and/or increases in the protective factors—emphasized by the model guiding development of the program's influential components; and (e) disordered eating, risk factors, protective factors, and program implementation are measured in reliable and valid ways. With some notable exceptions, few prevention studies meet these exacting criteria.

Stice and Shaw (2004) conducted a meta-analysis of 51 controlled prevention outcome studies (38 prevention programs). This widely cited review concluded that targeted or indicated prevention (which they referred to as "selected") for high-risk participants is more effective than universal prevention, especially for individuals ages 15 or older. Stice and Shaw also found stronger average effects when, instead of being didactic and psychoeducational, prevention programs are interactive and focus on developing skills for resisting unhealthy sociocultural influences or for increasing body satisfaction. However, less attention has been paid to Stice and Shaw's finding that universal-selective programs had small but statistically significant prevention effect sizes (r's range from +.06 to +.09) at follow-up (1–24 months after the program ended) for eating pathology and for the very important risk factors of body dissatisfaction and internalization of the slender beauty ideal (Cafri, Yamamiya, Brannick, & Thompson, 2005; Stice, 2002). For the latter factor the effect size at follow-up for universal programs was not statistically different from that for targeted programs.

Stice, Shaw, and Marti (2007) extended this meta-analysis, adding the results of 15 more studies, representing 13 more programs. The data reinforced the two most important sets of findings from Stice and Shaw's (2004) meta-analysis: (a) Both universal and targeted programs had beneficial and statistically significant effects—at follow-up and for young as well as older participants—on the measures of risk and of eating pathology; and (b) the most effective programs are designed for high-risk participants and use interactive, nondidactic methods to promote skills for improving eating and activity levels and/or for resisting sociocultural pressures to internalize the slender beauty ideal. Moderator analyses in the updated meta-analysis also indicated that thin ideal internalization and other risk factors (but not eating pathology) were more effectively reduced when the prevention programs were evaluated using well-validated measures and when the intervention was conducted by prevention specialists rather than teachers or others working in school settings. Interestingly, especially in light of Stice's dual-pathway model (Stice, Nemeroff, & Shaw, 1996) and the attention paid to his conclusions about the superiority of targeted prevention, at follow-up universal programs were less effective than targeted programs at decreasing dieting, but they were just as effective in reducing thin-ideal internalization and negative affect (Stice, Shaw, & Marti, 2007).

Another recent meta-analysis by Fingeret, Warren, Cepeda-Benito, and Gleaves (2006) also revealed that targeted prevention programs had greater effects on thin-ideal internalization and body dissatisfaction than did the programs they categorized as either universal or selective, although selective programs were more effective at reducing dieting. Fingeret et al.'s findings are largely in agreement with Stice and Shaw's conclusion that targeted programs have thus far shown better results, but that universal and selective (including universal-selective) programs continue to be viable.

Psychoeducation

In contrast to some of the findings reported by Stice and Shaw (2004), Fingeret et al. found no differences in effect sizes as a function of psychoeducational versus enhanced strategies. Again, there was no evidence of iatrogenesis, whether or not the program included specific information about eating disorders. These results challenge O'Dea's (2005) contention that, as a prevention methodology, psychoeducation is ineffective and potentially harmful. Fingeret et al.'s (2006) conclusion about the value of psychoeducation is supported by a series of experiments conducted by Wertheim and colleagues in Australia (see, e.g., Withers & Wertheim, 2004). They developed and evaluated a 24-minute videotape for seventh- and eighth-grade girls that addresses biological determinants of size and shape, natural weight gain during puberty, sociocultural influences on appearance and body image, and harmful consequences of dieting and emotional eating. Surprisingly, these investigators found that various forms of elaboration or discussion did not enhance the effects of the video, which, on its own, reduced drive for thinness and intention to diet. Other experiments (Durkin, Paxton, & Wertheim, 2005) indicate that 12- to 16-year-old girls find even 2- to 3-minute messages stating that "media images are not real" and "the ideal body changes throughout history and across cultures" to be persuasive and helpful.

Iatrogenesis

In the aftermath of Mann et al.'s (1997) prevention study with college students, a number of researchers (e.g., O'Dea, 2005) have been concerned with the possibility of inadvertently increasing body dissatisfaction or eating problems with prevention efforts. Both the Stice and Shaw (2004) and the Fingeret et al. (2006) meta-analyses explicitly examined this issue. Neither found any significant evidence of such iatrogenesis. Thus, concerns about inducing body image or eating problems should be carefully considered but should not deter the development of prevention programs.

UNIVERSAL-SELECTIVE PREVENTION CAN WORK

The meta-analyses by Stice and Shaw (2004) and Fingeret et al. (2006) both demonstrated small but significant effects of universal-selective prevention programs on not only knowledge, but attitudes and behaviors as well. In our own recent, extensive reviews (Levine & Smolak, 2006, 2007), we too concluded that universal-selective programs can work, particularly to actually prevent the onset of eating problems.

One very important target audience is 4- to 6-year-old children. Good evidence exists that many children in this age group already have developed (or are developing) clear, strong, and negative beliefs about fat and fat people, as well as a sense that thinness, dieting, and weight loss are all "good." Moreover, there is no doubt that many girls and some boys at ages 8 to 12 have developed at least some of the cognitive, emotional, and behavioral elements of significant body dissatisfaction and disordered eating (chap. 3, this volume). Consequently, as we have long argued (Smolak & Levine, 1994), it would be desirable to begin prevention efforts as early as ages 4 to 7.

Shapesville (Mills, Osborn, & Neitz, 2003) is a children's picture book that uses simple rhymes and bright, colorful illustrations to engage children in a story that "celebrates positive body image by encouraging self-acceptance and diversity" (Dohnt & Tiggemann, 2008, p. 224). As the text is read and each character (e.g., Cindy the [bright yellow] Circle) is introduced, the children are encouraged to comment on the character and to relate the characters' actions to their own lives. The combination of the text, illustrations, the invitations to elaborate, and the follow-up questions contained in *Shapesville* enables adults to use the proposition that "healthy bodies come in all sizes and shapes" as the foundation for developmentally appropriate discussions of body image, stereotyping on the basis of weight and shape, respect for individual differences (e.g., in size, talents, interests), self-esteem, healthy nutrition, and being active as part of a fun and fit lifestyle.

In a randomized controlled trial, Dohnt and Tiggemann (2008) evaluated the efficacy of the *Shapesville* "program" for small groups of south Australian girls, most of whom were 6 and 7 years old. In the control condition, girls commented on and discussed a colorful, enjoyable book whose content about an elephant and friends is irrelevant to *Shapesville*'s central messages. This pioneering, well-designed study of prevention for young children produced very encouraging data, all of which was based on interviews pre- and postintervention, and at 6-week follow-up. At posttest, relative to the control condition, girls participating in the *Shapesville*-based intervention learned more about nutrition, were more satisfied with their appearance, reduced their perceptions that normal-weight and overweight girls would have fewer friends than underweight girls, were less likely to want to look like TV and popular music stars, and reported being more aware of their own special talents. The program did not affect body image significantly, and at follow-up most of the between group differences were no longer significant. However, at 6-week follow-up girls participating in the *Shapesville* program were still reporting a lower desire to look like TV and pop stars and a greater awareness of their own special talents.

Other recent studies support the proposition that universal-selective programs can be successful with different, older age groups in reducing a variety of risk factors for disordered eating (Levine & Smolak, 2006, 2007; Piran, 2005; Pokrajac-Bulian, Zivcic-Becirevic, Calugi, & Dalle Grave, 2006). *Healthy Body Images: Teaching Kids to Eat and Love Their Bodies* (Kater, 2005) is a multilesson, integrated program designed for children in late elementary school (ages 9–12). In a controlled study, participating children improved in knowledge, body satisfaction, critical thinking about media, intentions to diet, and healthy nutrition and exercise choices (Kater, Rohwer, & Londre, 2002).

One emphasis of *Healthy Body Images* is media literacy. Based on our previous work with media and the work of Kater and colleagues, Wood (2005) constructed a pilot media literacy intervention for 5- to 11-year-old girls and boys. Wood compared the effects of a control discussion of peer pressure with a single lesson explaining how technology and fantasy are used to construct unrealistic and unhealthy media images of beauty. This brief media literacy intervention did not affect scores on the Eating Attitudes Test–Children's Version (ChEAT) but participants did report a significant increase in body esteem 2 weeks later.

The multilesson, more intensive *Free to Be Me* media literacy program for Girl Scouts (M_{age} = 10.6), their parents, and their troop leaders had several positive effects that were sustained for 3 months. For example, internalization of the thin ideal was reduced (Neumark-Sztainer, Sherwood, Coller, & Hannan, 2000). Another intensive, multilesson media literacy program, *GO GIRLS!* (Levine, Piran, & Stoddard, 1999) reduced emotional investment in and dissatisfaction with body weight in 13- to 14-year-old participants (Wade, Davidson, & O'Dea, 2003). In an evaluation of yet another media literacy program, aimed at both boys and girls, Wilksch, Tiggemann, and Wade (2006) reported immediate reductions, for both genders, in internalization of the general attractiveness ideal. Furthermore, the boys also reported significant immediate reductions in experienced pressures to manage weight and to look like athletes in the media. Finally, a media literacy program for 12- to 13-year-old boys (Stanford & McCabe, 2005) resulted in increased muscle satisfaction and self-esteem, as well as decreased negative affect, relative to a control group.

Thus, recent research demonstrates that universal-selective prevention can positively impact knowledge, attitudes, and, less frequently, behaviors (Levine & Smolak, 2006). Moreover, two significant components of all of these programs are psychoeducation and media literacy, each of which helps students understand, critically evaluate, and resist negative psychosocial influences. These universal-selective programs can be effective with both boys and girls. This is true whether the program is aimed at elementary or middle school programs. We have long argued (Smolak & Levine, 1994) that universal-selective prevention will be most effective with younger audiences. It is in these groups that a true prevention effect is most likely; with older audiences one is more likely to be attempting to reduce incipient or even established body image or eating problems. As will be seen in the section on ecological approaches, universal-selective programs can be useful with older adolescents. Nevertheless, as children and young adolescents get older, one is more likely to be addressing and identifying participants who already show body image or eating problems and hence are appropriate audiences for targeted prevention.

TARGETED PREVENTION CAN WORK

To our knowledge, there are no targeted prevention programs for elementary or middle school audiences, despite what appears to be a meaningfully high rate of eating disorders symptoms in the latter age group (McVey, Tweed, & Blackmore, 2005; Shisslak et al., 2006). Indeed, weight concerns among middle school-age girls are powerful predictors of the onset of eating disorders and their symptoms (chap. 3, this volume). And there are only a handful of programs for high school students; three of the newest ones are based on programs that have been successful with college women (Levine & Smolak, 2006, 2007).

The Cognitive Dissonance and Healthy Weight Programs

Stice and colleagues developed a cognitive dissonance-based (CD) program designed to reduce risk factors and eating disorder symptoms in high school girls who are concerned about negative body image. The reasonable "placebo" constructed for their controlled evaluations of the CD intervention with college students was a healthy weight management (HW) program that uses psychoeducation, motivational interviewing, and behavior modification to discourage food deprivation and calorie counting, while facilitating a healthier lifestyle in the form of a balanced diet and regular exercise (Stice, Shaw, Burton, & Wade, 2006, review the CD and HW programs). Stice, Presnell, Groesz, and Shaw (2005) randomly assigned 14- to 19-year-old girls with high initial levels of body dissatisfaction to the HW program or to an assessment-only control condition. As predicted on the basis of previous research with college students, the HW program had modest positive effects over a 1-year follow-up period in reducing bulimic symptoms, in increasing healthy eating, and in preventing weight gain and obesity onset.

In a particularly rigorous comparative outcome study, Stice et al. (2006) recruited 481 ethnically diverse girls ages 14 to 19 who, on average, had significantly elevated body dissatisfaction and thin-ideal internalization scores.

maker, 2005; Gortmaker et al., 1999; chap. 12, this volume). Its multifaceted curricular approach to limiting TV viewing, increasing moderate and vigorous activity, and improving eating habits is supported by teacher training and by attempts to modify the home environment. Among the 186 girls who were not dieting or eating disordered at baseline, only 1 (0.5%) who participated in *Planet Health* reported purging or using diet pills 2 years later, as compared with 9 (5.6%) of 162 in the control condition. This yields a preventive fraction ([incidence$_{control}$ – incidence $_{experimental}$] / incidence $_{control}$) of .91. That is, approximately 91% of the new cases of disordered eating among the nondieting girls could have been prevented by *Planet Health* (Austin et al., 2005).

Between 2002 and 2004, Austin and colleagues worked with the Massachusetts Department of Public Health to conduct a randomized controlled evaluation of an augmented form of *Planet Health* (Austin et al., 2007). More than 1,400 girls and boys in Grades 6 and 7 in 16 middle schools received no intervention or a combination of *Planet Health* and the Centers for Disease Control and Prevention's (n.d.) *School Health Index* [Program Guide] *for Physical Activity and Healthy Eating*. The program had no effect on boys. However, following the 2-year program only 1.2% girls in the 8 intervention schools began using diet pills, self-induced vomiting, or laxatives to manage weight. For girls in control schools the comparable figure was 3.6%. Even when the logistic regression model controlled for school-level baseline differences in disordered weight management behavior, the preventive fraction for *Planet Health* was .67. When the multivariate logistic regression model was expanded to include grade (6 vs. 7), White versus ethnic minority status, and whether a child was overweight at baseline, the resulting estimate of the prevention effect for *Planet Health* was only slightly less. However, the confidence intervals expanded to include the null effect. This statistic, coupled with sample sizes inadequate to test the three multivariate interactions (e.g., program × grade), means that future research is needed to establish with confidence that the augmented version of *Planet Health* had a preventive effect regardless of age, White versus ethnic minority status, or degree of overweight at baseline.

Very Important Kids (V.I.K.) is a multilevel ecological program designed to prevent all forms of teasing in an ethnically diverse, low-income group of students ages 9 to 12 (Haines, Neumark-Sztainer, Perry, Hannan, & Levine, 2006). In addition to student involvement in producing a play that was well attended by parents, there were educational workshops for teachers and a schoolwide anti-teasing campaign. V.I.K. reduced teasing at the intervention school relative to a matched comparison school (Haines et al., 2006). V.I.K. also increased students' self-efficacy in regard to changing weight-teasing norms and reduced negative peer norms and behavior about weight. Body satisfaction, unhealthy weight control, and internalization of media ideals were not affected. Hopefully, further evaluations of V.I.K. will include

These girls were randomly assigned to the CD program, the HW program, a control condition involving emotional expression through narrative writing, or an assessment-only control condition. In terms of absolute change, by posttest both the CD and HW interventions had produced significant reductions in risk factors for eating disorders, and in symptoms of eating disorders. In both conditions these desirable changes were maintained at 1-year follow-up. Yet the two control conditions also produced a host of positive and sustained changes, with the exception of the important variable of body dissatisfaction. Comparative analyses showed, however, that in general the CD and HW conditions produced greater decreases in risk factors than did the two control conditions. Moreover, at 1-year follow-up, as compared with the assessment-only controls, females in the CD and HW conditions were less likely to begin binge eating and to become obese. The girls in the HW condition were also less likely to begin using compensatory behaviors. Relative to the control conditions, both the CD and HW interventions reduced the risk of obesity onset.

The same research team examined the mediators of preventive changes (Stice, Presnell, Gau, & Shaw, 2007) and the extended long-term effects of these interventions (Stice, Marti, Spoor, Presnell, & Shaw, 2008). It appears that the positive 1-year effects of the CD program are mediated by its hypothesized ability to reduce idealization of the thin beauty standard for females. Interestingly, although the HW program did indeed increase healthy eating and physical activity, these benefits were not mediators of the program's positive effects on risk for eating disorders and on eating pathology. At 3-year follow-up both the CD and HW interventions produced a comparative reduction in the number of new cases of clinically significant eating pathology. In general, though, across a number of measures and across the four major assessment points, the CD program was the most effective in reducing internalization of the thin ideal, body dissatisfaction, negative affect, and psychological impairment.

Student Bodies

Student Bodies (Taylor, Winzelberg, & Celio, 2001) is a computer-assisted psychoeducational program based on the social cognitive and cognitive behavioral models. It also involves elements of feminist consciousness-raising as a critical social perspective (Levine & Piran, 2004). In addition to multimedia psychoeducation, participants also have the opportunity to provide and receive social support through online discussions. Using a pre–post only design, Abascal, Bruning Brown, Winzelberg, Dev, and Taylor (2004) evaluated the effects of internet delivery of a 6-week version of *Student Bodies* on private school girls aged 15 to 16. Students were categorized as high or low risk based on weight concerns. Although girls in the lower risk/lower motivation groups increased their knowledge and reduced their shape concerns, it appears that *Student Bodies* is more effective as a targeted prevention program. The higher risk/higher motivation groups showed improvements in knowledge and fairly large improvements (effect sizes ranged from .49–.75) in shape concerns, weight concerns, drive for thinness, and dietary restraint. A second study supports this conclusion about targeted prevention. Even an enhanced version of *Student Bodies*, including a Web site for parents, did not produce improvements in bulimic symptoms, weight concerns, or drive for thinness at posttest or 3-month follow-up in a group of 14- to 15-year-old girls who were not segmented or segregated by high or low risk (Bruning Brown, Winzelberg, Abascal, & Taylor, 2004).

Luce et al. (2005) used computer screening to identify at-risk high school girls for participation in a targeted program similar to *Student Bodies*. This raises the ethical question of potential distress to girls who find out online that they are considered at risk enough to participate in a program. Although girls categorized and labeled as high risk for eating disorders and/ or obesity reported mild, but significant, shame, approximately 60% of the high-risk girls indicated a desire to take part in the program. The core psychoeducational program combined with the targeted body image program resulted in a number of positive pre–post changes in scores on the questionnaire version of the Eating Disorders Examination and the Eating Disorder Inventory. However, so did the psychoeducational program alone.

Psychoeduational Approaches

In contrast to Stice and Shaw's (2004) often cited contention, Luce et al.'s (2005) data, as well as Stice's own evaluations of his HW program (Stice et al., 2005, 2006) support the following conclusion from Fingeret et al.'s (2006) meta-analysis: Targeted prevention programs that are psychoeducational and engaging can indeed be effective with high school students. Whether this would be true with younger elementary or middle school audiences is a question for future research.

THE VALUE OF FEMINIST APPROACHES

Feminist theories are a relative newcomer among the theoretical approaches used to underpin eating disorders programs. Furthermore, although they have not been heavily represented in eating disorders programs, when they have been used they have enjoyed some success (Levine & Smolak, 2006). Additionally, the risk factors for body image and eating problems emphasized by feminist theories have been supported by experimental and even some prospective data (Smolak & Murnen, 2007). Given the gendered nature of eating problems, it makes good sense that feminist theories offer promising approaches to the prevention of body image and eating problems (Levine & Piran, 2004; Levine & Smolak, 2006; Piran, 1999).

Girls Group is a universal prevention program for 10- to 11-year-old girls (Scime, Cook-Cottone, Kane, & Watson, 2006). It intentionally unites elements of Piran's (1999) feminist–relational model and O'Dea's (2005) interactive–constructionist approach to self-esteem development. The program seeks to "attune" the interconnections within and between girls' internal and external systems. In the initial, uncontrolled evaluation with three groups (Scime et al., 2006), the program produced statistically significant pre-to-post program reductions in the two important target risk factors: body dissatisfaction (effect size d for change = +.45) and drive for thinness (d for change = +.24).

Full of Ourselves: A Wellness Program to Advance Girl Power, Health, & Leadership is a prevention program for 12- to 14-year-old girls (Steiner-Adair & Sjostrom, 2006; Steiner-Adair et al., 2002). *Full of Ourselves* helps girls become more assertive and supportive of each other as they complete a psychoeducational prevention program. In a controlled evaluation with a 6-month follow-up, participants showed a sustained increase in knowledge about weightism, mass media, and health. Moreover, they also had sustained improvements in body satisfaction (Steiner-Adair et al., 2002). Although there were no significant effects on weight management behavior, the program increased global self-esteem while reducing both negative self-talk about the body and internalization of the slender beauty ideal.

These programs demonstrate the potential value of integrating feminist empowerment principles into universal-selective programs (Neumark-Sztainer et al., 2000). It is noteworthy that the programs have combined psychoeducational and interactive, discovery-based methods. Furthermore, there has been some success with both elementary and middle school-age girls.

ECOLOGICAL APPROACHES

Examination of efforts to prevent use and abuse of tobacco and alcohol strongly supports Piran's (1999) argument that programs designed to change the context within which body image and eating problems develop are likely to be particularly valuable (Levine & Smolak, 2006). Such programs not only guarantee support for the child's attempts at healthy eating and exercise and positive body attitudes, but reduce the presence of social and cultural risk factors, thereby decreasing the incidence of eating problems over time. Ecological programs can be difficult to plan and execute. Recent research, however, demonstrates the value of these efforts.

Planet Health is a social cognitive obesity prevention program for 11- to 13-year-olds (Grades 6 and 7; Austin, Field, Wiecha, Peterson, & Gort-

follow-up periods long enough to determine if a true prevention effect of the reduced teasing might be eventually realized.

Encouraged by the success of the *Everybody is a Somebody* curriculum in conjunction with the *Girl Talk* support-group-based prevention program (McVey, Lieberman, Voorberg, Wardrope, & Blackmore, 2003). McVey et al. (2007) developed *Healthy Schools–Healthy Kids*, an 8-month school-based intervention for middle school students. This pioneering project included an enhanced curriculum, teacher and staff training, parent education, gender-segregated support groups, posters and public service announcements, and student viewing and discussion of a 50-minute play about media and peer pressures. At 6-month follow-up, girls and boys in Grade 7 reported significantly less body dissatisfaction. Girls in the intervention schools also reduced their awareness and internalization of the slender beauty ideal, and skipped fewer meals.

A recent development related to the *Healthy Schools–Healthy Kids* program is *The Student Body: Promoting Health at Any Size* (McVey, 2006). This Web-based curriculum project, intended for teachers and public health staff who work with 9- to 12-year-olds, grew out of extensive training and research activities conducted in Ontario, Canada by a team of professionals at Toronto General Hospital and The Hospital for Sick Children (McVey, Davis, et al., 2005). Information and student activities available at the Web site build on the lessons in McVey's curriculum and are also well matched to the curriculum expectations of the Ontario and Nova Scotia Ministries of Education. Initial evaluation of *The Student Body: Promoting Health at Any Size* has yielded some encouraging results (McVey & Tweed, personal communication, August 12, 2006). After 60 days, compared with the control condition, the Web-based program significantly increased participants' belief that teaching practices could contribute to prevention of body image concerns, and it increased their own self-efficacy to fight weight-related social norms at school and in the workplace. Participants were also more likely to endorse the statements that "dieting may cause weight gain" and "girls who have friends who diet are more likely to diet themselves."

A Developmental, Communitywide Approach

The sequential development and assessment of McVey et al.'s ecological approach to school-based prevention is a very important advancement. In fact, McVey and colleagues in the province of Ontario, Canada, have fashioned a model of health promotion that integrates universal, selective, and targeted prevention, as well as treatment services (McVey, 2006; McVey, Davis, et al., 2005). This model brings together research, policy and program development, coalition-building and advocacy, and knowledge dissemination. In addition to the programs already described, McVey and colleagues are working on, for example, education and training of parents and teachers of elementary and middle school children, and a positive body image initiative for high school athletes and for their coaches and parents (Buchholz, Mack, McVey, Feder, & Barrowman, 2008).

Athletes Targeting Healthy Exercise and Nutrition Alternatives

Athletes Targeting Healthy Exercise and Nutrition Alternatives (ATHENA) is a multifaceted program designed to prevent eating problems and unhealthy weight/shape management or performance-enhancing practices, including use of diet pills, nicotine, "nutritional" supplements, and anabolic-androgenic steroids among high school female athletes, cheerleaders, and members of the dance and drill teams (Elliot et al., 2004; Elliot, Goldberg, et al., 2006; Elliot, Moe, et al., 2006). ATHENA is based on the *Adolescents Training and Learning to Avoid Steroids* (ATLAS) program, whose well-documented ability to prevent the use and abuse of anabolic steroids and food supplements by young male football players has made it a "model" program championed by the U.S. Department of Education (Elliot & Goldberg, 2008; Goldberg et al., 2000). ATHENA is a gender-specific adaptation of the ATLAS program because, in general, risk and protective factors for drug use are different for adolescent girls and boys, and because, more specifically, young female athletes tend to want to be "leaner and lighter," not bigger, more muscular, and much stronger (Elliot, Goldberg, et al., 2006).

ATHENA's ecological elements include training coaches and peers to administer the program within the framework of the team's usual practices. Using "sports teams" as a medium, the coaches and peers work closely with groups of six to eight student athletes to establish and reinforce each of the following: healthy norms within a cohesive group, clear expectations for healthy behavior in support of self and others, and desired skills. No information pertaining to eating disorders, body weight, or caloric intake is provided.

A large-scale pre-to-post–season randomized controlled evaluation of ATHENA (Elliot et al., 2004) produced a number of true prevention effects. Relative to girls on teams in the comparison schools, female athletes ages 14 to 16 participating in the program were significantly less likely to begin using diet pills and to continue using them. ATHENA participants were also only half as likely to begin using amphetamines, anabolic steroids, and muscle-building supplements. In addition to reporting healthier eating behaviors, ATHENA participants reduced their intentions to lose weight; to use tobacco and the "muscle-boosting" food supplement creatine; and to use self-induced vomiting and drugs for weight control. Moreover, as predicted, ATHENA successfully increased four potentially significant mediators: media literacy, drug resistance skills, self-efficacy in controlling mood, and the perception that few peers endorse and use body-shaping drugs.

Elliot, Goldberg, et al. (2006; Elliot & Goldberg, 2008) conducted a long-term follow-up of the ATHENA participants. Following the conclusion of the original program, female athletes not graduating from high school received five team "booster" sessions in what amounts to the second year of the program. A year after the booster sessions, all participants were sent a short follow-up survey, which slightly more than 50% completed and returned. Many of the relative gains demonstrated in the short-term were not maintained over the long follow-up. Nevertheless, relative to control participants, ATHENA participants reported a trend toward lower use of diet pills, diuretics, and laxatives. It is important to note that these girls also reported more adequate calcium intake and higher mood in general. In contrast to concerns about prevention programs affecting "only knowledge," longitudinal multivariate analysis showed that the comparative long-term reduction in intentions of ATHENA participants to use diet pills and other unhealthy weight management procedures was mediated by confidence in the nutritional knowledge generated and reinforced by the program (Wilke, MacKinnon, Elliot, & Moe, 2006).

The ATLAS and ATHENA programs are probably best considered a form of selective prevention, but their integration of psychoeducation, positive norm development, media literacy, and competence-building with a number of the well-established practices in the design and evaluation of drug prevention programs has very important and broad implications for construction of more universal programs for youth—girls *and* boys—ages 14 to 18. Furthermore, their attention to the broader ecology, including both peers and coaches, also provides an important model for future programs.

CONCLUSIONS, RECOMMENDATIONS, AND FUTURE DIRECTIONS

Since the beginning of the new millennium a number of exciting developments have contributed to substantial progress in theory and research concerning the prevention of negative body image and disordered eating in children and adolescents (Haines & Neumark-Sztainer, 2006; Levine & Smolak, 2006, 2007; Neumark-Sztainer et al., 2006; Taylor, 2005). We are pleased that all eight recommendations for "basic ingredients of an ideal prevention outcome study" that we made in the first edition of this book (Levine & Smolak, 2001) are now typically being followed (see Exhibit 11.1). On the basis of recent developments, we believe the following conclusions are merited and deserve the attention of researchers and activists in the field. These conclusions presume that prevention is not a luxury awaiting clarification of risk factors and perfection of treatment. Prevention is the only way to reduce the overall prevalence of a disorder, and it is a key aspect of demonstrating the status of some causal risk factors (Levine &

EXHIBIT 11.1
Basic Ingredients of an Ideal Prevention Outcome Study

Specification of goal as universal prevention and/or behavior change in children or adolescents already showing prodromal problems

Clear translation of a theoretical model for prevention into specific program components

Unbiased assignment of samples to experimental and comparison conditions, plus assessment of cross-fertilization of programmatic ideas to the comparison group

Valid measurement, using quantitative and qualitative data, of outcome variables pertaining to risk (e.g., belief in the importance of thinness), resilience (e.g., definition of self in terms of multiple interests and competencies unrelated to weight and shape), and the continuum of eating problems

Specification of program ingredients, how program staff were trained and supported in implementing them, and to what extent (e.g., in terms of attendance and completion of assignments) children participated in the program

Assessment of outcome variables and potential influences (e.g., body mass index, gender, ethnicity, depression) before the program (e.g., at age 10), immediately following the program (e.g., 3 months later), and during at least one follow-up wave that coincides with the period of risk (e.g., middle adolescence)

Assessment of changes in the ecology of the children's and the adult's lives (e.g., in the school system)

Data analyses that are sensitive to the possibility that some children in the experimental group may be negatively affected by the prevention program as well as to effect sizes

Note. "Primary Prevention of Body Image Disturbance and Disordered Eating in Childhood and Adolescence," by M. P. Levine and L. Smolak, 2001, in J. K. Thomson and L. Smolak (Eds.), *Body Image, Eating Disorders, and Obesity in Youth: Assessment, Prevention, and Treatment* (p. 255). Copyright 2001, American Psychological Association.

Smolak, 2006; Stice, 2002). Consequently, despite the many practical challenges of prevention work—and especially universal prevention—there is a continuing need for high-quality controlled outcome studies with sufficient sample sizes and follow-up periods long enough to determine whether prevention occurred: Did the intervention affect risk and resilience factors and thereby reduce the development of disordered eating?

Universal-Selective Prevention

There is substantial evidence that a variety of different types of universal-selective programs, implemented in schools or in organizations such as Girl Scouts, can have modest positive and sustained effects on the attitudes and behaviors of children and adolescents, that is, on more than "just knowledge." It is also clear that psychoeducation, as a form of consciousness-raising that encourages analytical thinking, can play an important role by fostering a critical perspective toward healthy and unhealthy influences on risk for disordered eating. The information and activities will, of course, need to be tailored to the developmental level of the audience (Levine & Smolak, 2006; Smolak, 1999), although certain themes such as an active, playful lifestyle, a nondieting approach to healthy eating, appreciation of diversity in weight and shape, elimination of teasing, and analysis and resistance of unhealthy sociocultural influences can be applied in general. Furthermore, although we need to be alert to the possibility that information alone may indeed backfire and inadvertently convey, for example, unhealthy weight management techniques (Levine & Smolak, 2006; O'Dea, 2005), evidence for iatrogenesis in prevention outcome studies is weak (Fingeret et al., 2006; Stice & Shaw, 2004) and should not detract from the value of psychoeducation and critical thinking.

Future research, building on progress in the prevention of substance use and abuse (Levine & Smolak, 2006; Perry, 1999) should aim to identify what techniques help to make universal-selective programs most effective. Furthermore, there continue to be questions as to which ages are best targeted by these programs. We also need more information concerning the theoretical models that work best in these programs. We have highlighted two: feminist theory and ecological systems models.

Feminist Theory

Body image and eating problems are gendered in their definition and etiology. So it should not be surprising that models that recognize and analyze the construction and role of gender by prominent sociocultural forces will be effective in preventing body image and eating problems. Recent research supports the argument that integrating elements of feminist theory into prevention programs aimed at elementary and middle school girls is a valuable approach.

Future research should continue to explore the relationship of the "lived experience" of being female or male to the development of body image and eating problems (chap. 7, this volume). Because gender is culturally defined, constructed, and reinforced, many of the elements of gender will be amenable to change. Such change will often require not only empowering girls—however, as programs like *Full of Ourselves* demonstrate, this is an important step—but also changing the actual environment that equates femininity with the thin body ideal and physical objectification (Levine & Smolak, 2006; Piran, 1999, 2005; Smolak & Murnen, 2007). This underscores the value of an ecological approach.

Ecological Models

Even a child well armed with new life skills and critical analysis tools is likely to have difficulty resisting cultural messages and pressures about body shape with no support from peers, parents, siblings, teachers, or coaches.

Changes in the environment, such as presenting more diverse body shapes in the media or reducing weight-related teasing, might also positively affect children who have not been in a specific prevention program. Work from other public health fields, such as drug abuse prevention, clearly demonstrates the value of changing the ecology in which children live (Levine & Smolak, 2006; Perry, 1999). Now we have results from body image and eating disorders programs that suggest the same is true in this field.

Once again, future research will need to identify which elements of the environment are most amenable to change and how to best change them. There is now considerable research establishing the impact of sociocultural factors, particularly media and peers, on the development of body image and eating problems (see chaps. 1, 3, 4, & 7, this volume). Thus, we must continue to clarify the most effective ways to involve community members, including busy parents and teachers, in prevention programs.

In the eating disorders area, engaging parents in prevention programming has proven to be very challenging (Haines et al., 2006; McVey et al., 2007; Varnado-Sullivan et al., 2001). But it is possible to involve substantial numbers of parents in ways that matter, as documented in Shepard and Carlson's (2003) review of school-based programs that have successfully applied an ecological approach to health promotion and drug abuse prevention. In regard to eating problems, the well-known Child and Adolescent Trial for Cardiovascular Health (CATCH; Luepker et al., 1996, cited in Shepard & Carlson, 2003; see also Perry, 1999) is noteworthy. Its integration of classroom curricula with home-based parent–child lessons and "family fun nights" at school is well established as being superior to control conditions in increasing nutritional knowledge and physical activity, while decreasing intake of dietary fat.

In a recent pilot project that attempted expressly to reduce risk factors for disordered eating, Gehrman, Hovell, Sallis, and Keating (2006) evaluated an 8-week educational and behavioral program for young adolescent boys and girls whose families were volunteers from the community. The researchers were successful in arranging for small groups of parents and small groups of children to participate in parallel in 2 hours weekly of education and behavioral training to improve the children's nutrition and level of physical activity. Although the program was not more significantly more successful than an injury prevention control, the children participating in the program demonstrated mean improvements in the predicted direction for all three dependent measures: drive for thinness (down 23% from baseline), body dissatisfaction (down 8%), and weight concerns (down 16%; p values for within group changes were not reported). These changes suggest that the parallel parental programming approach used by Gehrman et al. (2006) is deserving of further research attention, as it might easily be integrated into an expanded version of, for example, McVey et al.'s developmental communitywide project.

Targeted Prevention

There is now substantial evidence that the targeted interventions of cognitive dissonance induction and healthy weight management for high-risk adolescent girls and young women can generate reductions in risk factors and symptom levels that are sustained for 6 months to 1 year. Although a recent meta-analysis (Newton & Ciliska, 2006) of five controlled outcome studies (four of which were randomized) of the *Student Bodies* computer-assisted prevention program for older adolescents and university under-graduates revealed no significant overall effects for body satisfaction or for eating attitudes and behaviors, there is some evidence that computer-based interventions can have positive effects on risk factors and symptom levels in high-risk high school girls and female undergraduates (Taylor et al., 2001, 2006). Given that some eating disorders emerge during early and middle adolescence, these exciting advances in the efficacy of targeted prevention need to be extended to clarify if and how these programs can be instituted ethically and with long-term effectiveness for middle school and high school students. A tremendously important issue continues to be how to define "high risk" and how to communicate in nonstigmatizing ways the meaning of this category to those at risk, their families, professionals, and relevant personnel such as school staff (Levine & Smolak, 2006; Taylor, 2005).

A Word About Obesity Prevention

There is great public health concern about the increased rate of obesity among U.S. children, particularly ethnic minority children (see chaps. 8 & 12, this volume). We need to find ways for eating disorders prevention and obesity prevention advocates and researchers to work together effectively (Haines & Neumark-Sztainer, 2006; Neumark-Sztainer et al., 2006). Those concerned about obesity and eating disorders may find some common ground in helping children and youth to develop (a) a positive body image; (b) an active lifestyle; (c) better eating habits (e.g., more fruits and vegetables, less saturated fats, and fewer soft drinks); (d) life skills and social support for coping effectively with stress; (e) abstinence from tobacco and other appetite suppressants; (f) eating to satisfy hunger and to provide sufficient energy and nutrients for strength and stamina; (g) social norms that minimize teasing and maximize respect for diversity in size and shape; and (h) a critical social perspective (i.e., "literacy") in regard to mass media and other cultural factors that shape body image, eating, and weight management (Levine & Smolak, 2006).

We hope the next 10 years will see continuing developments in the field of prevention, accompanied by elimination of needless, and sometimes baseless, conflicts between "basic research versus prevention" and between "universal-selective versus targeted prevention." Projects in Canada (McVey,

2006), Australia (Paxton, 2006), Germany (Berger, Sowa, Bormann, Brix, & Strauss, 2008) and the United States (Abascal et al., 2004; Elliot & Goldberg, 2008) provide exciting examples of ways to address a continuum of disordered eating by integrating risk factor research, risk identification, and a continuum of prevention.

REFERENCES

Abascal, L., Bruning Brown, J., Winzelberg, A. J., Dev, P., & Taylor, C. B. (2004). Combining universal and targeted prevention for school-based eating disorder programs. *International Journal of Eating Disorders, 35,* 1–9.

Austin, S. B., Field, A. E., Wiecha, J., Peterson, K. E., & Gortmaker, S. L. (2005). The impact of a school-based obesity prevention trial on disordered weight-control behavior in early adolescent girls. *Archives of Pediatric & Adolescent Medicine, 159,* 225–230.

Austin, S. B., Kim, J., Wiecha, J., Troped, P. J., Feldman, H. A., & Peterson, K. E. (2007). School-based overweight preventive intervention lowers incidence of disordered weight-control behaviors in early adolescent girls. *Archives of Pediatric & Adolescent Medicine, 161,* 865–869.

Berger, U., Sowa, M., Bormann, B., Brix, C., & Strauss, B. (2008). Primary prevention of eating disorders: Characteristics of effective programmes and how to bring them to broader dissemination. *European Eating Disorder Review, 16,* 173–183.

Bruning Brown, J., Winzelberg, A. J., Absacal, L. B., & Taylor, C. B. (2004). An evaluation of an internet-delivered eating disorder prevention program for adolescents and their parents. *Journal of Adolescent Health, 35,* 290–296.

Buchholz, A., Mack, H., McVey, G. L., Feder, S., & Barrowman, N. (2008). An evaluation of the prevention project BODYSENSE: A positive body image initiative for female athletes. *Eating Disorders: Journal of Treatment and Prevention, 16,* 308–321.

Cafri, G., Yamamiya, Y., Brannick, M., & Thompson, J. K. (2005). The influence of sociocultural factors on body image: A meta-analysis. *Clinical Psychology: Science and Practice, 12,* 421–433.

Caplan, G. (1964). *Principles of preventive psychiatry.* New York: Basic Books.

Centers for Disease Control and Prevention. (n.d.). *Healthy Youth! School Health Index: An introduction.* Retrieved January 10, 2008, from http://www.cdc.gov/HealthyYouth/SHI/introduction.htm

Dohnt, H. K., & Tiggemann, M. (2008). Promoting positive body image in young girls: An evaluation of *Shapesville. European Eating Disorders Review, 16,* 222–233.

Durkin, S. J., Paxton, S. J., & Wertheim, E. H. (2005). How do adolescent girls evaluate body dissatisfaction prevention messages? *Journal of Adolescent Health, 37,* 381–390.

Elliot, D. L., & Goldberg, L. (2008). The ATHENA (Athletes Targeting Healthy Exercise and Nutrition Alternatives) harm reduction/health promotion program for female high school athletes. In C. LeCroy & J. E. Mann (Eds.), *Handbook of prevention and intervention programs for adolescent girls* (pp. 205–239). Hoboken, NJ: Wiley.

Elliot, D. L., Goldberg, L., Moe, E. L., DeFrancesco, C. A., Durham, M. B., & Hix-Small, H. (2004). Preventing substance use and disordered eating: Initial outcomes of the ATHENA (Athletes Targeting Healthy Exercise and Nutrition Alternatives) program. *Archives of Pediatric & Adolescent Medicine, 158*, 1043–1049.

Elliot, D. L., Goldberg, L., Moe, E. L., DeFrancesco, C. A., Durham, M. B., & McGinnis, W. J. (2006). *Long-term outcomes of the ATHENA (Athletes Targeting Healthy Exercise and Nutrition Alternatives) program for female high school athletes.* Manuscript submitted for publication.

Elliot, D. L., Moe, E. E., Goldberg, L., DeFrancesco, C. A., Durham, M. B., & Hix-Small, H. (2006). Definition and outcome of a curriculum to prevent disordered eating and body-shaping drug use. *Journal of School Health, 76*, 67–73.

Fingeret, M. C., Warren, C. S., Cepeda-Benito, A., & Gleaves, D. H. (2006). Eating disorder prevention research: A meta-analysis. *Eating Disorders: The Journal of Treatment & Prevention, 14*, 191–213.

Gehrman, C. A., Hovell, M. F., Sallis, J. F., & Keating, K. (2006). The effects of physical activity and nutrition intervention on body dissatisfaction, drive for thinness, and weight concerns in pre-adolescents. *Body Image, 3*, 345–351.

Goldberg, L., MacKinnon, D. P., Elliot, D. L., Moe, E. L., Clarke, G., & Cheong, J. (2000). The Adolescents Training and Learning to Avoid Steroids Program: Preventing drug use and promoting healthy behaviors. *Archives of Pediatrics & Adolescent Medicine, 154*, 332–338.

Gortmaker, S. L., Peterson, K., Wiecha, J., Sobol, A. M., Dixit, S., Fox, M. K., & Laird, N. (1999). Reducing obesity via a school-based interdisciplinary intervention among youth: Planet Health. *Archives of Pediatric & Adolescent Medicine, 153*, 409–418.

Haines, J., & Neumark-Sztainer, D. (2006). Prevention of obesity and eating disorders: A consideration of shared risk factors. *Health Education Research, 21*, 770–782.

Haines, J., Neumark-Sztainer, D., Perry, C. L., Hannan, P. J., & Levine, M. P. (2006). V.I.K. (Very Important Kids): A school-based program designed to reduce teasing and unhealthy weight control behaviors. *Health Education Research, 21*, 884–895.

Harrison, K., & Hefner, V. (2006). Media exposure, current and future body ideals, and disordered eating among preadolescent girls: A longitudinal panel study. *Journal of Youth and Adolescence, 3*, 146–156.

Jablensky, A. (2002). Research methods in psychiatric epidemiology: An overview. *Australian and New Zealand Journal of Psychiatry, 36*, 297–310.

Kater, K. J. (2005). *Healthy body images: Teaching kids to eat, and love their bodies, too!* (2nd ed.). Seattle, WA: National Eating Disorders Association.

Kater, K. J., Rohwer, J., & Londre, K. (2002). Evaluation of an upper elementary school program to prevent body image and weight concerns. *Journal of School Health, 72*, 199–204.

Levine, M. P., & Piran, N. (2004). The role of body image in the prevention of eating disorders. *Body Image, 1*, 57–70.

Levine, M. P., Piran, N., & Stoddard, C. (1999). Mission more probable: Media literacy, activism, and advocacy as primary prevention. In N. Piran, M. P. Levine, & C. Steiner-Adair (Eds.), *Preventing eating disorders: A handbook of interventions and special challenges* (pp. 3–25). Philadelphia: Brunner/Mazel.

Levine, M. P., & Smolak, L. (2001). Primary prevention of body image disturbance and disordered eating in childhood and adolescence. In J. K. Thompson & L. Smolak (Eds.), *Body image, eating disorders, and obesity in youth: Assessment, prevention, and treatment* (pp. 237–260). Washington, DC: American Psychological Association.

Levine, M. P., & Smolak, L. (2006). *The prevention of eating problems and eating disorders: Theory, research, and practice.* Mahwah, NJ: Erlbaum.

Levine, M. P., & Smolak, L. (2007). Prevention of negative body image, disordered eating, and eating disorders: An update. In S. Wonderlich, J. Mitchell, M. de Zwaan, & H. Steiger (Eds.), *Eating disorders review* (Part 3, pp. 1–13). Oxford, England: Radcliffe.

Luce, K. H., Osborne, M. I., Winzelberg, A. J., Das, S., Abascal, L. B., Celio, A. A., et al. (2005). Application of an algorithm-driven protocol to simultaneously provide universal and targeted prevention programs. *International Journal of Eating Disorders, 37,* 220–226.

Mann, T., Nolen-Hoeksema, S., Huan, K., Burgard, D., Wright, A., & Hanson, K. (1997). Are two interventions worse than none? Joint primary and secondary prevention of eating disorders in college females. *Health Psychology, 16,* 1–11.

McVey, G. L. (2006, June). *A developmental and community-wide approach to the prevention of disordered eating: Findings from outcome-based research.* Paper presented at the Academy for Eating Disorders International Conference on Eating Disorders, Barcelona, Spain.

McVey, G. L., Davis, R., Kaplan, A. S., Katzman, D. K., Pinhas, L., Heinmaa, M., et al. (2005). A community-based training program for eating disorders and its contribution to a provincial network of specialized services. *International Journal of Eating Disorders, 37*(Suppl. 1), 35–40.

McVey, G. L., Lieberman, M., Voorberg, N., Wardrope, D., & Blackmore, E. (2003). School-based peer support groups: A new approach to the prevention of eating disorders. *Eating Disorders: The Journal of Treatment and Prevention, 11,* 169–185.

McVey, G. L., Tweed, S., & Blackmore, E. (2005). Correlates of weight loss and muscle-gaining behavior in 10- to 14-year-old males and females. *Preventive Medicine, 40,* 1–9.

McVey, G. L., Tweed, S., & Blackmore, E. (2007). Healthy Schools–Healthy Kids: A controlled evaluation of a comprehensive universal eating disorder prevention program. *Body Image, 4,* 115–136.

Mills, A., Osborn, B., & Neitz, E. [Illustrator]. (2003). *Shapesville.* Carlsbad, CA: Gürze.

Mrazek, P. J., & Haggerty, R. J. (Eds.). (1994). *Reducing risks for mental disorders: Frontiers for prevention intervention research.* Washington, DC: National Academy Press.

Muñoz, R. F., Mrazek, P. J., & Haggerty, R. J. (1996). Institute of Medicine report on prevention of mental disorders: Summary and commentary. *American Psychologist, 51,* 1116–1122.

Neumark-Sztainer, D., Levine, M. P., Paxton, S. J., Smolak, L., Piran, N., & Wertheim, E. H. (2006). Prevention of body dissatisfaction and disordered eating: What next? *Eating Disorders: Journal of Treatment & Prevention, 14,* 265–285.

Neumark-Sztainer, D., Sherwood, N., Coller, T., & Hannan, P. J. (2000). Primary prevention of disordered eating among pre-adolescent girls: Feasibility and short-term impact of a community-based intervention. *Journal of the American Dietetic Association, 100,* 1466–1473.

Newton, M. S., & Ciliska, D. (2006). Internet-based innovations for the prevention of eating disorders: A systematic review. *Eating Disorders: Journal of Treatment & Prevention, 14,* 365–384.

O'Dea, J. A. (2005). School-based health education strategies for the improvement of body image and prevention of eating problems. *Health Education, 105,* 11–33.

Pokrajac-Bulian, A., Zivcic-Becirevic, I., Calugi, S., & Dalle Grave, R. (2006). School prevention program in Croatia: A controlled study with six months of follow-up. *Eating and Weight Disorders, 11,* 171–178.

Paxton, S. J. (2006, June). *Body dissatisfaction and eating disorder prevention in Australia: Current initiatives and research.* Paper presented at the Academy for Eating Disorders International Conference on Eating Disorders, Barcelona, Spain.

Perry, C. L. (1999). *Creating health behavior change: How to develop community-wide programs for youth.* Thousand Oaks, CA: Sage.

Piran, N. (1999). The reduction of preoccupation with body weight and shape in schools: A feminist approach. In N. Piran, M. P. Levine, & C. Steiner-Adair (Eds.), *Preventing eating disorders: A handbook of interventions and special challenges* (pp. 148–159). Philadelphia: Brunner/Mazel.

Piran, N. (2005). Prevention of eating disorders: A review of outcome evaluation research. *The Israel Journal of Psychiatry and Related Sciences, 42,* 172–177.

Scime, M., Cook-Cottone, C., Kane, L., & Watson, T. (2006). Group prevention of eating disorders with fifth-grade females: Impact on body dissatisfaction, drive for thinness, and media influence. *Eating Disorders: The Journal of Treatment & Prevention, 14,* 143–155.

Shepard, J., & Carlson, J. S. (2003). An empirical evaluation of school-based prevention programs that involve parents. *Psychology in the Schools, 40,* 641–656.

Shisslak, C. M., Mays, M. Z., Crago, M., Jirsak, J. K., Taitano, K., & Cagno, C. (2006). Eating and weight control behaviors among middle school girls in relationship to body weight and ethnicity. *Journal of Adolescent Medicine, 38,* 631–633.

Smolak, L. (1999). Elementary school curricula for the primary prevention of eating problems. In N. Piran, M. P. Levine, & C. Steiner-Adair (Eds.), *Preventing eating disorders: A handbook of interventions and special challenges* (pp. 85–104). Philadelphia: Brunner/Mazel.

Smolak, L., & Levine, M. P. (1994). Toward an empirical basis for primary prevention of eating problems with elementary school children. *Eating Disorders: Journal of Treatment & Prevention, 4,* 293–307.

Smolak, L., & Levine, M. P. (1996). Developmental transitions at middle school and college. In L. Smolak, M. P. Levine, & R. H. Striegel-Moore (Eds.), *The developmental psychopathology of eating disorders: Implications for research, prevention, and treatment* (pp. 207–233). Hillsdale, NJ: Erlbaum.

Smolak, L., & Murnen, S. K. (2007). Feminism and body image. In V. Swami & A. Furnham (Eds.), *The body beautiful: Evolutionary and socio-cultural perspectives* (pp. 236–258). London: Palgrave Macmillan.

Stanford, J., & McCabe, M. P. (2005). Sociocultural influences on adolescent boys' body image and body change strategies. *Body Image, 2*, 105–113.

Steiner-Adair, C., & Sjostrom, L. (2006). *Full of ourselves: A wellness program to advance girl power, health, and leadership.* New York: Teachers College Press.

Steiner-Adair, C., Sjostrom, L., Franko, D. L., Pai, S., Tucker, R., Becker, A. E., & Herzog, D. B. (2002). Primary prevention of eating disorders in adolescent girls: Learning from practice. *International Journal of Eating Disorders, 32*, 401–411.

Stewart, A. (2004). Prevention of eating disorders. In K. N. Dwivedi & P. B. Harper (Eds.), *Promoting the emotional well-being of children and adolescents and preventing their mental ill health: A handbook* (pp. 173–197). London: Jessica Kingsley.

Stice, E. (2002). Risk and maintenance factors for eating pathology: A meta-analytic review. *Psychological Bulletin, 128*, 825–848.

Stice, E., Marti, C. N., Spoor, S., Presnell, K., & Shaw, H. (2008). Dissonance and health weight eating disorder prevention programs: Long-term effects from a randomized efficacy trial. *Journal of Consulting and Clinical Psychology, 76*, 329–340.

Stice, E., Nemeroff, C., & Shaw, H. E. (1996). A test of the dual pathway model of bulimia nervosa: Evidence for restrained-eating and affect-regulation mechanisms. *Journal of Social and Clinical Psychology, 15*, 340–363.

Stice, E., Presnell, K., Gau, J., & Shaw, H. (2007). Testing mediators of intervention effects in randomized controlled trials: An evaluation of two eating disorder prevention programs. *Journal of Consulting and Clinical Psychology, 75*, 20–32.

Stice, E., Presnell, K., Groesz, L. M., & Shaw, H. (2005). Effects of a weight maintenance diet on bulimic symptoms in adolescent girls: An experimental test of the dietary restraint theory. *Health Psychology, 24*, 402–212.

Stice, E., & Shaw, H. (2004). Eating disorder prevention programs: A meta-analytic review. *Psychological Bulletin, 130*, 206–227.

Stice, E., Shaw, H., Burton, E., & Wade, E. (2006). Dissonance and healthy weight eating disorder prevention programs: A randomized efficacy trial. *Journal of Consulting and Clinical Psychology, 74*, 263–275.

Stice, E., Shaw, H., & Marti, C. N. (2007). A meta-analytic review of eating disorder prevention programs: Encouraging findings. *Annual Review of Clinical Psychology, 3*, 207–231.

Taylor, C. B. (2005). Update on the prevention of eating disorders. In S. Wonderlich, J. Mitchell, M. de Zwaan, & H. Steiger (Eds.), *Eating disorders review* (part 1, pp. 1–14). Oxford, England: Radcliffe.

Taylor, C. B., Bryson, S., Luce, K. H., Cunning, D., Doyle, A., Abascal, L. B., et al. (2006). Prevention of eating disorders in at- risk college-age women. *Archives of General Psychiatry, 63*, 881–888.

Taylor, C. B., Winzelberg, A. J., & Celio, A. A. (2001). The use of interactive media to prevent eating disorders. In R. H. Striegel-Moore & L. Smolak (Eds.), *Eating disorders: Innovative directions in research and practice* (pp. 255–269). Washington, DC: American Psychological Association.

Varnado-Sullivan, P. J., Zucker, N., Williamson, D. A., Reas, D., Thaw, J., & Netemeyer, S. B. (2001). Development and implementation of the Body Logic

Program for adolescents: A two-stage prevention program for eating disorders. *Cognitive and Behavioral Practice, 8*, 248–259.

Wade, T. D., Davidson, S., & O'Dea, J. A. (2003). A preliminary controlled evaluation of a school-based media literacy and self-esteem program for reducing eating disorder risk factors. *International Journal of Eating Disorders, 33*, 371–383.

Wilke, K., MacKinnon, D. P., Elliot, D. L., & Moe, E. L. (2006, June). *Mediating mechanisms of an intervention with high school female athletes.* Poster presented at the Society for Prevention Research national meeting, San Antonio, TX.

Wilksch, S. M., Tiggemann, M., & Wade, T. D. (2006). Impact of interactive school-based media literacy lessons for reducing internalization of media ideals in young adolescent girls and boys. *International Journal of Eating Disorders, 39*, 385–393.

Withers, G. F., & Wertheim, E. H. (2004). Applying the Elaboration Likelihood Model of persuasion to a videotape-based eating disorders primary prevention program for adolescent girls. *Eating Disorders: Journal of Treatment & Prevention, 12*, 103–124.

Wood, K. (2005). Effects of a media intervention program on body image and eating attitudes among children. *University of Wisconsin-La Cross Journal of Undergraduate Research, 7*, 1–6. Retrieved January 12, 2007, from http://www.uwlax.edu/URC/JUR-online/PDF/2004/wood.pdf

12

OBESITY PREVENTION: STRATEGIES TO IMPROVE EFFECTIVENESS AND REDUCE HARM

KATHERINE W. BAUER, JESS HAINES,
AND DIANNE NEUMARK-SZTAINER

Preventing and reducing overweight in children and adolescents is a public health priority. In the past three decades, the prevalence of overweight has doubled in young children, and at least tripled in older children and adolescents (Jolliffe, 2004). This increase is concerning because of the variety of physical, psychological, social, and economic implications of overweight and obesity during childhood and adulthood. Since the 1990s, numerous obesity prevention interventions have been implemented to help children and adolescents achieve a healthy weight, some with moderate success (Boon & Clydesdale, 2005; Summerbell et al., 2005). By building on this history, and developing innovative strategies to modify youths' behaviors and the environments in with they live, there is great potential to reduce the prevalence of childhood obesity.

Obesity prevention interventions are essential to protect the current and future health of our youth. However, professionals from the areas of obesity and eating disorders worry that this increased attention on weight

241

could lead to an excessive concern by youth about their weight, which could possibly increase the risk of disordered eating and interfere with obesity-reducing efforts (Harris, 1983; Irving & Neumark-Sztainer, 2002; O'Dea, 2005; Orbach, 2006). Clearly, an examination of the potential for obesity prevention interventions to lead to these consequences is needed. We must identify how obesity prevention interventions can accomplish their goals to reduce or prevent weight gain while avoiding negative outcomes.

In this chapter, we explore individual, peer, familial, school, community, and societal factors of potential relevance to weight-related outcomes and consider strategies for intervening at each of these levels. We address the increasing concerns about the rise in attention to weight status during childhood and adolescence, and examine potential mechanisms through which obesity prevention interventions may encourage behaviors that increase risk for disordered eating behaviors and paradoxically, lead to weight gain rather than weight loss. Select interventions are presented to show how obesity prevention programs can be designed to simultaneously help children and teens feel good about their bodies, and be motivated to eat healthier and be active. Finally, we offer suggestions of how obesity prevention interventions can accomplish their goals to reduce or prevent weight gain while taking into account concerns about the potential negative implications of heightened attention to weight.

USING THE ECOLOGICAL FRAMEWORK TO IDENTIFY AREAS FOR OBESITY PREVENTION INTERVENTIONS

An ecological framework can be useful for identifying factors of potential relevance to obesity and other weight-related outcomes that should be targeted within obesity prevention interventions. The ecological framework emphasizes the strong contribution of the physical and social environment and interactions between distal influences (e.g., societal factors) and more proximal influences (e.g., familial factors) on an individual's weight-related outcomes. Additionally, the ecological framework emphasizes the importance of intervening on multiple levels of influence to achieve the greatest results (McLeroy, Bibeau, Steckler, & Glanz, 1988; Sallis & Owen, 1997).

Figure 12.1 utilizes principles from the ecological framework to highlight the multiple levels of influence on weight status and related weight outcomes in children and adolescents (Neumark-Sztainer, 2005). Figure 12.1, originally developed to help parents understand the multitude of factors influencing weight-related outcomes, includes the following:

- Individual characteristics such as eating behaviors and genetics
- Family factors such as family meal patterns

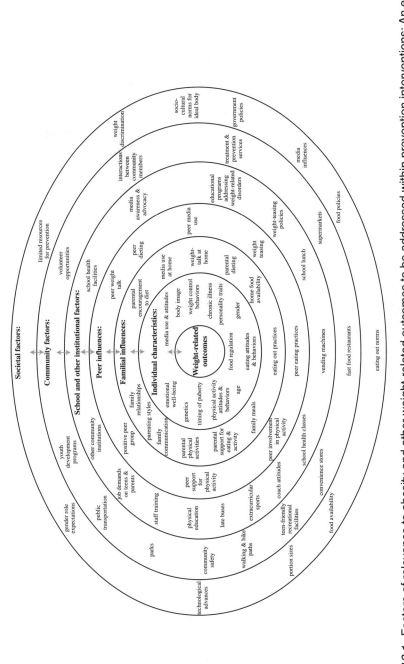

Figure 12.1. Factors of relevance to obesity and other weight-related outcomes to be addressed within prevention interventions: An ecological perspective. From *"I'm, Like, SO fat!" Helping Your Teen Make Healthy Choices about Eating and Exercise in a Weight-Obsessed World* (p. 25), by D. Neumark-Sztainer, 2005, New York: Guilford Press. Copyright 2005 by Guilford Press. Adapted with permission.

- Peer influences such as peer dieting norms
- School and other institutional factors
- Community factors such as community safety and accessibility of recreation facilities
- Societal factors such as media influences and public policy

Individual-Level Influences on Weight-Related Outcomes

The innermost level of the framework includes the individual's behaviors, attitudes, and biological and genetic propensities. Examples of individual factors of relevance to various weight-related outcomes include attitudes toward physical activity, eating behaviors, body image, and the existence of chronic health conditions.

Many obesity prevention interventions aim to modify personal attitudes and behaviors. These interventions often reach children and adolescents in school through classroom-based lessons and may work to modify a number of individual-level factors including children's self-efficacy for participating in healthy behaviors, their knowledge of healthy foods and eating habits, and their athletic skills. Examples of activities used within interventions to modify individual-level factors include conducting taste tests so children can try novel fruits and vegetables; providing walking clubs so youth can develop the habit of walking for exercise; and offering physical activity options that are an enjoyable substitute for television time (Davis et al., 1999; Gortmaker et al., 1999).

Familial and Peer-Level Influences on Weight-Related Outcomes

The next two levels of influence on children and adolescents' weight-related outcomes are their family and peer group. Interpersonal relationships at the familial and peer levels can have a significant impact on youth's dietary habits, physical activity levels, and other weight-related outcomes (Story, Neumark-Sztainer, & French, 2002). Families that eat meals together are supportive of each other being physically active, provide easy access to healthy foods, and provide a positive environment that is likely to promote a healthy weight status (Addessi, Galloway, Visalberghi, & Birch, 2005; Campbell, Crawford, & Ball, 2006; Hanson, Neumark-Sztainer, Eisenberg, Story, & Wall, 2005). Similarly, being engaged in a peer group that regularly participates in physical activity and engages in healthy behaviors while avoiding unhealthy dieting can have a positive impact on youths' weight-related behaviors (Contento, Williams, Michela, & Franklin, 2006; Eisenberg, Neumark-Sztainer, Story, & Perry, 2005; Grimm, Harnack, & Story, 2004).

Obesity prevention interventions working at the familial level can provide new opportunities for families to be active or eat together, such as hosting exercise and healthy cooking classes. Additionally, interventions can offer families tools so they can provide healthier options in their home such as coupons for fruits and vegetables or exercise equipment for family use. These strategies have the potential to allow youth to participate in positive activities as well as observe their parents engaging in healthy behaviors. In working with families regarding weight-related issues, it is important to help families take responsibility for providing a healthy home environment, without inducing feelings of shame or blame for having an overweight child (Neumark-Sztainer, 2005).

Possible strategies for targeting peer-group norms and behaviors include encouraging teens to engage in activities that they can do with their friends, such as taking a walk together or offering an afterschool drop-in group where discussions focus on the importance of positive body image and self-esteem. By modifying a peer group so that positive attitudes about diet, activity and other weight-related behaviors are the norm, youth may find it easier to engage in healthier behaviors for the long-term.

School and Other Institutional-Level Influences on Weight-Related Outcomes

Schools and other institutions, such as places of worship and community-based groups, also have the potential to influence children and adolescents' weight status. Messages about nutrition and physical activity provided by these institutions, whether explicitly taught or implicitly communicated through policies and norms, can greatly influence health behaviors and weight status (Kubik, Lytle, & Story, 2005). Some of the influential factors at this level include physical education requirements, health class curricula, and the presence of policies against weight-based teasing.

Schools are an excellent place for obesity prevention interventions because they have the potential to reach many children and adolescents. Examples of strategies for intervening at the school level include modifying policies regarding types of food allowed in the vending machines or on the a la carte line; requiring daily physical education; and making changes to the physical environment such as adding a new playing field or purchasing new sports equipment (Story, Kaphingst, & French, 2006). Additionally, modifying a school's policy regarding weight-related bullying and harassment has the potential to make overweight children feel more comfortable in their surroundings (Bauer, Patel, Prokop, & Austin, 2006), and, as discussed later, possibly decrease their risk for behaviors likely to lead to further weight gain, such as binge eating.

Community-Level Influences on Weight-Related Outcomes

Community factors of relevance to obesity prevention include the presence of safe parks; streets that are designed so it is easy to walk to schools;

community centers that provide opportunities for physical activity; and grocery stores, convenience stores, and restaurants that offer healthy, low-cost foods.

Assessing the impact of the community or "built environment" on overweight and obesity is a relatively new and exciting area. A growing body of literature is available that links proximity to parks, public transportation, and grocery stores to children and adolescents' dietary and activity habits, and weight status (Sallis & Glanz, 2006). Geographic information systems methodology has illuminated many opportunities for obesity prevention interventions in the community. For example, one study found that fast food restaurants are densely located near schools, presumably so students can stop in for food on their way to and from school, or grab a quick meal during the school day (Austin et al., 2005). Interventions to reduce the number of fast food outlets that are readily accessible to adolescents, or improve the quality of food available at these outlets, may have an impact on their weight status. Additional opportunities for obesity prevention interventions at the community level include developing public–private partnerships to increase reduced-cost access to athletic facilities and organizing a local farmer's market to facilitate the purchase of low-cost, high-quality food.

Societal-Level Influences on Weight-Related Outcomes

The outermost sphere of influence on youths' weight-related outcomes are societal norms and local, state, and federal government policies. These policies can impact factors such as physical education requirements, maintenance of local and state parks, and the cost of fruits and vegetables. Mass media can affect societal norms regarding desirable body shape and sizes and dietary patterns, which in turn impact youth's weight-related attitudes and behaviors. Children and adolescents can be highly influenced by media messages encouraging thinness or stigmatization of overweight people, and by advertisements for fast food restaurants, and foods of poor nutritional quality (Irving & Neumark-Sztainer, 2002; Lobstein & Dibb, 2005).

POTENTIAL UNINTENDED OUTCOMES OF OBESITY PREVENTION

Given the high prevalence of obesity and its adverse physical and psychological consequences, public health efforts focused on its prevention are warranted. Because of the multifactorial etiology of obesity, prevention efforts are needed at the societal, community, school, peer, familial, and individual levels. However, in developing obesity prevention interventions at each of these levels, we must also be cognizant of the potential adverse consequences of our actions.

Researchers and health-care practitioners have expressed concern that the recent emphasis on weight status and prevention of excessive weight gain among youth may have unintended adverse effects on youth's weight-related behaviors and outcomes (Harris, 1983; O'Dea, 2005; Orbach, 2006). Potential unintended adverse consequences include increases in unhealthy weight-control behaviors, body dissatisfaction, and further stigmatization of overweight youth. In addition to adversely affecting the physical and psychological health of youth, these potential adverse consequences also, ironically, have the potential to reduce the effectiveness of obesity prevention efforts.

Increase in Dieting and Unhealthy Weight Control Behaviors

By emphasizing weight status and encouraging weight loss, obesity prevention efforts may result in youth engaging in dieting or unhealthy weight control behaviors, such as skipping meals or using laxatives, in an attempt to lose weight. Evidence that well-intentioned prevention interventions may adversely affect dieting behaviors of youth is suggested by a recent study examining the impact of sending health report cards to parents of elementary school children. Chomitz, Collins, Kim, Kramer, and McGowan (2003) found that among parents who received a health card report informing them that their child was overweight, 19% reported that they planned to put their child on a diet. In contrast, only 9% of these parents reported that they planned to serve five servings of fruit and vegetables to their children.

Dieting and unhealthy weight-control behaviors have potentially serious consequences for the physical, psychological, and social well-being of youth. Physical symptoms associated with dieting behaviors among youth include fatigue, growth deceleration, and amenorrhea in girls (Dietz & Hartung, 1985; Johnson & Whitaker, 1992; Pugliese, Lifshitz, Grad, Fort, & Marks-Katz, 1983; Selzer, Caust, Hibbert, Bowes, & Patton, 1996). Dieting and unhealthy weight-control behaviors among youth have also been associated with inadequate intakes of essential nutrients (Crawley & Shergill-Bonner, 1995; Gibbons, Wertheim, Paxton, Petrovich, & Szmukler, 1995; Neumark-Sztainer, Story, Dixon, Resnick, & Blum, 1997; Story, Neumark-Sztainer, Sherwood, Stang, & Murray, 1998). Mental and psychological symptoms associated with dieting and unhealthy weight-control behaviors include anxiety, depression, and mental sluggishness (Grant, Lyons, Landis, & Cho, 1999; Siegel, Yancey, Aneshensel, & Schuler, 1999; Stice, Hayward, Cameron, Killen, & Taylor, 2000).

In addition to adversely affecting the well-being of youth, dieting and unhealthy weight control behaviors also have implications for eating disorder risk. Numerous longitudinal studies of adolescents have found that self-reported dieting is associated with an increased risk of disordered eating behavior (Field, Camargo, Taylor, Berkey, & Colditz, 1999; Killen et al.,

1996) and subthreshold eating disorders (Leon, Fulkerson, Perry, Keel, & Klump, 1999; Patton, Johnson-Sabine, Wood, Mann, & Wakeling, 1990).

The possible impact of obesity prevention interventions inadvertently increasing the use of dieting behaviors may also have the seemingly contradictory effect of placing youth at greater risk for weight gain over time. As discussed in chapter 8, several large, observational studies have shown that dieting predicts weight gain among adolescents (Field et al., 2003; Neumark-Sztainer, Wall, et al., 2006; Stice & Agras, 1999). The largest of these three prospective studies followed 8,203 girls and 6,769 boys over 3 years and found that adolescents who reported dieting at baseline gained more weight than nondieters, adjusting for baseline body mass index (BMI), pubertal development, dietary intake, and physical activity/inactivity (Field et al., 2003). Engaging in unhealthy weight-control behaviors has been found to increase risk for weight gain over time. In one large prospective study, adolescents who reported using unhealthy weight-control behaviors at baseline were approximately three times more likely to be overweight 5 years later compared with those who did not report using these behaviors (Neumark-Sztainer, Wall, et al., 2006).

One potential explanation of this seemingly contradictory association between dieting and weight gain is that engaging in behaviors that involve severe caloric restrictions may lead to periods of overeating or binge eating (Stice, 2001; Stice, Presnell, Shaw, & Rohde, 2005). This cycle of restriction and overeating would likely result in a net caloric gain that could lead to weight gain. A related explanation is that dieting is adopted as a short-term behavior in lieu of long-term behavior change. For example, a teenage girl may "go on a diet to lose weight for prom" and then "go off her diet" once the date has passed. For long-term weight management it would be more effective to integrate fruits and vegetables, breakfast, and physical activity into her lifestyle. Another proposed mechanism is that dietary restrictions lead to an increase in metabolic efficiency. Therefore, those who have restricted caloric intake for a certain period of time may alter their metabolism such that they require fewer calories to maintain their weight (Klesges, Isbell, & Klesges, 1992). An important aim of obesity prevention efforts should be to help children and adolescents avoid ineffective and possibly harmful dieting behavior. Instead, youth should be provided with the skills and support to engage in sustained healthy eating and physical activity.

Increase in Body Dissatisfaction

Obesity prevention efforts that focus excessively on weight have the potential to lead to increased body dissatisfaction among youth. Body dissatisfaction during early adolescence (i.e., age 10–14 years), a critical period of identity formation, is of concern in that body image and a more global self-image tend to be closely intertwined (Keery, van den Berg, & Thompson,

2004). Longitudinal analyses have shown that low levels of body satisfaction during key developmental periods of adolescence are predictive of later signs of more global mental distress including lower self-esteem and depressive symptoms (Holsen, Kraft, & Roysamb, 2001; Johnson & Wardle, 2005; Stice & Bearman, 2001).

An increase in body dissatisfaction could also place youth at increased risk for the development of eating disorders. Two recent meta-analytic reviews examining the evidence for a range of putative risk and maintenance factors for eating pathology, body dissatisfaction emerged as one of the most consistent and potent risk factors for disordered eating behaviors among youth (Jacobi, Hayward, de Zwaan, Kraemer, & Agras, 2004; Stice, 2002).

Although study findings are not definitive, body dissatisfaction has also been found to be predictive of behaviors that can lead to obesity. Recent results from a large, prospective study of adolescents found that increased body dissatisfaction at baseline predicted increased dieting, unhealthy weight control behaviors, binge eating, and decreased physical activity and fruit and vegetable intake. After controlling for BMI, many of these relationships remained (Neumark-Sztainer, Paxton, Hannan, Haines, & Story, 2006). As evidenced by the previous discussion, outcomes such as dieting and increased unhealthy weight-control behaviors can increase risk for obesity. This research provides preliminary evidence that body dissatisfaction does not successfully motivate adolescents to engage in behaviors with benefits for long-term weight management. On the contrary, if obesity prevention interventions increase body dissatisfaction among youth, these findings suggest that they may be less effective in their obesity prevention efforts. An important challenge facing researchers and public health practitioners is to develop interventions that simultaneously help children and adolescents appreciate and feel good about their bodies, while also taking steps toward making their bodies healthier through changes in their physical activity and eating behaviors.

Further Stigmatization and Weight-Related Teasing

Studies show that overweight children are at higher risk for weight stigmatization including becoming victims of weight-related teasing (Neumark-Sztainer et al., 2002; Neumark-Sztainer, Story, & Faibisch, 1998). Weight-related teasing has been found to be associated with lower levels of body dissatisfaction, low self-esteem, anxiety, depressive symptoms, and suicidal behavior (Eisenberg, Neumark-Sztainer, & Story, 2003; Fabian & Thompson, 1989; Grilo, Wilfley, Brownell, & Rodin, 1994; Roth, Coles, & Heimberg, 2002).

Interventions that inadvertently lead to increased stigma and weight-related teasing could potentially lead to greater use of unhealthy weight control behaviors among affected youth. Weight-related teasing has been found to be associated with higher levels of disordered eating behaviors among adolescents in cross-sectional as well as prospective studies (e.g., Cattarin & Thompson, 1994; Haines, Neumark-Sztainer, Eisenberg, & Hannan, 2006; Wertheim, Koerner, & Paxton, 2001).

Additionally, weight-related teasing is associated with behaviors that may lead to increased weight gain among youth. A large, cross-sectional survey of adolescents found that, among overweight adolescents, those who experienced weight-related teasing had two times the odds of binge eating as compared with youth who did not report being teased (Neumark-Sztainer et al., 2002). Longitudinally, weight-related teasing is predictive of binge eating among adolescent boys and girls after adjustment for age, race/ethnicity, and socioeconomic status (Haines et al., 2006). Being teased about one's weight has also been identified by youth as a barrier to engaging in physical activity (Bauer, Yang, & Austin, 2004; O'Dea, 2003). The finding that weight-related teasing may be associated with increased levels of binge eating and decreased physical activity among youth suggests that obesity prevention interventions may be counterproductive if they inadvertently lead to increased weight-related teasing among youth. Thus, care needs to be taken when developing obesity prevention interventions to ensure that overweight children and adolescents are not stigmatized. Furthermore, it may be appropriate to provide participants with skills for dealing with weight-related mistreatment when it does occur.

RECOMMENDATIONS FOR A MORE INTEGRATED APPROACH

As evidenced by this review, child and adolescent obesity prevention efforts could adversely affect youth by increasing their risk for body dissatisfaction, unhealthy weight-control behaviors, and use of behaviors (e.g., binge eating) that are antithetical to the programs' goals of weight loss and maintenance. Thus, in order for the interventions to be as effective as possible while avoiding potentially dangerous outcomes, obesity prevention programs aimed at youth should ensure that their messages (a) improve participants' body satisfaction (or at least not lower their body satisfaction); (b) do not lead participants to engage in short-term dieting practices or various unhealthy weight control behaviors; and (c) do not further stigmatize youth based on their weight status. Programs that are able to avoid these unintended adverse outcomes while promoting the adoption of healthy eating and physical activity will likely be successful in helping youth achieve a healthy BMI and develop lifelong healthy habits.

Two important steps that researchers and practitioners can take to ensure the development of such programs are to (a) explicitly integrate messages that improve body satisfaction and that reduce dieting and weight-related stigmatization; and (b) measure the impact of the prevention effort on these potentially adverse outcomes. By designing interventions that take these steps into account, it is hoped that adolescents will lose or maintain their weight without engaging in unhealthy behaviors. Additionally, using this integrated approach may have the secondary benefit of providing some protection against the development of eating disorders given that body dissatisfaction, dieting and unhealthy weight-control behaviors are known risk factors for anorexia nervosa, bulimia nervosa, and binge eating disorder. Evaluating the impact that obesity prevention interventions have on participants' body dissatisfaction, dieting behaviors, and level of weight-related teasing can help to ensure that the prevention strategies and messages are not causing harm. Process evaluation measures are important given that early attempts at interventions using this integrated approach will likely need to be modified to determine the messages and strategies that can most effectively address factors of relevance for both obesity and prevention of eating disorders.

OBESITY PREVENTION INTERVENTIONS

Some preliminary evidence exists that programs addressing factors of relevance to a broad spectrum of weight-related disorders including obesity, eating disorders, and disordered eating, can be effective both at preventing obesity and supporting healthy weight-control behaviors. In this section we present two examples of obesity prevention interventions that measured the impact of their programming on changes in body satisfaction, and dieting or unhealthy weight-control behaviors, the Stanford Girls Health Enrichment Multi-site Studies (GEMS) pilot study and Planet Health. Chapter 11 discussed additional interventions that have shown success in preventing obesity while encouraging body satisfaction.

The Stanford GEMS pilot study aimed to test an afterschool and family-based obesity prevention intervention with Black girls aged 8 to 10 years. The girls participated in an afterschool dance class that was fun and culturally appropriate. Additionally, individual sessions were conducted with the girls' families to help them reduce time in front of the television. The messages provided to the girls and their families focused on increasing girls' time participating in fun and healthy activities and did not make reference to the girls' weight or to weight-loss and maintenance being the goal of the intervention (Robinson et al., 2003).

Because Black women generally report higher body satisfaction than women from other racial groups, the researchers felt it was important to monitor the participants' weight concerns, desired body shape, and self-esteem throughout the study. Although this was a pilot study to test the feasibility and acceptability of the program, positive changes were seen in girls' level of body satisfaction and weight concerns, compared with girls in the control condition. Girls also reported liking physical activity more, trying more physical activities, decreasing television use, and eating fewer meals in front of the television. Finally, although the findings were not significant, at follow-up, girls in the treatment group tended to have lower BMI than those in the control group (Robinson et al., 2003).

Outcomes of the Stanford GEMS pilot study suggest that by helping girls and their families increase their activity levels and decrease their sedentary behavior time using enjoyable, culturally appropriate methods that did not focus on weight or weight loss, girls can lose weight and decrease factors that put them at risk for disordered eating behaviors. Additionally, this pilot study intervened on multiple levels of the girls' environment, at their school, with their peers, and at home with their families, effectively reinforcing messages throughout the girls' days (Robinson et al., 2003).

Planet Health is a middle school-based intervention program designed to prevent obesity by increasing students' energy expenditure and promoting several healthy dietary habits. Implemented in four ethnically diverse communities in Massachusetts, *Planet Health* was comprised of activities designed to improve dietary quality, increase physical activity and reduce television time. The activities were integrated into students' academic and physical education classes. As with the Stanford GEMS intervention, *Planet Health* did not involve discussions about students' weight status or indicate to the students within the curricula that the goal of the intervention was to decrease weight. The intervention was specifically designed to work on a population level and did not target overweight students. This was done so all students would engage in behaviors to prevent obesity and the risk of stigma against overweight students would be reduced (Gortmaker et al., 1999).

Planet Health was successful in reducing the prevalence of obesity among female participants, although no difference was seen among boys participating in the intervention compared with those in the control schools. Further analysis revealed that decreases in sedentary behavior accompanying the intervention mediated weight loss among the girls (Gortmaker et al., 1999).

Austin et al. (2005) evaluated the impact of *Planet Health* on two extreme weight-control behaviors, self-induced vomiting and diet pill use among girls. At the end of the intervention, girls who had participated in *Planet Health* were 60% less likely to report self-induced vomiting or diet pill use compared with girls in the control schools. It was estimated that 59% of these extreme weight-control behaviors among girls in the control schools could have been prevented if those girls had participated in *Planet Health*. It has been hypothesized that *Planet Health* was successful in reducing extreme weight-control behaviors among the girls because it focused on healthy and sustainable ways of eating and being active.

NEW MOVES

We are currently in the process of refining and evaluating an obesity prevention program for adolescent girls that integrates principles from both the eating disorder and obesity prevention fields. New Moves, a school-based intervention for girls who are at risk for overweight, integrates messages of obesity prevention with improving body satisfaction, and avoiding dieting and unhealthy weight-control behaviors. Initial findings demonstrated that the program was well received by adolescent girls, their parents, and school staff. However, findings also indicated a need for a more intensive, multi-component intervention and a more comprehensive evaluation in order to detect a change in behavioral and physical outcomes (Neumark-Sztainer, Story, Hannan, & Rex, 2003).

The revised New Moves has eight behavioral objectives for girls participating in the intervention, with the ultimate goal of helping girls maintain a healthy weight. The eight objectives are as follows:

1. Aim to be physically active at least 1 hour each day.
2. Limit television/video watching to no more than 1 hour a day.
3. Eat at least five servings of fruits and vegetables each day.
4. Choose water or low-calorie drinks instead of soda or sweetened beverages.
5. Eat breakfast every day.
6. Pay attention to portion size and to your body's signs of hunger and fullness.
7. Avoid unhealthy weight-control practices.
8. Focus on your positive traits.

To achieve these objectives, the intervention is delivered primarily during a girls-only physical education class. During class time, girls participate in three of the intervention's components, including:

1. physical activity lessons that focus on life-long activity within a noncompetitive environment;
2. nutrition education sessions that stress a nondieting approach to healthy weight management; and
3. social support sessions that focus on enhancing self-esteem and body image.

There are four additional components of New Moves designed to complement the skills gained during the classroom components. These are:

1. Individual counseling sessions with New Moves staff to help girls identify any barriers to health behavior change and discuss means of reducing such barriers using motivational enhancement techniques.
2. Weekly maintenance sessions that include activities designed to reinforce New Moves messages.
3. Parental outreach via postcards highlighting the New Moves messages and that include ways parents can be supportive of their daughter's behavior change goals. Additionally, parents are invited to an informal get-together to meet the study investigator, hear about study highlights, and participate in activities promoting healthy eating and physical activity.
4. Staff training to introduce school staff involved in delivering the program to the goals of New Moves.

Through the combined action of these seven components, New Moves aims to modify girls' self-perceptions, eating and physical activity behaviors, and body composition, by intervening at the individual, peer, familial, and school levels of the ecological framework.

CONCLUSIONS

The outcomes of the Stanford GEMS Pilot Study, *Planet Health*, and the initial New Moves program, suggest that it is possible to work toward obesity prevention by helping youth engage in weight-management behaviors while supporting a positive body image and discouraging extreme weight-loss behaviors. These interventions also support the premise that obesity prevention interventions can avoid increased stigma against overweight children and adolescents through the use of population-based or targeted interventions that include sensitive and appropriate messages.

In order to enhance the effectiveness of obesity prevention interventions using an integrated view of the predictors' weight-related outcomes, the ecological model can used to guide areas for future efforts. Within each of the levels of influence, interventions can be implemented to encourage obesity prevention while also improving body satisfaction, and decreasing unhealthy weight-control behaviors and stigma. Table 12.1 illuminates potential interventions at each of the ecological levels. Building from these suggestions, future obesity prevention interventions can likely curb the trend of increasing obesity prevalence among children and adolescents.

TABLE 12.1
Examples of Strategies for Obesity Prevention at the Individual, Family, Peer, School/Institutional, Community, and Society Levels

Individual level	Discourage use of unhealthy weight-control behaviors by providing youth with skills and support to engage in regular physical activity and make healthy food choices.
	Provide opportunities for youth to learn about and challenge sociocultural ideals of body size and shape.
	Educate youth about the advertising process and provide them with skills to critically analyze the media/advertising they consume.
	Provide individual counseling on healthy eating, physical activity, and positive body image in a sensitive and nonstigmatizing manner.
Family level	Within clinical settings, provide parents written materials promoting healthy eating and physical activity. Materials can be provided in the waiting room and as part of routine pediatric care.
	Offer parent groups as an add-on component to school-based programs and address topics such as "Weight–Doing not Talking" or "Making Family Meals a Reality in Your Home."
	Work with parents of young children to help them establish family routines around eating and physical activity to prevent excessive weight gain. Examples include limiting TV viewing and eating fast foods, and providing family meals and active time together.
Peer level	Work with peer groups to reduce the level of body comparison, negative body talk, and weight-related teasing.
	Provide youth with opportunities to be physically active within their peer groups as a way to influence norms regarding physical activity and the level of support for these behaviors.
School/institutional level	Implement institutional policies and programs that
	prohibit weight-based teasing among youth;
	provide high-quality breakfast, lunch, and snacks to all youth;
	remove non-nutritive snack foods and sweetened beverages;
	require instruction on weight stigmatization and healthy weight management for school/program staff;
	only allows media that promotes healthy behaviors, as well as healthy and diverse body sizes and shapes; and
	provide noncompetitive, enjoyable physical activities for all youth regardless of their skill level.

Community level	Provide well-maintained, safe spaces where youth can be physically active.
	Include weight tolerance when implementing community programs to increase tolerance of individual differences.
	Pressure media outlets to stop stigmatizing overweight individuals in advertising and in various television shows.
Society level	Provide federal funding to public health departments for mass media campaigns that discourage the use of unhealthy dieting practices and promote healthful eating and regular physical activity.
	Restrict advertising of high-calorie, low-nutrient foods on television shows commonly watched by children or provide equal time for messages promoting healthy eating and regular physical activity, as well as messages that discourage the use of unhealthy dieting.
	Modify zoning requirements to designate areas as pedestrian walkways or bike paths and modify neighborhoods to promote pedestrian traffic.
	Provide tax incentives to encourage food outlets (e.g., supermarkets, convenience stores) to provide healthy food choices.

REFERENCES

Addessi, E., Galloway, A. T., Visalberghi, E., & Birch, L. L. (2005). Specific social influences on the acceptance of novel foods in 2-5-year-old children. *Appetite*, *45*(3), 264–271.

Austin, S. B., Melly, S. J., Sanchez, B. N., Patel, A., Buka, S., & Gortmaker, S. L. (2005). Clustering of fast-food restaurants around schools: A novel application of spatial statistics to the study of food environments. *American Journal of Public Health*, *95*(9), 1575–1581.

Bauer, K. W., Patel, A., Prokop, L. A., & Austin, S. B. (2006). Swimming upstream: Faculty and staff members from urban middle schools in low-income communities describe their experience implementing nutrition and physical activity initiatives. *Preventing Chronic Disease*, *3*(2), A37.

Bauer, K. W., Yang, Y. W., & Austin, S. B. (2004). "How can we stay healthy when you're throwing all of this in front of us?" Findings from focus groups and interviews in middle schools on environmental influences on nutrition and physical activity. *Health Education and Behavior*, *31*(1), 34–46.

Boon, C. S., & Clydesdale, F. M. (2005). A review of childhood and adolescent obesity interventions. *Critical Reviews in Food Science and Nutrition*, *45*(7–8), 511–525.

Campbell, K. J., Crawford, D. A., & Ball, K. (2006). Family food environment and dietary behaviors likely to promote fatness in 5–6 year-old children [Electronic Version]. *International Journal of Obesity*, *30*(8), 1272–1280.

Cattarin, J., & Thompson, J. K. (1994). A three-year longitudinal study of body image, eating disturbance, and general psychological functioning in adolescent females. *Eating Disorders: The Journal of Treatment and Prevention, 2*(2), 114–125.

Chomitz, V. R., Collins, J., Kim, J., Kramer, E., & McGowan, R. (2003). Promoting healthy weight among elementary school children via a health report card approach. *Archives of Pediatrics and Adolescent Medicine, 157*(8), 765–772.

Contento, I. R., Williams, S. S., Michela, J. L., & Franklin, A. B. (2006). Understanding the food choice process of adolescents in the context of family and friends. *Journal of Adolescent Health, 38*(5), 575–582.

Crawley, H., & Shergill-Bonner, R. (1995). The nutrient and food intakes of 16–17 year old female dieters in the UK. *Journal of Human Nutrition, 8*, 25–34.

Davis, S. M., Going, S. B., Helitzer, D. L., Teufel, N. I., Snyder, P., Gittelsohn, J., et al. (1999). Pathways: A culturally appropriate obesity-prevention program for American Indian schoolchildren. *American Journal of Clinical Nutrition, 69*(4), 796S–802S.

Dietz, W. H., Jr., & Hartung, R. (1985). Changes in height velocity of obese pre-adolescents during weight reduction. *American Journal of Diseases of Children, 139*(7), 705–707.

Eisenberg, M. E., Neumark-Sztainer, D., & Story, M. (2003). Associations of weight-based teasing and emotional well-being among adolescents. *Archives of Pediatrics and Adolescent Medicine, 157*, 733–738.

Eisenberg, M. E., Neumark-Sztainer, D., Story, M., & Perry, C. (2005). The role of social norms and friends' influences on unhealthy weight-control behaviors among adolescent girls. *Social Science and Medicine, 60*, 1165–1173.

Fabian, L. J., & Thompson, J. K. (1989). Body image and eating disturbance in young females. *International Journal of Eating Disorders, 8*(1), 63–74.

Field, A. E., Austin, S. B., Taylor, C. B., Malspeis, S., Rosner, B., Rockett, H. R., et al. (2003). Relation between dieting and weight change among preadolescents and adolescents. *Pediatrics, 112*(4), 900–906.

Field, A. E., Camargo, C. A., Jr., Taylor, C. B., Berkey, C. S., & Colditz, G. A. (1999). Relation of peer and media influences to the development of purging behaviors among preadolescent and adolescent girls. *Archives of Pediatric & Adolescent Medicine, 153*(11), 1184–1189.

Gibbons, K. L., Wertheim, E. H., Paxton, S. J., Petrovich, J., & Szmukler, G. I. (1995). Nutrient intake of adolescents and its relationship to desire for thinness, weight loss behaviours, and bulimic tendencies. *Australian Journal of Nutrition and Dietetics, 52*, 69–74.

Gortmaker, S. L., Peterson, K., Wiecha, J., Sobol, A. M., Dixit, S., Fox, M. K., et al. (1999). Reducing obesity via a school-based interdisciplinary intervention among youth: Planet Health. *Archives of Pediatrics and Adolescent Medicine, 153*(4), 409–418.

Grant, K., Lyons, A., Landis, D., & Cho, M. H. (1999). Gender, body image, and depressive symptoms among low-income African American adolescents. *Journal of Social Issues, 55*(2), 299–316.

Grilo, C. M., Wilfley, D. E., Brownell, K. D., & Rodin, J. (1994). Teasing, body image, and self-esteem in a clinical sample of obese women. *Addictive Behaviors, 19*(4), 443–450.

Grimm, G. C., Harnack, L., & Story, M. (2004). Factors associated with soft drink consumption in school-aged children. *Journal of the American Dietetic Association, 104*(8), 1244–1249.

Haines, J., Neumark-Sztainer, D., Eisenberg, M. E., & Hannan, P. J. (2006). Weight-teasing and disordered eating behaviors in adolescents: Longitudinal findings from Project EAT (Eating Among Teens). *Pediatrics, 117*, e209–215.

Hanson, N. I., Neumark-Sztainer, D., Eisenberg, M. E., Story, M., & Wall, M. (2005). Associations between parental report of the home food environment and adolescent intakes of fruits, vegetables, and dairy foods. *Public Health Nutrition, 8*, 77–85.

Harris, M. B. (1983). Educating students about obesity: An ounce of prevention, a pound of cure, and a ton of prejudice. *Health Education, 14*(4), 44–46.

Holsen, I., Kraft, P., & Roysamb, E. (2001). The relationship between body image and depressed mood in adolescence: A 5-year longitudinal panel study. *Journal of Health Psychology, 6*, 613–627.

Irving, L. M., & Neumark-Sztainer, D. (2002). Integrating primary prevention of eating disorders and obesity: Feasible or futile? *Preventive Medicine, 34*(3), 299–309.

Jacobi, C., Hayward, C., de Zwaan, M., Kraemer, H. C., & Agras, W. S. (2004). Coming to terms with risk factors for eating disorders: Application of risk terminology and suggestions for a general taxonomy. *Psychological Bulletin, 130*(1), 19–65.

Johnson, F., & Wardle, J. (2005). Dietary restraint, body dissatisfaction, and psychological distress: A prospective analysis. *Journal of Abnormal Psychology, 114*, 119–125.

Johnson, J., & Whitaker, A. H. (1992). Adolescent smoking, weight changes, and binge–purge behavior: Associations with secondary amenorrhea. *American Journal of Public Health, 82*(1), 47–54.

Jolliffe, D. (2004). Extent of overweight among US children and adolescents from 1971 to 2000. *International Journal of Obesity and Related Metabolic Disorders, 28*(1), 4–9.

Keery, H., van den Berg, P., & Thompson, J. K. (2004). An evaluation of the tripartite influence model of body dissatisfaction and eating disturbance with adolescent girls. *Body Image, 1*, 237–251.

Killen, J. D., Taylor, C. B., Hayward, C., Haydel, K. F., Wilson, D. M., Hammer, L., et al. (1996). Weight concerns influence the development of eating disorders: A 4-year prospective study. *Journal of Consulting and Clinical Psychology, 64*(5), 936–940.

Klesges, R. C., Isbell, T. R., & Klesges, L. M. (1992). Relationship between dietary restraint, energy intake, physical activity, and body weight: A prospective analysis. *Journal of Abnormal Psychology, 101*(4), 668–674.

Kubik, M. Y., Lytle, L. A., & Story, M. (2005). Schoolwide food practices are associated with body mass index in middle school students. *Archives of Pediatrics and Adolescent Medicine, 159*(12), 1111–1114.

Leon, G. R., Fulkerson, J. A., Perry, C. L., Keel, P. K., & Klump, K. L. (1999). Three to four year prospective evaluation of personality and behavioral risk factors for later disordered eating in adolescent girls and boys. *Journal of Youth and Adolescence, 28*, 181–196.

Lobstein, T., & Dibb, S. (2005). Evidence of a possible link between obesogenic food advertising and child overweight. *Obesity Reviews, 6*(3), 203–208.

McLeroy, K. R., Bibeau, D., Steckler, A., & Glanz, K. (1988). An ecological perspective on health promotion programs. *Health Education Quarterly, 15*(4), 351–377.

Neumark-Sztainer, D. (2005). *"I'm, like, so fat!" Helping your teen make healthy choices about eating and exercise in a weight-obsessed world.* New York: Guilford Press.

Neumark-Sztainer, D., Falkner, N., Story, M., Perry, C., Hannan, P. J., & Mulert, S. (2002). Weight-teasing among adolescents: Correlations with weight status and disordered eating behaviors. *International Journal of Obesity and Related Metabolic Disorders, 26*(1), 123–131.

Neumark-Sztainer, D., Paxton, S. J., Hannan, P. J., Haines, J., & Story, M. (2006). Does body satisfaction matter? Five-year longitudinal associations between body satisfaction and health behaviors in adolescent females and males. *Journal of Adolescent Health, 39*(2), 244–251.

Neumark-Sztainer, D., Story, M., Dixon, L. B., Resnick, M., & Blum, R. (1997). Correlates of inadequate consumption of dairy products among adolescents. *Journal of Nutrition Education, 29,* 12–20.

Neumark-Sztainer, D., Story, M., & Faibisch, L. (1998). Perceived stigmatization among overweight African-American and Caucasian adolescent girls. *Journal of Adolescent Health, 23*(5), 264–270.

Neumark-Sztainer, D., Story, M., Hannan, P. J., & Rex, J. (2003). New Moves: A school-based obesity prevention program for adolescent girls. *Preventive Medicine, 37,* 41–51.

Neumark-Sztainer, D., Wall, M., Guo, J., Story, M., Haines, J., & Eisenberg, M. (2006). Obesity, disordered eating, and eating disorders in a longitudinal study of adolescents: How do dieters fare five years later? *Journal of the American Dietetic Association, 106,* 559–568.

O'Dea J. A. (2003). Why do kids eat healthful food? Perceived benefits of and barriers to healthful eating and physical activity among children and adolescents. *Journal of the American Dietetic Association, 103*(4), 497–501.

O'Dea, J. A. (2005). Prevention of child obesity: "First, do no harm". *Health Education Research, 20*(2), 259–265.

Orbach, S. (2006). Commentary: There is a public health crisis—its not fat on the body but fat in the mind and the fat of profits. *International Journal of Epidemiology, 35*(1), 67–69.

Patton, G. C., Johnson-Sabine, E., Wood, K., Mann, A. H., & Wakeling, A. (1990). Abnormal eating attitudes in London schoolgirls—a prospective epidemiological study: Outcome at twelve month follow-up. *Psychological Medicine, 20*(2), 383–394.

Pugliese, M. T., Lifshitz, F., Grad, G., Fort, P., & Marks-Katz, M. (1983). Fear of obesity: A cause of short stature and delayed puberty. *New England Journal of Medicine, 309*(9), 513–518.

Robinson, T. N., Killen, J. D., Kraemer, H. C., Wilson, D. M., Matheson, D. M., Haskell, W. L., et al. (2003). Dance and reducing television viewing to prevent weight gain in African-American girls: The Stanford GEMS pilot study. *Ethnicity and Disease, 13*(1 Suppl. 1), S65–S77.

Roth, D. A., Coles, M. E., & Heimberg, R. G. (2002). The relationship between memories for childhood teasing and anxiety and depression in adulthood. *Journal of Anxiety Disorders, 16*(2), 149–164.

Sallis, J. F., & Glanz, K. (2006). The role of built environments in physical activity, eating, and obesity in childhood. *Future of Children, 16*(1), 89–108.

Sallis, J. F., & Owen, N. (1997). Ecological models. In K. Glanz, F. M. Lewis, & B. K. Rimer (Eds.), *Health behavior and health education: Theory, research and practice* (2nd ed., pp. 403–424). San Francisco: Jossey-Bass.

Selzer, R., Cause, J., Hibbert, M., Bowes, G., & Patton, G. (1996). The association between secondary amenorrhea and common eating disordered weight control practices in an adolescent population. *Journal of Adolescent Health, 19*, 56–61.

Siegel, J. M., Yancey, A. K., Aneshensel, C. S., & Schuler, R. (1999). Body image, perceived pubertal timing, and adolescent mental health. *Journal of Adolescent Health, 25*(2), 155–165.

Stice, E. (2001). A prospective test of the dual-pathway model of bulimic pathology: Mediating effects of dieting and negative affect. *Journal of Abnormal Psychology, 110*(1), 124–135.

Stice, E. (2002). Risk and maintenance factors for eating pathology: A meta-analytic review. *Psychological Bulletin, 128*(5), 825–848.

Stice, E., & Agras, W. S. (1999). Subtyping bulimic women along dietary restraint and negative affect dimensions. *Journal of Consulting & Clinical Psychology, 67*(4), 460–469.

Stice, E., & Bearman, S. K. (2001). Body-image and eating disturbances prospectively predict increases in depressive symptoms in adolescent girls: A growth curve analysis. *Developmental Psychology, 37*(5), 597–607.

Stice, E., Hayward, C., Cameron, R. P., Killen, J. D., & Taylor, C. B. (2000). Body-image and eating disturbances predict onset of depression among female adolescents: A longitudinal study. *Journal of Abnormal Psychology, 109*(3), 438–444.

Stice, E., Presnell, K., Shaw, H., & Rohde, P. (2005). Psychological and behavioral risk factors for obesity onset in adolescent girls: A prospective study. *Journal of Consulting & Clinical Psychology, 73*(2), 195–202.

Story, M., Kaphingst, K. M., & French, S. (2006). The role of schools in obesity prevention. *The Future of Children, 16*(1), 109–142.

Story, M., Neumark-Sztainer, D., & French, S. (2002). Individual and environmental influences on adolescent eating behaviors. *Journal of the American Dietetic Association, 102*, S40–51.

Story, M., Neumark-Sztainer, D., Sherwood, N., Stang, J., & Murray, D. (1998). Dieting status and its relationship to eating and physical activity behaviors in a representative sample of U.S. adolescents. *Journal of the American Dietetic Association, 98*(10), 1127–1135.

Summerbell, C. D., Waters, E., Edmunds, L. D., Kelly, S., Brown, T., & Campbell, K. J. (2005). Interventions for preventing obesity in children. *Cochrane Database Syst Rev (3)* (pp. CD001871).

Wertheim, E., Koerner, J., & Paxton, S. J. (2001). Longitudinal predictors of restrictive eating and bulimic tendencies in three different age groups of adolescent girls. *Journal of Youth and Adolescence, 30*(1), 69–81.

13

TREATMENT OF EATING DISORDERS IN CHILDHOOD AND ADOLESCENCE

STEFFANIE SPERRY, MEGAN ROEHRIG, AND J. KEVIN THOMPSON

Since the 2001 publication of the first edition of this volume, there has been a substantial increase in research attention devoted to the treatment of children and adolescents with eating disorders. Two dominant approaches, family-based treatment and cognitive–behavioral therapy, have emerged as the strategies that are receiving the most empirical evaluation and practical dissemination. In this chapter, we initially review the key elements and empirical evidence for each treatment, followed by an overview of the essential components of these two approaches. Finally, we provide an overview of other issues pertinent to the treatment of eating disorders in youth, including: inpatient and outpatient treatment, developmental considerations, the context of treatment, compliance issues, comorbidity, and pharmacological treatments.

KEY ELEMENTS OF TREATMENT

Family-Based Treatment for Anorexia Nervosa and Bulimia Nervosa

Family-based treatment (FBT) is a highly symptom-focused approach with weight restoration and abstinence from binging and purging being its primary goals for treatment of anorexia nervosa (AN) and bulimia nervosa (BN), respectively (Lock, le Grange, Agras, & Dare, 2001; le Grange & Lock, 2007). FBT takes an agnostic view on the etiology of the eating disorder and uses parents as the principal facilitators of change. The entire family is encouraged to participate in treatment, and parents are initially put in charge of their child's eating and weight (much like a nurse in an inpatient unit would be). As symptoms improve, the focus of treatment shifts to teaching adolescents how to maintain these improvements and gain control over their own eating and weight. The last phase of treatment focuses on addressing typical developmental issues (e.g., autonomy) that have likely been stunted due to the eating disorder.

Cognitive–Behavioral Therapy for Bulimia Nervosa

Cognitive–behavioral therapy (CBT) for BN is an active treatment approach that emphasizes the modification of maladaptive cognitions and behaviors that maintain the disorder (Fairburn, Marcus, & Wilson, 1993; Gore, Vander Wal, & Thelen, 2001; Pike, Devlin, & Loeb, 2004). The initial goals of CBT include the introduction of the cognitive model of BN and the establishment of a regular eating pattern. Once a relatively normal eating pattern has been instated and the frequency of binge and purge episodes has been reduced, treatment focuses on the identification and modification of maladaptive thought patterns that proliferate the disorder. The final goal of CBT for BN is relapse prevention and the maintenance of change after treatment. Although the number of sessions devoted to each phase of treatment is not crucial, the process is additive and treatment techniques should be introduced in order (Fairburn et al., 1993).

TWO EMERGENT TREATMENTS FOR EATING DISORDERS IN YOUTH

Family-Based Treatment for Eating Disorder

FBT for eating disorders has been studied most frequently in AN, and the Maudsley approach is the most promising intervention for adolescent AN to date (Eisler et al., 1997; Lock & le Grange, 2005; Russell, Szmuckler, Dare, & Eisler, 1987). Five, small randomized controlled trials (RCTs) of variations of the Maudsley approach have been published supporting the efficacy of FBT with adolescents with AN (Eisler et al., 2000; le Grange, Eisler, Dare, & Russell, 1992; Lock, Agras, Bryson, & Kraemer, 2005; Robin, Siegel, Koepke, Moye, & Tice, 1994; Robin et al., 1999) (see Table 13.1 for details on these studies). A preliminary case series study also suggests the Maudsley approach can successfully improve weight and eating-disordered cognitions in 9- to 12-year olds with AN (Lock, le Grange, Forsberg, & Hewell, 2006). The National Institute for Health and Clinical Excellence (NICE) guidelines for treatment of child and adolescent AN reflect these research findings and recommend FBT as the preferred treatment of choice (NICE, 2004).

le Grange and Lock (2007) adapted the Maudsley approach to the treatment of adolescent BN based on preliminary case series research supporting the efficacy of family-based approaches (see le Grange & Schmidt, 2005, for review). In addition, two RCTs of FBT in adolescent BN and girls with subthreshold BN provide partial support for the efficacy of FBT (le Grange, Crosby, Rathouz, & Leventhal, 2007; Schmidt et al., 2007). In an RCT comparing FBT and individual supportive psychotherapy, FBT was found to produce greater abstinence from binging and purging than the supportive psychotherapy condition at post-treatment and 6-month follow-up (le Grange et al., 2007). In contrast, a controlled comparison of FBT and CBT that was administered in a guided self-help format found that CBT produced higher rates of abstinence from binge eating at post-treatment than FBT (41.9% vs. 25%, respectively; Schmidt et al., 2007); however, the treatments were equivalent at the 6-month follow-up with binge-eating abstinence rates of 55% for FBT and 52% for CBT guided self-help. No differences in purging abstinence emerged between the two treatment groups at either assessment point.

Research on the Maudsley approach has many of the same methodological limitations as other eating disorder treatment studies, including small sample sizes and high attrition rates (le Grange & Lock, 2005). Treatment manuals have been published for the application of the Maudsley approach to the treatment of adolescent AN (Lock et al., 2001) and BN (le Grange & Lock, 2007). These manuals will be important in standardizing research protocols across trials and also in helping clinicians implement outpatient FBT for adolescents with eating disorders. The following sections provide a brief overview of the Maudsley approach as well as the three phases of treatment for both AN and BN (see Lock et al., 2001; le Grange & Lock, 2007, for more extensive guidelines).

Maudsley Approach to the Treatment of AN

FBT considers parents to be a resource in the treatment of adolescent patients with AN and takes an agnostic view of the etiology of the disorder.

TABLE 13.1
Summary of Treatment Outcome Studies

Author, date	Participants	Diagnoses	Purpose	Major findings
FBT Studies				
Russell, Szmukler, Dare, & Eisler (1987); Eisler et al. (1997)	Adolescents (N = 21)	AN	RCT of conjoint FBT vs. individual therapy	End of Treatment Outcome (% Good or Intermediate on Morgan-Russell): Conjoint FBT: 90% Individual Therapy: 18 % 5-Year Follow-Up: Conjoint FBT: 90% Individual Therapy: 54%
le Grange et al. (1992)	Adolescents (N = 18)	AN	RCT of conjoint FBT vs. separated FBT	End of Treatment Outcome (% Good or Intermediate on Morgan-Russell): Conjoint FBT: 70% Separated FBT: 90%
Robin et al. (1999)	Adolescents (N = 37)	AN	RCT of conjoint FBT vs. ego-oriented individual therapy (EOIT)	End of Treatment Outcome (% Good or Intermediate): Conjoint FBT: 65% EOIT: 69% 1-Year Follow-Up: Conjoint FBT: 80% EOIT: 93%
Eisler et al. (2000)	Adolescents (N = 40)	AN	RCT of conjoint FBT vs. separated FBT	End of Treatment Outcome (% Good or Intermediate on Morgan-Russell): Conjoint FBT: 47% Separated FBT: 76 %

Study	Sample	Diagnosis	Design/Focus	Results
Lock, Agras, Bryson, & Kraemer (2005); Lock, Couturier, & Agras (2006)	Adolescents (N = 86)	AN	RCT of short-course (6 mo) or long-course (12 mo) of FBT	Equivalent improvements between short- & long-course on BMI, EDE Global, or EDE subscales over course of treatment Moderators of outcome: Long-course > short-course for: • Those from non-intact families • Those with higher Yale Brown Cornell Eating Disorder Scale scores Follow-Up Outcome (M = 3.96 years) 89% of P's were >90% ideal body weight 74% of P's were within normal limits of all EDE scales No differences between short- & long-course on BMI, EDE Global, EDE subscales
Lock, Couturier, Bryson, & Agras (2006)	Adolescents (N = 86)	AN	Predictors of drop-outs and remission in FBT	Drop-out rates 12-month > 6-month; OR = 1.14 Co-morbidity > No Co-morbidity; OR = .85 Remission at 12 months Co-morbidity < No Co-morbidity; OR = -.76 Early weight gain > No early response psych functioning at 6-mo > no improvements
Lock, le Grange, Forsberg, & Hewell (2006)	Children & Adol (N = 110)	AN or EDNOS/R	FBT outcome in children vs. adolescents	• No significant differences between children and adolescents in response to FBT • Clinically significant weight gain in both adolescents and children (6.9 kg vs 6.8 kg, respectively) • Significant improvements on all EDE scales in both children and adolescents

TABLE 13.1
Summary of Treatment Outcome Studies

Author, date	Participants	Diagnoses	Purpose	Major findings
le Grange, Crosby, Rathouz, & Leventhal (2007)	Adolescents ages 12–19 (N = 80)	BN or EDNOS/BN	RCT of FBT vs. supportive therapy	Binge-purge abstinence rates: Post-treatment: • FBT (39%) vs. SPT (18%) p = .049 6-month follow-up: • FBT (29%) vs. SPT (10%). p = .05
CBT Studies				
Schapman-Williams, Lock, & Couturier (2006)	Female Adolescents (N = 7) Age: M = 16.29	BN or EDNOS	Case series of CBT for binge eating and purging in adolescents	Pre-Post Differences: 90%: reduction of binge/purge symptoms 57%: abstinent from binge eating 71%: abstinent from purging 57% abstinent from binging and purging Significant reductions in all EDE scales
Lock (2005)	Female Adolescents (N = 34) Age: M = 15.8	BN	Case series of CBT for BN in adolescents	Pre-Post Differences: 78%: reduction of binge/purge symptoms 56%: abstinent from binge/purge symptoms
FBT vs. CBT Studies				
Schmidt et al. (2007)	Female Adolescents (N = 85); Ages 13–20	BN or EDNOS/ BN	RCT of FBT vs. CBT, guided self-help	Post-Treatment: Binge abstinence: CBT (41.9%) > FBT (25%) Purging abstinence: CBT (32.3%) = FBT (28%) 6-Month Follow-Up: Binge abstinence: CBT (52%) = FBT (55%) Purging abstinence: CBT (56%) = FBT (51.7%)

According to Lock et al. (2001), the Maudsley approach assumes that the adolescent is embedded in the family and that it is essential to involve the parents in treatment by having them take charge of the eating disorder, which has taken control of the AN adolescent. The eating disorder has halted typical adolescent development, and the adolescent with AN is viewed as regressed. Weight restoration is the primary goal of therapy, and family members are instructed to put other conflicts and issues on hold until the eating disorder is resolved. Once this has been achieved, control should be returned to the adolescent, and the remainder of therapy can then focus on typical developmental issues of adolescence with the family. The Maudsley treatment of AN typically lasts about 1 year and consists of three phases, although recent findings have demonstrated equivalent outcomes between short-term (6 months) and long-term therapy (1 year) at the end of treatment and follow-up (Lock, Agras, Bryson, & Kraemer, 2005; Lock, Couturier, & Agras, 2006).

Phase 1. Refeeding the patient is the sole focus of Phase 1. A family meal is conducted early on in treatment to provide direct observation of the family dynamics surrounding food and meals. The parents are encouraged to refeed their child in a unified manner, and the therapist is nondirective on how this goal should be achieved. Parents are encouraged to generate their own solutions for refeeding their child, and the therapist aims to provide support and encouragement by telling them that they know how to help their child best. Enhancing the bond between the parental and sibling subsystems is also a large component of the first phase of therapy, and the therapist strives to reduce any guilt or blame that the family feels over the eating disorder. Phase 1 typically lasts approximately 3 to 5 months and is conducted on a weekly basis typically during a 50- to 60-minute session.

Phase 2. The second phase of the Maudsley approach begins after the patient has begun regaining weight, and the family is in less crisis over the eating disorder. The goal of Phase 2 is to restore the patient's physical health and begin to return control of eating and weight back to the adolescent. Symptoms of eating disorders remain a central component of therapy; however, other family issues related to the eating disorder and adolescent development can now be reviewed and discussed. Phase 2 sessions are conducted every 2 to 3 weeks, and can be concluded when (a) the adolescent's weight is stable and between 90% and 100% of ideal body weight; (b) the adolescent is eating regular meals without supervision; (c) the family can discuss noneating-disordered adolescent development issues; and (d) the patient has increased peer relationships.

Phase 3. The goal of Phase 3 is to address more general family and adolescent issues and to develop healthy parent–adolescent relationships in which eating-disordered patterns are not the basis of interaction. Each family is unique and issues discussed will vary from family to family. Typical topics include increased autonomy for the adolescent, establishing appropriate intergenerational family boundaries, sexuality, and future challenges associated with leaving home for college or work. This phase is brief, and only a few major themes can be addressed. Monthly sessions are generally advised.

Maudsley Approach to the Treatment of Adolescent BN

The Maudsley approach assumptions—(a) parents are an asset to treatment, (b) the eating disorder has taken control of the adolescent, and (c) parents are not to blame for the eating disorder—are also applied to the treatment of adolescent BN. Although much of the treatment protocol for FBT of AN can be applied directly to the treatment of adolescent BN, le Grange and Lock (2007) highlighted important differences in clinical presentations of AN and BN that require adaptation and flexibility in the Maudsley treatment of adolescent BN. First, given the ego-dystonic nature of BN (as opposed to the ego-syntonic nature of AN), the adolescent is asked to take a more active role in collaborating with his or her parents in their efforts against the eating disorder. Furthermore, adolescents with BN likely experience significant shame and guilt surrounding the binging and purging behaviors (as opposed to little shame experienced by patients with AN), and the therapist should make efforts to help reduce these feelings.

Second, adolescents with BN may be less regressed developmentally than their counterparts with AN, and adolescent issues such as peer pressure, romantic relationships, sexuality, and experimentation with drugs and/or alcohol may arise throughout treatment, posing challenges to the therapist and the family to stay focused on the eating disorder. Similarly, adolescents with BN frequently have serious comorbidities and/or suicidal or self-injurious behavior that may become severe enough to warrant immediate attention during treatment.

FBT for adolescent BN consists of three phases over a period of 6 months. Phase 1 occurs weekly for approximately 10 sessions, and the primary goal is to reestablish healthy eating patterns by helping the parents and the adolescent find ways to disrupt binging, excessive dietary restraint, and purging behaviors. The primary goal of Phase 2 is to transfer the eating control back to the adolescent once her eating has been normalized. Identification of adolescent development issues that may be related to the BN is also a goal of this phase of treatment. Phase 2 typically occurs between sessions 11 and 16, and sessions are held every other week. Phase 3 begins once there is abstinence from all binging and purging symptoms. The goal of Phase 3 is to address more general adolescent issues, including personal autonomy and family boundaries, and termination of treatment. Sessions 17 to 20 are allotted for Phase 3, and it is recommended to hold these sessions on a monthly basis.

Cognitive–Behavioral Therapy for Bulimia Nervosa

CBT has received substantial support as an effective treatment approach and is considered the intervention of choice for adults with BN (NICE, 2004). Numerous RCTs and systematic reviews have endorsed the advantages of CBT over placebo or waiting-list controls in terms of abstinence rates and clinically significant reductions in binging and purging (Wilson & Fairburn, 2002). Overall, it can be concluded that a specific form of CBT that focuses on modifying weight- and shape-related cognitions and abnormal eating behaviors is the most effective treatment for adult BN (Fairburn & Harrison, 2003).

Notably, there is considerable evidence to suggest that fluoxetine, a selective serotonin reuptake inhibitor (SSRI), can decrease binge and purge episodes and improve mood in adults with BN in the short-term (Berkman et al., 2006). Additionally, dialectical behavior therapy has received modest support in the treatment of adults with BN (Fairburn & Harrison, 2003), and forms of interpersonal therapy have led to decreases in bulimic symptoms, although symptom reduction is comparatively slower than that reported with CBT (Tantleff-Dunn, Gokee-LaRose, & Peterson, 2004). Although other psychological and pharmacological treatments have shown varying degrees of effectiveness in decreasing bulimic symptoms, CBT has received the most empirical support in treating adults with BN, and recent attention has focused on the adaptation of CBT for use with adolescents.

In light of the research base supporting the efficacy of CBT with adult patients with BN, Gowers and Bryant-Waugh (2004) proposed several reasons why extrapolating from the adult research is warranted. First, adolescence is a developmental stage that is not defined solely by age, and many young adults with eating disorders (as well as some young adults without an eating disorder) are struggling with the challenges typically confronted in adolescence. It is also suggested that the primary features of AN and BN are consistent from adolescence to early adulthood and many of the adult trials have included adolescents in their samples. Finally, the treatments receiving the most empirical support for adult clients with eating disorders are effective in treating adolescents with other disorders (e.g., CBT for adolescents with depression), and are therefore not developmentally inappropriate for that age group.

Fairburn et al. (1993) created one of the most widely used and empirically supported CBT manuals for adults with BN. They suggested a three-stage treatment program consisting of 20 sessions occurring over the course of approximately 6 months. Stage 1 is focused on the normalization of eating patterns. Stage 2 targets the correction of distorted cognitions, and Stage 3 is comprised primarily of relapse-prevention techniques and anticipatory problem solving. Most efficacy studies have shown a complete remission rate of approximately 40% for individuals who completed the CBT treatment with overall reduction in binge eating and purging occurring in approximately 80% of study participants (Wilson & Fairburn, 2002).

Lock (2005) adapted the Fairburn et al. (1993) manual for use with adolescents. None of the suggested modifications alters the fundamental features of CBT as designed for adults. Consistent with the original version, the adolescent CBT approach consists of approximately 20 sessions over a 6-month period. Preliminary studies have supported the effectiveness of the modified CBT protocol with adolescent clinical samples suggesting that the approach led to significant reductions in the behavioral, cognitive, and emotional characteristics of BN (Lock, 2005; Schapman-Williams, Lock, & Couturier, 2006). Additionally, in a recent RCT comparing individual guided self-help CBT versus FBT for adolescents with BN or eating disorder not otherwise specified, patients in the CBT group achieved a greater binge-abstinence rate at post-treatment than their FBT counterparts, and comparable purge-abstinence rates were reported at post-treatment and at a 12-month follow-up (Schmidt et al., 2007; see Table 13.1 for details regarding studies and specific findings).

The following is a specific overview of the three treatment phases along with the suggested modifications for adolescent clients (see Lock, 2005, for more extensive guidelines).

Stage 1. Stage 1 of the adolescent protocol consists of approximately 10 sessions. Consistent with the adult approach, this initial phase of treatment aims to introduce the client to the therapy process, establish therapist–client rapport, normalize eating habits, and decrease binge frequency via self-monitoring and engagement in alternative behaviors. Several adjustments to the adult CBT approach are suggested for the adolescent client with BN to address potential motivational and developmental barriers commonly seen in this age group. The modifications are as follows:

- Additional time is spent assessing the adolescent client's motivation to change.
- Special attention is given to the establishment of rapport and collaboration in treatment.
- Psychoeducation on the physical and psychological aspects and consequences of BN is provided in a clear and often repetitive manner.
- A comprehensible explanation of the therapeutic process and the cognitive–behavioral view of BN are provided.
- The therapist should acknowledge the environmental contexts in which the adolescent client is operating and should express interest in the client's experiences (e.g., family, friends, school).
- The therapist should spend extra time explaining the importance of self-monitoring.

Parental support and involvement is often needed if not essential to improve treatment outcome.

Stage 2. Stage 2 of adolescent CBT consists of approximately seven or eight sessions. This stage aims to maintain or progress toward a normalized eating pattern and to explain the role of feared foods in proliferating the disorder. The client, often with the help of parents, is slowly reintroduced to previously avoided foods. Cognitive restructuring and problem-solving techniques are also introduced during Stage 2 to address common binge triggers. Some of the primary adolescent protocol adjustments for this stage of treatment are listed here:

- Extra time should be spent helping the adolescent to identify, label, and process her emotional states, especially surrounding binge–purge episodes.
- The therapist generally needs to take on an active role in the cognitive-restructuring process.
- Problem solving with the adolescent is more direct, requires less judgment, and is practical.
- The therapist should consider the adolescent's limited independence when prescribing behavioral experiments and may find it necessary to more actively facilitate such experiences.
- Parents are usually a great resource in the problem-solving process and can be effective behavioral experiment facilitators.

Stage 3. The remaining sessions comprise Stage 3 of the adjusted CBT protocol. The primary goal of this stage is relapse prevention and the maintenance of positive change following termination. The client is prepared for possible setbacks and is provided effective ways of coping with stressors or triggers in order to prevent or disrupt a relapse episode. Important considerations when working through Stage 3 with an adolescent client are summarized here:

- The therapist should discuss the potential for relapse in ways that are directly relevant to the adolescent by targeting specific developmental challenges likely to be faced by the client (e.g., going away to college).
- In preparation for termination, the therapist should recognize the possibility for a wide range of client responses to the cessation of treatment. A strong attachment is often formed between an adolescent client and the therapist. On the other hand, some adolescent clients are ready to get on with their lives by the end of treatment and may appear indifferent to the prospect of termination.
- It is often helpful for the therapist to remain available for future contact by the client or the client's family.

EFFICACY OF CBT AND FT TREATMENTS: SUMMARY

Researchers have been very active in evaluating the efficacy of the above two strategies for the treatment of eating disorders (Lock & le Grange, 2005; see Table 13.1). However, it is very difficult to conduct RCTs of these treatments, given the difficulty of recruiting a large enough sample size of young individuals with AN or BN for meaningful treatment comparisons. To date, five RCTs using the Maudsley approach or recent variations for AN (FBT) have been completed and two more are ongoing (Lock & le Grange, 2005). Two RCTs also evaluated the efficacy of FBT for BN in adolescents. Although sample sizes have often been small, the results have generally been encouraging. Additionally, CBT is showing promising results for the treatment of adolescent BN and has been evaluated in two recent case series and an RCT of a guided self-help version of CBT (Lock, 2005; Schapman-Williams et al., 2006; Schmidt et al., 2007).

However, some critics have suggested that the optimism associated with the findings in treatments of childhood and adolescent eating disorders outstrips the actual data (Fairburn, 2005). Specifically, there are few studies on which to base any decision regarding efficacy and the studies conducted thus far were performed by a limited number of research groups. Part of the problem is that there is currently no agreed upon definition of remission of symptoms for younger patients (Couturier & Lock, 2006). Additionally, most of the research in the area is being conducted by a very small number of research groups, so the generalizability of the findings to other locales and evaluation teams has not been demonstrated.

ISSUES IN THE TREATMENT OF EATING DISORDERS IN YOUTH

There are a variety of important issues to consider when treating an eating disturbance in younger individuals. These are considered below.

Inpatient and Outpatient Treatment

The NICE (2004) guidelines note that the majority of patients with eating disorders can be treated on an outpatient basis with adequate psychological and physical management provided. Patients requiring inpatient care are generally those with concomitant physiological or psychological problems (Nicholls & Bryant-Waugh, 2003). Patients who are unstable and present with syncopal episodes, cardiac arrhythmias, severe fluid and electrolyte imbalances, severe dehydration, extreme fatigue, or continued weight loss, should be considered for inpatient treatment as a first course of action (Hill & Pomeroy, 2001). Without such intervention, development and growth may be affected and damage may be permanent (Katzman, 2005; Sokol et al., 2005).

Developmental Considerations

Children, adolescents, and adults with eating disorders may present with different clinical features. A comparison of adolescent and adult patients found that adolescents had greater denial, less desire for help, and report a shorter period of more rapid weight loss; whereas adults were more likely to engage in binge eating and laxative use and report a prior use of psychiatric medication and therapy (Fisher, Schneider, Burns, Symons, & Mandel, 2001). Similarly, recent research has revealed several important differences in clinical presentation between adolescents and prepubertal children. Peebles, Wilson, and Lock (2006) found that children in a treatment-seeking sample were less likely to binge, purge, or use laxatives or diuretics, more likely to be boys, have a faster rate of weight loss, and a shorter duration of illness than adolescents.

Developmental issues should also inform the use and reliance on diagnostic criteria. For instance, variability in the rate, timing, and degree of growth during normal puberty makes application of the weight criterion for AN very difficult (Robin, Gilroy, & Dennis, 1998). Substantiating the presence of an intense fear of gaining weight and body image disturbance are also problematic, as these symptoms are often dependent on a developmentally achieved level of cognitive functioning and abstract reasoning (Robin et al., 1998; chap. 2, this volume). This issue certainly has relevance for the CBT approach, wherein a certain level of cognitive development may be necessary to engage in cognitive strategies.

Cognitive functioning is also an issue in treatment planning; it is important to ascertain that the patient's cognitive abilities are at a level to handle the therapeutic strategies (in particular, cognitive therapies). We suggest that developmental considerations be taken into account before treating any adolescent or child with an eating disorder. It is normal for young individuals (and older adults, for that matter) to have limited abstract reasoning and goal-setting abilities, and a careful understanding of developmental changes is essential for the delineation of an effective treatment plan (Lock, 2005).

Finally, it may be important to include an assessment of relevant peer, parental, and media influences for consideration as potential topics to add to the standardized treatment protocols. Research strongly suggests that peer and parental pressures, manifested in appearance-related comments and modeling of body image concern, are strongly connected to levels of body image and eating disturbances in adolescence (e.g., Keery, van den Berg, & Thompson, 2004; Shroff & Thompson, 2006). Additionally, media pressures and the images and messages that connote the desirability of an unrealistic appearance ideal that are present in many forms of media (including the Internet), should be considered as potential treatment topics (Harper, Sperry, & Thompson, 2008; Levine & Harrison, 2004).

Family Issues

Regardless of the therapeutic approach that will be used to treat the patient, it is almost always important to enlist the entire family, including siblings, in the treatment process by sharing information, facilitating communication, and helping with the behavioral management plan (NICE, 2004). Parents are often overwhelmed by guilt or frustrated by the lack of control they have over their child's behavior. The clinician should emphasize to parents that their role in their child's recovery is essential (Lask, 2000) and that they should not blame themselves for the patient's problems. (Of course, if an assessment reveals that, indeed, parents perhaps did have a role in the onset or perpetuation of the child's problems, this should be considered as integral to the therapy intervention.)

Alliance With Patient

The therapeutic alliance with an adult who has an eating disorder is very important and the situation is even more critical when the patient is a child or adolescent (Constantino, Arnow, Blasey, & Agras, 2005; Pereira, Lock, & Oggins, 2006). It is common for the patient to be guarded with the therapist and to minimize problems. In order to enhance the relationship, the initial interview might begin with open-ended, general questions about family, school, interests, and friends (Lock et al., 2001). Questions could then proceed into problems related to eating and weight. Young patients may want to discuss other issues in their lives (i.e, school, friends, dating) and this should be encouraged. Lock (2005) recommended spending extra time on alliance-building by expressing interest in the adolescent's perspective and experiences. Pereira et al. (2006) found that a strong early therapy alliance with the child was associated with higher weight gain. Additionally, a stronger alliance with the parents prevented dropout and higher overall weight gain for the patient.

Compliance

Self-monitoring is a large component of CBT and young patients may not comply with this homework for a variety of reasons, including difficulty understanding how to complete the task, embarrassment of their eating patterns, fear that others will see the log, lack of time, or trouble labeling their experiences. Lock (2005) recommended that the therapist spend extra time in early sessions completing the food record together (if not completed outside of session) and stressing the importance of self-monitoring. Parents can be a help in increasing compliance, especially in tasks such as food shopping, meal planning, meal monitoring, and in helping the patient follow the prescribed eating routine. Poor academic performance or issues at school may emerge and the therapist may need to become involved with the school in order to make special arrangements for missed classes or the timing of meals (Lock, 2005).

Part of the compliance problem may emanate from the resistance and denial that are common in young patients (Couturier & Lock, 2006). Motivational interviewing may be one approach for increasing motivation in adolescents with eating disorders, and may even be sufficient to induce behavioral change in a subset of patients (Gowers & Smyth, 2004; Wilson & Schlam, 2004). This is a strategy used prior to active treatment, designed to engage the individual in dialogue regarding their readiness for treatment and motivation for active engagement in treatment procedures.

Comorbidity

As is the case with adults, comorbidity is a prime concern when treating eating disorders in young patients. When such co-occurring problems as depression, anxiety disorders, or other conditions occur, it is important to consider the best available treatments and integrate the strategies into the ongoing eating disorder-related treatment protocol. Lock, Couturier, Bryson, and Agras (2006) found that comorbid psychiatric disorder was predictive of treatment dropout and remission of adolescents receiving family therapy.

Pharmacological Treatments

To date, no pharmacological treatment has been supported as a first-line form of treatment for eating disorders in youth (NICE, 2004). Notably, however, the use of fluoxetine in adults with BN has resulted in significant decreases in core bulimic symptomatology and improved mood (Berkman et al., 2006). There may also be an indication for the consideration of medication in the case of comorbidity. For instance, anti-anxiety or anti-depressant medications may be considered when such comorbid conditions are interfering with participation in the psychological treatments. However, it is important to consider the physical status of the individual and it is not recommended that individuals at a very low weight be prescribed drugs that might compromise metabolic or cardiac functioning (NICE, 2004).

SUMMARY AND CONCLUSIONS

We are still at a very early stage in knowing just what types of treatments are effective for children and adolescents. Recent work has provided a solid foundation for further work in the area, which was missing from the field only a few short years ago. Strategies are now available in the form of CBT and FBT that appear to be beneficial in improving symptomatology, at least from an analysis of the few RCTs and the case series that have been published. Although much has yet to be ascertained about the best available treatments for the specific presentations of eating disorders in youth, future work in this area is rapidly accelerating and, hopefully, by the time of the publication of the third edition of this book, the information available will vastly exceed what we now know.

REFERENCES

Berkman, N. D., Bulik, C. M., Brownley, K. A., Lohr, K. N., Sedway, J. A., Rooks, A., & Gartlehner, G. (2006). Management of eating disorders. *Evidence Report Technology Assessment, 135,* 1–166.

Consantino, M. J., Arnow, B. A., Blasey, C., & Agras, W. S. (2005). The association between patient characteristics and the therapeutic alliance in cognitive-behavioral and interpersonal therapy for bulimia nervosa. *Journal of Consulting and Clinical Psychology, 73,* 203–211.

Couturier, J., & Lock, J. (2006). What is recovery in adolescent anorexia nervosa? *International Journal of Eating Disorders, 39*(7), 550–555.

Eisler, I., Dare, C., Hodes, M., Russell, G., Dodge, E., & le Grange, D. (2000). Family therapy for adolescent anorexia nervosa: The results of a controlled comparison of two family interventions. *Journal of Child Psychology and Psychiatry, 41,* 727–736.

Eisler, I., Dare, C., Russell, G., Szmukler, G., le Grange, D., & Dodge, E. (1997). A five-year follow-up of a controlled trial of family therapy in severe eating disorders. *Archives of General Psychiatry, 54,* 1025–1030.

Fairburn, C. G. (2005). Evidence-based treatment of anorexia nervosa. *International Journal of Eating Disorders, 37*(Suppl.), S26–S30.

Fairburn, C. G., & Harrison, P. J. (2003). Eating disorders. *The Lancet, 361,* 407–416.

Fairburn, C. G., Marcus, M. D., & Wilson, G. T. (1993). Cognitive-behavioral therapy for binge eating and bulimia nervosa: A comprehensive treatment manual. In C. G. Fairburn & G. T. Wilson (Eds.), *Binge eating: Nature, assessment, and treatment* (pp. 361–404). New York: Guilford Press.

Fisher, M., Schneider, M., Burns, J., Symons, H., & Mandel, F. S. (2001). Differences between adolescents and young adults at presentation to an eating disorders program. *Journal of Adolescent Health, 28,* 222–227.

Gore, S. A., Vander Wal, J. S., & Thelen, M. H. (2001). Treatment of eating disorders in children and adolescents. In J. K. Thompson & L. Smolak (Eds.), *Body image, eating disorders, and obesity in youth: Assessment, prevention, and treatment* (pp. 293–312). Washington, DC: American Psychological Association.

Gowers, S., & Bryant-Waugh, R. (2004). Management of child and adolescent eating disorders: The current evidence base and future directions. *Journal of Child Psychology and Psychiatry, 45*(1), 63–83.

Gowers, S. G., & Smyth, B. (2004). The impact of motivational assessment interview on initial response to treatment in adolescent anorexia nervosa. *European Eating Disorders Review, 12,* 87–93.

Harper, K., Sperry, S., & Thompson, J. K. (2008). Viewership of pro-eating disorder websites: Associations with body image and eating disturbances. *International Journal of Eating Disorders, 41*(1), 92–95.

Hill, K., & Pomeroy, C. (2001). Assessment of physical status of children and adolescents with eating disorders and obesity. In J. K. Thompson & L. Smolak (Eds.), *Body image, eating disorders, and obesity in youth: Assessment, prevention, and treatment* (pp. 171–191). Washington, DC: American Psychological Association.

Katzman, D. K. (2005). Medical complications in adolescents with anorexia nervosa: A review of the literature. *International Journal of Eating Disorders, 37*(Suppl.), S52–S59.

Keery, H., van den Berg, P., & Thompson, J. K. (2004). An evaluation of the Tripartite Influence Model of body dissatisfaction and eating disturbance with adolescent girls. *Body Image: An International Journal of Research, 1,* 237–251.

Lask, B. (2000). Aetiology. In B. Lask & R. Bryant-Waugh (Eds.), *Anorexia nervosa and related eating disorders in childhood and adolescence* (pp. 63–79). East Sussex, England: Psychology Press.

le Grange, D., Crosby, R. D., Rathouz, P. J., & Leventhal, B. L. (2007). A randomized controlled comparison of family-based treatment and supportive psychotherapy for adolescent bulimia nervosa. *Archives of General Psychiatry, 64*(9), 1049–1056.

le Grange, D., Eisler, I., Dare, C., & Russell, G. F. M. (1992). Evaluation of family treatments in adolescent anorexia nervosa: A pilot study. *International Journal of Eating Disorders, 12,* 347–357.

le Grange, D., & Lock, J. (2005). The dearth of psychological treatment studies for anorexia nervosa. *International Journal Eating Disorders, 37,* 79–91.

le Grange, D., & Lock, J. (2007). *Treating bulimia in adolescents: A family-based approach.* New York: Guilford Press.

le Grange, D., & Schmidt, U. (2005). The treatment of adolescents with bulimia nervosa. *Journal of Mental Health, 14,* 587–597.

Levine, M. P., & Harrison, K. (2004). Media's role in the perpetuation and prevention of negative body image and eating disorders. In J. K. Thompson (Ed.), *Handbook of eating disorders and obesity* (pp. 695–717). New York: Wiley.

Lock, J. (2005). Adjusting cognitive behavior therapy for adolescents with bulimia nervosa: Results of a case series. *American Journal of Psychotherapy, 59*(3), 267–281.

Lock, J., Agras, W. S., Bryson, S., & Kraemer, H. C. (2005). Short versus long-term family treatment of anorexia nervosa. *Journal of the American Academy of Child and Adolescent Psychiatry, 44,* 632–639.

Lock, J., Couturier, J., & Agras, W. S. (2006). Comparison of long term outcomes in adolescents treated with family therapy. *Journal of the American Academy of Child and Adolescent Psychiatry, 45,* 666–672.

Lock, J., Couturier, J., Bryson, S., & Agras, S. (2006). Predictors of dropout and remisssion in family therapy for adolescent anorexia nevosa in a randomized clinical trial. *International Journal of Eating Disorders, 39*(8), 639–647.

Lock, J., & le Grange, D. (2005). Family-based treatment of eating disorders. *International Journal of Eating Disorders, 37*(Suppl.), S64–S67.

Lock, J., le Grange, D., Agras, W. S., & Dare, C. (2001). *Treatment manual for anorexia nervosa: A family-based approach.* New York: Guilford Press.

Lock, J., le Grange, D., Forsberg, S., & Hewell, K. (2006). Is family therapy useful for treating children with anorexia nervosa? Results from a case series. *Journal of the American Academy of Child and Adolescent Psychiatry, 45,* 1323–1328.

National Institute for Health and Clinical Excellence. (2004). *Eating disorders: Core interventions in the treatment and management of anorexia nervosa, bulimia nervosa, and related eating disorders.* London: National Collaborating Centre for Mental Health.

Nicholls, D., & Bryant-Waugh, R. (2003). Children and young adolescents. In J. Treasure, U. Schmidt, & E. Van Furth (Eds.), *Handbook of eating disorders* (2nd ed., pp. 415–434). Chichester, England: Wiley.

Peebles, R., Wilson, J. L., & Lock, J. D. (2006). How do children with eating disorders differ from adolescents with eating disorders at initial evaluation? *Journal of Adolescent Health, 39,* 800–805.

Pereira, T., Lock, J., & Oggins, J. (2006). The role of therapeutic alliance in family therapy for adolescent anorexia nervosa. *International Journal of Eating Disorders, 39*(8), 677–684.

Pike, K. M., Devlin, M. J., & Loeb, K. L. (2004). Cognitive-behavioral therapy in the treatment of anorexia nervosa, bulimia nervosa, and binge eating disorder. In J. K. Thompson (Ed.), *Handbook of eating disorders and obesity* (pp. 130–162). Hoboken, NJ: Wiley.

Robin, A. L., Gilroy, M., & Dennis, A. B. (1998). Treatment of eating disorders in children and adolescents. *Clinical Psychology Review, 18,* 421–446.

Robin, A. L., Siegel, P. T., Koepke, T., Moye, A. W., & Tice, S. (1994). Family therapy versus individual therapy for adolescent females with anorexia nervosa. *Journal of Developmental and Behavioral Pediatrics, 15,* 111–116.

Robin, A. L., Siegel, P. T., Moye, A. W., Gilroy, M., Dennis, A. B., & Sikand, A. (1999). A controlled comparison of family versus individual therapy for adolescents with anorexia nervosa. *Journal of the American Academy of Child and Adolescent Psychiatry, 38,* 1428–1489.

Russell, G. F. M., Szmukler, G. I., Dare, C., & Eisler, I. (1987). An evaluation of family therapy in anorexia nervosa and bulimia nervosa. *Archives of General Psychiatry, 44,* 1047–1056.

Schapman-Williams, A. M., Lock, J., & Couturier, J. (2006). Cognitive-behavioral therapy for adolescents with binge eating syndromes: A case series. *International Journal of Eating Disorders, 39*(3), 252–255.

Schmidt, U., Lee, S., Beecham, J., Perkins, S., Treasure, J., Yi, I. et al., (2007). A randomized controlled trial of family therapy and cognitive behavior therapy guided self-care for adolescents with bulimia nervosa and related disorders. *American Journal of Psychiatry, 164*, 591–598.

Shroff, H., & Thompson, J. K. (2006). The Tripartite Influence Model of body image and eating disturbance: A replication with adolescent girls. *Body Image: An International Journal of Research, 3*, 17–23.

Sokol, M. S., Jackson, T. K., Selser, C. T., Nice, H. A., Christiansen, N. D., & Carroll, A. K. (2005). Review of clinical research in child and adolescent eating disorders. *Primary Psychiatry, 12*, 52–58.

Tantleff-Dunn, S., Gokee-LaRose, J., & Peterson, R. D. (2004). Interpersonal psychotherapy for the treatment of anorexia nervosa, bulimia nervosa, and binge eating disorder. In J. K. Thompson (Ed.), *Handbook of eating disorders and obesity* (pp. 163–185). New York: Wiley.

Wilson, G. T., & Fairburn, C. G. (2002). Treatments for eating disorders. In P. E. Nathan & J. M. Gorman (Eds.), *A guide to treatments that work* (pp. 559–592). New York: Oxford University Press.

Wilson, G. T., & Schlam, T. R. (2004). The transtheoretical model and motivational interviewing in the treatment of eating and weight disorders. *Clinical Psychology Review, 24*, 361–378.

14

BEHAVIORAL TREATMENT OF CHILDHOOD AND ADOLESCENT OBESITY

MYLES S. FAITH, JULIA KERNS, AND LISA DIEWALD

Childhood obesity is a major focus of attention for practitioners and public health officials and will remain so in the foreseeable future. There are several reasons for this trend. Data from the 2003 to 2004 National Health and Nutrition Examination Survey (NHANES) show that overweight increased from 7.2% to 13.9% among 2- to 5-year-olds and from 11% to 19% among 6- to 11-year-olds between 1988 and 1994 and 2003 and 2004 (overweight being defined as body mass index [BMI] values at or above the 95th percentile of the sex-specific BMI growth charts; Centers for Disease Control and Prevention, n.d.). Among 12- to 19-year-olds, overweight increased from 11% to 17.1% during the same period (Ogden et al., 2006). A second reason concerns the health complications associated with childhood obesity (Dietz, 1998), including elevated blood pressure, hyperinsulinemia and glucose intolerance, respiratory abnormalities, poor body image, and increased adulthood mortality in females. The increasing prevalence of type 2 diabetes mellitus (T2DM) in children is of particular concern because of the long-term health consequences associated with the disease. In 1990, T2DM accounted for less than 3% of new cases of diabetes among adolescents. By 2005, up to 45% of new-onset cases in adolescents were T2DM (Pinhas-Hamiel & Zeitler, 2005). Childhood obesity is also associated with metabolic syndrome, and was found to be present in approximately 1 of 10 U.S. children aged 12 to 19 years using a pediatric definition based on the Adult Treatment Panel III (de Ferranti et al., 2004). Third, as this chapter illustrates, many questions concerning treatment efficacy, strategies, and maintenance remain unanswered (Epstein, Myers, Raynor, & Saelens, 1998).

This chapter addresses current approaches to the behavioral treatment of childhood and adolescent obesity. It begins with a discussion of identifying the children who may be the most appropriate candidates for treatment, followed by an overview of the effectiveness of current behavioral interventions for childhood obesity. Data on core treatment components are then presented along with practical recommendations. Following this, potential barriers to behavioral intervention are outlined.

DETERMINING WHICH CHILDREN REQUIRE TREATMENT

Guidelines for identifying children who may benefit from treatment are available from an expert panel consensus report (Spear et al., 2007). The panel's recommendations include monitoring and addressing weight-management and healthy lifestyle measures annually in all children and teens to evaluate trends in weight and dietary intake, and to recognize and improve potentially detrimental lifestyle patterns. In contrast to prior reports, the panel recommends classifying those children exceeding the 95th percentile of BMI-for-age as obese, and those over the 85th and below the 95th percentile as overweight, replacing the former terms "overweight and "at risk for overweight" in classifying child BMI status. Given the rising prevalence of weight-related comorbidities in youth, the expert panel recommended the addition of a fourth cutoff point in BMI classification, the ">99th percentile," to provide the most appropriate treatment prescription and to better tailor the treatment intensity according to each child's needs. The following BMI values correspond to the 99th percentile for boys: 20.1 (age 5), 21.6 (age 6), 23.6 (age 7), 25.6 (age 8), 27.6 (age 9), 29.3 (age 10), 30.7 (age 11), 31.8 (age 12), 32.6 (age 13), 33.2 (age 14), 33.6 (age 15), 33.9 (age 16), 34.4 (age 17). The following BMI values correspond to the 99th percentile for girls: 21.5 (age 5), 23.0 (age 6), 24.6 (age 7), 26.4 (age 8), 28.2 (age 9), 29.9 (age 10), 31.5 (age 11), 33.1 (age 12), 34.6 (age 13), 36.0 (age 14), 37.5 (age 15), 39.1 (age 16), 40.8 (age 17).

Identifying those children and adolescents 2 to 18 years of age who are at risk is also dependent on a number of other factors, including age, physical and emotional development, presence of weight-related comorbidities, family history of cardiovascular disease and T2DM, and readiness to change. Spear et al. (2007) outlined a model that represents a strategy for identifying children and adolescents in need of intervention as well as a four-stage intervention plan, discussed later in this section. The four stages of treatment are prevention plus (PP), structured weight management (SWM), comprehensive multidisciplinary intervention (CMI), and tertiary care (TC). These stages provide a systematic and progressive plan of care for children and youth identified as overweight or obese by their primary care provider (PCP). Although the staged approach has not yet been formally evaluated, there is evidence to support the core components of each stage.

Several other indices are also available to track the growth and development of children and provide referents for childhood overweight and obesity. For example, the National Center for Health Statistics (NCHS) published revised growth charts for individuals 2 to 20 years old (refer to Figures 14.1 and 14.2). Originally developed in 1977, these charts have been used widely by pediatricians and other health professionals to gauge the developmental trajectory of individual children. In the most current release (NCHS, 2000), growth charts pertaining to the 5th, 10th, 25th, 50th, 75th, 85th, 90th, and 95th percentiles are presented for various growth parameters: weight-for-age, length-for-age, stature-for-age, weight-for-stature, head circumference-for-age, and BMI-for-age. This last category, BMI-for-age, is most pertinent for the classification of overweight and obesity. Figures 14.1 and 14.2 present BMI-for-age percentile growth charts for girls and boys.

In 2000, the first set of international guidelines for defining overweight and obesity in children and adolescents was published (Cole, Bellizzi, Flegal, & Dietz, 2000). Using data from Brazil, Great Britain, Hong Kong, Netherlands, Singapore, and the United States, growth curves were constructed for each age group to identify those BMI scores that would "project" to a BMI of 25 (i.e., overweight) or 30 (i.e., obese) at 18 years of age. Thus, they provide BMI cutoffs for overweight and obesity from age 2 to 18 by half years for males and females. Table 14.1 illustrates several gender-specific cutoffs for defining overweight and obesity in children and adolescents. Alternatively, one could use the aforementioned BMI cutoffs that were developed by Must, Dallal, and Dietz (1991) on a nationally representative U.S. sample (also see Barlow & Dietz, 1998), or most recently, the cutoff points for 99th percentile of BMI based on age and gender (see Table 3 in Spear et al., 2007) At the present time, the practical implications of using one set of criteria versus the other may be negligible.

Finally, in 2006, the World Health Organization (WHO) released new Child Growth Standards for children from birth to age 5. Using a prescriptive approach, the WHO standards include guidelines for normal child growth and development that were normalized on breastfed children. This is the first time that global normative data were provided for infants and toddlers younger than 2 years of age.

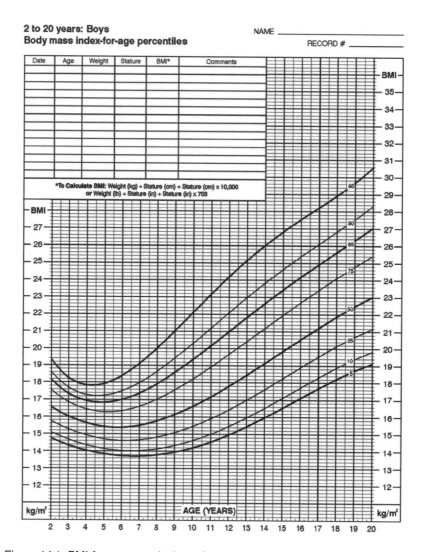

Figure 14.1. BMI-for-age growth charts for 2 to 20-year-old males. From "National Health and Nutritional Examination Survey," developed by the National Center for Health Statistics in collaberation with the National Center for Chronic Disease Prevention and Health Promotion, 2000. Retrieved from http://www.cdc.gov/growthcharts/

TREATMENT RECOMMENDATIONS

Children aged 2 to 18 with a BMI percentile between 5 and 84 are encouraged to follow standard recommendations for child overweight prevention, including a screen time limit of 1 to 2 hours daily, minimal sugar-sweetened beverage intake, promotion of physical activity, liberal fruit and vegetable consumption, portion control, regular family meals, daily breakfast consumption, removal of televisions and computers from bedrooms, and at

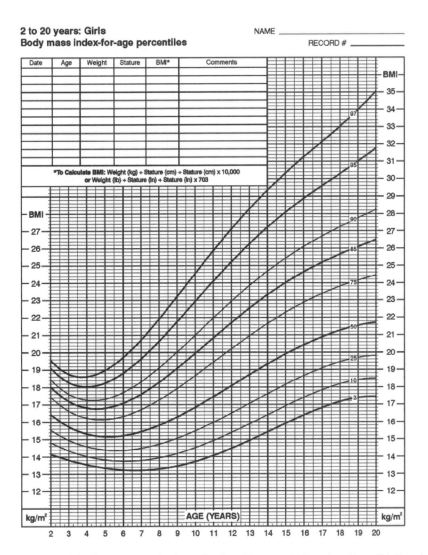

2 to 20 years: Girls
Body mass index-for-age percentiles

NAME _____

RECORD # _____

Date	Age	Weight	Stature	BMI*	Comments

*To Calculate BMI: Weight (kg) ÷ Stature (cm) ÷ Stature (cm) x 10,000
or Weight (lb) ÷ Stature (in) ÷ Stature (in) x 703

AGE (YEARS)

Figure 14.2. BMI-for-age growth charts for 2 to 20-year-old females. From "National Health and Nutritional Examination Survey," developed by the National Center for Health Statistics in collaberation with the National Center for Chronic Disease Prevention and Health Promotion, 2000. Retrieved from http://www.cdc.gov/growthcharts/

least 60 minutes of physical activity daily. Based on the expert panel recommendations, children with a BMI above the 85th percentile should be referred for Stage 1, PP care, which involves adopting the core principles outlined in standard prevention guidelines, as well as monitoring by the health care provider on a monthly basis, with a goal of gradual improvement leading to an improvement in BMI to below the 85th percentile for age.

In accordance with the expert panel recommendations, those children not responding to PP after 3 to 6 months should be referred to Stage 2,

TABLE 14.1
International Body Mass Index Cutoffs for Defining Overweight and Obesity in Children and Adolescents

Age (years)	Males		Females	
	Overweight	Obesity	Overweight	Obesity
5	17.4	19.3	17.1	19.2
6	17.6	19.8	17.3	19.7
7	17.9	20.6	17.8	20.5
8	18.4	21.6	18.3	21.6
9	19.1	22.8	19.1	22.8
10	19.8	24.0	19.9	24.1
11	20.6	25.1	20.7	25.4
12	21.2	26.0	21.7	26.7
13	21.9	26.8	22.6	27.8

Note. "Establishing a Standard Definition for Child Overweight and Obesity Worldwide: International Survey, by T. J. Cole, M. C. Bellizzi, K. M. Flegel, and W. H. Dietz, 2000, *British Medical Journal, 320,* p. 1242. Copyright 2000 by the *British Medical Journal.* Adapted with permission.

SWM for a more intense, structured eating and activity plan with greater emphasis on patient and family self-monitoring and behavior modification principles by the parent and child, under the guidance of the health care provider. Successful treatment is defined as a gradual decrease in BMI to less than the 85th percentile. Weight losses of up to 1 lb monthly for 2- to 5-year-olds and up to 2 lb per week for older children are acceptable. Lack of progress, as indicated by stable or rising BMI, should trigger the referral of the child to Stage 3, the CMI, which ideally involves a team of professionals on an obesity team. Intensive behavioral modification and more frequent monitoring by the health-care team is suggested, along with training with parent or caregiver and child for children under 12 years, consistent food and activity monitoring and goal-setting and parental training. Goals for weight loss and BMI are similar as those outlined in Stage 2.

Children and teens with a BMI falling above the 99th percentile, who have not responded positively to treatment under Stages 1 through 3, and with the presence of comorbidities, should be referred to Stage 4, TC, for assistance with meal planning and the design of an individualized plan that may include meal replacements, a very-low-calorie diet, adjunctive medication management, and/or surgery within the setting of a multidisciplinary weight-management center. Weight losses of up to 2 lb per week are encouraged and acceptable in this age group due to degree of impairment from obesity. Prior to initiating any intervention, however, the expert panel recommends assessing self-efficacy and readiness to change to best predict successful outcome.

Barriers exist that make implementation of this coordinated approach to child obesity management difficult. Poor insurance reimbursement, inadequate practitioner training and time, and few specialty obesity treatment centers, make access to appropriate treatment daunting. Because pediatric PCPs focus more heavily on acute, rather than chronic disease management, most are not equipped to provide the monitoring and behavioral counseling required to promote sustained lifestyle change. Despite these limitations, efforts are underway to better equip pediatric PCPs with the training, community resources, and referral services to improve the quality of care provided and to expand insurance reimbursement for child obesity treatment.

PARENTAL PERCEPTION OF CHILD OVERWEIGHT

Despite these guidelines, many parents of overweight children do not perceive their child to have a weight problem and, therefore, may not be inclined to make changes. Evidence to support this comes primarily from focus group studies with parents from low-income families, who were enrolled in the federal Supplemental Program for Women Infants and Children (WIC) (Baughcum, Chamberlin, Deeks, Powers, & Whitaker, 2000). For example, Baughcum, Burklow, Deeks, Powers, and Whitaker (1998) conducted focus groups with more than 600 low-income mothers of young children to assess their attitudes concerning child feeding. Results indicated three major themes including (a) long-held parental belief that a heavy child is a healthy child, (b) parental concerns that a child is not getting enough to eat, and (c) use of food by parents to influence children's behavior.

Similarly, Jain et al. (2001) reported that mothers of children who were overweight and at risk for overweight did not use the definition of child overweight based on the standard growth charts. Instead, these mothers related their children's weight status to weight-related teasing and their ability to partake in physical activity. Finally, in a survey study of 277 mothers whose perceptions about childhood obesity were assessed, 33% of the mothers of overweight or obese children reported that their child's weight was "about right" (Jeffery, Voss, Metcalf, Alba, & Wilkin, 2005).

Most clinic-based weight-control interventions have studied motivated individuals or family members who were willing to undergo time-intensive treatments. These individuals perceived obesity as a problem and were motivated to make necessary individual behavior changes. However, this may not be the case for all overweight or obese individuals in the broader population. Some people who are generally motivated to lose weight may have limited readiness to undertake the specific behavior changes required for weight loss. How these issues are negotiated on an individual-by-individual, or community-by-community, basis warrants additional research to empower family behavior change.

EFFICACY OF BEHAVIORAL TREATMENT
FOR CHILDHOOD OBESITY

Family-based behavioral treatment is the "treatment of choice" for childhood obesity, and has reliably produced the best short- and long-term treatment effects on weight (Jelalian & Saelens, 1999). Moreover, treatment of childhood obesity is associated with significant health benefits including decreases in systolic and diastolic blood pressure, better physical fitness, and improved lipid profiles. The most effective behavioral weight-control programs show promising results even at 10-year follow-up for overweight children, but not for their overweight parents despite initial weight-loss success (Epstein, Valoski, Kalarchian, & McCurley, 1995). Three indices traditionally have been used in evaluating family-based treatment outcomes: (a) change in average percent overweight, with 20% change considered the standard for a large effect (Epstein et al., 1995); as this measure accounts for changes in expected weight as a result of developmental increases in height (Epstein, Valoski, Wing, & McCurley, 1990); (b) the proportion of children maintaining large changes in percent overweight (Epstein et al., 1995); and (c) follow-up of at least 1 year or longer, as many obesity treatment programs are able to delay relapse for approximately 6 months (Wilson, 1994).

Reviews of the pediatric obesity treatment literature (Epstein et al., 1998; Haddock, Shadish, Klesges, & Stein, 1994; Jelalian & Saelens, 1999) identified 14 published studies that evaluated changes in percent overweight for at least 1 year and included some follow-up evaluation. Of these studies, three reported poor maintenance (i.e., subjects maintained less than a 10% decrease in percent overweight), eight reported moderate maintenance (i.e., subjects maintained a 10%–20% decrease in percent overweight) and only three studies reported good maintenance (i.e., subjects maintained a 20% or greater decrease in percent overweight). Among those achieving good maintenance, one treatment study by Brownell, Kelman, and Stunkard (1983) achieved an average of 20.5% change in percent overweight in the most effective treatment group for the 12 of 14 adolescents who were still available for follow-up. Another study (Epstein, Wing, Koeske, & Valoski, 1985) reported an average 20% decrease in children's percent overweight that was even maintained at 10-year follow-up (Epstein, Valoski, Wing, & McCurley, 1994).

The most effective interventions included parental involvement within the treatment program. More consistent evidence for the role of family support comes from family-based intervention studies for pediatric obesity. Reviews of this literature are provided elsewhere (Epstein et al., 1998), however there is compelling evidence that obese children lose more weight when their parents are actively involved in treatment than when they are not. Epstein et al. (1994) provided 10-year follow-up data on children who are obese and their parents who were randomly assigned to one of three family-based behavioral weight-loss interventions: (a) an intervention that targeted the parent and child together; (b) an intervention that just targeted the child; or (c) a nonspecific intervention that reinforced the families for attendance. Parents in the first group were trained actively in the behavioral change strategies (see next section) that could be applied to their children to guide them in achieving better lifestyle changes. Results indicated that 43% of the children in this group reduced their percent overweight by at least 20% (a relatively large treatment effect), in comparison to only 22% of the children in the second group and 29% of the children in the third group.

Golan, Weizman, Apter, and Fainaru (1998) compared the effects of a behavioral weight-control intervention for 6- to 11-year-old children who were obese. The intervention targeted either the parent or the obese child as the active "agent" of behavior change. Both interventions used the same behavior change principles, including self-monitoring, stimulus control, and reinforcement. After 1 year, reduction in child percent overweight was significantly greater among the intervention targeting parents (mean reduction = 14.6%) compared to the intervention targeting children (mean reduction = 8.1%). After 7 years, the superior outcome of the parent intervention group remained significant (mean reductions = 29% vs. 20.2% in the two groups, respectively, $p < 0.05$; Golan & Crow, 2004).

Most studies testing family behavioral modification programs have evaluated 8- to 12-year-old children; however, a handful of studies have tested behavioral modification in children under 8 years of age and have found comparable findings. For example, in the mid-1980s, Epstein, Wing, Woodall, et al. (1985) demonstrated the efficacy of family-based behavioral modification (FBM) compared with nutrition education for weight loss among a sample of 5- to 8-year-old children who were overweight. Children receiving FBM reduced their mean percentage overweight from 41.9% to 15.6%, whereas children receiving nutrition education showed a smaller reduction in percentage overweight from 39.2% to 28%. Aragona, Cassady, and Drabman (1975) randomly assigned 5- to 11-year-old overweight children to one of two behavioral treatment groups (response cost or response cost plus reinforcement) or to a control intervention. Mean reductions in percentage overweight were significantly greater in the two behavioral groups (–11.8% and –7.1%, respectively) compared with the control (–2.5%). Wheeler and Hess (1976) randomly assigned 2- to 10-year-old overweight children to either behavioral modification or control. The former group showed a mean reduction in percentage overweight of –4.1%, whereas the latter group showed a mean increase of +6.3%. Senediak and Spence (1985) randomly assigned 6- to 13-year-old overweight children to one of four conditions: two conditions were active behavioral treatments (rapid schedule behavior modification or gradual schedule behavior modification), one condition was attention control, and the remaining condition was no treatment control. Mean reductions in percent overweight for the two behavioral treatments were −5.3% and −13.6%, respectively, both of which were significantly greater than the mean changes for children in the attention control (−1.4%) and the no treatment control (+2.3%). Graves, Meyers, and Clark (1988) randomized 6- to 12-year-old overweight children to one of three treatments: parent problem-solving training, no parent problem-solving training, and education only. Mean reduction in child percent overweight was significantly greater for the parent problem-solving training (−11.2%) compared with the latter two treatments (−3.9% and −0.5%, respectively).

In summary, the balance of evidence supports FBM as the treatment of choice for childhood overweight. This holds true not only for 8- to 12-year old children (i.e., the most commonly studied age group), but also for younger children.

EFFICACY AND PRACTICAL RECOMMENDATIONS FOR KEY TREATMENT COMPONENTS

FBM has been extensively studied over the past three decades and as outlined earlier, is generally considered to be the "treatment of choice" for childhood overweight (Epstein et al., 1998; Faith, Fontaine, Cheskin &, Allison, 2000; Jelalian & Saelens, 1999). FBM includes a package of strategies consisting of parental skills training (Golan & Crow, 2004; Golan et al., 1998; Wrotniak, Epstein, Paluch, & Roemmich, 2004), reduced sedentary behavior and increased physical activity (Epstein, Paluch, Consalvi, Riordan, & Scholl, 2002; Epstein, Paluch, Gordy, & Dorn, 2000; Epstein, Roemmich, Paluch, & Raynor, 2005), and prescriptions for reduced energy-dense food and increased nutrient-dense food intake (Epstein et al., 2001). We discuss these components next. The most extensively studied program has been Epstein's Traffic Light, or Stoplight Diet (Epstein & Squires, 1988) that has been well supported in randomized clinical trials (Epstein et al., 1998), with treatment effects lasting up to 10 years in long-term follow up studies (Epstein et al., 1994).

We now review the components of effective FBM for childhood obesity.

Diet Modification

Research suggests that dietary modification is a powerful and necessary component for child weight loss. There are short- (Epstein, Wing, Penner, & Kress, 1985; Rocchini et al., 1988) and long-term decreases in adiposity (Epstein et al., 1994) for treatments focusing solely on dietary modification. Short-term effects for interventions lacking a dietary component are mixed (Blomquist, Borjeson, Larsson, Persson, & Sterky, 1965; Epstein, Wing, Koeske, Ossip, & Beck, 1982), but there is no evidence to date of long-term efficacy for the outcome of percent overweight among treatments lacking a dietary component.

Nutrition education/instruction alone as a dietary component of treatment appears inadequate for overweight children to incur weight loss. Behavior modification strategies, such as behavioral contracting, stimulus control, and/or a specific dietary plan, are required to help children lose weight (Coates, Jeffery, Slinkard, Killen, & Danaher, 1982; Epstein, Wing, Steranchak, Dickson, & Michelson, 1980; Johnson et al., 1997). Many different dietary components have been attempted, including moderate caloric restriction, protein-sparing modified fast, and very-low-calorie diets. Aside from differences in prescribed caloric restriction (e.g., Amador, Ramos, Morono, & Hermelo, 1990), few studies have evaluated different nutrition plans or tested particular aspects of the overall dietary component while keeping constant other treatment components (Epstein et al., 1998). In their meta-analysis, Haddock and colleagues (1994) found little evidence that any particular aspect of dietary intervention is maximally effective for inducing child weight loss. Because long-term outcomes remain unknown for some dietary modification plans, the need for controlled trials continues (e.g., Brown, Klish, Hollander, Campbell, & Forbes, 1983).

The most extensively studied dietary intervention package to date has been Epstein's Stoplight Diet (Epstein & Squires, 1988). The Stoplight Diet is a family-based nutritional "game plan" for facilitating healthy, low-fat food selections by children and adults with the aim of promoting weight control. Foods are categorized based on their relative energy and nutrient densities. "Red light foods," for example, contribute few nutrients for the calories they provide. According to Stoplight Diet principles, energy-dense red light foods, such as french fries, ice cream, and sugar-sweetened beverages should be selected infrequently because of their high-fat, sugar, and total calorie content. Although moderate in calories, "yellow light foods" are rich in nutrients and tend to be lower in fat and sugar than their red light counterparts. Consumed in recommended portion sizes, yellow light foods contribute essential nutrients and form the foundation of a well-balanced diet. "Green light foods" contain few calories yet contribute significantly to overall vitamin, mineral, and nutrient intake and are also low in sugar and fat. Liberal consumption of these foods is encouraged, and parents are advised to make these foods readily available in the home.

The Stoplight Diet effectively shifts the emphasis from calorie counting to making smarter food choices, monitoring portion sizes, and "budgeting" red light selections. Red light foods are not forbidden; the child is simply taught to select these foods infrequently (four or fewer times per week) and is encouraged to substitute green and yellow light foods for red light foods whenever possible. Parents are encouraged to gradually limit access to red light foods, and to stock the family's kitchen with more selections from the yellow and green light food lists. Although initially designed and tested on 6-

to 12-year-old children, this program may easily be taught to older children and adults as well. The flexible approach to preventing excess energy intake makes this an attractive and effective family-based plan.

In 2005, the U.S. Department of Agriculture released dietary guidelines in the form of *MyPyramid*, another tool designed to assist individuals in making healthy food and activity choices. *MyPyramid for Kids* follows the guidelines but is presented in an age-appropriate form for 6- to 11-year-olds. The recommendations include eating 1.5 and 2.5 cups of fruits and vegetables per day, respectively, making whole grains 50% of daily grain consumption and choosing lean meats that are baked, broiled, or grilled.

Researchers have begun to look beyond low-fat, energy-restricted diets for weight loss in adolescents. Alternate interventions have been created based on the glycemic index (GI) of food. The GI indicates how quickly the carbohydrate in that food will be converted to sugar in the body. Glycemic load (GL) is the amount of carbohydrate in a food multiplied by the GI of that carbohydrate. In a study comparing an energy-restricted reduced fat diet to a reduced glycemic load diet, BMI and fat mass decreased significantly more in the experimental group compared with the conventional group at 12 months (Ebbeling, Leidig, Sinclair, Hangen, & Ludwig, 2003). However, there is a paucity of studies comparing the effectiveness of varying dietary interventions in adolescents (Gibson, Peto, Warren, & dos Santos Silva, 2006). Additionally, dietary studies with adolescents vary in size, outcome measures, and length of follow-up and often are tested in combination with other lifestyle interventions (Collins, Warren, Neve, McCoy, & Stokes, 2006). In 2005, a review of 22 interventions designed to prevent obesity in children through modification of diet, physical activity, and/or lifestyle found no significant reduction in BMI in most of the interventions. The major finding was that many intervention studies involving adolescents are inadequately powered, too short in duration, fail to take into consideration participants' environment and lack thorough evaluation (Summerbell et al., 2005).

Lacking consensus, Dietz and Robinson (2005) recommended that clinicians work with the child and family to establish dietary goals that are realistic and feasible for the family. More restrictive dietary plans have been recommended only in combination with careful monitoring by a physician for severely obese adolescents or less overweight adolescents with major health complications secondary to obesity (Stallings, Archibald, Pencharz, Harrison, & Bell, 1988).

Physical Activity

In addition to diet modification, increased activity is the other hallmark component of behavior therapy for childhood obesity. This section summarizes research on physical activity prescribed as treatment and offers some practical clinical suggestions.

Physical activity appears essential to the maintenance of weight loss among adults (National Institutes of Health: National Heart, Lung, and Blood Institute, 1998), but the long-term impact of physical activity in the treatment of childhood obesity is less clear (Kohl & Hobbs, 1998). The most successful pediatric obesity programs have included a physical activity component (e.g., Epstein, Wing, Koeske, et al., 1985; Epstein et al., 1994), but physical activity components have not always augmented the effects of dietary modification (Hills & Parker, 1988; Rocchini, Katch, Schork, & Kelch, 1987). There appear to be consistent short-term effects of physical activity interventions on both children's weight status as well as their cardiorespiratory fitness (e.g., Epstein, Valoski, Vara, et al., 1995) and other cardiovascular health benefits (Rocchini et al., 1988; Sasaki, Shindo, Tanaka, Ando, & Arakawa, 1987). However, more research is needed to clarify the long-term effects on overweight children's weight status after receiving physical activity modification alone and to determine physical activity programs that maximize outcomes (Epstein & Goldfield, 1999).

Programmed exercise programs that stress planned aerobic bouts of physical activity seem to contribute to children's weight loss more significantly than lower energy expenditure calisthenics programs (Epstein, Wing, Koeske, et al., 1985; Epstein et al., 1994). Epstein and colleagues (Epstein et al., 1982; Epstein, Wing, Koeske, et al., 1985; Epstein et al., 1994) reported some success with lifestyle physical activity interventions, but few other studies have explored such approaches. Lifestyle interventions work to integrate more physical activity into daily activities, such as climbing stairs instead of taking the elevator. Recent research suggests that targeting reductions in sedentary activity (e.g., positively reinforcing decreases in television-viewing time), an innovative strategy for increasing physical activity (Epstein, Saelens, & Giancola O'Brien, 1995), can produce weight loss (Epstein, Valoski, Vara, et al., 1995; Epstein et al., 2000). There seems to be a reliable, albeit moderate, association between the sedentary activity of television watching and adiposity among children (Andersen, Crespo, Bartlett, Cheskin, & Pratt, 1998). Based on these data, one study tested a home-based exercise device designed to increase physical activity while decreasing children's television viewing. This device consists of a cycle ergometer electronically connected to a television, thus rendering television viewing fully contingent upon pedaling. When placed in the homes of children who are obese, their physical activity increased and television viewing decreased (Faith et al., 2001). Another study compared energy expenditure in children in four situations: watching television seated, playing a traditional video game seated, watching television while walking on a treadmill at 1.5 miles per hour, and playing activity-promoting video games. The activity-promoting video games included a floor dance pad (Dance Dance Revolution Ultramix 2, Konami Digital Entertainment) used as a remote control where children earn points by dancing in a particular pattern and a small USB camera (EyeToy, Sony Computer Entertainment) that "inserts" the child into the video game (Lanningham-Foster et al., 2006). All activities increased energy expenditure above resting values; however, Dance Dance Revolution and the Eyetoy resulted in the greatest increases at 108% and 172%, respectively.

Based on the Dietary Guidelines for Americans 2005, the Centers for Disease Control and Prevention recommends that children and adolescents participate in at least 1 hour of moderate intensity physical activity most days of the week, preferably daily. However, this recommendation is for the goal of long-term health promotion and no specific physical activity guidelines exist for weight loss in adults, adolescents, or children. In fact, others have recommended higher levels of physical activity for youth and the inclusion of physical activity focusing on maintaining or increasing strength as well as cardiorespiratory fitness, particularly among adolescents (Pate, Trost, & Williams, 1998). It is reasonable to assume that the level of physical activity of most overweight children is initially inadequate for weight loss and that approaches to increase duration, frequency, and ultimately intensity of physical activity are warranted.

As with dietary modification, self-monitoring of children's physical activity is a reasonable initial step in modifying their physical activity. Additionally, helping children become more cognizant of their sedentary behaviors may provide them the opportunity to consider changes in physical activity patterns. In our experience, effective strategies include identifying physical activities that can be done by the family (e.g., family hikes, bicycle rides), increasing cues for and providing access to physical activity (e.g., bringing children to the park instead of the video arcade), parental modeling of habitual physical activity, and initiating lifestyle and moderate physical activity (e.g., walking) before moving into more vigorous physical activity (e.g., running, swimming laps). Parents can be instrumental in providing opportunities, safe environments, and support for their children's physical activity, particularly when physical activity is perceived as a family health priority.

Parent Participation

Review of Empirical Literature

The benefits of parental participation in childhood and adolescent weight-loss programs has received considerable attention. Some treatments have targeted parents exclusively (Golan et al., 1998), the child or adolescent exclusively (e.g., Brownell et al., 1983; Kirschenbaum, Harris, & Tomarken, 1984), the parent and the child or adolescent seen primarily together (e.g., Wadden et al., 1990), or most commonly the parent and child or adolescent participating separately for at least part of the treatment session (e.g., Epstein, Valoski, Vara, et al., 1995). Some studies found that parental participation did not improve effects found for treating children alone, although other data suggest that treating parents alone may be more effective for inducing child weight loss (Golan et al., 1998). However, the most robust weight-control programs for prepubertal children have included at least some separate, but concurrent participation by parents (Epstein et al., 1990). Among obese adolescents, there is some evidence that parents' separate but concurrent participation is valuable (Brownell et al., 1983), but not all studies support this conclusion (Coates, Killen, & Slinkard, 1982; Wadden et al., 1990).

Clinical experience also suggests that active parent participation is an important component of children's long-term weight control. Parenting skills training is a common component of treatment (e.g., Barlow & Dietz, 1998; Epstein, Wing, Koeske, et al., 1985; Israel, Stolmaker, & Andrian, 1985), particularly focusing on increasing praise for children's healthful eating and activity choices, better control of the family eating and physical activity environment, and parental modeling. Others highlight additional parenting skills frequently taught in child and adolescent weight-control programs (Barlow & Dietz, 1998). Parental participation is likely especially necessary when young children are involved in the intervention. Barlow and Dietz (1998) and others (e.g., Satter, 2004) provided practical recommendations for parental feeding practices. Among other practices, these researchers recommended the following: Never use food as a reward; establish daily family meal and snack times; offer only healthy food options; be a role model for children; and parents or caregivers should determine what food is offered and when, and the child should decide whether to eat.

PHARMACOLOGICAL TREATMENT OF ADOLESCENT OBESITY

There have been studies examining drug treatments for adolescent obesity as an adjunct to behavioral intervention. In a randomized, double-blind trial, Berkowitz et al. (2006) compared sibutramine (an appetite suppressant) with a placebo in a study of 12- to 16-year-olds. Both groups received behavioral therapy. At 1 year, the youths given sibutramine had a statistically significant reduction in BMI compared with the placebo group. Additionally, compared with placebo, the use of sibutramine was associated with greater improvements in triglyceride levels, insulin levels, high-density lipoprotein cholesterol levels, and insulin sensitivity. In a 2005 double-blind study, subjects between 12 and 16 years of age were randomized to receive orlistat (a lipase inhibitor that reduces fat absorption) or placebo (Chanoine, Hampl, Jensen, Boldrin, & Hauptman, 2005). Both groups received behavioral therapy, prescribed caloric intake, and guidelines for physical activity.

At 1 year, the orlistat group had a significantly greater reduction in BMI, waist circumference, and body fat compared with those taking a placebo. It is worth mentioning that participants in both studies had BMIs that were two units higher than U.S. weighted mean for the 95th percentile based on age and sex. Current pharmacological treatments may be most appropriate for obese adolescents who have attempted conventional weight control programs but have not been successful.

CONCLUSIONS

Compared with the behavioral treatment of adult obesity, family-based interventions for childhood obesity have yielded much more encouraging results at short- and long-term follow-up (Epstein et al., 1998). Nonetheless, there is considerable interindividual variation in response to interventions such that not all children maintain weight loss and the needs of the heaviest children still need to be addressed. Future developments in behavioral theory, body composition measurement, and insights into the genetics of obesity are expected to enhance the development of more effective and comprehensive interventions.

REFERENCES

Amador, M., Ramos, L. T., Morono, M., & Hermelo, M. P. (1990). Growth rate reduction during energy restriction in obese adolescents. *Experimental & Clinical Endocrinology, 96*, 73–82.

Andersen, R. E., Crespo, C. J., Bartlett, S. J., Cheskin, L. J., & Pratt, M. (1998). Relationship of physical activity and television watching with body weight and level of fatness among children: Results from the third National Health and Nutrition Examination Survey. *JAMA, 279*, 938–942.

Aragona, J., Cassady, J., & Drabman, R. S. (1975). Treating overweight children through parental training and contingency contracting. *Journal of Applied Behavior Analysis, 8*, 269–278.

Barlow, S. E., & Dietz, W. H. (1998). Obesity evaluation and treatment: Expert committee recommendations. *Pediatrics, 102*(e.29). Retrieved July 31, 2008, from http://www.pediatrics.org /cgi/content/full/102/3/e29

Baughcum, A. E., Burklow, K. A., Deeks, C. M., Powers, S. W., & Whitaker, R. C. (1998). Maternal feeding practices and childhood obesity: A focus group study of low-income mothers. *Archives of Pediatrics & Adolescent Medicine, 152*(10), 1010–1014.

Baughcum, A. E., Chamberlin, L. A., Deeks, C. M., Powers, S. W., & Whitaker, R. C. (2000). Maternal perceptions of overweight preschool children. *Pediatrics, 106*(6), 1380–1386.

Berkowitz, R. I., Fujioka, K., Daniels, S. R., Hoppin, A. G., Owen, S., Perry, A. C., et al. (2006). Sibutramine Adolescent Study Group. Effects of sibutramine treatment in obese adolescents: A randomized trial. *Annals of Internal Medicine*, *145*(2), 81–90.

Blomquist, B., Borjeson, M., Larsson, Y., Persson, B., & Sterky, G. (1965). The effect of physical activity on the body measurements and work capacity of overweight boys. *Acta Paediatrica Scandinavica*, *54*, 566–572.

Brown, M. R., Klish, W. J., Hollander, J., Campbell, M. A., & Forbes, G. B. (1983). A high protein, low calorie liquid diet in the treatment of very obese adolescents: Long-term effect on lean body mass. *American Journal of Clinical Nutrition*, *38*, 20–31.

Brownell, K. D., Kelman, J. H., & Stunkard, A. J. (1983). Treatment of obese children with and without their mothers: Changes in weight and blood pressure. *Pediatrics*, *71*, 515–523.

Centers for Disease Control and Prevention. (n.d.). *Prevalence of overweight among children and adolescents: United States, 2003–2004*. Retrieved February 3, 2007, from http://www.cdc.gov/nchs/products/pubs/pubd/hestats/overweight/overwght_child_03.htm

Chanoine, J. P., Hampl, S., Jensen, C., Boldrin, M., & Hauptman, J. (2005). Effect of orlistat on weight and body composition in obese adolescents: A randomized controlled trial. *JAMA*, *293*(23), 2873–2883.

Coates, T. J., Jeffery, R. W., Slinkard, L. A., Killen, J. D., & Danaher, B. G. (1982). Frequency of contact and monetary reward in weight loss, lipid change, and blood pressure reduction with adolescents. *Behavior Therapy*, *13*(2), 175–185.

Coates, T. J., Killen, J. D., & Slinkard, L. A. (1982). Parent participation in a treatment program for overweight adolescents. *International Journal of Eating Disorders*, *1*, 37–48.

Cole, T. J., Bellizzi, M. C., Flegal, K. M., & Dietz, W. H. (2000). Establishing a standard definition for child overweight and obesity worldwide: International survey. *British Medical Journal*, *320*, 1240–1243.

Collins, C. E., Warren, J., Neve, M., McCoy, P., & Stokes, B. J. (2006). Measuring effectiveness of dietetic interventions in child obesity: A systematic review of randomized trials. *Archives of Pediatrics & Adolescent Medicine*, *160*(9), 906–922.

de Ferranti, S. D., Gauvreau, K., Ludwig, D. S., Neufeld, E. J., Newburger, J. W., & Rifai, N. (2004). Prevalence of the metabolic syndrome in American adolescents: Findings from the Third National Health and Nutrition Examination Survey. *Circulation*, *110*(16), 2494–2497.

Dietz, W. H. (1998). Health consequences of obesity in youth: Childhood predictors of adult disease. *Pediatrics*, *101*(3), 518–525.

Dietz, W. H., & Robinson, T. N. (2005). Overweight children and adolescents. *New England Journal of Medicine*, *352*(20), 2100–2109.

Ebbeling, C. B., Leidig, M. M., Sinclair, K. B., Hangen, J. P., & Ludwig, D. S. (2003). A reduced-glycemic load diet in the treatment of adolescent obesity. *Archives of Pediatrics & Adolescent Medicine*, *157*(8), 773–779.

Epstein, L. H., & Goldfield, G. S. (1999). Physical activity in the treatment of childhood overweight and obesity: Current evidence and research issues. *Medicine and Science in Sports and Exercise*, *31*, S553–559.

Epstein, L. H., Gordy, C. C., Raynor, H. A., Beddome, M., Kilanowski, C. K., & Paluch, R. A. (2001). Increasing fruit and vegetable intake and decreasing fat and sugar intake in families at risk for childhood obesity. *Obesity Research, 9*(3), 171–178.

Epstein, L. H., Myers, M. D., Raynor, H. A., & Saelens, B. E. (1998). Treatment of pediatric obesity. *Pediatrics, 101,* 554–570.

Epstein, L. H., Paluch, R. A., Consalvi, A., Riordan, K., & Scholl, T. (2002). Effects of manipulating sedentary behavior on physical activity and food intake. *Journal of Pediatrics, 140,* 334–339.

Epstein, L. H., Paluch, R. A., Gordy, C. C., & Dorn, J. (2000). Decreasing sedentary behaviors in treating pediatric obesity. *Archives of Pediatric and Adolescent Medicine, 154,* 220–226.

Epstein, L. H., Roemmich, J. N., Paluch, R. A., & Raynor, H. A. (2005). Physical activity as a substitute for sedentary behavior in youth. *Annals of Behavioral Medicine, 29,* 200–209.

Epstein, L. H., Saelens, B. E., & Giancola O'Brien, J. (1995). Effects of reinforcing increases in active behavior versus decreases in sedentary behavior for obese children. *International Journal of Behavioral Medicine, 2,* 41–50.

Epstein, L. H., & Squires, S. (1988). *The stoplight diet for children: An eight-week program for parents and children.* Boston: Little, Brown.

Epstein, L. H., Valoski, A. M., Kalarchian, M. A., & McCurley, J. (1995). Do children lose and maintain weight easier than adults: A comparison of child and parent weight changes from six months to ten years. *Obesity Research, 3,* 411–417.

Epstein, L. H., Valoski, A. M., Vara, L. S., McCurley, J., Wisniewski, L., Kalarchian, M. A., et al. (1995). Effects of decreasing sedentary behavior and increasing activity on weight change in obese children. *Health Psychology, 14,* 109–115.

Epstein, L. H., Valoski, A., Wing, R. R., & McCurley, J. (1990). Ten-year follow-up of behavioral, family-based treatment for obese children. *Journal of the American Medical Association, 264,* 2519–2523.

Epstein, L. H., Valoski, A., Wing, R. R., & McCurley, J. (1994). Ten-year outcomes of behavioral family-based treatment for childhood obesity. *Health Psychology, 13,* 373– 383.

Epstein, L. H., Wing, R. R., Koeske, R., Ossip, D., & Beck, S. (1982). A comparison of lifestyle change and programmed aerobic exercise on weight and fitness changes in obese children. *Behavior Therapy, 13,* 651–665.

Epstein, L. H., Wing, R. R., Koeske, R., & Valoski, A. (1985). A comparison of lifestyle exercise, aerobic exercise, and calisthenics on weight loss in obese children. *Behavior Therapy, 16,* 345–356.

Epstein, L. H., Wing, R. R., Penner, B. C., & Kress, M. J. (1985). Effect of diet and controlled exercise on weight loss in obese children. *Journal of Pediatrics, 107,* 358–361.

Epstein, L. H., Wing, R. R., Steranchak, L., Dickson, B., & Michelson, J. (1980). Comparison of family-based behavior modification and nutrition education for childhood obesity. *Journal of Pediatric Psychology, 5*(1), 25–36.

Epstein, L. H., Wing, R. R., Woodall, K., Penner, B. C., Kress, M. J., & Koeske, R. (1985). Effects of family-based behavioral treatment on obese 5-to-8- year-old children. *Behavior Therapy, 16,* 205–212.

Faith, M. S., Berman, N., Heo, M., Pietrobelli, A., Gallagher, D., Epstein, L. H., et al. (2001). Effects of contingent television on physical activity and television viewing in obese children. *Pediatrics, 107*(5), 1043–1048.

Faith, M. S., Fontaine, K. R., Cheskin, L. J., & Allison, D. B. (2000). Behavioral approaches to the problems of obesity. *Behavior Modification, 24*(4), 459–493.

Gibson, L. J., Peto, J., Warren, J. M., & dos Santos Silva, I. (2006). Lack of evidence on diets for obesity for children: A systematic review. *International Journal of Epidemiology, 35,* 1544–1552.

Golan, M., & Crow, S. (2004). Targeting parents exclusively in the treatment of childhood obesity: Long-term results. *Obesity Research, 12*(2), 357–361.

Golan, M., Weizman, A., Apter, A., & Fainaru, M. (1998). Parents as the exclusive agents of change in the treatment of childhood obesity. *American Journal of Clinical Nutrition, 67,* 1130–1135.

Graves, T., Meyers, A. W., & Clark, L. (1988). An evaluation of parental problem-solving training in the behavioral treatment of childhood obesity. *Journal of Consulting and Clinical Psychology, 56,* 246–250.

Haddock, C. K., Shadish, W. R., Klesges, R. C., & Stein, R. J. (1994). Treatments for childhood and adolescent obesity. *Annals of Behavioral Medicine, 16,* 235–244.

Hills, A. P., & Parker, A. W. (1988). Obesity management via diet and exercise intervention. *Child: Care, Health, and Development, 14,* 409–416.

Israel, A. C., Stolmaker, L., & Andrian, C. A. (1985). The effects of training parents in general child management skills on a behavioral weight loss program for children. *Behavior Therapy, 16*(2), 169–180.

Jain, A., Sherman, S. N., Chamberlin, L. A., Carter, Y., Powers, S. W., & Whitaker, R. C. (2001). Why don't low-income mothers worry about their preschoolers being overweight? *Pediatrics, 107*(5), 1138–1146.

Jeffery, A. N., Voss, L. D., Metcalf, B. S., Alba, S., & Wilkin, T. J. (2005). Parents' awareness of overweight in themselves and their children: Cross sectional study within a cohort (EarlyBird 21). *British Medical Journal, 330*(7481), 23–24.

Jelalian, E., & Saelens, B. E. (1999). Empirically supported treatments in pediatric psychology: Pediatric obesity. *Journal of Pediatric Psychology, 24,* 223–248.

Johnson, W. G., Hinkel, L. K., Carr, R. E., Anderson, D. A., Lemmon, C. R., Engler, L. B., & Bergeron, K. C. (1997). Dietary and exercise interventions for juvenile obesity: Long-term effects of behavioral and public health models. *Obesity Research, 5,* 257–261.

Kirschenbaum, D. S., Harris, E. S., & Tomarken, A. J. (1984). Effects of parental involvement in behavioral weight loss therapy for preadolescents. *Behavior Therapy, 15,* 485–500.

Kohl, H.W., III, & Hobbs, K. E. (1998). Development of physical activity behaviors among children and adolescents. *Pediatrics, 101,* 549–554.

Lanningham-Foster, L., Jensen, T. B., Foster, R. C., Redmond, A. B., Walker, B. A., Heinz, D., & Levine, J. A. (2006). Energy expenditure of sedentary screen time compared with active screen time for children. *Pediatrics, 118*(6), e1831–1835.

Must, A., Dallal, G. E., & Dietz, W. H. (1991). Reference data for obesity: 85th and 95th percentiles of body mass index (wt/ht^2) and triceps skinfold. *American Journal of Clinical Nutrition, 53,* 839–846.

National Institutes of Health: National Heart, Lung, and Blood Institute. (1998). Clinical guidelines on the identification, evaluation, and treatment of overweight and obesity in adults—the evidence report. *Obesity Research, 6,* 51S–209S.

National Center for Health Statistics. (2000). *2000 CDC growth charts: United States.* Retrieved August 28, 2008, from http://www.cdc.gov/growthcharts

Ogden, C. L., Carroll, M. D., Curtin, L. R., McDowell, M. A., Tabak, C. J., & Flegal, K. M. (2006). Prevalence of overweight and obesity in the United States, 1999–2004. *JAMA, 295*(13), 1549–1555.

Pate, R., Trost, S., & Williams, C. (1998). Critique of existing guidelines for physical activity in young people. In S. Biddle, J. Sallis, & N. Cavill (Eds.), *Young and active? Young people and health-enhancing physical activity—evidence and implications* (pp. 162–176). London: Health Education Authority.

Pinhas-Hamiel, O., & Zeitler, P. (2005). The global spread of type 2 diabetes mellitus in children and adolescents. *Journal of Pediatrics, 146*(5), 693–700.

Rocchini, A. P., Katch, V., Anderson, J., Hinderliter, J., Becque, D., Martin, M., & Marks, C. (1988). Blood pressure in obese adolescents: Effect of weight loss. *Pediatrics, 82,* 16–23.

Rocchini, A. P., Katch, V., Schork, A., & Kelch, R. P. (1987). Insulin and blood pressure during weight loss in obese adolescents. *Hypertension, 10,* 267–273.

Sasaki, J., Shindo, M., Tanaka, H., Ando, M., & Arakawa, K. (1987). A long-term aerobic exercise program decreases the obesity index and increases the high-density lipoprotein cholesterol concentration in obese children. *International Journal of Obesity, 11,* 339–345.

Satter, E. (2004). Children, the feeding relationship, and weight. *Maryland Medicine, 5*(3), 26–28.

Senediak, C., & Spence, S. H. (1985). Rapid versus gradual scheduling of therapeutic contact in a family based behavioural weight control programme for children. *Behavioural Psychotherapy, 13,* 265–287.

Spear, B. A., Barlow, S. E., Ervin, C., Ludwig, D. S., Saelens, B. E., Schetzina, K. E., & Taveras, E. M. (2007). Recommendations for treatment of child and adolescent overweight and obesity. *Pediatrics, 120,* S254–S288.

Stallings, V. A., Archibald, E. H., Pencharz, P. B., Harrison, J. E., & Bell, J. E. (1988). One-year follow-up of weight, total body potassium, and total body nitrogen in obese adolescents treated with the protein-sparing modified fast. *American Journal of Clinical Nutrition, 48,* 91–94.

Summerbell, C. D., Waters, E., Edmunds, L. D., Kelly, S., Brown, T., & Campbell, K. J. (2005). Interventions for preventing obesity in children. *Cochrane Database of Systematic Reviews, 3,* CD001871.

Wadden, T. A., Stunkard, A. J., Rich, L., Rubin, C. J., Sweidel, G., & McKinney, S. (1990). Obesity in black adolescent girls: A controlled clinical trial of treatment by diet, behavior modification, and parental support. *Pediatrics, 85,* 345–352.

Wheeler, M. E., & Hess, K. W. (1976). Treatment of juvenile obesity by successive approximation control of eating. *Journal of Behavior Therapy & Experimental Psychiatry, 7,* 235–241.

Wilson, G. T. (1994). Behavioral treatment of obesity: Thirty years and counting. *Advances in Behaviour Research & Therapy, 16*(1), 31–75.

Wrotniak, B. H., Epstein, L. H., Paluch, R. A., & Roemmich, J. N. (2004). Parent weight change as a predictor of child weight change in family-based behavioral obesity treatment. *Archives of Pediatrics & Adolescent Medicine, 158,* 342–347.

15

PLASTIC SURGERY FOR CHILDREN AND ADOLESCENTS

DAVID B. SARWER, ALISON L. INFIELD, AND CANICE E. CRERAND

Plastic surgery is an umbrella term that covers both cosmetic and reconstructive surgery. Cosmetic surgery is designed to improve the appearance of an individual with a "normal" appearance, and includes procedures such as liposuction, rhinoplasty (nose surgery), and breast augmentation. Each year, thousands of children also undergo reconstructive surgical procedures, such as cleft lip and palate repair, in an attempt to turn an "abnormal" appearance into a "normal" one. Due to the lack of agreement as to what constitutes a normal appearance, the line between cosmetic and reconstructive surgery is often unclear.

The popularity of plastic surgery has increased dramatically since the 1990s. Surgeons and mental health professionals have long been interested in the psychological characteristics of adults who undergo plastic surgery, as well as the psychosocial outcomes of these procedures (Crerand, Cash, & Whitaker, 2006; Sarwer, Didie, & Gibbons, 2006). As reviewed here, there is a relatively well-developed body of research on the psychological aspects of reconstructive procedures for children. In contrast, there has been very little research on the psychological characteristics of children and adolescents who seek cosmetic surgery and, similarly, little thoughtful consideration of the appropriateness of cosmetic procedures on individuals whose bodies and body images are still developing. This chapter provides an overview of the psychological aspects of plastic surgery for young people, and uses the findings from the adult literature as a framework to consider relevant psychological issues for children and adolescents who undergo these procedures.

BODY IMAGE AND PLASTIC SURGERY IN ADOLESCENTS

Body image, defined as perceptions and attitudes toward one's own physical appearance, is the largest contributor to self-esteem and self-concept in children and adolescents (Cash, 2006). Adolescence is thought to be a key time in the development of body image, namely because of the number of normative developmental challenges that influence and are influenced by body image (e.g., pubertal development, identity formation, emergence of sexuality; Cash, 2006). The experience of having an objective visible appearance difference, such as a scar, or the adolescent's subjective perception that a physical feature is outside the "norm" (e.g., small breast size compared with one's peers) can potentially leave adolescents vulnerable to teasing, feelings of self-consciousness, confusion about sexual identity, and body image dissatisfaction. Body image dissatisfaction in particular has been associated with depression, low self-esteem, social anxiety, and poor quality of life.

Since the late 1990s, a great deal of attention has been paid to the relationship between body image and plastic surgery (Sarwer & Crerand, 2004; Sarwer, Pruzinsky, et al., 2006; Sarwer, Wadden, Pertschuk, & Whitaker, 1998a). Body image is thought to motivate many self-improvement behaviors, including dieting, exercise, and cosmetic surgery (Sarwer & Crerand, 2004; Sarwer, Pruzinsky, et al., 2006; Sarwer et al., 1998a). Several studies have documented that patients who undergo cosmetic surgery report increased body image dissatisfaction prior to surgery (e.g., Didie & Sarwer, 2003; Sarwer et al., 2003) Other studies have found improvements in body image within the first 2 postoperative years (e.g., Banbury et al., 2004; Bolton, Pruzinsky, Cash, & Persing, 2003; Cash, Duel, & Perkins, 2002; Sarwer, Wadden, & Whitaker, 2002; Sarwer et al., 2005).

The relation between body image and psychosocial functioning in children and adolescents presenting for plastic surgery has received little empirical attention. In one of the few studies of adolescent cosmetic surgery patients, they, like adults, reported increased body image dissatisfaction with the feature for which they desired treatment (Simis, Verhulst, & Koot, 2001). Otherwise, the majority of adolescents were judged to be psychologically healthy. Postoperatively, they reported satisfaction with their appearance and improved self-confidence (Simis, Hovius, de Beaufort, Verhulst, & Koot, 2002). Thus, there is preliminary evidence to suggest that adolescent patients appear to be similar to adults—the majority appear to be psychologically appropriate for surgery and may experience psychological benefit postoperatively. Nonetheless, more research is needed to examine the psychological impact of plastic surgery in pediatric populations.

COSMETIC SURGICAL AND MINIMALLY INVASIVE PROCEDURES

In 2007, the American Society of Plastic Surgeons (ASPS) reported that 224,658 individuals under the age of 19 underwent cosmetic surgical or minimally invasive procedures (ASPS, 2008). This is likely an underestimation of the actual number of cosmetic procedures performed annually, as many non-plastic surgeon physicians now perform these procedures. Although the majority of these procedures are performed to treat acne and other skin problems, adolescents do undergo other procedures such as liposuction and breast augmentation, amid some controversy. If other methods to alter one's appearance (e.g., tattoos, body piercing, branding, and orthodontia) are considered, it is likely that even more children and adolescents are modifying their appearance now than at any other time in history.

Attitudes about and Motivations for Cosmetic Procedures

With the rise in popularity of cosmetic surgery since the 1990s, studies have attempted to assess attitudes about cosmetic surgery in the general population. A recent online survey of 52,677 adults (aged 18–65 years) found that 48% of women and 23% of men expressed interest in pursuing cosmetic surgery if they could afford it (Frederick, Lever, & Peplau, 2007). Similarly, nearly 50% of female college students reported that they would consider cosmetic surgery in the near future or in middle age (Sarwer et al., 2005). Cosmetic surgery is on the mind of younger adolescents as well. In a sample of 130 high school students, 30% reported that they would consider having cosmetic surgery (Pearl & Weston, 2003). The most frequently desired procedures were liposuction, breast augmentation, and rhinoplasty. Body image dissatisfaction, concern with social standing, and greater internalization of mass media standards of beauty have been associated with more positive attitudes toward surgery (Henderson-King & Henderson-King, 2005; Sarwer et al., 2005).

Although body image dissatisfaction may play an important role in a young person's decision to undergo cosmetic surgery, children and adolescents may be motivated by other reasons as well. Some young people may be driven by parental pressure to improve their appearance, particularly in families in which a parent has had cosmetic procedures. Mass media, either through the unrealistic images of beauty or through stories promoting the benefits of cosmetic surgery, may also influence adolescents' interest in cosmetic (Pearl & Weston, 2003).

Adolescents also may feel some direct or indirect pressure from their peers to have surgery. For example, a teenager may suggest cosmetic surgery to a peer who is unhappy with his or her appearance. An adolescent may live in a community in which cosmetic surgery is seen as a "rite of passage" or is sometimes given as a sweet 16 or graduation present. In these situations, there is clinical concern about the adolescent's ability to independently evaluate and understand the long-term risks and benefits of cosmetic procedures (Sarwer, 2006).

These attitudes and motivations, coupled with the increase in the number of cosmetic procedures undergone by adolescents over the past several years, raise some interesting ethical issues as well (Hilhorst, 2002; Laneader & Wolpe, 2006). Given the lack of data supporting the long-term psychosocial benefits of cosmetic surgery (Sarwer, Pruzinsky, et al., 2006), plastic surgeons need to consider if it is appropriate to operate on an adolescent during a period of rapid physical and psychological development. Typically, cosmetic surgery is recommended only for those adolescents who are able to thoughtfully participate in the surgery decision-making process. The extent to which this is assessed by the treating plastic surgeon is unknown.

Issues of informed assent and consent are particularly relevant. Adolescent patients must be informed about the procedure and its risks in an understandable manner, be given sufficient time to ask questions, and not be subjected to undue pressure to make a decision. The existence of a psychiatric disorder, such as body dysmorphic disorder (BDD; discussed later in this chapter), or family dysfunction may make it difficult to determine a patient's ability to make an autonomous decision about surgery. It becomes the cosmetic surgeon's ethical responsibility to make that determination before agreeing to perform surgical procedures on an adolescent (Laneader & Wolpe, 2006).

Rhinoplasty

Rhinoplasty is the most commonly performed cosmetic surgical procedure for adolescents; more than 38,000 procedures were performed in 2007 (ASPS, 2008). Typically performed to reduce the overall size of the nose, rhinoplasty also reshapes the tip and/or bridge, narrows the span of the nostrils, or changes the angle between the nose and upper lip. Mental health professionals have long been interested in the psychological characteristics of patients who have rhinoplasty. Early descriptions suggested that patients were highly psychopathological (Crerand, Cash, et al., 2006). The nose was often thought to symbolize the penis, and the desire for rhinoplasty was believed to represent the patient's unconscious displacement of sexual conflicts onto the nose. Subsequent studies during the 1970s and 1980s, which began to include reliable and valid self-report psychometric measures, suggested that patients had lower rates of psychopathology than previously believed. For example, studies incorporating the use of the Minnesota Multiphasic Personality Inventory reported that the personality profiles of these patients were essentially normal preoperatively (Micheli-Pellegrini & Manfrida, 1979; Wright & Wright, 1975) and no changes in personality were noted postoperatively (Wright & Wright, 1975). Studies also documented improvements in psychosocial function postoperatively (Marcus, 1984; Wright & Wright, 1975). These results have been replicated in numerous studies (e.g., Borges-Dinis, Dinis, & Gomes, 1998; Ercolani, Baldaro, Rossi, Trombini, & Trombini, 1999; Hern, Rowe-Jones, & Hinton, 2003).

Given the relative popularity of rhinoplasty for adolescents, it is somewhat surprising that no study has specifically examined the pre- or postoperative psychological characteristics of adolescents who undergo rhinoplasty. Perhaps because of its popularity, rhinoplasty is considered to be far less controversial than other surgical procedures (i.e., breast augmentation), so much so that the appropriateness of adolescent rhinoplasty is rarely, if ever, debated among plastic surgeons. Regardless, research is clearly needed before this procedure is deemed psychologically appropriate and beneficial for adolescents.

Otoplasty

Otoplasty is a surgical procedure that is used to correct prominent or protruding ears. In 2007, otoplasty was the third most frequently performed procedure for adolescents (ASPS, 2008). Prominent ears are typically not associated with any physiological consequences (Janis, Rohrich, & Gutowski, 2005). However, children with prominent ears are frequently targets of ridicule from others, particularly peers (Bradbury, Hewison, & Timmons, 1992; Sheerin, MacLeod, & Kusumakar, 1995). Poor self-esteem, negative perceptions of appearance, and social difficulties also have been noted (Sheerin et al., 1995). Thus, surgery is typically performed in an effort to reduce or prevent psychological distress and negative social responses (e.g., teasing). Bradbury et al. (1992) conducted a prospective study that examined the effectiveness of surgery to reduce psychosocial distress in a sample of 30 children with prominent ears. At 12 months postoperatively, 90% of children reported improvements in well-being, although there was a small group of children who were dissatisfied with the results of surgery. These children were more socially isolated prior to surgery. Thus, although otoplasty may have psychosocial benefits for many children with prominent ears, it may not be sufficient to resolve all psychosocial difficulties.

Body-Contouring Procedures

The prevalence of obesity in children and adolescents has increased at alarming rates. Of children between the ages of 2 and 19 years, 16.5% are at risk for overweight, and 17.1% are overweight (Ogden et al., 2006). Behavioral interventions that emphasize reduction of caloric intake and increased physical activity are the mainstays of treatment for childhood obesity, and to a lesser extent, pharmacological agents such as orlistat and sibutramine (Cooperberg & Faith, 2004; Sarwer, Foster, & Wadden, 2004). In adults, bariatric surgery has become a popular treatment option. Although considered controversial, bariatric surgery is performed on selected adolescents with extreme obesity (body mass index >40). In 2003, more than 1,000 bariatric procedures were performed on adolescents and this number is expected to increase, perhaps dramatically, in the coming years (Xanthakos, Daniels, & Inge, 2006).

In 2007, almost 67,000 body-contouring procedures were performed on adults who had experienced massive weight loss (ASPS, 2008). Although statistics for body-contouring procedures in adolescents are unavailable, it is likely that a similar trend will also be seen among adolescents who experience massive weight loss.

The massive weight loss associated with bariatric surgery can result in loose, hanging skin, which can subsequently lead to physical discomfort and body image dissatisfaction (Sarwer & Fabricatore, 2008; Sarwer, Thompson, Mitchell, & Rubin, 2008). Unfortunately, little is known about the physical and psychological impact of these procedures in either adults or adolescents (Sarwer & Fabricatore, 2008; Sarwer et al., 2008).

Liposuction

In 2007, liposuction, the removal of unwanted fat from specific areas of the body, was the fourth most frequently performed cosmetic procedure for adolescents (it was the second most commonly performed procedure for adults; ASPS, 2008). Despite its popularity, several misconceptions about the procedure exist. Liposuction is widely believed to only remove excess fat from the torso. In reality, the procedure can be used to remove fat cells throughout the body. Another misconception is that liposuction produces a significant weight loss. Unfortunately, this misconception was recently publicized in media reports of liposuction and abdominoplasty being used as treatments for childhood obesity (Sarwer, Allison, et al., 2006). The actual weight losses following liposuction are quite modest. A study of 14 overweight women reported a mean weight loss of approximately 11 lb by 6 weeks postoperatively and an additional 3-lb weight loss by 4 months (Giese, Bulan, Commons, Spear, & Yanovski, 2001). Many patients erroneously believe that fat deposits will never return to the treated areas.

Although liposuction reduces the number of fat cells in a specific area, the remaining cells may still expand if weight increases. Between 40% and 50% of patients who received liposuction reported weight gain after surgery and up to 29% claimed that their fat returned to the surgical site (Rohrich et al., 2004).

Individuals with excessive weight or shape concerns, or those with eating disorders, require particular attention prior to liposuction (Sarwer, 2006). Adolescents with anorexia nervosa (AN) or bulimia nervosa (BN; discussed later) may mistakenly seek liposuction as an inappropriate compensatory behavior to control their weight. Willard, McDermott, and Woodhouse (1996) described the cases of two women with BN who underwent liposuction with the unrealistic expectation that surgery would result in an improvement of their eating disorder symptoms. Postoperatively, both women reported worsening of their bulimic and depressive symptoms, and one woman reported a weight gain of 25 lb in 3 months. Unfortunately, little else is known about the relationship between eating disorders and liposuction. Adolescent patients interested in liposuction should be asked about their history of weight fluctuations, binge eating, amenorrhea, and dieting and purging behaviors.

Cosmetic Breast Augmentation

In 2007, 10,505 of the 347,524 women who underwent cosmetic breast augmentation were 18 or 19 years old (ASPS, 2008). The enduring popularity of breast augmentation surprises many individuals, particularly given the concerns about the safety and efficacy of silicone gel-filled breast implants over the past 15 years. In 2006, the U.S. Food and Drug Administration (FDA) limited the use of silicone gel-filled breast implants to women 22 years of age and older and has approved use of saline-filled breast implants in women 18 years of age and older. These recommendations are based on concerns about adolescents' abilities to consider the risks associated with breast implants. For example, an adolescent may not realize that secondary surgeries could be needed to address complications or to replace implants over the course of her lifetime. Given that cosmetic procedures are not covered by insurance, adolescents also may not fully grasp the future financial implications of having breast implants. The FDA recommendations also reflect concerns that the adolescents may not have finished physical development, as well as concerns about emotional maturity to handle the potential physical and psychological outcomes of surgery.

Despite the FDA's recommendations that breast augmentation candidates should be at least 18 years of age, it is still possible for surgeons to perform cosmetic breast augmentation on younger patients as an "off-label" use of the device. The ASPS does not endorse the use of breast implants for cosmetic purposes in adolescent girls; thus, the number of these procedures are not tracked. Some plastic surgeons will use breast implants with adolescent girls who have experienced abnormal breast development secondary to a congenital abnormality, illness, or traumatic injury (Greydanus, Matytsina, & Gains, 2006). The use of breast implants in these cases illustrates the overlap between the cosmetic and reconstructive aspects of plastic surgery.

In part because of the controversy surrounding cosmetic breast augmentation for adolescents, little is known about the psychological characteristics of young women who undergo the procedure. In contrast, a large body of research has examined the psychosocial characteristics of adult women who receive cosmetic breast implants, as well as the psychosocial outcomes associated with breast augmentation. Early studies of the personality characteristics of women who underwent breast augmentation, similar to studies of women who underwent rhinoplasty, described patients as experiencing increased symptoms of depression, anxiety, guilt, and low self-esteem (Edgerton, Meyer, & Jacobson, 1961; Ohlsen, Ponten, & Hambert, 1978; Schlebusch & Levin, 1983). Subsequent studies have found fewer symptoms of psychopathology, although women typically report heightened dissatisfaction with their breasts (Didie & Sarwer, 2003; Sarwer et al., 2003; Sarwer et al., 2005; Schlebusch, 1989).

Other studies have found several demographic differences between women who receive breast implants and those who do not. Women with breast implants are more likely to have had more overall lifetime sexual partners, report a greater use of oral contraceptives, be younger at their first pregnancy, and have a history of terminated pregnancies as compared to other women (Cook et al., 1997; Fryzek et al., 2000; Kjøller et al., 2003). They also have been found to be more frequent users of alcohol and tobacco, as well as have a higher divorce rate (Cook et al., 1997; Fryzek et al., 2000; Kjøller et al., 2003). Finally, they have been reported to have a below-average body weight, leading to concern that some may be experiencing eating disorders (Cook et al., 1997; Didie & Sarwer, 2003; Fryzek et al., 2000; Kjøller et al., 2003).

Postoperative clinical reports and empirical studies suggest that the vast majority of women are satisfied with the outcome of breast augmentation (Cash et al., 2002; Park, Chetty, & Watson, 1996; Sarwer et al., 2005; Wells et al., 1994; Young, Nemecek, & Nemecek, 1994). A limited number of studies have reported improvements, or at least no change, in self-esteem and depressive symptoms (Cash et al., 2002; Ohlsen et al., 1978). Additionally, women who undergo breast augmentation also experience improvements in their body image postoperatively (Cash et al., 2002; Sarwer et al., 2002, 2005). These body image improvements, however, may be tempered by the occurrence of a postoperative complication, which occurs in 24% to 31% of patients (Cash et al., 2002; Fryzek et al., 2001; Gabriel et al., 1997).

Recently, seven large epidemiological studies designed to investigate the relationship between breast implants and mortality found an unexpected relationship between breast implants and suicide (Brinton, Lubin, Burich, Colton, & Hoover, 2001; Brinton, Lubin, Murray, Colton, & Hoover, 2006; Jacobsen et al., 2004; Koot, Peeters, Granath, Grobbee, & Nyren, 2003; Lipworth et al., 2007; Pukkala et al., 2003; Villeneuve et al., 2006). The suicide rate (as obtained from patients' death records) was two to three times greater among patients with breast implants as compared with either patients who underwent other cosmetic surgical procedures or population estimates.

Presently, the specific nature of the relationship between breast implants and suicide is unclear (Sarwer, 2007; Sarwer, Brown & Evans, 2007). Some women may enter into surgery with unrealistic expectations about the effect that breast augmentation will have on their lives. When these expectations are not met, they may become despondent, depressed, and potentially sui-cidal. Alternatively, women who experience medical conditions (such as autoimmune and connective tissue diseases) not statistically associated with breast implants may believe these complications are a consequence of their implants. These women may become depressed as a result of a lack of perceived or real attention from the medical community. Although speculative, both of these hypotheses have some intuitive appeal. In their study, Jacobsen and colleagues (2004) found an increased prevalence of preoperative psychiatric hospitalizations in women who received breast implants as compared with women who underwent other forms of plastic surgery. These results suggest that the increase suicide rate among women who have breast implants may reflect some underlying psychopathology rather than a direct relationship with the implants (McLaughlin, Lipworth, & Tarone, 2003; Sarwer, 2007; Sarwer et al., 2007). Furthermore, specific demographic characteristics have been noted among women seeking breast augmentation. Several—such as increased use of alcohol and tobacco—are, in and of themselves, associated with an increased risk of suicide and could actually account for an even higher suicide rate than found in the epidemiological investigations (Joiner, 2003).

Clearly, additional studies of the relationship between breast implants and suicide are needed. In light of these current findings, young women and adolescents who pursue cosmetic breast augmentation should be screened for depression and substance use, as well as disorders with body image compo-nents, such as eating disorders and BDD. Those who present with a history of psychiatric hospitalizations or significant psychopathology should undergo a mental health evaluation prior to breast augmentation surgery (Sarwer, 2007; Sarwer et al., 2007).

Acne Treatment

Acne affects at least 80% of adolescents (Krowchuk, 2000). Thus, many adolescents and young adults present to cosmetic surgeons, dermatologists, or other professionals complaining of active acne or acne-related scarring. Laser skin resurfacing, chemical peels, microdermabrasion, and other treatments for acne are among the most frequently performed treatments on adolescent patients (ASPS, 2008).

Psychological effects of acne are frequently dismissed. More health professionals are now recognizing the impact acne may have on psychosocial functioning. As many as 50% of adolescents report psychological difficulties associated with acne, including body image concerns, poor self-esteem, depressive symptoms, and social impairment (e.g., Gupta & Gupta, 1998; Koo, 1995; Papadopoulos, Walker, Aitken, & Bor, 2000). More than 80% of young adult patients with severe acne reported significant distress and impairment in their daily lives because of their skin concerns (Bowe, Leyden, Crerand, Sarwer, & Margolis, 2007). Impairments in quality of life are comparable with those of other chronic medical conditions, such as epilepsy and diabetes (Mallon et al., 1999); suicidal ideation or suicide attempts are not uncommon (Cotterill & Cunliffe, 1997; Gupta & Gupta, 1998).

Patients with facial acne, compared with those with truncal acne, appear to be more susceptible to the psychological effects of the disease, experiencing lower self-esteem and greater body image dissatisfaction (Papadopoulos et al., 2000). Consistent with theories of body image, the distress appears to be related to the self-perceived, rather than objective, acne severity.

Acne treatment appears to result in improvements in psychosocial functioning (Rubinow, Peck, Squillace, & Gantt, 1987). However, studies examining acne treatment with isotretinoin (Retin A) suggest that the psychological effect of the acne may remain despite the successful treatment (Kellett & Gawkrodger, 1999). A recent study of 128 patients with acne found that those with a history of isotretinoin treatment were twice as likely to report distress and impairment in social or occupational functioning compared to those who were never treated with the medication (Bowe et al., 2007). Although some of this distress may be related to the "memory" of the active acne or fear of its return, for others it may be attributed to residual scarring.

PSYCHIATRIC DISORDERS AMONG COSMETIC SURGERY PATIENTS

All of the psychiatric diagnoses likely appear within the large population of individuals who now seek cosmetic surgery. Given the relationship between body image dissatisfaction and cosmetic surgery, conditions with a significant body image component, such as BDD and the eating disorders, may appear with greater frequency and be associated with poor postoperative outcomes.

Body Dysmorphic Disorder

BDD is described as a preoccupation with an imagined or slight defect in appearance that results in significant emotional suffering and disruption in daily functioning (American Psychiatric Association [APA], 2000). It is characterized by intrusive thoughts about the perceived defect and compulsive behaviors (e.g., excessive grooming, mirror checking) related to the feature. The disorder is believed to affect approximately 1% of the general population (APA, 2000), although rates from 2% to 5% have been reported in high school and college students (Bienvenu et al., 2000; Bohne et al., 2002; Cansever, Uzun, Donmez, & Ozsahin, 2003; Faravelli et al., 1997; Mayville, Katz, Gipson, & Cabral, 1999; Otto, Wilhelm, Cohen, & Harlow, 2001; Rief, Buhlmann, Wilhelm, Borkenhagen, & Brahler, 2006; Sarwer et al., 2005).

Among adolescents with BDD, the skin and hair are the most commonly reported features of concern (Albertini & Phillips, 1999). However, any body part may become the focus, and preoccupation with more than one body part is common (Phillips, Menard, Fay, & Weisberg, 2005). Symptom severity and level of impairment can vary, ranging from mild disruption in quality of life to suicidal ideation and completed suicides (Phillips, Coles, et al. 2005). The onset of the disorder is typically during adolescence and the course tends to be chronic. Because some concern about physical appearance is normative during adolescence, it may be challenging to diagnose BDD during this developmental period. Careful assessment of an adolescent's appearance concerns and their impact on school and social performance is needed in order to differentiate "normal" from pathological appearance concerns (Hadley, Greenberg, & Hollander, 2002).

Like their adult counterparts, adolescents with BDD frequently pursue cosmetic surgery and related treatments (Crerand, Phillips, Menard, & Fay, 2005; Phillips, Grant, Siniscalchi, & Albertini, 2001). Among 200 persons with BDD, 71% sought and 64% received cosmetic treatments (e.g., dermatological and surgical procedures; Crerand et al., 2005). Of the 16 adolescents included in this sample, 10 sought cosmetic treatments and 9 received them. The mean age at which adolescents first pursued cosmetic treatments was 14.8 years. Dermatological treatment was the most commonly sought and received procedure.

Not surprisingly, BDD is relatively common among those who seek cosmetic surgical or dermatological treatments. Studies have found that 7% to 15% of adult patients who seek these treatments meet criteria for BDD

(Aouizerate et al., 2003; Bowe et al., 2007; Crerand et al., 2004; Dufresne, Phillips, Vittorio, & Wilkel, 2001; Phillips & Dufresne, 2000; Sarwer, Wadden, Pertschuk, & Whitaker, 1998b). No studies have investigated the rate of BDD among adolescent patients. Retrospective studies of cosmetic treatment among persons with BDD suggest that most experienced either no change or a worsening in symptoms (Crerand et al., 2005; Phillips et al., 2001). As a result, BDD is believed to contrainidicate cosmetic surgery (Crerand, Franklin, & Sarwer, 2006; Sarwer, 2006). Given the typical age of onset and the increasing number of young people who seek cosmetic treatments, providers should routinely screen for BDD (Sarwer, 2006).

Eating Disorders

As a result of the disproportionate focus individuals diagnosed with AN or BN typically place on their appearance, these disorders also may appear among those who seek cosmetic surgery (Sarwer, Didie, et al., 2006). Individuals with both disorders may erroneously believe that cosmetic surgery will improve their dissatisfaction with their bodies.

Unfortunately, there is little information on the prevalence rate of AN or BN among patients undergoing cosmetic surgery; what information does exist has been limited to case reports. One of the earliest reports (Yates, Shisslak, Allender, & Wolman, 1988) described two young female college students, a 19-year old with AN and BN who underwent rhinoplasty and chin augmentation; and a 20-year-old with BN who had breast augmentation. Both women experienced temporary remission of their eating disorder symptoms in the first few months after surgery. However, in both cases, symptoms returned and worsened, and in one case, hospitalization was required. Similarly, other case reports have described young women with AN or BN who underwent breast augmentation (McIntosh, Britt, & Bulik, 1994) as well as reports of women with BN who sought liposuction (Willard et al., 1996). In these case reports, motivations for surgery were described as being directly related to the body image distortions that characterize eating disorders. Willard et al. noted that liposuction was essentially a variant of purging for women with BN. Women in both case series also experienced exacerbations of eating disorder symptoms postoperatively.

Although data are limited on the prevalence of eating disorders in plastic surgery populations, these case reports demonstrate that surgery is not a cure for eating pathology and its associated body image disturbances. In some instances, surgery may even exacerbate symptoms. Screening for eating disorders among patients presenting for plastic surgery is recommended, particularly among young patients, given that eating disorders typically emerge during adolescence and young adulthood (Sarwer, 2006).

RECONSTRUCTIVE SURGICAL PROCEDURES

Over 5 million of the surgical procedures performed by ASPS members in 2007 were reconstructive in nature (ASPS, 2008). These procedures ranged from treatment of developmental abnormalities to treatment of physical insults from illness or traumatic injury.

Breast Reduction

In 2005, according to the ASPS (2007) 5,312 adolescent females underwent breast reduction surgery. (The ASPS did not report the number of breast reductions performed in 2006 or 2007 on women under the age of 18). Although there are no data on the average age of persons who underwent this surgery, patients are typically in their late teens, as surgeons usually delay surgery until breast development has stopped. Women who seek breast reduction typically report physical limitations and pain associated with their large breasts (Young & Watson, 2006). Following surgery, they desire average-sized breasts proportional to the rest of their bodies. Others report significant psychosocial concerns, including body image dissatisfaction, low self-esteem, and social isolation. Teenage girls, in particular, may be the target of teasing comments and mean-spirited jokes. Others may experience a great deal of unwanted attention from male peers, who concentrate more on their breasts than the person behind them. As a result, many adolescent females adopt strategies to hide, or camouflage, their breasts such as wearing baggy clothing, adopting a hunched posture, or intentionally gaining weight.

Patient satisfaction following breast reduction is typically high; more than 90% report they would have surgery again or recommend it to others (Brown, Hill, & Khan, 2000; Dabbah, Lehman, Parker, Tantri, & Wagner, 1995). Studies examining psychosocial changes postoperatively show significant improvements in self-esteem, depressive symptoms, and quality of life (Behmand, Tang, & Smith, 2000; Shakespeare & Cole, 1997). Two case studies have examined the outcome of breast reduction in adolescent and young adult women with BN (Kreipe, Lewand, Dukarm, & Caldwell, 1997; Losee, Serletti, Kreipe, & Caldwell, 1997). In both reports, patients noted that their eating-disordered behaviors were performed in an attempt to reduce the size of their breasts and to achieve a more proportionate body. The majority of patients in both reports experienced improvements in their eating disorder symptoms postoperatively (Kreipe et al., 1997; Losee, Serletti, Kreipe, & Caldwell, 1997). Improvements in eating pathology (including remission of symptoms) were still apparent 10 years postoperatively (Losee et al., 2004). These reports suggest that objectively large breast size may be a contributory factor in the development of eating disorders, and surgery to reduce breast size may play a role in the treatment of eating pathology. However, surgery should be considered as a potential adjunctive treatment and not a substitute for established psychological and psychiatric interventions for eating disorders.

Gynecomastia Correction

In 2007, 16,400 surgical procedures were performed in the United States for the correction of gynecomastia in males aged 13 to 19 years (ASPS, 2008). Gynecomastia is defined as abnormal proliferation of breast tissue in males that results in breast enlargement of one or both breasts (Greydanus et al., 2006). The condition can result in discomfort, nipple irritation, painful swelling, and skin redundancy (ASPS, 2002). Additionally, males with this condition frequently experience psychosocial distress because of the feminine appearance of their chest (ASPS, 2002; Greydanus et al., 2006). Significant distress and embarrassment about appearance are considered to be indications for surgery (ASPS, 2002; Fisher & Fornari, 1990). Anecdotally, patients with gynecomastia have reported embarrassment in social situations, low self-esteem, teasing related to breast enlargement, and avoidance of situations and/or activities in which their chest may be exposed (e.g., locker room, athletic activities; Fisher & Fornari, 1990).

Case reports have documented social isolation as well as eating disorders, depressive symptoms, and social anxiety among adolescent males with gynecomastia (Storch et al., 2004). These individuals may also be at risk for body image dissatisfaction and low self-esteem. Despite these concerns, no studies to date have examined pre- or postoperative psychosocial status in these adolescents. Many of the psychosocial problems associated with gynecomastia are thought to resolve postoperatively. However, clinical experience suggests that surgery does not improve psychosocial functioning for all patients, and some patients report dissatisfaction with postoperative outcome even after technically successful procedures (Fisher & Fornari, 1990). Such reports suggest that psychosocial factors may play an important role in predicting postoperative outcomes for this condition.

Craniofacial Surgery

In 2007, more than 27,000 craniofacial surgical procedures were performed on children born with birth defects of the head and face. These procedures play a large role in addressing the functional and aesthetic concerns associated with congenital craniofacial conditions (e.g., cleft lip and palate, craniosynostosis). Patients typically undergo several surgical procedures over the course of childhood and adolescence in order to restore function (e.g., improve ability to eat, speak, and hear) and appearance (e.g., creation of a more normal skull shape). As physical growth ends, additional procedures may be performed for primarily aesthetic purposes (e.g., scar revision).

An extensive body of research exists regarding the psychosocial aspects of congenital craniofacial conditions (e.g., Endriga & Kapp-Simon, 1999; Kapp-Simon, 2006). Anxiety, social inhibition, and externalizing behaviors appear to be more common in these children compared to their nondisfigured peers. Residual, often permanent disfigurement (typical for most of these patients) and speech difficulties can leave some vulnerable to peer teasing and rejection. Patients face treatment-related challenges similar to those with other chronic medical conditions, including frustration with the timing of interventions and coping with the stress of numerous surgeries and hospitalizations. Psychosocial factors, such as developmental stage and psychological adjustment, are believed to play integral roles in the timing of surgical interventions and ultimately, satisfaction with treatment outcome.

Traumatic Injuries and Disease

Each year, tens of thousands of children and adolescents sustain injuries from traumatic events (e.g., motor vehicle accidents, dog bites, burns) or develop chronic and potentially severe illnesses (e.g., cancer). Improvements in medical technology have resulted in increased survival rates for those affected by such events. Nonetheless, the medical interventions used to ensure survival may result in lasting physical changes (e.g., scarring, tissue loss, amputation) that affect physical appearance and body image.

In addition to the potential for long-term physical changes and disability, traumatic injury or illness may exacerbate preexisting psychosocial problems for children and their families (Kazak et al., 2006). Children who require reconstructive procedures may be at risk for psychosocial problems, such as posttraumatic stress, body image dissatisfaction, depression, social anxiety, and social stigmatization, particularly if the injury, disease, or related treatment results in disfigurement. More research is needed to further understand the psychosocial concerns of children and adolescents who undergo reconstructive procedures and their potential impact on treatment outcome.

CONCLUSIONS

Tens of thousands of adolescents undergo plastic surgical treatment each year. As with other areas of Western culture, the popularity of plastic surgery has raced ahead of thoughtful consideration of the appropriateness of performing these procedures on adolescents whose bodies and body images are still developing. On the one hand, one could argue that adolescent patients are just like adults—that the majority are psychologically appropriate for surgery and may experience psychosocial benefits from the procedure postoperatively. However, given the central role of body image in the pursuit of cosmetic surgery, coupled with the often turbulent nature of body image during adolescence, it is clear that more research is needed before we can confidently state that cosmetic surgery is psychologically beneficial to the majority of adolescents who now seek it.

A larger body of research has investigated the psychosocial issues in reconstructive surgery. In general, children and adolescents with a disfigured appearance appear to be at increased risk for suffering from a range of psychosocial difficulties, although it is clear that the experience of being disfigured does not necessarily predict psychosocial difficulties later in life. Future research in this area should include an assessment of the body image concerns of these children and adolescents, an area that has been infrequently investigated to date. Furthermore, disappointingly little is known about how best help disfigured children and adolescents successfully grow into an adult world that puts such a premium on physical beauty.

REFERENCES

Albertini, R. S., & Phillips, K. A. (1999). Thirty-three cases of body dysmorphic disorder in children and adolescents. *Journal of the American Academy of Child and Adolescent Psychiatry, 38,* 453–459.

American Psychiatric Association. (2000). *Diagnostic and statistical manual of mental disorders* (4th ed., text rev.). Washington, DC: Author.

American Society of Plastic Surgeons. (2002). *Position paper: Gynecomastia.* Arlington Heights, IL: Author.

American Society of Plastic Surgeons. (2004). *Policy statement on breast augmentation in teenagers.* Arlington Heights, IL: Author.

American Society of Plastic Surgeons. (2007). *2006 report of the 2005 National Clearinghouse of Plastic Surgery Statistics.* Arlington Heights, IL: Author.

American Society of Plastic Surgeons. (2008). *2008 report of the 2007 National Clearinghouse of Plastic Surgery Statistics.* Arlington Heights, IL: Author.

Aouizerate, B., Pujol, H., Grabot, D., Faytout, M., Suire, K., Braud, C., et al. (2003). Body dysmorphic disorder in a sample of cosmetic surgery applicants. *European Psychiatry, 18,* 365–368.

Banbury, J., Yetman, R., Lucas, A., Papay, F., Graves, K., & Jins, J. E. (2004). Prospective analysis of the outcome of subpectoral breast augmentation: Sensory changes, muscle function, and body image. *Plastic and Reconstructive Surgery, 113,* 701–707.

Behmand, R. R., Tang, D. H., & Smith, D. J., Jr. (2000). Outcomes in breast reduction surgery. *Annals of Plastic Surgery, 45,* 575–580.

Bienvenu, O. J., Samuels, J. F., Riddle, M. A., Hoehn-Saric, R., Liang K. Y., Cullen, B. A., et al. (2000). The relationship of obsessive-compulsive disorder to possible spectrum disorders: Results from a family study. *Biological Psychiatry, 48,* 287–293.

Bohne, A., Wilhelm, S., Keuthen, N. J., Florin, I., Baer, L., & Jenike, M. A. (2002). Prevalence of body dysmorphic disorder in a German college student sample. *Psychiatry Research, 109,* 101–104.

Bolton, M. A., Pruzinsky, T., Cash, T. F., & Persing, J. A. (2003). Measuring outcomes in plastic surgery body image and quality of life in abdominoplasty patients. *Plastic and Reconstructive Surgery, 112,* 619–625.

Borges-Dinis, P., Dinis, M., & Gomes, A. (1998). Psychosocial consequences of nasal aesthetic and functional surgery: A controlled prospective study in an ENT setting. *Rhinology, 36,* 32–36.

Bowe, W. P., Leyden, J. J., Crerand, C. E., Sarwer, D. B., & Margolis, D. J. (2007) Body dysmorphic disorder symptoms among patients with acne vulgaris. *Journal of the American Academy of Dermatology, 57,* 222–230.

Bradbury E. T., Hewison, J., & Timmons, M. J. (1992). Psychological and social outcome of prominent ear correction surgery in children. *British Journal of Plastic Surgery, 45,* 97–100.

Brinton, L. A., Lubin, J. H., Burich, M. C., Colton, T., & Hoover, R. N. (2001). Mortality among augmentation mammaplasty patients. *Epidemiology, 12,* 321–326.

Brinton, L. A., Lubin, J. H., Murray, M. C., Colton, T., & Hoover, R. N. (2006). Mortality rates among augmentation mammaplasty patients: An update. *Epidemiology, 17,* 162–169.

Brown, A. P., Hill, C., & Khan, K. (2000). Outcome of reduction mammaplasty—A patients' perspective. *British Journal of Plastic Surgery, 53,* 584–587.

Cansever, A., Uzun, O., Donmez, E., & Ozsahin, A. (2003). The prevalence and clinical features of body dysmorphic disorder in college students: A study in a Turkish sample. *Comprehensive Psychiatry, 44,* 60–64.

Cash, T. F. (2006). Body image and plastic surgery. In D. B. Sarwer, T. Pruzinsky, T. F. Cash., R. M. Goldwyn, J. A. Persing, & L. A. Whitaker (Eds.), *Psychological aspects of reconstructive and cosmetic surgery* (pp. 37–59). Philadelphia: Lippincott, Williams, & Wilkins.

Cash, T. F., Duel, L. A., & Perkins, L. L. (2002). Women's psychosocial outcomes of breast augmentation with silicone gel-filled implants: A 2-year prospective study. *Plastic and Reconstructive Surgery, 109,* 2112–2121.

Cook, L. S., Daling, J. R., Voigt, L. F., deHart, M. P., Malone, K. E., Stanford, J. L., et al. (1997). Characteristics of women with and without breast augmentation. *Journal of the American Medical Association, 277,* 1612–1617.

Cooperberg, J., & Faith, M. S. (2004). Treatment of obesity II: Childhood and adolescent obesity. In J. K. Thompson (Ed.), *Handbook of eating disorders and obesity* (pp. 443–460). Hoboken, NJ: Wiley.

Cotterill, J. A., & Cunliffe, W. J. (1997). Suicide in dermatological patients. *British Journal of Dermatology, 137,* 246–250.

Crerand, C. E., Cash, T. F., & Whitaker, L. A. (2006). Cosmetic surgery of the face. In D. B. Sarwer, T. Pruzinsky, T. F. Cash, R. M Goldwyn, J. A. Persing, & L. A. Whitaker (Eds.), *Psychological aspects of reconstructive and cosmetic plastic surgery: Clinical, empirical, and ethical perspectives* (pp. 233–250). Philadelphia: Lippincott, Williams, & Wilkins.

Crerand, C. E., Franklin, M. E., & Sarwer, D. B. (2006). Body dysmorphic disorder and cosmetic surgery. *Plastic and Reconstructive Surgery, 118*, 167e–180e.

Crerand, C. E., Phillips, K. A., Menard, W., & Fay, C. (2005). Nonpsychiatric medical treatment of body dysmorphic disorder. *Psychosomatics, 46*, 549–555.

Crerand, C. E., Sarwer, D., Magee, L., Gibbons, L. M., Lowe, M. R., Bartlett, S. P., et al. (2004). Rate of body dysmorphic disorder among patients seeking facial cosmetic procedures. *Psychiatric Annals, 34*, 958–965.

Dabbah, A., Lehman, J. A., Jr., Parker, M. G., Tantri, D., & Wagner, D. S. (1995). Reduction mammaplasty: An outcome analysis. *Annals of Plastic Surgery, 35*, 337–341.

Didie, E. R., & Sarwer, D. B. (2003). Factors that influence the decision to undergo cosmetic breast augmentation surgery. *Journal of Women's Health, 12*, 241.

Dufresne, R. G., Phillips, K. A., Vittorio, C. C., & Wilkel, C. S. (2001). A screening questionnaire for body dysmorphic disorder in a cosmetic dermatologic surgery practice. *Dermatologic Surgery, 27*, 457–462.

Edgerton, M. T., Meyer, E., & Jacobson, W. E. (1961). Augmentation mammaplasty II: Further surgical and psychiatric evaluation. *Plastic and Reconstructive Surgery, 27*, 279.

Endriga, M. C., & Kapp-Simon, K. A. (1999). Psychological issues in craniofacial care: State of the art. *Cleft Palate and Craniofacial Journal, 36*, 3–9.

Ercolani, M., Baldaro, B., Rossi, N., Trombini, E., & Trombini, G. (1999). Short-term outcome of rhinoplasty for medical or cosmetic indication. *Journal of Psychosomatic Research, 47*, 277–281.

Faravelli, C., Salvatori, S., Galassi, F., Aiazzi, L., Drei, C., & Cabras, P. (1997). Epidemiology of somatoform disorders: A community survey in Florence. *Social Psychiatry and Psychiatric Epidemiology, 32*, 24–29.

Fisher, M., & Fornari, V. (1990). Gynecomastia as a precipitant of eating disorders in adolescent males. *International Journal of Eating Disorders, 9*, 115–119.

Frederick, D. A., Lever, J., & Peplau, L. A. (2007). Interest and cosmetic surgery and body image: Views in men and women across the lifespan. *Plastic and Reconstructive Surgery, 120*, 1407–1415.

Fryzek, J. P., Signorello, L. B., Hakelius, L., Lipworth, L., McLaughlin, J. K., Blot, W. J., & Nyren, O. (2001). Local complications and subsequent symptom reporting among women with cosmetic breast implants. *Plastic and Reconstructive Surgery, 107*, 214–221.

Fryzek, J. P., Weiderpass, E., Signorello, L. B., Hakelius, L., Lipworth, L., Blot, W. J., et al. (2000). Characteristics of women with cosmetic breast augmentation surgery compared with breast reduction surgery patients and women in the general population of Sweden. *Annals of Plastic Surgery, 45*, 349–356.

Gabriel, S. E., Woods, J. E., O'Fallon, W. M., Beard, C. M., Kurland, L. T., & Melton, L. J. (1997). Complications leading to surgery after breast implantation. *New England Journal of Medicine, 336*, 677–682.

Giese, S. Y., Bulan, E. J., Commons, G. W., Spear, S. L., & Yanovski, J. A. (2001). Improvements in cardiovascular risk profile with large-volume liposuction: A pilot study. *Plastic and Reconstructive Surgery, 108*, 510–519.

Greydanus, D. E., Matytsina, L., & Gains, M. (2006). Breast disorders in children and adolescents. *Primary Care: Clinics in Office Practice, 33*, 455–502.

Gupta, M. A., & Gupta, A. K. (1998). Depression and suicidal ideation in dermatology patients with acne, alopecia areata, atopic dermatitis, and psoriasis. *British Journal of Dermatology, 139,* 846–850.

Hadley, S. J., Greenberg J., & Hollander, E. (2002). Diagnosis and treatment of body dysmorphic disorder in adolescents. *Current Psychiatry Reports, 4,* 108–113.

Henderson-King, D., & Henderson-King, E. (2005). Acceptance of cosmetic surgery: Scale development and validation. *Body Image, 2,* 137–149.

Hern, J., Rowe-Jones, J., & Hinton, A. (2003). Nasal deformity and interpersonal problems. *Clinical Otolaryngology, 28,* 121–124.

Hilhorst, M. T. (2002). Philosophical pitfalls in cosmetic surgery: A case of rhinoplasty during adolescence. *Medical Humanities, 28,* 61–66.

Jacobsen, P. H., Hölmich, L. R., McLaughlin, J. K., Johansen, C., Olsen, J. H., Kjøller, K., & Friis, S. (2004). Mortality and suicide among Danish women with cosmetic breast implants. *Archive of Internal Medicine, 164,* 2450–2455.

Janis, J. E., Rohrich, R. J., & Gutowski, K. A. (2005). Otoplasty. *Plastic and Reconstructive Surgery, 115,* 60e–72e.

Joiner, T. E. (2003). Does breast augmentation confer risk of or protection from suicide? *Aesthetic Surgery Journal, 23,* 370–375.

Kapp-Simon, K. A. (2006). Craniofacial conditions. In D. B. Sarwer, T. Pruzinsky, T. F. Cash, R. M. Goldwyn, J. A. Persing, & L. A. Whitaker (Eds.), *Psychological aspects of reconstructive and cosmetic plastic surgery: Clinical, empirical, and ethical perspectives* (pp. 63–81). Philadelphia: Lippincott, Williams, & Wilkins.

Kazak A. E., Kassam-Adams N., Schneider S., Zelikovsky N., Alderfer M. A., & Rourke M. (2006). An integrative model of pediatric medical traumatic stress. *Journal of Pediatric Psychology, 31,* 343–355.

Kellett, S. C., & Gawkrodger, D. J. (1999). The psychological and emotional impact of acne and the effect of treatment with isotretinoin. *British Journal of Dermatology, 140,* 273–282.

Kjøller, K., Hölmich, L. R., Fryzek, J. P., Jacobsen, P. H., Friis, S. McLaughlin, J. K., et al. (2003). Characteristics of women with cosmetic breast implants compared with women with other types of cosmetic surgery and population-based controls in Denmark. *Annals of Plastic Surgery, 50,* 6–12.

Koo, J. (1995). The psychosocial impact of acne: Patients' perceptions. *Journal of the American Academy of Dermatology, 32,* S26–30.

Koot, V. C., Peeters, P. H., Granath, F., Grobbee, D.E ., & Nyren, O. (2003). Total and cause specific mortality among Swedish women with cosmetic breast implants: A prospective study. *British Medical Journal, 326,* 527–528.

Kreipe, R. E., Lewand, A. G., Dukarm, C. P., & Caldwell E. H. (1997). Outcome for patients with bulimia and breast hypertrophy after reduction mammaplasty. *Archives of Pediatrics and Adolescent Medicine, 151,* 176–180.

Krowchuk, D. P. (2000). Managing acne in adolescents. *Pediatric Clinics of North America, 47,* 841–857.

Laneader, A. M., & Wolpe, P. R. (2006). Ethical considerations in cosmetic surgery. In D. B. Sarwer, T. Pruzinsky, T. F. Cash, R. M. Goldwyn, J. A. Persing, & L. A. Whitaker (Eds.), *Psychological aspects of reconstructive and cosmetic plastic surgery: Clinical, empirical, and ethical perspectives* (pp. 301–313). Philadelphia: Lippincott, Williams, & Wilkins.

Lipworth, L., Nyren, O., Weimen, Y., Fryzek, J. P., Tarone, R. E., & McLaughlin, J. K. (2007). Excess mortality from suicide and other external causes of death among women with cosmetic breast implants. *Annals of Plastic Surgery, 59,* 119–123.

Losee, J. E., Jian, S., Long, D. E., Kreipe, R. E., Caldwell, E. H., & Serletti, J. M. (2004). Macromastia as an etiologic factor in bulimia nervosa: 10-year follow up after treatment with reduction mammaplasty. *Annals of Plastic Surgery, 52,* 452–457.

Losee, J. E., Serletti, J. M., Kreipe, R. E., & Caldwell, E. H. (1997). Reduction mammaplasty in patients with bulimia nervosa. *Annals of Plastic Surgery, 39,* 443–446.

Mallon, E., Newton, J. N., Klassen, A., Stewart-Brown, S. L., Ryan, T. J., & Finlay, A. Y. (1999). The quality of life in acne: A comparison with general medical conditions using generic questionnaires. *British Journal of Dermatology, 140,* 672–676.

Marcus, P. (1984). Psychological aspects of cosmetic rhinoplasty. *British Journal of Plastic Surgery, 37,* 313–318.

Mayville, S. B., Katz, R. C., Gipson, M. T, & Cabral, K. (1999). Assessing the prevalence of body dysmorphic disorder in an ethnically diverse group of adolescents. *Journal of Child and Family Studies, 8,* 357–362.

McIntosh, V. V., Britt, E., & Bulik, C. M. (1994). Cosmetic breast augmentation and eating disorders. *New Zealand Medical Journal, 107,* 151–152.

McLaughlin, J. K., Lipworth, L., & Tarone, R. E. (2003). Suicide among women with cosmetic breast implants: A review of the epidemiologic evidence. *Journal of Long-Term Effects of Medical Implants, 13,* 445–450.

Micheli-Pellegrini, V., & Manfrida, G. M. (1979). Rhinoplasty and its psychological implications. Applied psychology observations in aesthetic surgery. *Aesthetic Plastic Surgery, 3,* 299–319.

Ogden, C. L., Carroll, M. D., Curtin, L. R., McDowell, M. A., Tabak, C. J., & Flegal, K. M. (2006). Prevalence of overweight and obesity in the U.S., 1999–2004. *JAMA, 295,* 1549–1555.

Ohlsen, L., Ponten, B., & Hambert, G. (1978). Augmentation mammaplasty: A surgical and psychiatric evaluation of the results. *Annals of Plastic Surgery, 2,* 42–52.

Otto, M. W., Wilhelm, S., Cohen, L. S., & Harlow, B. L. (2001). Prevalence of body dysmorphic disorder in a community sample of women. *American Journal of Psychiatry, 158,* 2061–2063.

Papadopoulos, L., Walker, C., Aitken, D., & Bor, R. (2000). The relationship between body location and psychological morbidity in individuals with acne vulgaris. *Psychology, Health, and Medicine, 5,* 431–438.

Park, A. J., Chetty, U., & Watson, A. C. H. (1996). Patient satisfaction following insertion of silicone breast implants. *British Journal of Plastic Surgery, 49,* 515–518.

Pearl, A., & Weston, J. (2003). Attitudes of adolescents about cosmetic surgery. *Annals of Plastic Surgery, 50,* 628–630.

Phillips, K. A., Coles, M. E., Menard, W., Yen, S., Fay, C., & Weisberg, R. B. (2005). Suicidal ideation and suicide attempts in body dysmorphic disorder. *The Journal of Clinical Psychiatry, 66,* 717–725.

Phillips, K. A., & Dufresne, R. G. (2000). Body dysmorphic disorder: A guide for dermatologists and cosmetic surgeons. *American Journal of Clinical Dermatology, 4*, 235–243.

Phillips, K. A., Grant, J., Siniscalchi, J., & Albertini, R. S. (2001). Surgical and nonpsychiatric medical treatment of patients with body dysmorphic disorder. *Psychosomatics, 42*, 504.

Phillips, K. A., Menard, W., Fay, C., & Weisberg, R. (2005). Demographic characteristics, phenomenology, comorbidity and family history in 200 individuals with body dysmorphic disorder. *Psychosomatics, 46*, 317–325.

Pukkala, E., Kulmala, I., Hovi, S. L., Hemminki, E., Keskimäki, I. Pakkanen, M., et al. (2003). Causes of death among Finnish women with cosmetic breast implants, 1971–2001. *Annals of Plastic Surgery, 51*, 39–342.

Rief, W., Buhlmann, U., Wilhelm, S., Borkenhagen, A., Brahler, E. (2006). The prevalence of body dysmorphic disorder: A population-based survey. *Psychological Medicine, 36*, 877–885.

Rohrich, R. J., Broughton, G., Horton, B., Lipschitz, A., Kenkel, J. M., & Brown, S. A. (2004). The key to long-term success in liposuction: A guide for plastic surgeons and patients. *Plastic and Reconstructive Surgery, 114*, 1945–1952.

Rubinow, D. R., Peck, G. L., Squillace, K. M., & Gantt, G. G. (1987). Anxiety and depression in cystic acne patients after successful treatment with isotretinoin. *Journal of the American Academy of Dermatology, 17*, 25–32.

Sarwer, D. B. (2006). Psychological assessment of cosmetic surgery patients. In D. B. Sarwer, T. Pruzinsky, T. F. Cash, R. M. Goldwyn, J. A. Persing, & L. A. Whitaker (Eds.), *Psychological aspects of reconstructive and cosmetic plastic surgery: Clinical, empirical, and ethical perspectives* (pp. 267–283). Philadelphia: Lippincott, Williams, & Wilkins.

Sarwer, D. B. (2007). The psychological aspects of cosmetic breast augmentation. *Plastic and Reconstructive Surgery, 120*, 110S–117S.

Sarwer, D. B., Allison, K. C., Fabricatore, A. N., Faith, M. S., Tsai, A. G., & Wadden, T. A. (2006). Childhood obesity and cosmetic surgery. *Plastic and Reconstructive Surgery, 119*, 106–1107.

Sarwer, D. B., Brown, G. K., & Evans, D. L. (2007). Cosmetic breast augmentation and suicide: A review of the literature. *American Journal of Psychiatry, 164*, 1006–1113.

Sarwer, D. B., Cash, T. F., Magee, L., Williams, E. F., Thompson, J. K., Roehrig, M., et al. (2005). Female college students and cosmetic surgery: An investigation of experiences, attitudes, and body image. *Plastic and Reconstructive Surgery, 115*, 931–938.

Sarwer, D. B., & Crerand, C. E. (2004). Body image and cosmetic medical treatments. *Body Image, 1*, 99–111.

Sarwer, D. B., Didie, E. R., & Gibbons, L. M. (2006). In D. B. Sarwer, T. Pruzinsky, T. F. Cash, R. M. Goldwyn, J. A. Persing, & L. A. Whitaker (Eds.), *Psychological aspects of reconstructive and cosmetic plastic surgery: Clinical, empirical, and ethical perspectives* (pp. 251–266). Philadelphia: Lippincott, Williams, & Wilkins.

Sarwer, D. B., & Fabricatore, A. N. (2008). Psychiatric considerations of the massive weight loss patient. *Clinics in Plastic Surgery, 35*, 1–10.

Sarwer, D. B., Foster, G. D., & Wadden, T. A. (2004). Treatment of obesity I: Adult obesity. In J. K. Thompson (Ed.), *Handbook of eating disorders and obesity* (pp. 421–442). Hoboken, NJ: Wiley.

Sarwer, D. B., LaRossa, D., Bartlett, S. P., Low, D. W., Bucky, L. P., & Whitaker, L. A. (2003). Body image concerns of breast augmentation patients. *Plastic and Reconstructive Surgery, 112,* 83–90.

Sarwer, D. B., Pruzinsky, T., Cash, T. F., Goldwyn, R. M., Persing, J. A., & Whitaker, L. A. (2006). *Psychological aspects of reconstructive and cosmetic plastic surgery: Clinical, empirical, and ethical perspectives.* Philadelphia: Lippincott, Williams, & Wilkins.

Sarwer, D. B., Thompson, J. K., Mitchell, J. E., & Rubin, J. P. (2008). Psychological considerations of the bariatric surgery patient undergoing body contouring surgery. *Plastic and Reconstructive Surgery, 121*(6), 423e–434e.

Sarwer, D. B., Wadden, T. A., Pertschuk, M. J., & Whitaker, L. A. (1998a). Body image dissatisfaction and body dysmorphic disorder in 100 cosmetic surgery patients. *Plastic and Reconstructive Surgery, 101,* 1644–1649.

Sarwer, D. B., Wadden, T. A., Pertschuk, M. J., & Whitaker, L. A. (1998b). The psychology of cosmetic surgery: A review and reconceptualization. *Clinical Psychology Review, 18,* 1–22.

Sarwer, D. B., Wadden, T. A., & Whitaker, L. A. (2002). An investigation of changes in body image following cosmetic surgery. *Plastic and Reconstructive Surgery, 109,* 636–639.

Schlebusch, L. (1989). Negative bodily experience and prevalence of depression in patients who request augmentation mammaplasty. *South African Medical Journal, 75,* 323.

Schlebusch, L., & Levin, A. (1983). A psychological profile of women selected for augmentation mammaplasty. *South African Medical Journal, 64,* 481.

Shakespeare, V., & Cole, R. P. (1997). Measuring patient-based outcomes in a plastic surgery service: Breast reduction surgical patients. *British Journal of Plastic Surgery, 50,* 242–248.

Sheerin, D., MacLeod, M., & Kusumakar, V. (1995). Psychosocial adjustment in children with port-wine stains and prominent ears. *Journal of the American Academy of Child & Adolescent Psychiatry, 34,* 1637–1647.

Simis, K. J., Hovius, S. E. R., de Beaufort, I. D., Verhulst, F. C., & Koot, H. M. (2002). After plastic surgery: Adolescent reported appearance ratings and appearance-related burdens in patient and general population groups. *Plastic and Reconstructive Surgery, 109,* 9–17.

Simis, K. J., Verhulst, F. C., & Koot, H. M. (2001). Body image, psychosocial functioning, and personality: How different are adolescents and young adults applying for plastic surgery? *Journal of Child Psychology and Psychiatry and Allied Disciplines, 42,* 669–678.

Storch, E. A., Lewin A. B., Geffken, G. R., Heidgerken, A. D., Stawser M. S., Baumeister, A., & Silverstein, J. H. (2004). Psychosocial adjustment of two boys with gynecomastia. *Journal of Pediatrics and Child Health, 40,* 331.

Villeneuve, P. J., Holowaty, E. J., Brisson, J., Xie, L., Ugnat, A. M., Latulippe, L., & Mao, Y. (2006). Mortality among Canadian women with cosmetic breast implants. *American Journal of Epidemiology, 164,* 334–341.

Wells, K. E., Cruse, C. W., Baker, J. L., Jr., Daniels, S. M., Stern, R. A., Neuman, C., et al. (1994). The health status of women following cosmetic surgery. *Plastic and Reconstructive Surgery, 93*, 907–912.

Willard, S. G., McDermott, B. E., & Woodhouse, L. (1996). Lipoplasty in the bulimic patient. *Plastic and Reconstructive Surgery, 98*, 276–278.

Wright, M. R., & Wright, W. K. (1975). A psychological study of patients undergoing cosmetic surgery. *Archives of Otolaryngology, 101*, 145–151.

Xanthakos, S. A., Daniels, S. R., & Inge, T. H. (2006). Bariatric surgery in adolescents: An update. *Adolescent Medicine Clinics, 17*, 589–612.

Yates, A., Shisslak, C. M., Allender, J. R., & Wolman, W. (1988). Plastic surgery and the bulimic patient. *International Journal of Eating Disorders, 7*, 557–560.

Young, V. L., Nemecek, J. R., & Nemecek, D. A. (1994). The efficacy of breast augmentation: Breast size increase, patient satisfaction, and psychological effects. *Plastic and Reconstructive Surgery, 94*, 958–969.

Young, L. V., & Watson, M. E. (2006). Breast reduction. In D. B. Sarwer, T. Pruzinsky, T. F. Cash, R. M. Goldwyn, J. A. Persing, & L. A. Whitaker (Eds.), *Psychological aspects of reconstructive and cosmetic plastic surgery: Clinical, empirical, and ethical perspectives* (pp. 189–206). Philadelphia: Lippincott, Williams, & Wilkins.

IV

CONCLUSION

MORE QUESTIONS: SOME CONCLUDING THOUGHTS ON BODY IMAGE, EATING DISORDERS, AND OBESITY IN YOUTH

LINDA SMOLAK AND J. KEVIN THOMPSON

It is evident throughout this volume that tremendous progress has been made in understanding body image, eating disorders, and obesity among children and adolescents. For example, researchers have become much more cognizant of the links among the three phenomena. Awareness of how body image, eating problems, and obesity develop cross-culturally, in boys, and in various American ethnic groups has grown. Indeed, this edition has chapters on boys and on cross-cultural research that did not appear in any form in the first edition.

Researchers are making particular progress in understanding the risk factors and precursors that might contribute to the development of these problems, though there are startling gaps in the research. For example, the genetics and neuroscience approaches that are "hot" topics in the adult literature are almost without child and adolescent data. There is still much ground to cover in terms of outlining the developmental course of all three problems, particularly in the younger age groups. For example, researchers are still hard pressed to say whether boys' investment in muscularity emerges at the same early ages that girls' commitment to thinness does. There is even more work to be done in identifying successful intervention programs, be it prevention or treatment. There are virtually no targeted prevention programs for children who are younger than high school age, despite claims that these are the most effective types of programs to prevent eating disorders. One wonders whether this claim even applies to young children who are still quite positive about their bodies. Psychopharmacological approaches remain largely unevaluated among children, despite their likely use with this population.

We certainly do not want to ignore or even underestimate the substantial advances in the field that this book showcases. The expert authors of the various chapters have noted some areas for future research. That is the thread we wish to pick up in this concluding chapter. The purpose of this chapter is to identify 4 major topics in each of the areas covered in this edition: body image, eating disorders, and obesity. Of course, the focus is exclusively on children and adolescents and there is no assumption that information about adults will automatically transfer to younger populations.

BODY IMAGE

The study of body image has expanded to include research about preschool age children (< 6 years), boys, and previously under-represented groups (e.g., cross-cultural data). Such growth has underscored the need for more accurate, psychometrically tested assessment; the lack of information about developmental course of body image development; the relationship of body image to the later development of eating disorders and disordered eating; and the identification of universal prevention programs that might work with children.

Assessment

Anderson, Lavender, Milnes, and Simmons (chap. 10, this volume) include several available body image measures for use with adolescents. These measures often have considerable psychometric validity information, although there is important variability. However, the younger the children, the fewer measures that researchers can use. For example, the figure silhouettes so commonly used with adolescents and adults appear to lack stability and, perhaps, validity with preschool children (Collins, 1991; Musher-Eizenman, Holub, Edwards-Leeper, Persson, & Goldstein, 2003; Smolak, 2004). Researchers have not established what information children use to answer these questions. Preschoolers perceived body shape is not related to their actual body mass index (BMI), for example (Holub, 2008). Thus, when they select a figure that indicates their current body shape, it is based on something other than their actual weight. Whether this reflects perceptual or cognitive development, social desirability, or a misunderstanding of the task is unknown. Similarly, preschool children do not seem to fully comprehend the word "diet" although they do report dieting behaviors (Holub et al., 2005).

Similarly, questionnaire and interview measures are not clearly useful with very young children. Even scales designed for children, such as the Body Esteem Scale (Mendelson, Mendelson, & White, 2001), have not been validated for use with preschoolers. Some measures that have been devised to assess body image related attitudes in young children do not meet standard criteria for internal consistency (Holub, 2008; Musher-Eizenman, Holub, Miller, Goldstein, & Edwards-Leeper, 2004). There is a particular gap in measures of investment of muscularity; the Drive for Muscularity Scale (McCreary & Sasse, 2000), apparently has a different factor structure with young adolescents than with older adolescents and adults (Smolak & Stein, 2006). There is not a muscularity measure that has demonstrated validity with preschool or early elementary school children. It will be impossible to describe the developmental progression of body image without such measures.

Developmental Progression and Future Disordered Eating

Because there is a dearth of longitudinal data, particularly for groups other than White girls, it is difficult to describe when body dissatisfaction becomes problematic. If a 5-year-old expresses weight and shape dissatisfaction, how likely is she to report such concerns at 8, 10, or 14? In other words, at what point does body dissatisfaction become stable? In a related vein, although the research is quite clear that adolescent weight concerns predict disordered eating, does childhood body dissatisfaction or weight concerns do this? Or are there some groups of children for whom body dissatisfaction predicts disordered eating while for others there is no relationship? It needs to be ascertained whether there may be moderator variables in the relationship between body dissatisfaction and disordered eating.

The possibility of moderating variables reinforces the importance of describing body image development among ethnic minority children and adolescents as well as in boys (of all ethnic groups). Research has clearly established that boys and ethnic minority children do indeed suffer from body dissatisfaction. Yet, there are surprisingly new data concerning the age of onset of muscle or weight and shape concerns, the stability of such concerns, or their predictive ability.

It is not reasonable to expect to identify etiological factors in body dissatisfaction, much less effective treatment or prevention programs, without a clear description of the developmental progression. Future research should try to trace both positive and negative aspects of body image in order to better identify potential protective factors.

Universal Prevention

Two meta-analyses examining eating disorders prevention programs (Fingeret, Warren, Cepeda-Benito, & Gleaves, 2006; Stice and Shaw, 2004) have found that targeted prevention has produced larger effect sizes in reducing body dissatisfaction and eating problems than universal or universal-selective programs have (Levine & Smolak, chap. 11, this volume; in press). Targeted prevention has been virtually nonexistent with young adolescents or with children. In the case of children, this may be at least partly because it is difficult to definitively identify "at risk" cases, a prerequisite for targeted prevention.

Does the relative success of targeted prevention mean that attempts at universal prevention should be abandoned? There are at least two reasons why researchers should not do so. First, few would agree that it is acceptable to let the behaviors and attitudes "targeted" in targeted prevention develop. For example, in a recent article, Stice, Presnell, Gau, and Shaw (2007) evaluated the efficacy of targeted prevention in reducing thin ideal internalization, body dissatisfaction, restrained eating, and bulimic symptoms among 14- to 19-year-old girls and women. Universal prevention (or universal–selective) programs hold the possibility of intervening with young enough children to prevent the onset of thin ideal internalization, body dissatisfaction, restrained eating, and bulimic symptoms rather than seeking to reduce them as targeted prevention does. Given the psychological and physical risks of these attitudes and behaviors, it would certainly be better if they never occurred.

Second, there are enough methodological problems in the extant literature to argue that universal prevention outcomes have yet to be effectively measured. Most studies employ a design that will be more favorable to documenting effects of targeted than universal prevention. In this normative design, there are pre-post assessments, with the posttest measures taken upon completion of the program, with short-term follow-up of 6 to 24 months. The goal, typically, is to lower "risk factors" from pre-to-post and then to hold (or increase) those improvements at the follow-up. This goal is best achieved if the pretest scores are high enough to easily decline. This is not to say that it is easy to design a successful targeted prevention program. However, if body image and disordered eating scores are relatively low (i.e., indicative of good health), it will be more difficult to see immediate or short-term declines.

Instead, what one would be looking for is the failure of body image or eating problems to onset. To establish this type of prevention effect, healthy childhood participants would be followed into developmental risk periods (e.g., adolescence). For example, a program might be directed at 5- to 6-year olds and the children would be followed into at least early adolescence. Data like these are currently not available but remain a challenge for future researchers. Again, information concerning the developmental progression of body image and disordered eating would be very helpful in designing such a study.

EATING DISORDERS

Eating disorders (ED) in children are poorly understood in part because they are even rarer than in adults. However, ED clearly occurs among children. Indeed, the current diagnostic criteria may be leading to under-estimates or misdiagnosis of ED in children. Furthermore, researchers are increasingly arguing that genetics and neurochemistry create predispositions for eating disorders. There is almost no genetic or neurological research with children and adolescents. Indeed, even the psychopharmacological research that might yield clues about neurochemistry is rare with child participants. Despite the great need to investigate these biological factors, it is equally critical to recognize that there are important gender and ethnic group differences in childhood ED. Thus, the four issues we will consider here are nosology, genetic and neurochemical factors, psychopharmacological (and other) treatments, and the influence of gender and ethnicity.

Nosology

ED diagnostic criteria are often simply not applicable to young children. They do not have the cognitive or self-development (or, in the case of amenorrhea, physical development) necessary to meet the criteria. This does not mean that children have no clinically significant eating problems. Indeed, Watkins and Lask (chap. 2, this volume) outline the Great Ormand Street Criteria that propose diagnostic criteria not only for anorexia nervosa (AN) and bulimia nervosa (BN) but other childhood eating disorders. There are some validity data available for the Great Ormand Street criteria but much more psychometric research is needed.

In addition, epidemiological data concerning AN, BN, and the other disorders in the Great Ormand Street list must be collected. Both frequency information and developmental progressions are needed. There are already limited data suggesting that childhood eating problems, e.g., "picky" eating, are risk factors for the later development of ED (Marchi & Cohen, 1990). Much more research is needed.

Neurochemistry and Genetic Influences

With the field of neuroscience growing by leaps and bounds, it is no surprise that neurochemistry has been hypothesized to be instrumental in the development of various psychological disorders, including ED and the comorbid mood disorders (Jimerson & Wolfe, 2006; Kaye, Frank, Bailer, & Henry, 2005). Genetics have also been hypothesized to play an etiological role in ED (Bulik & Tozzi, 2004) perhaps by establishing a vulnerable neurochemical (e.g., serotonin) system (Steiger, 2004). Both genetics and neurochemistry are receiving increasing attention from funding agencies, therapeutic approaches, and even the popular press.

At the present time, neither genetics nor neurochemistry can be established as etiological factors via experimental design. Therefore, researchers must try to investigate the potential causal role of these biological factors by first establishing temporal precedence. The proposed serotonin vulnerability, for example, must predate the onset of symptoms of BN. If the vulnerability is genetically induced, as opposed to caused by an environmental experience such as trauma, then the genes involved must be identified prior to the onset of BN. All of these and related possibilities must be investigated in children and adolescents in order to establish such precedence.

It is further noteworthy that research has yet to establish that genetic-ED or neurochemistry-ED links are the same in children as in adults or adolescents. While ED is rare among children and adolescents, it occurs frequently enough to do these investigations, particularly through collaborative research. It would even be interesting to assess whether girls who appear to be at risk for developing ED (e.g., girls who score unusually high on weight concerns scales) have unusual levels of serotonin or other neurotransmitters.

Psychopharmacology

In general, therapeutic techniques for ED have not been widely tested with children and adolescents. It is not clear that the techniques widely used with adults, including cognitive–behavioral therapy and interpersonal therapy, work well with children and adolescents. Thus, all forms of therapy, including those that are commonly used with adolescents (e.g., the Maudsley approach; Rhodes, Gosbee, Madden, & Brown, 2005) need to be investigated more fully, particularly with children.

Psychopharmacology is commonly used to treat a variety of disorders, including depression. Serious questions have been raised regarding the cost–benefit ratio of using antidepressants with children and adolescents (Bridge et al., 2007). The FDA's decision to add a black box warning about the risk of suicide in adolescents using SSRIs underscores the importance of testing drugs with various age groups. While no single drug or set of drugs has been found to be consistently useful in ending ED symptoms, testing of pharmacological approaches should include the youngest clients.

Such psychopharmacological research may also provide some clues concerning the neurochemistry of ED. The specific action of most drugs is not sufficiently understood to claim that pharmacological experiments will definitively establish underlying etiology. Nonetheless they can provide suggestive evidence. Certainly there are ethical challenges in this research but if a drug has been established as efficacious with adults, it becomes reasonable, perhaps even imperative, that its usefulness with children and adolescents be investigated.

Gender and Ethnicity

Research has clearly established that the rate and type of ED varies by gender as well as by ethnicity. The gender differences are particularly large and robust. Research that explains these effects is desperately needed.

Gender and ethnicity are social constructs. They summarize a variety of experiences, opportunities, and expectations. Researchers need to analyze the components of gender and ethnicity to try to pinpoint the sources of the group effects. This work is only beginning with adults (Smolak & Murnen, 2004, 2007). Objectification as a "lived experience" of being female (Fredrickson & Roberts, 1997) is particularly receiving attention in the adult literature. Scales to measure objectification in adolescents have been developed (Lindberg, Hyde, & McKinley, 2006; Tolman, Impett, Tracy, & Michael, 2006) enabling examination of this factor in a younger group. Whether objectification is a meaningful construct with younger children remains an open question. Other potential risk factors associated with gender, including sexual abuse and sexual harassment, have received surprisingly little attention in child and adolescent research.

Protective factors are also interesting to consider. Non-elite sports participation in high school may be associated with lower body dissatisfaction (Smolak, Murnen, & Ruble, 2000). This link requires further investigation. Among adults, feminist identity is correlated with lower internalization of thin ideal, body dissatisfaction, and disordered eating (Hurt et al., 2007; Myers & Crowther, 2007). Whether and how this effect might translate to children and adolescents is unclear. However, the prevention literature suggests a factor related to feminism, critiquing social images of women, might reduce risk (Piran & Cormier, 2005). Research with elementary school children suggests that girls who reject media images of the thin ideal have more positive body images (Murnen, Smolak, Mills, & Good, 2003). All of these protective factors may be related to empowerment, a component of feminism that may make girls and women feel more in control of their life circumstances, social support systems, and decision making (Worell, 2006). Such control may prove protective against body image and eating problems.

The research with children will be challenging because of developmental shifts in gender role and ethnic identity (Ruble et al., 2007; Whitesell, Mitchell, Kaufman, Spicer, & the Voices of America, 2006). This underscores the importance of longitudinal research as well as the importance of developing age appropriate measures (Smolak, 1996). Furthermore, it is evident that relationships between risk factors and outcomes may change with age, sometimes in ways that reflect deep structure changes in the self or cognitive system (Dittmar, Halliwell, & Ive, 2006). Thus, the relationships between distal and proximal risk factors as well those between risk–protective factors and outcomes across development must be considered (McCartney, Burchinal, & Bub, 2006).

OBESITY

Public health officials routinely describe childhood and adolescent obesity as an epidemic with serious health consequences. Yet, there continues to be some debate about the health consequences of obesity, particularly in childhood. This is partly because it has been challenging to define obesity and overweight in children. Furthermore, although there is evidence of a relationship between childhood and adult obesity, there is limited information on what creates (or undermines) this link. Finally, in the interest of public health, it is important to examine and understand the relationships between disordered eating and obesity, including efforts to prevent both.

Defining Overweight and Obesity

The Centers for Disease Control and Prevention (CDC; 2007a) does not currently recognize "obesity" per se among children and adolescents; instead they define "overweight" and "at risk for overweight". A child whose BMI is equal to or greater than the 95th percentile for age and gender is considered overweight. One whose BMI is equal to or greater than the 85th percentile but less than the 95th percentile for age and gender is considered at risk for overweight (CDC, 2007a). These standards have been widely used in research concerning etiology, treatment, and prevention of childhood obesity. Yet, recent discussions and recommendations calling for a clearer definition of *obesity* per se, highlight the controversy surrounding the criteria (Barlow & the Expert Committee, 2007; Spear et al., 2007).

Some of the problem arises from concern that the use of the word "obese" will lead to stigmatization of the child (O'Dea, 2005). Yet, particularly the "at risk for overweight" category leaves some people, including some physicians, unsure of the importance of the child's weight "problem" (Dilley, Martin, Sullivan, Seshadri, & Binns, 2007). However, some of the definitional problems echo those of adult obesity. In adulthood, overweight is defined as a BMI over 25 while obesity is defined as a BMI exceeding 30 (CDC, 2007b). It is assumed that the risk of illness, disability, and even morbidity linearly rises with BMI such that overweight people face more problems that normal weight people do with even higher risks associated with obesity. Yet, some research (Romero-Corral et al., 2006) suggests that being slightly overweight may actually be protective against some diseases and disorders. In other words, the BMI values used to define overweight and obesity appear to be somewhat arbitrary vis-à-vis health risks.

Research needs to establish the BMIs that are associated with real health risks among children and adolescents. These risks may be short-term or long-term; they may be greater for some groups than for others; and they may depend on whether or not the overweight status is maintained. It is crucially important to investigate these links among ethnic minority children since, even as preschoolers, they have higher rates of overweight than white children do. Definitions of overweight and obesity should be tied to actual medical risk.

Relatedly, researchers need to ascertain whether BMI is actually the best predictor of health problems in children. Particularly around puberty, when some children's weight spurt will precede their height spurt while others will grow taller before gaining weight, children's BMIs can be unreliable indicators of their eating and exercise habits as well as their health status. Perhaps fat to muscle ratios would be more adequate indicators, for example. Furthermore, given the changes associated with growth, there may also need to be a criterion that the overweight status persists for some appointed amount of time.

Health Consequences of Overweight and Obesity

The popular press has frequently trumpeted findings that diabetes is increasing among young children because of obesity. While some research shows it is the nonoverweight related Type I diabetes that has increased (Kemper, Dombkowski, Menon, & Davis, 2006), others have demonstrated an increase in Type II diabetes (Dabeles et al., 1998). The question is whether it is amount of body fat per se that is creating this problem or poor nutrition or exercise or some interaction of these. It is possible that even environmental stress is playing a role.

The timing of onset of overweight status as well as its duration may also play a role in the development of health problems. Furthermore, the presence of other health problems as well as medical support and care may be instrumental in determining the long-term outcomes of obesity. Longitudinal research tracing patterns of obesity and their outcomes is essential to this endeavor as are experimental design studies demonstrating the effects of weight loss on child health.

Mediators of the Childhood–Adult Obesity and the Obesity–Health Risk Links

Successful treatment and prevention of adult obesity and its accompanying health problems relies on understanding when and why childhood obesity leads to these problems. The greater risk of obesity among ethnic minority children and adults provides a starting point for this research. More attention needs to be given to how lifestyle factors of ethnic minority groups might create this risk.

Genetics is a particularly interesting and important potential mediator. Researchers have long claimed that weight is heavily genetically determined, with perhaps 25% to 40% of weight variability attributable to genetics (Wadden, Brownell, & Foster, 2002). Others note that obesity has risen precipitously during the past two decades without a concomitant change in the gene pool. While the latter claim is certainly true and underscores the role of nutritional and exercise pattern changes in the United States, it is also possible that the presence of certain genes creates a vulnerability to the relatively high-fat and calorie and low-exercise lifestyle of many Americans. Genetic studies that focus on children can help to answer this question. Such studies can help us to ascertain whether genetic influence is important at all stages of development or whether it is only triggered at certain times. For example, puberty, with its weight gain, may be a time of particular genetic risk. Or the genetic risk may be greater throughout childhood, when there are many periods of active growth, than in adulthood. Such possibilities deserve more research attention.

Obesity and Disordered Eating

Too frequently, the prevention and treatment of eating disorders seems to be at odds with treating and preventing obesity (Bauer, Haines, & Neumark-Sztainer, chap. 12, this volume). Eating disorders specialists want to minimize restrictive eating while obesity experts want to encourage at least watching fat or calories. Thus, eating disorders prevention researchers may be concerned that obesity prevention encourages body dissatisfaction and focus on eating and so encourages eating disorders. Obesity prevention program designers, on the other hand, may be concerned that eating disorders programs encourage body acceptance at any size and critiques of caloric restriction and so may be fostering obesity.

There is common ground for eating disorder and obesity researchers, however. In both types of prevention programs, for example, there is emphasis on healthy eating and exercise. There is also commonly a discussion of self-esteem and self-acceptance. Both prevention efforts may encourage a critical reading of the media, albeit from somewhat different angles. Thus, one can envision programs that integrate both perspectives into one program, an effort that would improve the cost–benefit ratio of prevention.

CONCLUSION

Despite a growing body of empirical literature and substantial progress in understanding the assessment, etiology, outcomes, treatment, and prevention of body image, eating, and obesity problems in children and adolescents, childhood remains something of a frontier for researchers concerned with weight and shape. In this chapter we have tried to highlight some of the broad, unanswered questions about childhood body image and eating problems. The list is by necessity selective; there are many other possibilities for future research.

Researchers need to continue to use their data to lobby for increased funding for research, treatment, and prevention. Body image problems, disordered eating, and obesity appear to have long term costs psychologically and physically. As more information becomes available concerning etiology and outcomes, treatment and prevention will become more effective. Finding the links among body image, eating disorders, and obesity as well as between basic and applied research needs to continue as a goal for our research endeavors.

REFERENCES

Barlow, S., & the Expert Committee. (2007). Expert Committee recommendations egarding the prevention, assessment, and treatment of child and adolescent overweight and obesity: Summary report. *Pediatrics, 120*, S164-S192.

Bridge, J., Iyengar, S., Salary, C. B., Barbe, R., Birmaher, B., Pincus, H. A., et al. (2007). Clinical response and risk for reported suicidal ideation and suicide attempts in pediatric antidepressant treatments: A meta-analysis of randomized controlled trials. *Journal of the American Medical Association, 297*, 1683–1697.

Bulik, C., & Tozzi, F. (2004). Genetics in eating disorders: State of the science. *CNS Spectrums, 9*, 511–515.

Centers for Disease Control and Prevention. (2007a). *About BMI for children and teens.* Retrieved February 13, 2008, from www.cdc.gov/nccdphp/dnpa/bmi/childrens_BMI/about_children_BMI.htm

Centers for Disease Control and Prevention. (2007b). *Defining overweight and obesity.* Retrieved February 13, 2008, from www.cdc.gov/nccdphp/dnpa/obesity/defining.htm

Collins, M. E. (1991). Body figure perceptions and preferences among preadolescent children. *International Journal of Eating Disorders, 10*, 100–108.

Dabeles, D., Hanson, R., Bennett, P., Roumain, J., Knowler, W., & Pettitt, D. (1998). Increasing prevalence of Type II diabetes in American Indian children. *Diabetologia, 41*, 904–910.

Dilley, K., Martin, L., Sullivan, C., Seshadri, R., & Binns, H. J. (2007). Identification of overweight status is associated with higher rates of screening for comorbidities of overweight in pediatric primary care practice. *Pediatrics, 119*, e148-e155.

Dittmar, H., Halliwell, E., & Ive, S. (2006). Does Barbie make girls want to be thin? The effect of experimental exposure to images of dolls on the body image of 5- to 8-year-old girls. *Developmental Psychology, 42*, 283–292.

Fingeret, M. C., Warren, C. S., Cepeda-Benito, A., & Gleaves, D. H. (2006). Eating disorder prevention research: A meta-analysis. *Eating Disorders: The Journal of Treatment & Prevention, 14*, 191–213.

Fredrickson, B. L., & Roberts, T. A. (1997). Objectification theory: Toward understanding women's lived experiences and mental health risks. *Psychology of Women Quarterly, 21*, 173–206.

Holub, S. (2008). The anti-fat attitudes of pre-school children: The importance of perceived body size. *Body Image, 5*, 317–321.

Holub, S. C., Musher-Eizenman, D. R., Persson, A. V., Edwards-Leeper, L. A., Goldstein, S. E., & Barnhart, A. (2005). Do preschool children understand what it means to "diet" and do they do it? *International Journal of Eating Disorders, 38*, 91–93.

Hurt, M. M., Nelson, J. A., Turner, D. L., Haines, M. E., Ramsey, L. R., Erhcull, M. J., & Liss, M. (2007). Feminism: What is it good for? Feminine norms and objectification as the link between feminist identity and clinically relevant outcomes. *Sex Roles, 57*, 355–363.

Jimerson, D., & Wolfe, B. (2006). Psychobiology of eating disorders. In S. Wonderlich, J. Mitchell, M. de Zwaan, & H. Steiger (Eds.), *Annual review of eating disorders part 2–2006* (pp. 1–15). Oxford, England: Radcliffe Publishing.

Kaye, W., Frank, G., Bailer, U., & Henry, S. (2005). Neurobiology of anorexia nervosa: Clinical implications of alterations of the function of serotonin and other neuronal systems. *International Journal of Eating Disorders, 37*, S15–S19.

Kemper, A., Dombkowski, K., Menon, R., & Davis, M. M. (2006). Trends in diabetes mellitus among privately insured children, 1998–2002. *Ambulatory Pediatrics, 6*, 178–181.

Levine, M. P., & Smolak, L. (in press). "What exactly *are* we waiting for?" The case for universal-selective eating disorders prevention programs. *IJDHD.*

Lindberg, S., Hyde, J. S., & McKinley, N. M. (2006). A measure of objectified body consciousness for preadolescent and adolescent youth. *Psychology of Women Quarterly, 30*, 65–76.

Marchi, M., & Cohen, P. (1990). Early childhood eating behaviors and adolescent eating disorders. *Journal of the American Academy of Child and Adolescent Psychiatry, 29*, 112–117.

McCartney, K., Burchinal, M., & Bub, K. (2006). Best practices in quantitative methods for developmentalists. *Monographs of the Society for Research in Child Development, 71*(3), Serial # 285.

McCreary, D. R., & Sasse, D. K. (2000). An exploration of the drive for muscularity in adolescent boys and girls. *Journal of American College Health, 48*, 297–304.

Mendelson, B. K., Mendelson, M. J., & White, D. R. (2001). Body-Esteem Scale for adolescents and adults. *Personality Assessment, 76*, 90–106.

Musher-Eizenman, D. R., Holub, S. C., Edwards-Leeper, L., Persson, A. V., & Goldstein, S. E. (2003). The narrow range of acceptable body types of preschoolers and their mothers. *Journal of Applied Developmental Psychology, 24*, 259–272.

Musher-Eizenman, D. R., Holub, S. C., Miller, A., Goldstein, S. E., & Edwards-Leeper, L. (2004). Body size stigmatization in preschool children: The role of control attributions. *Journal of Pediatric Psychology, 29*, 613–620.

Murnen, S. K., Smolak, L., Mills, J. A., & Good, L. (2003). Thin, sexy women and strong, muscular men: Grade-school children's responses to objectified images of women and men. *Sex Roles, 49,* 427–437.

Myers, T. A., & Crowther, J. H. (2007). Sociocultural pressures, thin-ideal internalization, self-objectification, and body dissatisfaction: Could feminist beliefs be a moderating factor? *Body Image, 4,* 296–308.

O'Dea, J. A. (2005). Prevention of child obesity: 'First, do no harm'. *Health Education Research, 20,* 259–265.

Piran, N., & Cormier, H. C. (2005). The social construction of women and disordered eating patterns. *Journal of Counseling Psychology, 52,* 549–558.

Rhodes, P., Gosbee, M., Madden, S., & Brown, J. (2005). 'Communities of Concern' in the family-based treatment of anorexia nervosa: Towards a consensus in the Maudsley Model. *European Eating Disorders Review, 13,* 392–398.

Romero-Corral, A., Montori, V. M., Somers, V. K., Korinek, J., Thomas, R. J., Allison, T. G., et al. (2006). Association of bodyweight with total mortality and with cardiovascular events in coronary artery disease: A systematic review of cohort studies. *Lancet, 368,* 666–678.

Ruble, D., Taylor, L., Cyphers, L., Greulich, F., Lurye, L., & Shrout, P. (2007). The role of gender constancy in early gender development. *Child Development, 78,* 1121–1136.

Smolak, L. (1996). Methodological implications of developmental approaches. In L. Smolak, M. Levine, & R. Striegel-Moore (Eds.), *The developmental psychopathology of eating disorders.* Mahwah, NJ: Erlbaum.

Smolak, L. (2004). Body image in children and adolescents: Where do we go from here? *Body Image, 1,* 15–28.

Smolak, L., & Murnen, S. K. (2004). Feminist perspectives on eating problems. In J. K. Thompson (Ed.), *Handbook of eating disorders and obesity* (pp. 590–606). New York: Wiley.

Smolak, L., & Murnen, S. K. (2007). Feminism and body image. In V. Swami & A. Furnham (Eds.), *The body beautiful: Evolutionary and sociocultural perspectives* (pp. 236–258). New York: Palgrave Macmillan.

Smolak, L., Murnen, S. K., & Ruble, A. (2000). Female athletes and eating disorders: A meta-analysis. *International Journal of Eating Disorders, 27,* 371–381.

Smolak, L., & Stein, J. A. (2006). The relationship of drive for muscularity to sociocultural factors, self-esteem, physical attributes gender role, and social comparison in middle school boys. *Body Image, 3,* 121–129.

Spear, B. A., Barlow, S. E., Ervin, C., Ludwig, D. S., Saelens, B. E., Schetzina, K. E., et al. (2007). Recommendations for the treatment of child and adolescent overweight and obesity. *Pediatrics, 120,* S254–S288.

Steiger, H. (2004). Eating disorders and the serotonin connection: State, trait and developmental effects. *Journal Psychiatry Neuroscience, 29,* 20–29.

Stice, E., Presnell, K., Gau, J., & Shaw, H. (2007). Testing mediators of intervention effects in randomized controlled trials: An evaluation of two eating disorder prevention programs. *Journal of Counseling and Clinical Psychology, 75,* 20–32.

Stice, E., & Shaw, H. E. (2004). Eating disorder prevention programs: A meta-analytic review. *Psychological Bulletin, 130,* 206–227.

Tolman, D., Impett, E., Tracy, A., & Michael, A. (2006). Looking good, sounding good: Femininity ideology and adolescent girls' mental health. *Psychology of Women Quarterly, 30,* 85–95.

Wadden, T., Brownell, K. D., & Foster, G. D. (2002). Obesity: Responding to the global epidemic. *Journal of Consulting and Clinical Psychology, 70,* 510–525.

Whitesell, N. R., Mitchell, C., Kaufman, C., Spicer, P., & the Voices of America. (2006). Developmental trajectories of personal and collective self-concept among American Indian adolescents. *Child Development, 77,* 1487–1503.

Worell, J. (2006). Pathways to healthy development: Sources of strength and empowerment. In J. Worell & C. D. Goodheart (Eds.), *Handbook of girls' and women's psychological health* (pp. 25–35). New York: Oxford.

AUTHOR INDEX

Numbers in italics refer to listings in the reference sections.

Bodor, J., 101, *111*
Bohne, A., 313, *319*
Bohr, Y., 200, *210*
Boice, R., 182, 185, *189*
Bojorquez, I., 120, 125, *129*
Boldrin, M., 295, *297*
Bolton, M. A., 304, *319*
Bond, B. J., 80, 86, *92*
Bond, M., 122, *131*
Bonds-Raacke, J., 86, *91*
Bonzheim, K. A., *171*
Boon, C. S., 241, *256*
Bor, R., 312, *322*
Borges-Dinis, P., 307, *319*
Borjeson, M., 290, *297*
Borkenhagen, A., 313, *323*
Bormann, B., 234, *234*
Borovoy, A., 114, 117, *132*
Borowiecki, J., 86, *94*
Bosveld, J., *130*
Bouchard, C., *169*
Boutelle, K., 52, *71*
Bove, C. F., 25, *29*
Bowe, W. P., 312, 314, *319*
Bowes, G., 247, *260*
Bowie, D., 207, *211*
Bowman, B. A., *110*
Bowman, J., 48, *71*
Bowman, S. A., 163, 164, *169*
Bradbury, E. T., 307, *319*
Bradlee, M. L., *172–73*
Bradley, J. S., 88, *91*
Bradley, R., *12, 153*
Braet, C., 166, *170*, 196, 199, *209*
Brahler, E., 313, *323*
Brannick, M., 218, *234*
Braud, C., *318*
Breen, A., 118, *131*
Breis, A., 165, *169*
Brennan, N., 178, *189*
Brewerton, T. D., 178, *189*, 201, *208*
Bridge, J., 334, *339*
Bridgwater, C. A., 205, *208*
Brindis, C. D., 108, *110*
Brinton, L. A., 311, *319*
Brisson, J., *324*
Britt, E., 314, *322*
Britten, C., 43, *45*
Britton, M., 102, *109*
Brix, C., 234, *234*
Brody, J., *13*
Bronner, Y., 83, *96*

Brooks-Gunn, J., 7, *12*, 51, 57–59, 61, 64, 68, 69, *71, 73*
Broughton, G., *323*
Brown, A. P., 315, *319*
Brown, G., *210*
Brown, G. K., 311, *323*
Brown, J., 334, *341*
Brown, K. M., 104, *108*
Brown, L., 144, *151*
Brown, M. R., 291, *297*
Brown, S. A., *323*
Brown, T., *260, 300*
Brownell, K. D., 7, *13*, 100, *112*, 141, *155, 169*, 249, *257*, 288, 294, 295, *297*, 338, *342*
Brownley, K. A., *276*
Brownson, R. C., *110*
Brubaker, P. H., 159, *173*
Bruning Brown, J., 223, 224, *234*
Bryant-Waugh, R., 5, 6, *11, 12*, 35, 36, 38–41, 43, *45*, 184, *189*, 194, 195, 198, *208, 210*, 212, 269, 272, 277, *278*
Brylinsky, J. A., 56, *69*
Bryson, S., *75*, 238, 263, 265, 267, 275, *277, 278*
Bryson, S. W., *210*
Bub, K., 336, *340*
Buchan, T., 124, *129*
Buchholz, A., 228, *234*
Bucky, L. P., *324*
Buhlmann, U., 313, *323*
Buka, S., *256*
Bulan, E. J., 308, *320*
Bulik, C., 140, *151, 153*, 334, *339*
Bulik, C. M., 48, *70*, 276, 314, *322*
Bunnell, D., *189*
Burchinal, M., 336, *340*
Burgard, D., *236*
Burich, M. C., 311, *319*
Burke, D., *128*
Burklow, K. A., 161, *169*, 287, *296*
Burns, J., 273, *276*
Burrows, A., 27, *29*
Burton, E., 222, *238*
Burwell, R., 115, 121, *128*
Burwinkle, T. M., 164, *173*
Busey, S. L., 83, *95*
Butler, R., 62, *72*
Button, E. J., 53, *69*
Byely, L., 59, 68, *69*
Byrne, B., 84, *91*
Byrne, N. M., *95*

Cabral, K., 186, *190, 322*
Cabras, P., 313, *320*
Cafri, G., 5, *11, 13,* 77–80, *92,* 182, 185, 186, *189, 191,* 218, *234*
Cagno, C., *237*
Caldwell, E. H., 315, *321, 322*
Calfas, K. J., *111*
Calnan, A., 189
Calogero, R. M., 140, 147, *151*
Calugi, S., 221, *237*
Camargo, C. A., Jr., *31, 70,* 247, *257*
Cameron, N., 206, *210*
Cameron, R., 136, *155*
Cameron, R. P., 68, *74,* 136, *155,* 167, *173,* 247, *260*
Campbell, K. J., 244, *256, 260, 300*
Campbell, M., 203, *208*
Campbell, M. A., 291, *297*
Campbell, R., *112*
Campra, D., *130*
Cano-Prous, A., *130*
Cansever, A., 313, *319*
Cantwell, M. M., *32*
Caplan, G., 216, *234*
Caradas, A., 115, *129*
Cardoso-Saldana, G., *133*
Carlson, J. S., 232, *237*
Carney, C. P., 196, *208*
Carr, R. E., *299*
Carroll, A. K., *279*
Carroll, D., 178, *189*
Carroll, M. D., *12,* 97, 98, *110,* 157, *172, 300, 322*
Carson, A., 115, *129*
Carter, J., 149, *155*
Carter, Y., *299*
Carvajal, S. C., 106, *109*
Cash, T. F., 51–53, *69,* 103, *108,* 180, 183, *187, 189,* 303, 304, 306, 310, 311, *319, 323, 324*
Cassady, J., 289, *296*
Castro, C., *110*
Cattarin, J., 59, *69,* 250, *257*
Cauderay, M., 88, *91*
Caust, J., 247, *260*
Celio, A. A., 207, *213,* 223, 236, *238*
Cella, J., *111*
Centers for Disease Control and Prevention (CDC), 98, *108,* 159, 160, *169, 170, 172, 173,* 234, *297,* 336, 337, *339*
Cepeda-Benito, A., 218, *235,* 332, *340*

Cervera-Enguix, S., *130*
Chabanet, C., 20, *31*
Chamberlin, L. A., 287, *296, 299*
Chamorro, R., 126, *129*
Chandarana, P., 116, *130*
Chang, J. Y., 105, *111*
Chanoine, J. P., 295, *297*
Charlton, K., 115, *129*
Chater, R., 37, *46,* 195, *211*
Chaturvedi, S., 116, *130*
Chen, E. H., 164, *169*
Cheong, J., *235*
Cherman, C., *191*
Cheskin, L. J., 102, *108,* 290, 293, 296, *299*
Chetty, U., 310, *322*
Childress, A. C., 178, *189,* 201, *208*
Chipkin, S. R., 101, *112*
Cho, M. H., 247, *257*
Chomitz, V. R., *170,* 247, *257*
Chrisler, J. C., 85, *91*
Christiansen, N. D., *279*
Christie, D., 43, *46*
Christoffel, K. K., 164, *169*
Chuang, S., *108*
Chumlea, W. C., 98, *110*
Cichetti, D., 142, 143, *151*
Ciliska, D., 233, *237*
Clair, S., 149, *155*
Clark, L., 51–53, *69,* 290, *299*
Clark, L. S., *69*
Clarke, G., *235*
Clarke, S., *13*
Cleveland, G. E., 23, *32*
Cleveland, L., *31, 32*
Clifford, E., 142, *151*
Clydesdale, F. M., 241, *256*
Coakley, E. H., *110*
Coates, T. J., *210,* 291, 295, *297*
Cohen, D., 8, *12*
Cohen, H., 116, 126, *130*
Cohen, L. S., 313, *322*
Cohen, M. L., *33, 212*
Cohen, P., 333, *340*
Cohen-Tovée, E. M., 181, 182, *189, 192*
Colditz, G., *110*
Colditz, G. A., *70,* 162, *169,* 247, *257*
Cole, D. A., 68, *69*
Cole, R. P., 315, *324*
Cole, T. J., 283, 286, *297*
Coles, M. E., 249, *260,* 313, *322*
Coller, T., 221, *237*

Colleran, E. G., 159, *170*
Collins, C. E., 292, *297*
Collins, J., 247, *257*
Collins, M. E., 81, 83, *91*, 178, *189*, 330, *339*
Collins, W. J., 35, *45*
Colton, T., 311, *319*
Commons, G. W., 308, *320*
Connors, M., 25, *30*
Consalvi, A., 290, *298*
Consantino, M. J., 274, *276*
Contento, I. R., 23, *32*, 244, *257*
Conway, T. L., 164, *171*
Cook, D. A., *31*
Cook, L. S., 310, *319*
Cook-Cottone, C., 225, *237*
Cooke, L., 20, *29*
Cooper, L., 88, *91*
Cooper, M., 27, *29*
Cooper, M. J., 181, *191*
Cooper, P., 39, 42, *45*, 46, *189*
Cooper, P. J., 39, 41–43, *45*, 180, 183, 184, *189*, 198, *208*
Cooper, Z., 39, *45*, 180, 183, 184, *189*, 198, *208, 209*
Cooperberg, J., 308, *319*
Coovert, M., 51, *75*
Cormier, H. C., 335, *341*
Cornell, C. E., 95, *112*
Cornsweet, T. N., 185, *189*
Coronado, G. D., 164, *172*
Corwin, S. J., 83, 90, *95*
Costanzo, P. R., 22, 23, *29*
Cotterill, J. A., 312, *319*
Couturier, J., 265–267, 270, 272, 275, 276, *278*
Covington, C. Y., 160, *170*
Cowell, C., *13*
Cowen, P., 142, 147, *151*
Cox, C., *33*
Cozzi, M., *130*
Crago, M., 84, *91*, 139, *154, 191, 211, 237*
Cramer, P., 56, *69*
Cramer, S., 21, *33*
Crawford, D. A., 244, *256*
Crawford, J. K., 87, *92*
Crawford, P., 56, 57, 72, *75*, 104, *108*
Crawford, P. A., *74*
Crawley, H., 247, *257*
Crerand, C. E., 303, 304, 306, 312–314, *319, 320, 323*
Crespo, C. J., 102, *108*, 293, *296*

Crisp, A., 35, *45*
Crisp, A. H., 36, *45*, 124, *133*
Croll, J., 72, 107, *108, 110*
Crosby, R., 142, *152*
Crosby, R. D., *172*, 206, 209, 263, 266, *277*
Crosnoe, R., *12, 153*
Crossan, S., 179, *190*
Crow, R., 19, *33*
Crow, S., 196, *208*, 289, 290, *299*
Crow, S. J., *172*
Crowther, J. H., 56, *74*, 196, 197, *208*, 335, *341*
Cruse, C. W., *325*
Cullen, B. A., *318–319*
Cunliffe, W. J., 312, *319*
Cunning, D., *238*
Cupples, L. A., *171–173*
Curbow, B., 115, *133*
Curtin, L. R., *12*, 300, *322*
Curtis, W. J., 142, 143, *151*
Cusumano, D. L., 84, *91*
Cutting, T. M., 26, *30*, 165, *170*
Cuzzolaro, M., 181, 184, *189*
Cybulski, M. J., *170*
Cyphers, L., *341*

Dabbah, A., 315, *320*
Dabeles, D., 337, *339*
Dafoe, J. L., 23, *31*
Daling, J. R., *319*
Dallal, G. E., 283, *299*
Dalle Grave, R., 221, *237*
Danaher, B. G., 291, *297*
Dancyger, I., 128, *129*
Daniels, S. M., *325*
Daniels, S. R., 100, *109, 171*, 200, *210*, 296, 308, *325*
Daniluk, J., 57, *75*
Dare, C., *45*, 262–264, *276–278*
Das, S., 210, *236*
da Veiga, G. V., 25, *30*
Davidson, S., 221, *239*
Davies, J., 53, *69*
Davies, M., 106, *108, 212*
Davis, D., *110*
Davis, M. M., 3, *11*, 337, *340*
Davis, R., 149, *153*, 227, *236*
Davis, S. M., 244, *257*
Davis, T. L., *170*
Davis, W. N., 147, *151*

Ellison, R. C., 32, 171–173
Elton, M., 209
Emery, J. L., 181, 182, 189, 192
Endriga, M. C., 317, 320
Engel, K., 209
Engel, S. G., 206, 209
Engler, L. B., 299
English and Romanian Adoptees Study
        Team, 143, 154
Engstrom, I.
Engström, I., 180, 186, 192, 201, 212
Eppers, K., 107, 110
Eppers-Reynolds, K., 200, 210
Eppright, T. D., 88, 91
Epstein, L. H., 282, 288–291, 293, 295,
        296, 297–299, 301
Ercolani, M., 307, 320
Erhcull, M. J., 340
Ericksen, A. J., 84, 91
Ervin, C., 13, 300, 341
Estes, L. S., 75
Evans, D. L., 311, 323
Evans, M., 95, 112
Evenson, K., 8, 12
Expert Committee, 3, 11, 336, 339
Eyler, A. A., 110

Fabian, L. J., 249, 257
Fabricatore, A. N., 308, 323
Faibisch, L., 249, 259
Fainaru, M., 289, 299
Fairburn, C. G., 39, 45, 142, 149, 151, 155,
        166, 170, 180, 183, 184, 189, 198,
        209, 262, 269, 270, 272, 276, 279
Faith, M. S., 30, 164, 165, 170, 290, 293,
        299, 308, 319, 323
Falk, L. W., 25, 30
Falkner, N., 259
Fallon, A. E., 178, 189
Faravelli, C., 147, 151, 313, 320
Fariburn, C. G., 208
Farmer, J., 200, 212
Farnill, D., 48, 74
Farrell, E. B., 170
Faulkner, P., 163, 173
Favaro, A., 57, 65, 68, 74, 75
Fawcett, J., 19, 33
Fay, C., 49, 73, 313, 320, 322, 323
Faytout, M., 318
Fear, J. L., 48, 70
Feder, S., 228, 234

Feldman, H. A., 170, 234
Feldman, J., 108
Ferrara, S., 57, 74
Ferreira, C., 115, 129
Ferron, C., 88, 91
Fichter, M. M., 125, 129, 198, 199, 209
Field, A. E., 4, 12, 24, 30, 49, 51, 57, 58, 60,
        70, 110, 136, 151, 162, 169, 225,
        234, 247, 248, 257
Finemore, J., 78, 94
Fingeret, M. C., 218, 219, 231, 235, 332,
        340
Finlay, A. Y., 322
Fiorito, L., 20, 21, 31
Firo, F., 13
Fisher, D., 11, 151
Fisher, J., 27, 31
Fisher, J. O., 23–26, 29, 163, 165, 169, 170
Fisher, M., 129, 273, 276, 316, 320
Fitzgibbon, M., 103, 104, 109
Flannery-Schroeder, E. C., 85, 91
Flegal, K. M., 12, 97, 99, 110, 112, 157,
        172, 283, 297, 300, 322
Fleitlich-Bilyk, B., 115, 132
Flejal, 98
Flett, G. L., 89, 92
Flodmark, C. E., 102, 109
Flores-Ortiz, Y., 126, 129
Florin, I., 319
Floro, J. N., 206, 209
Flynn, K. J., 103, 104, 109
Flynn, M. A. T., 81, 92
Foehr, V., 101, 111
Fontaine, K. R., 290, 299
Forbes, D., 116, 130
Forbes, G. B., 291, 297
Ford, E. S., 110
Ford, K., 83, 92
Foreyt, J., 169
Forman, M. R., 32
Forman-Hoffman, V., 106, 109
Fornari, V., 129, 316, 320
Forsberg, S., 263, 265, 278
Fort, P., 247, 259
Fosson, A., 35–38, 41, 45
Foster, G. D., 7, 13, 100, 112, 141, 155,
        164, 170, 308, 324, 338, 342
Foster, R. C., 299
Fox, M. K., 235, 257
Frampton, I., 198, 212
Francis, L. A., 20, 23, 26, 28, 30, 31
Frank, G., 142, 152, 334, 340

Frank, S., *129*
Franklin, A. B., 244, *257*
Franklin, M. E., 314, *320*
Franko, D. L., *13*, 97, 103, 104, *108, 109,*
    155, 238
Frazier, A. L., *31, 70*
Frederick, D. A., 305, *320*
Fredrickson, B. L., 143–145, 147, *151,* 335,
    340
Freedman, D. S., 3, 8, *12,* 98, *109, 172*
Freedman, R. J., *212*
Freeman, C., 115, *129*
Freeman, C. P., *212*
French, S., 244, 245, *260*
French, S. A., *72, 95,* 103, 105, 107, *109,*
    110, 111
Friday, J., *31*
Friederici, S., 65, 68, *74*
Friedman, B. N., 80, 89, *91,* 106, *109*
Friend, R., *173*
Friestad, C., 58, 60, 68, *70*
Friis, S., *321*
Frisen, A., 79, *93*
Fryzek, J. P., 310, 311, *320, 322*
Fthenakis, E., 125, *129,* 199, *209*
Fujioka, K., *296*
Fukui, K., *190*
Fukuyama, S., 121, 125, *129*
Fulkerson, J. A., 58, 61, 62, 68, *71, 73,* 89,
    92, 248, *258*
Furham, A., *189*
Furnham, A., 116, *129*
Furst, T., 25, *30*

Gabriel, S. E., 311, *320*
Gains, M., 310, *320*
Galassi, F., *320*
Gallagher, D., *299*
Galloway, A. T., 20, 21, 25, 28, *30,* 244, *256*
Gance-Cleveland, B., *11*
Gantt, G. G., 312, *323*
Gao, D., *172–73*
Garber, C. E., *171*
Gardner, R. M., 80, 82, 89, *91,* 106, *109,*
    182, 185, 187, *189*
Garfinkel, P. E., 41, *45,* 51, *70,* 181, *189,*
    199, 200, *209–210*
Garner, D. M., 41, *45,* 51, *70,* 118, *130,*
    179, 180, 183, 186, *190,* 199–201,
    209–210 (check that this format is
    correct)

Garrahie, E. J., *32*
Gartin, M., 165, *169*
Gartlehner, G., *276*
Garton, M., 40, *46*
Gau, J., 223, 238, 332, *341*
Gauvreau, K., *297*
Gawkrodger, D. J., 312, *321*
Geffken, G. R., *324*
Gehrman, C. A., 232, *235*
Gehrman, G. A., 79, *91*
Georgieff, M., 142, *154*
Georgopoulou, E., 125, *129,* 199, *209*
Ghee, K. L., 104, *108*
Giancola O'Brien, J., 293, *298*
Gibbons, K., 49, *72, 73*
Gibbons, K. L., 247, *257*
Gibbons, L. M., 303, 314, *320, 323*
Gibson, L. J., 292, *299*
Gidding, S., *109*
Giese, S. Y., 308, *320*
Gillberg, C., 40, *46*
Gilligan, C., 144, *151*
Gillis, L., 159, *171*
Gillman, M. W., 19, *31, 32, 70,* 162, *169*
Gilman, S., 115, 121, *128*
Gilroy, M., 273, *278*
Gipson, M. T., 186, *190,* 313, *322*
Girard, B., 162, *173*
Gittelsohn, J. J., *95, 112, 257*
Giugni, A., 147, *151*
Glanz, K., 242, 246, *259, 260*
Glass, S. C., *171*
Gleaves, D. H., 218, *235,* 332, *340*
Gleeson, C., 178, *189*
Glynn, N. W., *171*
Goff, G., 42, *46*
Going, S. B., *257*
Gokee-LaRose, J., 269, *279*
Golan, M., 289, 290, 294, 295, *299*
Goldberg, L., *151,* 228, 229, 234, *234, 235*
Golden, N. H., 194, 195, *210*
Goldfield, G. S., 293, *297*
Golding, C., 56, *75*
Goldschmidt, A. B., 24, *31*
Goldstein, N., 48, *70*
Goldstein, S. E., 79, *94,* 330, 331, *340*
Goldwyn, R. M., *324*
Gomes, A., 307, *319*
Good, L., 86, *93,* 145, *153,* 335, *341*
Goodman, R., 115, *132*
Goodyer, L., 36, *45*
Goran, M. I., 164, *171*

Harrison, P. J., 269, 276
Harter, S., 79, 92
Hartung, R., 247, 257
Harvey, S., 121, 129
Haselhuhn, G., 85, 92
Hasin, D., 212
Haskell, W. L., 259
Haslam, D., 36, 45
Hassink, S., 11
Hathaway, J., 146, 154
Hau, K. T., 80, 93
Hauptman, J., 295, 297
Havens, P. L., 83, 95
Hawley, R., 41, 45
Haydel, K. F., 71, 105, 111, 258
Hayden, H., 52, 72
Hayman, L., 109
Hayward, C., 50, 68, 71, 74, 136, 139, 152,
    155, 167, 173, 247, 249, 258, 260
He, J., 92
Heatherton, T. F., 89, 92
Hebl, M., 147, 152
Hediger, M. L., 19, 31
Hefner, V., 217, 235
Heidgerken, A. D., 324
Heimberg, R. G., 249, 260
Heinberg, L., 115, 133, 138, 155, 184, 191
Heinberg, L. J., 4, 13, 47–48, 75, 185, 191
Heinig, 19
Heinmaa, M., 236
Heinz, D., 299
Helenius, H., 90
Helitzer, D. L., 257
Hemminki, e., 323
Henderson-King, D., 305, 321
Henderson-King, E., 305, 321
Hendy, H. M., 22, 31, 78, 87, 92
Henig, M. J., 30
Henker, B., 206, 209
Hennessey, M., 118, 129
Henry, S., 142, 152, 334, 340
Heo, M., 299
Hergenrather, K., 207, 211
Hermann, J., 179, 190
Hermans, K., 123, 130
Hermelo, M. P., 291, 296
Hern, J., 307, 321
Herpertz, S., 198, 209
Herpertz-Dahlmann, B., 198, 209
Hertz, S., 189
Herzog, D. B., 97, 109, 115, 128, 155, 238
Heshka, S., 170

Hess, K. W., 289, 300
Hess, M. S., 210
Hewell, K., 263, 265, 278
Hewison, J., 307, 319
Hewitt, P. L., 89, 92
Hibbert, M., 247, 260
Hickey, J. S., 210
Higgs, J., 36, 37, 41, 42, 45
Hilhorst, M. T., 306, 321
Hill, A. J., 24, 26, 30, 31
Hill, C., 315, 319
Hill, K., 272, 277
Hill, K. K., 200, 210
Hill, P., 12
Hillier, L., 73
Hills, A. P., 84, 95, 293, 299
Hind, H., 23, 29
Hinderliter, J., 300
Hinkel, L. K., 299
Hinton, A., 307, 321
Hix-Small, H., 151, 235
Ho, T., 117, 126, 131
Hobbs, K. E., 293, 299
Hodes, M., 116, 133, 276
Hodges, E. L., 178, 189, 201, 208
Hoehn-Saric, R., 318–319
Hoek, H., 123, 124, 130
Hoelscher, D. M., 204, 211
Hofer, S. M., 23, 30
Hoffman, K., 68, 69
Hogansen, J., 147, 153
Holbert, D., 120, 131
Ho Lee, Y., 130
Holland, L., 147, 154
Hollander, E., 313, 321
Hollander, J., 291, 297
Hollis-Neely, T., 112
Holmes, N., 112
Hölmich, L. R., 321
Holowaty, E. J., 324
Holsen, I., 68, 71, 249, 258
Holt, K., 79, 82, 87, 88, 92, 93
Holt, K. E., 78, 92, 94
Holub, S. C., 79, 94, 330, 331, 340
Holzer, B., 210
Hood, M. Y., 165, 171–173
Hooper, M., 118, 130
Hoover, R. N., 311, 319
Hopkins, V., 78, 88, 92
Hoppin, A. G., 296
Horowitz, T., 21, 32
Horton, B., 323

Houts, R., *12*, *153*
Hovell, M. F., 79, *91*, 232, *235*
Hovi, S. L., *323*
Hovius, S. E. R., 304, *324*
Hsu, L., 117, *131*
Hu, K., 55, *72*
Hu, X., 79, *93*
Huan, K., *236*
Huddy, D. C., 180, *190*
Hulse, G., 116, *130*
Huon, G. F., 50, *71*, 123, *133*
Hurdle, D., 106, *110*
Hurt, M. M., 335, *340*
Hwang, C. P., 79, *93*
Hyde, J. S., 104, *109*, 144, 145, 147, 149,
    151–153, 180, 184, *190*, 335, *340*

Iacono, W. G., 123, *130*, 141, *152*, 178, *191*
Impett, E., 144, *155*, 335, *342*
Inaoka, T., *129*
Inge, T. H., 3, 7, *14*, 308, *325*
Iniewicz, G., 115, *130*
Ireland, M., 107, *108*
Irving, L. M., 4, *12*, 242, 246, *258*
Irwin, C. E., 108, *110*
Irwin, M., 39, *45*
Isaacs, S., 36, 37, 41, *45*
Isbell, T. R., 24, *31*, 248, *258*
Israel, A. C., 295, *299*
Issanchou, S., 20, *31*
Ive, S., 5, *11*, 51, 70, 336, *339*
Iyengar, S., *339*

Jablensky, A., 217, *235*
Jack, D. C., *152*
Jackman, L. P., 200, *213*
Jackson, N. A., 80, 89, *91*, 106, *109*
Jackson, S., 126, *130*
Jackson, S. R., 200, *213*
Jackson, T. K., *279*
Jacobi, C., 50, 68, *71*, 139, 140, 146, *152*,
    249, *258*
Jacobs, B., 36, 37, 41, *45*
Jacobsen, P. H., 311, *321*
Jacobson, W. E., 310, *320*
Jaffa, T., *12*, 97, *110*
Jagnow, C. P., 18, *32*
Jahns, L., 162, *171*
Jain, A., 287, *299*
Jamner, L. D., 206, *209*

Janis, J. E., 307, *321*
Jarrell, M. P., 178, *189*, 201, *208*
Jeffers, S., *92*
Jeffery, A. N., 287, *299*
Jeffery, R. W., 291, *297*
Jeffrey, D. B., 205, *208*, *213*
Jeffrey, D. G., 204, *210*
Jelalian, E., 288, 290, *299*
Jenike, M. A., *319*
Jennings, P., 116–117, 126, *130*
Jensen, C., 295, *297*
Jensen, H. H., 164, *172*
Jensen, P., *152*
Jensen, T. B., *299*
Ji, M., *111*
Jian, S., *322*
Jimerson, D., 142, *152*, 334, *340*
Jins, J. E., *318*
Jirsak, J. K., *237*
Johansen, C., *321*
Johnson, A., 18, *32*, 116, *130*
Johnson, C. L., 97, 105, *110*, 157, *172*
Johnson, F., 249, *258*
Johnson, J., 46, *212*, 247, *258*
Johnson, M., 7, *14*
Johnson, R., *11*
Johnson, R. L., 180, *190*
Johnson, S., 27, *31*
Johnson, S. B., 83, *92*
Johnson, S. L., 23, 27, 29, *31*
Johnson, W. G., *110*, 202, *210*, 291, *299*
Johnson-Sabine, E., 57, 64, *73*, 248, *259*
Joiner, T. E., 311, *321*
Jolliffe, D., 241, *258*
Jonat, L., 125, *130*
Jones, D. C., 51–53, *71*, 87, *92*
Jones, L. R., 164, *171*
Jones, M. B., 23, *29*
Jones-Rodriguez, G., 106, *109*
Joughin, N., 35, *45*, 124, *133*
Juhaeri, *95*
Juniper, S., 116, *130*

Kachi, K., *45*
Kahle, L. L., *31*
Kahn, R., 7, *12*
Kalarchian, M. A., 166, *172*, 288, *298*
Kalat, J. W., 20, *31*
Kalikow, K., 46, *212*
Kaltiala-Heino, R., 41, *46*
Kaminsky, L. A., 158, *171*

Nickel, C., 142, 153
Nielson, S. J., 162, 172
Nieman, D. C., 180, 190
Nieri, T., 106, 110
Nikolic, S., 50, 72
Nobakht, M., 50, 73
Nolen-Hoeksema, S., 236
Noll, S. M., 147, 151
Nommsen, L. A., 19, 30
Norman, G. J., 111
Norris, M., 53, 73
Nunn, K. P., 44, 46
Nyren, O., 311, 320, 322

Obarzanek, E., 13, 57, 72, 75
O'Bien, M., 12
Obremski-Brandon, K., 51, 75
O'Brien, M., 153
O'Dea, J. A., 215, 219, 221, 225, 231, 237, 239, 242, 247, 250, 259, 336, 341
O'Fallon, W. M., 320
Offord, D., 152
Ogden, C. L., 3, 7, 12, 97–99, 109,110, 157, 172, 281, 300, 308, 322
Oggins, J., 274, 278
Ohashi, Y., 45
O'Herlihy, A., 6, 12
Ohlsen, L., 310, 322
Ohring, R., 51, 53, 57, 58, 64, 68, 73
Okamoto, A., 190
Olivardia, R., 77, 86, 94, 186, 190
Oliver, K., 50, 71
Oliver, S., 190
Oliveria, S. A., 25, 32
Olmsted, M. P., 200, 210
O'Loughlin, J., 165, 172
Olsen, J. H., 321
Olvera, N., 79, 81, 83, 84, 94
O'Neill, S. J., 189
Openshaw, C., 203, 211
Orbach, S., 242, 247, 259
Orzol, S. M., 7, 14, 99, 112
Osborn, B., 220, 236
Osborne, M. I., 210, 236
Osganian, S. K., 170
Ossip, D., 290, 298
Oster, H., 21, 32
Otto, M. W., 313, 322
Otto, R. M., 159, 173
Overpeck, M. D., 19, 31
Owen, N., 242, 260

Owen, S., 296
Oyewumi, L., 118, 132
Ozsahin, A., 313, 319

Paavonen, E. J., 201, 209
Padgett, J., 103, 108
Pai, S., 155, 238
Paige, D. M., 83, 96
Paikoff, R. L., 58, 61, 71
Paionni, A., 211
Pakkanen, M., 323
Palti, H., 62, 72
Paluch, R. A., 290, 298, 301
Panchoo, K., 133
Papadopoulos, L., 312, 322
Papay, F., 318
Paradis, G., 11, 165, 172
Park, A. J., 310, 322
Park, M. J., 108, 110
Parker, A. W., 293, 299
Parker, M. G., 315, 320
Parker, S., 104, 110
Parsons, E., 135, 153
Pate, R., 294, 300
Patel, A., 245, 256
Patrick, K., 99, 111
Patterson, T. L., 210
Patton, G., 247, 260
Patton, G. C., 57, 58, 64, 73, 248, 259
Paulosky, C. A., 195, 197, 198, 200, 201, 203, 204, 207, 208
Pawlak, D. B., 100, 109
Paxton, S. J., 5, 12, 48–53, 55, 57, 58, 63, 67, 68, 70, 72–76, 78, 81, 95, 148, 153,172, 179, 192, 219, 234, 234, 237, 247, 249, 250, 257, 259, 260
Pearl, A., 305, 306, 322
Peck, G. L., 312, 323
Pedrosa Gil, F., 153
Peebles, R., 6, 12, 273, 278
Peeke, L., 68, 69
Peeters, P. H., 311, 321
Pellai, A., 130
Pelletier, R. L., 164, 171
Pena, M., 120, 131
Pencharz, P. B., 292, 300
Penner, B. C., 290, 298
Pennington, B., 48, 75, 192
Pepe, M. S., 158, 173
Peplau, L. A., 305, 320
Pepper, A., 97, 111

Sala, A., 57, *74*

Salary, C. B., *339*

Salbe, A. D., *169*

Saling, M., 88, 89, *91*

Sallis, J. F., 79, *91, 110–111*, 159, 164, *173, 210*, 232, *235*, 242, 246, *260*

Sallis, J. R., *171*

Saltzberg, E., 184, *191*

Salvatori, S., 147, *151, 320*

Samuels, J. F., *318–319*

Sanchez, B. N., *256*

Sanders, M., 41, *45*, 81, *91, 194, 211*

Sands, R., 82, *91*, 178, *191*

Sandy, J., 202, *210*

Sanfacon, J. A., 88, *91*

Sanftner, J. L., 56, *74*

Sansbury, L. B., *32*

Sanson, A., 57, *75*

Santonastaso, P., 57, 65, 68, *74, 75*

Sargent, R. G., 83, 90, *95*

Sarwer, D. B., 49, *74*, 146, *152*, 303–306, 308–312, 314, *319, 320, 323, 324*

Sasaki, J., 293, *300*

Sasse, D. K., 77, 80, *93*, 182, 185, *190*, 331, *340*

Satter, E., 295, *300*

Saucier, D. M., 80, *93*

Sawyer, S. M., *210*

Scanlon, K. S., 19, *33, 172*, 204, *211*

Schaal, B., 20, *31*

Schafer, E., 25, *32*

Schafer, R. B., 25, *32*

Schapman-Williams, A. M., 266, 270, 272, *278*

Schermer, F., 5, *13*

Schetzina, K. E., *13, 300, 341*

Schilkel, C., 81, *91*

Schlam, T. R., 275, *279*

Schlebusch, L., 310, *324*

Schlundt, D. G., 204, *211*

Schlusinger, F., 178, *191*

Schmidt, A., 142, *154*

Schmidt, U., 263, 266, 270, 272, 277, *278–279*

Schneider, M., *129*, 273, *276*

Schneider, S., *321*

Scholl, T., 290, *298*

Schork, A., 293, *300*

Schreiber, G. B., *75*, 104, *108*

Schuler, R., 181, *191*, 247, *260*

Schulz, A., *112*

Schumacher, H., 161, *173*

Schumaker, J., 125, *133*

Schur, E. A., 81, *91, 194, 211*

Schutz, H. K., 49, 51–53, *73–74*

Schwartz, D., 51, 56, *70*

Schwartz, M. B., *72*

Schwenger, S., *169*

Schwimmer, J. B., 164, *173*

Scime, M., 225, *237*

Scott, M., 8, *12*

Sedway, J. A., *276*

Seidel, K. D., 158, *173*

Seifert, S., 162, *171*

Selser, C. T., *279*

Selzer, R., 247, *260*

Semega-Janneh, M., *212*

Senediak, C., 289, *300*

Serdula, M. K., 98, *109*, 204, *211*

Serletti, J. M., 315, *322*

Seroczynski, A. D., 68, *69*

Serpell, L., 203, *208*

Seshadri, R., 336, *339*

Shadish, W. R., 288, *299*

Shaffer, D., *46*, 212

Shakespeare, V., 315, *324*

Shapiro, J. R., 195, *207*

Sharpe, M., 115, *129*

Sharpe, T., *75, 191, 211*

Shaw, B. P., 149, *153*

Shaw, H., 4, *13*, 66, *74*, 102, *111*, 136, *155*, 218, 219, 222–224, 231, 238, 248, *260*, 332, *341*

Shaw, H. E., 58, 65, *75*, 218, 238, 332, *341*

Shea, S., 23, *32*

Sheerin, D., 307, *324*

Sheffield, C., 145, *154*

Shenker, I., *189*

Shepard, J., 232, *237*

Shergill-Bonner, R., 247, *257*

Sherman, C., 82, *91*

Sherman, D. K., 178, *191*

Sherman, S. N., *299*

Sherrodd, J., 107, *110*

Sherry, B., *170*

Sherwood, N., 221, *237*, 247, *260*

Sherwood, N. E., 196, 197, *208*

Shetty, P., 119, *128*

Shibata, S., 181, *191*

Shiffman, K. S., 86, 87, *92*

Shiffman, S., 206, *212*

Shin, C., 149, *155*

Shindo, M., 293, *300*

Shisslak, C., *75*, 139, *154*

Steinberg, A. R., 87, *94*
Steinberg, E., 202, *212*
Steinberg, L., 20, *29*
Steinegger, C., 36, *46*
Steiner, H., 41, *45*, 81, *91*, 194, *211*
Steiner-Adair, C., 149, *155*, 225, *238*
Steinwert, T., 56, *69*
Steranchak, L., 291, *298*
Sterky, G., 290, *297*
Stern, R. A., *325*
Stevens, J., 79, 81, *95*, *112*
Stevens, S. L., *210*
Stewart, A., 215, *238*
Stewart, D., 149, *155*
Stewart-Brown, S. L., *322*
Stice, E., 4, 5, *13*, 26, *33*, 51, 53, 58, 65, 66, 68, *74–75*, 82, *95*, 102, *111*, 124, *133*, 136, 139, 140, 144, 146, 147, *153*, *155*, 167, *173*, 218, 219, 222–224, 230–231, *238*, 247–249, 260, 332, *341*
Stoddard, C., 221, *236*
Stokes, B. J., 292, *297*
Stolmaker, L., 295, *299*
Stone, A., 206, *212*
Stone, M., 6, *13*
Storch, E. A., 316, *324*
Storey, M., 30, *170*
Story, M., *12*, 50, 52, 58, 63, 70–73, 84, *95*, 107, *108–111*, 149, *152*, *153*, *163*, *166*, *171*, *172*, *173*, 244, 245, 247, 249, 253, *257–260*
Strauss, B., 79, 81, *91*, 234, *234*
Strauss, J., *91*
Strauss, R. S., 164, *173*
Striegel-Moore, R., 142, 149, *154*, *155*
Striegel-Moore, R. H., 58, *75*, 103, 104, 108, *109*, *238*
Strong, E., 123, *133*
Stroud, J. M., *210*
Stubbs, M. L., 68, *73*
Stunkard, A., 178, *191*, *212*
Stunkard, A. J., 30, 56, *72*, 100, *112*, *170*, 288, *297*, *300*
Sturgeon-Tillisch, J., *210*
Subar, A. F., *31*
Suire, K., *318*
Sullivan, C., 336, *339*
Sullivan, P., 48, *70*
Sullivan, S. A., 20, *33*
Suminski, R., 79, *94*
Summerbell, C. D., 241, 260, 292, *300*

Summers, J. A., 204, *208*
Sundarajan-Ramamurti, A., *171*
Sung, R. Y. T., 80, *93*
Surgeon General of the United States, *174*
Susman, E., *12*
Susser, E., *130*
Swain, R. M., 164, *170*
Swan-Kremeier, L., 207, *211*
Sweidel, G., *300*
Swift, W. J., 41, *46*
Swigart, S., 196, *208*
Swinburn, B., 101, *109*
Symons, H., 273, *276*
Szabo, C., 118, *133*
Szmukler, G., *45*, 262, 264, *276*
Szmukler, G. I., 49, *72*, *73*, 247, *257*, *278*

Tabak, C. J., *12*, 300, *322*
Tadai, T., *190*
Taitano, K., *237*
Takei, N., *45*
Tanaka, H., 293, *300*
Tang, D. H., 315, *318*
Tanner, J. M., 39, *46*
Tanofksy-Kraff, *24*
Tanofsky-Kraff, M., *24*, *31*, *33*, 196, 199, *212*
Tantleff-Dunn, S., 4, *13*, 48, *75*, 138, *155*, 185, *191*, 269, *279*
Tantri, D., 315, *320*
Tareen, A., 116, 117, *133*
Tarone, R. E., 311, *322*
Taveras, E. M., *13*, 19, *33*, *300*
Taylor, C., 39, 44, *45*
Taylor, C. B., 30, 52, 68, 70, *74*, *75*, 136, 151, *155*, 167, *173*, 207, *210*, 213, 215, 223, 224, 229, 233, *234*, *238*, 247, *257*, 258, 260
Taylor, C. L., 184, *189*, 198, *208*
Taylor, L., *341*
Taylor, M. J., 180, 183, *189*
Taylor, S., *46*
Taylor, W. C., 159, *173*
Teasley, N., *173*
Telama, R., 158, *173*
Telch, C., 118, *131*
Teufel, N. I., *257*
Thaw, J., *238–239*
Theeboom, M., 88, *95*
Theim, K. R., *33*
Thelen, M., 180, 183, *191*

Williamson, D. A., 178, 182, 183, 185, *190, 192,* 195, 196, 200, 204, *211, 213,* 236–239
Williamson, S., 78, 96
Willows, N., 7, 8, *14*
Wilson, D. K., 162, *173*
Wilson, D. M., *71, 111,* 258, 259
Wilson, G. L., 205, *213*
Wilson, G. T., 56, *72,* 262, 269, 270, 275, *276, 279,* 288, *301*
Wilson, J., 6, *13*
Wilson, J. L., 273, 278
Wing, R., *212*
Wing, R. R., 288–291, 293, 295, 298
Winzelberg, A. J., *210,* 223, 224, *234, 236,* 238
Wiseman, C. V., 51, 76
Wisniewski, L., 298
Wisotsky, W., *129*
Withers, G. F., 219, *239*
Wolfe, B., 142, *152,* 334, *340*
Wolman, W., 314, *325*
Wolpe, P. R., 306, *321*
Wonderlich, S., 140, 142, 146, *152, 155,* 200, 207, *211, 212*
Wonderlich, S. A., 206, 209
Wood, K., 57, 64, *73, 239,* 248, *259*
Wood, K. C., *192*
Woodall, K., 289, 298
Woodfield, L. A., *189*
Woodhouse, L., 309, *325*
Woods, J. E., *320*
Woodward, H., 81, 82, 89, 95
Woody, E. Z., 22, 23, 29
Worell, J., 336, *342*
Work Group on Eating Disorders, 194, 196, 197, 199, 204, *213*
World Health Organization (WHO), 36, 46, 113, 122, *133,* 199, *213*
World Health Organization Expert Consultation, 99, *112*
Worrall, A., *12*
Wright, A., 236
Wright, J. A., 158, *173*
Wright, M. R., 307, *325*
Wright, P., 19, *33*
Wright, W. K., 307, *325*
Wroten, Cori, *170*
Wrotniak, B. H., 290, *301*
Wu, H., *133*

Wu, J., 55, *72, 79, 93*
Wyson, Andrea C., *170*
Wyson, C., *170*

Xanthakos, S. A., 3, 7, *14,* 308, *325*
Xepapadakos, F., 125, *129,* 199, 209
Xiao, G., 50, *71*
Xie, L., *324*

Yamamiya, Y., 218, *234*
Yamamoto, M., *132*
Yamamoto-Kimura, L., 125, *133*
Yamashita, T., *190*
Yamauchi, Y., *129*
Yamazaki, O., *132*
Yancey, A. K., 181, *191,* 247, *260*
Yang, X., 158, *173*
Yang, Y. W., 250, 256
Yanovski, J. A., 106, *110,* 212, 308, *320*
Yanovski, S. J., 202, *212–13*
Yanovski, S. Z., *33, 212*
Yates, A., 124, *133,* 314, *325*
Yellowlees, A., *212*
Yen, S., *322*
Yesalis, C., *91*
Yetman, R., *318*
Yi, I., *278–279*
Yip, R., *172*
Young, L. R., 163, *173*
Young, L. V., 310, 315, *325*
Young, V. L., *325*
Younger, K. M., 81, 92
Yu, C. W., 80, *93*

Zabinski, M. F., *111,* 207, *213*
Zamora-Gonzalez, J., *133*
Zanetti, T., 57, *74*
Zeitler, P., 282, *300*
Zelikovsky, N., *321*
Zenk, S., 101, *112*
Zhang, J., *133*
Zimmerman, S. I., 23, 29
Zivcic-Becirevic, I., 221, *237*
Zucchi, T., *211*
Zucker, N., *238–239*
Zybert, P., 23, *32*

SUBJECT INDEX

with parent participation, 294–295
and pharmacological treatment,
    295–296
with physical activity, 292–294
stages of, 284–286
Behaviors of Eating and Activity for
    Children's Health Evaluation
    System (BEACHES), 205–206
Belize, 121, 124, 126
Bermuda, 120–121
BET. See Behavioral Eating Test
Beverage consumption, 161–162, 164
Beverage guidelines, 168
Binge eating, 6
    abstinence from, 262
    and body dissatisfaction, 5
    defined, 166
    and denial/minimization of eating
        disorders, 195
    frequency of, 104, 105
    in Pacific Island societies, 121
    and teasing, 250
Binge-eating disorders (BED), 166–167
    genetic factors in, 140
    in Pacific Island societies, 121
Biological factors, in development of body
    dissatisfaction, 51
Biological sex, 143
Birth defects, 316
Bitter taste (per Smolak), rejection of, 19
Blacks. See African-American children and
    adolescents
Blood pressure, 281, 288
BMI. See Body mass index
BMI-for-age, 283–285
BMI status, 282
BN. See Bulimia nervosa
Bob and Tom's Method of Assessing
    Nutrition (BATMAN), 205
Body Attitude Test (BAT)—Japanese
    Version, 181, 186
Body-Cathexis Scale, 179
Body Change Inventory, 186
Body change strategies
    assessment of, 185
    and body image in preadolescent boys,
        89
    of boys, 87
Body Concept Scale, 179
Body-contouring procedures, 308
Body dissatisfaction, 5
    cross-cultural issues with, 115–116

defined, 103
and eating disorders in girls, 137
emergence of, 56
internalization, 117
measures of, 78, 179, 180
obesity prevention and increased,
    248–249
and sexual harassment, 145
universal prevention of, 332–333
Body dissatisfaction in boys. See Boys; Risk
    factors
Body dissatisfaction in girls
    biological/physical factors in
        development of, 51
    individual characteristics influencing
        development of, 52–53
    risk factors for development of, 50–55
    sociocultural influences on
        development of, 51–52
    synthesized model of development of,
        53–55
Body Dissatisfaction Scale, 179, 180
Body dysmorphic disorder (BDD)
    assessment of, 186
    and body image problems, 49
    and cosmetic surgery, 313–314
    in males and females, 115
Body esteem, 52
Body Esteem Scale, 79, 179, 183
Body Esteem Scale for Adolescents and
    Adults, 181
Body fat, 80, 123
Body image, 4–6, 330–333. See also Body
    image in girls; Body image in
    preadolescent boys
    in African American children/
        adolescents, 103–105
    assessment of. See Assessment of body
        image
    cross-cultural issues in. See Cross-
        cultural issues in body image
    defined, 4, 103, 104
    developmental progression of, 331–332
    and eating disorders, 331–332
    in ethnic children, 102–107
    gender differences with, 49–50
    influences on, 5
    in Latino/Asian/Native-American
        children/adolescents, 105–107
    measurement of, 78–81
    and plastic surgery, 304–305
    risk factors for problems with, 138

efficacy of treatment for, 272
family-based treatment of, 262, 263,
    266, 268
genetic factors in, 140, 141
GOS criteria for rating, 40
"hidden," 42
in Latin America/Caribbean, 120
and liposuction, 309
Maudsley approach to treatment of,
    268
in the Middle East, 119
neurochemical abnormalities with, 142
in Pacific Island societies, 121
peak onset of, 6
pharmacological treatment of, 275
structured interview for, 198–199
symptomology of, 37
theories about, 114
in urban contexts, 124
Bulimia Test—Revised (BULIT-R), 197,
    200
Bulimic symptomology, 106
BULIT-R. *See* Bulimia Test—Revised
Bullying, 245
BUT. *See* Body Uneasiness Test

Cadbury Schweppes, 168
Calcium, 25, 229
Calories. *See also* High-calorie foods
    from beverages, 162
    and portion sizes, 163–164
Campbell Soup Co., 168
Canada, 117
Cardiorespiratory fitness, 293
Cardiovascular disease, 8
Cardiovascular health, 293
The Caribbean, 106, 120–121
"Caring for Children and Adolescents with
    Mental Disorders" (WHO), 113
Carrots, 18
CATCH (Child and Adolescent Trial for
    Cardiovascular Health), 232
Causal relationship, establishing, 140
CBT. *See* Cognitive-behavioral therapy
CDC. *See* Centers for Disease Control and
    Prevention
CDC growth charts, 7, 8
CD programs. *See* Cognitive dissonance-
    based programs
Celebrities, 102

Centers for Disease Control and Prevention
    (CDC), 7, 160, 226, 294
ChEAT. *See* Eating Attitudes Test—
    Children's Version
ChEDE. *See* Eating Disorder Examination—
    Children
Cheerleading, xii
Chemical peels, 312
Child and Adolescent Trial for
    Cardiovascular Health (CATCH),
    232
Child development
    of body image, 304
    and cognitive-behavior therapy, 269
    and eating disorders, 6–7
    and food acceptance patterns, 20–22
    normal feeding problems in, 36
    and treatment of eating disorders,
        273–274
Child Growth Standards, 283
Childhood overweight
    and adult obesity, 338
    and eating disorders in girls, 137
Child Nutrition and WIC Reauthorization
    Act of 2004, 167
Children's Body Image Scale, 78, 179
Child sexual abuse (CSA)
    and boys' body image problems, 138
    and eating disorders in girls, 137
    and girls' body image problems, 136
    and obesity, 139
    as risk factor for body dissatisfaction
        and eating disorders, 146
Chile, 120
China, 50, 55, 84, 116, 117
Choking, fear of, 43
Cholesterol, 8, 100, 295
Classroom-based prevention programs, 217
Clinton, Bill, 168
CMI. *See* Comprehensive multidisciplinary
    intervention
Coca Cola, 168
Cognitive-behavioral therapy (CBT)
    for bulimia nervosa, 262, 269–271
    compliance with, 274–275
    developmental considerations with,
        273
    efficacy of, 272
    family-based treatment vs., 266, 270
    research on, 263, 266
Cognitive development, 194

Cognitive dissonance-based (CD) programs, 222–223, 233
Cognitive functioning, 273
Collectivistic societies, 123
Comfort, food for, 161
Communal societies, 123
Communicate, unwillingness to, 43
Community centers, 246
Community-level influences
  and obesity, 8
  and obesity prevention, 164, 245–246, 256
Communitywide prevention programs, 227–228
Comorbidity, 275
Compliance, 274–275
Comprehensive multidisciplinary intervention (CMI), 283, 286
Compulsive behaviors, 313
Computer-assisted psychoeducational programs, 223–224, 233
Computer game playing, 102
Computerized video projection techniques, 80
Computer-use time, 159
Contour Drawing Rating Scale, 178
Control beliefs, 144–145
Control of eating
  and breast- vs. bottlefeeding, 18–19
  consequences of excessive parental, 23–25
  parent—child balance in, 22–23
  and parenting skills, 295
  and treatment of eating disorders, 267
Coronary heart disease, 100
Cosmetic surgery, 305–314
  acne treatment, 312
  attitudes/motivations for, 305–306
  body-contouring procedures, 308
  and body dysmorphic disorder, 313–314
  breast augmentation, 309–311
  defined, 303
  and eating disorders, 314
  liposuction, 308–309
  otoplasty, 307
  prevalence of, 305
  psychiatric disorders among patients of, 312–314
  rhinoplasty, 306–307
Craniofacial surgery, 316–317
Crash dieting, 52
Creatine, 228

Cree Indian children, 7, 8
Croatia, 50, 115
Cross-cultural issues in body image, 113–128
  during adolescence, 122–124
  in Asia, 116–117
  and cultural change/acculturation, 125–127
  global trends with, 122–127
  in Latin America/Caribbean, 119–121
  in the Middle East, 119
  in North America/Australia/Europe, 115–116
  in Pacific Island societies, 121–122
  in sub-Saharan Africa, 118–119
  and upward mobility, 124
  in urban contexts, 124–125
CSA. *See* Child sexual abuse
Cuisine rules, 21
Cultural change, 113, 125–127
Cultural conflict, 127
Cultural issues and differences. *See also* Cross-cultural issues in body image
  with boys' body image, 83–84
  with food-related traditions, 164
  with girls' body image, 50
Curaçao, 120, 123
Cutting behaviors, 41
Cycle ergometer, 293

Daily lifestyle activities, 159
Dance Dance Revolution Ultramix 2, 293–294
Dannon, 168
Dating, onset of, 57
Dating violence, 137, 146–147
Demographic factors, of obesity, 164–165
Denial, of eating disorder symptoms, 195
Depression and depressed mood, 4
  and body dissatisfaction, 5, 53
  and body image, 69
  and boys' body image problems, 138
  and breast augmentation, 311
  and eating disorders, 275
  and obesity, 139
  and objectification, 147
Dermatological treatment, 313
Desserts, 27
Developmental prevention programs, 227–228
Developmental psychopathology, 4

Diabetes, 100, 281–282
Diagnostic and Statistical Manual of Mental Disorders (DSM–III), 201
Diagnostic and Statistical Manual of Mental Disorders (DSM–IV–TR), 36–38, 42, 114, 194, 195
Diagnostic issues, with eating disturbances, 194–195, 273
Dialectical behavior therapy, 269
Dietary factors, of obesity, 161–164
    beverage consumption as, 161–162
    fast food consumption as, 163
    meal patterns/frequency as, 162
    portion sizes as, 163–164
    and television viewing, 163
Dietary guidelines, 292
Dietary Guidelines for Americans 2005, 294
Dietary restraint, 26
Dieting
    and body dissatisfaction, 89
    childhood understanding of, 55
    crash, 52
    frequency of, 104
    maternal, 142
    naturalistic, 136, 137, 139
    and obesity, 136, 167
    obesity prevention and increased, 247–248
Diet modification, 290–292
Diet pills, 6, 147, 228, 229, 252
Disfigurement, 317
Disinhibited eating, mothers', 26
Diuretics, 229
Diversity, 220
Dopamine, 136–138
Drive for Bulk, 182
Drive for Muscularity scale, 80, 182, 185
Drug resistance skills, 228
DSM–III (Diagnostic and Statistical Manual of Mental Disorders), 201
DSM–IV–TR. See *Diagnostic and Statistical Manual of Mental Disorders*
Dual-pathway model, 218
Dysphagia, 40

Early childhood
    and body image in girls, 55–56
    feeding/eating patterns in, 137
    parental influences during, 20–28
Early-onset AN, 39–41
Ears, 307

Eastern Europe, 115
EAT. See Eating Attitudes Test
EAT-26, 200
Eating attitudes and behaviors, 163
    assessment of, 205–206
    and body change strategies, 89
    and culture, 164
    and diet, 161
    and fast food, 163
    intergenerational transfer of, 25–28
    modeling of, 165
    and television viewing, 163
Eating Attitudes Test (EAT), 197, 199–200
Eating Attitudes Test—Children's Version (ChEAT), 197, 199–200
Eating Disorder Belief Questionnaire, 181
Eating Disorder Examination (EDE), 39, 184
Eating Disorder Examination—Children (ChEDE), 39, 197, 198
Eating Disorder Inventory (EDI), 79, 179, 186
Eating Disorder Inventory—2 (EDI–2), 201
Eating Disorder Inventory—3 (EDI–3), 197, 200–201
Eating disorder not otherwise specified (EDNOS), 6, 38, 42, 195
Eating disorders, 6–7
    classification problems with, 117
    and cosmetic surgery, 314
    cross-cultural issues in. See Cross-cultural issues in body image
    and developmental progression of body image, 331–332
    and dieting, as risk factor, 142
    gender differences in, 115
    health problems with, 3–4
    and obesity, 338
    obesity prevention programs and increased risk for, 247–248
    prevalence of, 3
    risk factors for development of, 137
    treatment of. See Treatment of eating disorders
Eating disorders in children, 35–44, 333–336
    anorexia nervosa, 39–41
    bulimia nervosa, 41–42
    classification problems with, 35–39, 333
    food avoidance emotional disorder, 42

General appearance concerns, 58–69
General well-being, 69
Genetics
    and boys' body image problems, 138
    and eating disorders, 137, 140–141, 334
    and girls' body image problems, 136
    and obesity, 139
    as protective factor, 148–149
Ghana, 118–119
GI (glycemic index), 292
Girl Scouts, 221 (changed from "Girls Scouts" to "Girl Scouts" per Smolak)
Girls. *See also* African-American girls; Body dissatisfaction in girls; Body image in girls
    binge eating in, 105
    BMI values for, 285
    obesity in, 157
    prevalence of eating disturbances in adolescent, 104
    risk factors for body image problems in, 136
    risk factors for eating disorders in, 137
Girls Group program, 225
Girl Talk program, 227
GL (glycemic load), 292
Globalization, 126–127
Global trends, in body image and eating disorders, 122–127
Glucose intolerance, 281
Glycemic index (GI), 292
Glycemic load (GL), 292
GO GIRLS! program, 221
GOS criteria, 38–40
Goteberg, Sweden, 40
Government policies, 246
Great Ormond Street Hospital, London, 38
Greece, 125
Greek adolescents in Germany, 125
Green light foods, 291
Growth charts, 283–285
Guilt, 268
Gynecomastia correction, 316

Hair, 313
Harassment, 245. *See also* Sexual Harrassment (per Smolak)
Hawaii, 99

Health consequences, of overweight/obesity, 100, 337
Health report cards, 247
Healthy Body Images program, 221
Healthy culture, 149
Healthy eating and exercise
    parental/peer influence on, 149
    role models for, 21–22, 27, 166
Healthy foods
    access to/availability of, 101, 245, 246
    choosing, 291
    providing options for, 295
Healthy Kids—Healthy Weight, 161
Healthy lifestyle, 166, 295. *See also* Athletes Targeting Healthy Exercise and Nutrition Alternatives
Healthy Schools—Healthy Kids program, 227
Healthy weight management (HW) program, 222–223, 233
Helplessness, learned, 44
"Hidden" bulimia nervosa, 42
High-calorie foods, 101, 102, 162
High cholesterol, 100
High-density lipoprotein, 8, 295
High infant weight, 139
High School Musical (film), xii
Hispanic children
    binge eating in, 105–106
    overweight in, 7, 99
    weight-loss efforts of, 107
Hong Kong, 116, 117
HW program. *See* Healthy weight management program
Hydration, 39
Hyperinsulinemia, 281
Hypertension, 100

Iatrogenesis, 219
ICD (International Classification of Diseases), 199
ICD-10 (International Classification of Diseases and Health Problems, 10th edition), 36, 38, 199
Identity formation, 123, 248–249
Immigrants and immigration
    and acculturation, 125–126
    and eating disorders, 123
    number of years in United States and overweight increases in, 99
Income levels, 101

India, 117, 125
Individual characteristics
    and body image in preadolescent boys,
        88–89
    and development of body
        dissatisfaction in girls, 52–53
    and development of eating disorders in
        girls, 27
    and obesity prevention outcomes, 244,
        255
Individuation, 123
Indoor activities, 161
Infant growth patterns
    and obesity, 139, 141
    WHO standards for, 283
Infant weight, 139, 141
Informed assent and consent, 306
Inpatient treatments, 272–273
Institute of Medicine (IOM), 216
Institutional-level influences, on obesity
        prevention outcomes, 245, 255
Insulin, 295
Insulin sensitivity, 295
Internalization, of body dissatisfaction, 117
International Classification of Diseases
        (ICD), 199
International Obesity Task Force (IOTF), 8
Internet-based assessments, 206–207
Interoceptive awareness, 137
Interpersonal therapy, 269
Interviews
    for body image assessment, 184
    for eating disturbances assessment,
        196–199
Intimidation, 145
Intrusive thoughts, 313
In utero, taste/flavor experiences, 18
IOM (Institute of Medicine), 216
IOTF (International Obesity Task Force), 8
Iran, 50, 126
Iranian immigrants in Los Angeles, 126
Isotretinoin, 312
Israel, 119, 123
Italy, 115

Japan, 116
Japanese (language), 186

Kids' Eating Disorders Survey (KEDS), 178,
        197, 201

Korea, 84, 116, 126
Korean Americans, 126
Kraft Foods, Inc., 168

The Lancet, 35
Larger body size
    Black acceptance of, 83, 103–105
    boys' desire for, 81
Laser skin resurfacing, 312
Late-onset AN, 39, 41
Latin America, 119–121
Latino/a children and adolescents. See
        also Hispanic children; Mexican
        Americans
    body image and eating disturbances in,
        105–107
    overweight in, 99–102
Laxative abuse, 147
Laxatives, 6, 229
Learned helplessness, 44
Lifestyle
    as energy-imbalance factor, 158
    healthy, 166, 295
Lifestyle-based behavior change, 167
Lifestyle physical activity, 293, 294
Lipid profiles, 288
Liposuction, 308–309
Lived experience, 143, 147, 231
Low-density lipoprotein, 8

Malaysia, 122
Male bodies, 143–144
Males. See also Body image in preadolescent
        boys
    body image of, 77
    gynecomastia in, 316
    testosterone in, 37–38
Malnutrition, 125, 142
Manners, 21
Mars, Inc., 168
Masculinity, 143
Massachusetts Department of Health, 226
Maternal comments, 136–138
Maternal diet, 18, 20, 142, 165
Maternal eating behavior, 21–22, 26
Maternal modeling, 136–138
Maudsley approach
    to anorexia nervosa treatment, 263,
        267–268
    assumptions of, 268

to bulimia nervosa treatment, 268
to eating disorders, 262–263
efficacy of, 272
MBSRQ. *See* Multidimensional Body Self-
Relations Questionnaire
McKnight Risk Factor Survey III (MFRS-
III), 180
McKnight Risk Factor Survey IV (MFRS-
IV), 201–202
Meal patterns and frequency, 21, 162
Meaning-centered work, 127
Measures
issues with, 187–188
lack of standardized, 36–37
Media exposure. *See also* Western television
programming
and body image, 53
of celebrity weight fluctuations, 102
and overweight in children, 101–102
in Pacific Island societies, 121
in United Arab Emirates, 123
in urban settings, 124–125
Media images, 51, 135
Media influences
on body image in preadolescent boys,
84–87
and body image problems in boys, 138
and body image problems in girls, 136
with cosmetic surgery, 305–306
on eating disorders, 273–274
and eating disorders in girls, 137
research on, 232
on weight-related outcomes, 246
Media Influence Scale for Adolescent Boys
(MISAB), 85
Media literacy, 221, 228
Melanesia, 121
Menarche, 57
Menstrual cycles, 194
Menstrual status, 56–57
Meta-analyses, of prevention programs,
218–219
Metabolic syndrome, 282
Mexican Americans
acculturation of, 126
and BMI, 83
body dissatisfaction among young male,
84
overweight in, 98
Mexico, 120, 125
MFRS-III. *See* McKnight Risk Factor Survey
III

MFRS-IV. *See* McKnight Risk Factor Survey
IV
Microdermabrasion, 312
Micronesia, 121
The Middle East, 119
Minimization, of eating disorder symptoms,
195
MISAB (Media Influence Scale for
Adolescent Boys), 85
Modeling
of body image acceptance, 83
and body image problems in boys, 138
and body image problems in girls, 136
of eating behavior, 165
and eating disorders in girls, 137
of healthy eating patterns, 21–22, 27,
166
of healthy lifestyles, 295
maternal, 136–138
paternal, 136–138
peer, 136–138
of physical activity, 294
Moderate physical activity, 158, 294
Modernization, 117, 121
Morbidity rates, obesity-related, 7
Mortality rates, obesity-related, 7
Mothers
body image acceptance by Black, 83,
104
body image influenced by, 52
and body image in preadolescent boys,
87
overweight perceptions of, 287
Motivational interviewing, 275
Motivations, for plastic surgery, 305–306
Motor skills, lack of, 159
MRFS-IV, 197
Multidimensional Body Self-Relations
Questionnaire (MBSRQ)
Appearance Evaluation subscale, 180,
183, 187–188
Appearance Orientation subscale, 188
Multidimensional Media Influence Scale, 84
Muscle Appearance Satisfaction Scale, 182,
185
Muscle-building supplements, 228
Muscle gain strategies, 82
Muscular dissatisfaction, 185
Muscular ideal
awareness of, 86
internalization of, 138
in media, 85

and increased dieting/unhealthy weight
control behaviors, 247–248
individual-level influences on
outcomes of, 244, 255
integrated approach to, 250–251
New Moves program for, 253–254
school-/institutional-level influences
on outcomes of, 245, 255
societal-level influences on outcomes
of, 246, 256
and stigmatization/teasing, 249–251
strategies for, 255–256
Objectification, 143–145, 147
Objectification Theory, 143–144, 147
Objectified Body Conciousness—Youth,
180, 184
Objectified body consciousness (OBC),
144–145, 147
Oman, 119
Ontario Ministry of Health, 227
Orlistat, 295–296
Otoplasty, 307
Outcome research, prevention-program, 217
Outpatient treatments, 272
Overweight
as classification, 282
defined, 7
health consequences of, 337
problems with defining, 336–337
Overweight in children and adolescents,
98–102
and body dissatisfaction, 107
in ethnic children, 100–102
factors contributing to, 97, 100–102
health implications of, 100
parental perception of child, 287
prevalence of, 98–100

Pacific Island societies
body image issues in, 121–122
overweight in, 99
sedentary behavior in, 125
Parental disinhibition, 165
Parental feeding patterns, 164
Parental influence, 17–28
on body dissatisfaction, 52
on body image, 83, 87, 104
on boys' body image, 83, 87
with breast milk and formula, 18–19
on control of eating, 22–25
with cosmetic surgery, 305

in early childhood, 20–28
on eating attitudes/behaviors, 25–28
on food acceptance patterns, 19–20
on healthy eating and exercise, 149
of maternal diet, 18
on obesity, 165–166
on obesity prevention outcomes,
244–245, 255
on physical activity, 294
on taste/flavor experiences in utero, 18
during transition to solid foods, 19–20
Parenting skills training, 290, 295
Parent participation
in behavioral treatment of obesity,
288–289, 294–295
in family-based treatments of eating
disorders, 262, 263, 267, 268, 274,
275
in prevention programs, 232
Parents
alliance with, 274
control of child's eating behavior by,
165
overweight in, 139
perception of child overweight by, 287
weight -focus of, 167
Parents' working hours, 160
Parks, 245, 246
Paternal comments, 136–138
Paternal modeling, 136–138
Patient alliance, 274
PCP. See Primary care provider
Peer appearance culture, 52
Peer conversations, 136–138
Peer modeling, 136–138
Peers and peer influences
on body image in girls, 52
on body image in preadolescent boys,
87–88
with cosmetic surgery, 306
eating behaviors learned from, 22
on healthy eating and exercise, 149
on obesity prevention outcomes,
244–245, 255
perception of drug use by, 228
research on, 232
support of, 104
PepsiCo, 168
Perfectionism, 53, 89
Pervasive refusal syndrome (PRS), 40,
43–44
Pharmacological treatment

Puberty
  and anorexia nervosa, 36, 39
  and body image in girls, 56–57
  and eating disorders, 123
  objectification during, 145
Public health issue, 3, 7, 115
Punishment, food as, 161
Purging behavior
  abstinence from, 262
  cultural differences with, 106
  and early- vs. late-onset AN, 41
  frequency of, 104
  neurochemical abnormalities
    associated with, 142
  and sexual violence, 147

QEWP-A. *See* Questionnaire on Eating
    and Weight Patterns—Adolescent
    Version
QEWP-A/P, 197
QEWP-P. *See* Questionnaire on Eating and
    Weight Patterns—Parent Version
Quebec, Canada, 7
Questionnaire on Eating and Weight
    Patterns—Adolescent Version
    (QEWP-A), 202–203
Questionnaire on Eating and Weight
    Patterns—Parent Version
    (QEWP-P), 202–203

Randomized controlled trials (RCTs),
    262–266, 272
Rape, 145, 147
RCTs. *See* Randomized controlled trials
Reconstructive surgical procedures, 315–317
  breast reduction, 315–316
  craniofacial surgery, 316–317
  defined, 303
  gynecomastia correction, 316
  and traumatic injuries/disease, 317
Red light foods, 291
Relapse prevention, 271
Respiratory abnormalities, 281
Restrained eating, 22–23, 27
Restrictive eating
  and child development, 6–7
  cycle of overeating and, 248
  and eating disorders in girls, 137
  and excessive parental control, 23–25

and obesity, 139, 165
Retin A, 312
Rewards, food, 23, 161, 295
Rhinoplasty, 306–307
Risk factor(s), 135–150
  biological/physical factors in
    development of body dissatisfaction
    in girls, 51
  child sexual abuse as, 146
  dating violence as, 146–147
  defining, 139–140
  for development of body dissatisfaction
    in girls, 50–55
  for development of body image
    problems in boys, 138
  for development of body image
    problems in girls, 136
  for development of eating disorders in
    girls, 137
  for development of obesity in children/
    adolescents, 139
  gender as, 143–148
  genetics as, 140–141
  neurochemical abnormalities as,
    142–143
  objectification as, 143–145
  and protective factors, 148–150
  sexual harassment as, 145
Risk status, 216
"Rite of passage," 306
Role models
  for healthy eating, 21–22, 27, 166
  for healthy lifestyles, 295
Romanian orphans, 143
Running, 294
Rural areas, 125

Safety, 160, 245
Saline-filled breast implants, 309
Salt, taste of, 19
Sami adolescents, 116
Samoa, 99, 100, 122
Sampling problems, 124
Scar effects, 142
Scarring, 312
Scheduling activities, 161
*School Health Index for Physical Activity and
    Healthy Eating* (CDC), 226
School lunches, 245
Schools and school settings

family fun nights in, 232
healthy snacks/beverages in, 168
obesity prevention programs in, 245,
    255
physical activity in, 159, 160
and treatment of eating disorders, 275
School wellness policies, 160, 167–168
Secondary prevention, 216
Sedentary behavior
    awareness of, 294
    behavior modification of, 290
    of ethnic minority children, 101–103
    and obesity, 159–160
    in urban settings, 125
    and weight loss, 252
SEDS. *See* Stirling Eating Disorders Scales
Selective eating, 40, 43
Selective prevention programs, 216, 217
Selective serotonin reuptake inhibitor
    (SSRI), 269
Self-acceptance, 220
Self-confidence, 159
Self-efficacy, 226–228
Self-esteem
    in African-American children/
        adolescents, 103
    and body dissatisfaction, 5, 53, 69
    and boys' body image problems, 88, 138
    and bulimia nervosa, 41
    and girls' body image problems, 136
Self-evaluation, 24–25
Self-harming behaviors, 41
Self-monitoring
    of eating patterns, 203–204, 274–275
    obsessive, 147
    of physical activity, 294
Self-objectification, 144, 147
Self-Perception Profile for Children, 79
Self-regulation, of energy intake, 23
Self-report instruments, 183–184, 197,
    199–203
Self weighing, 137
Sensory exposure, 18
Serotonin
    and anorexia nervosa, 142–143
    and body image problems in boys, 138
    and body image problems in girls, 136
    and eating disorders in girls, 137
    and trauma, 147
SES. *See* Socioeconomic status
Sexual abuse, 146. *See also* Child sexual
    abuse

Sexual harassment
    and body image problems in boys, 138
    and body image problems in girls, 136
    gender differences with, 145
Sexual victimization, 147
Sexual violence, 140
Shame, 224, 268
Shapesville (Mills, Osborn, & Neitz), 220
SIAB. *See* Structured Interview for
    Anorexia and Bulimic Disorders
SIAB-EX See Structured Interview for
    Anorexia and Bulimic Disorders for
    Expert Ratings
Siblings, 22, 274
Sibutramine, 295
Sidewalks, 160
Silicone gel-filled breast implants, 309
Singapore, 116
Single-item scales, 80–81
Single-parent households, 164
Size perception. measurement of, 185
Skin, 308, 312, 313
Sleep, 139
Sleep apnea, 100
Snacking, 160, 162, 295
Snacks, 21, 168
Social age, 119
Social comparisons, 87
    and body image problems in boys, 138
    and body image problems in girls, 136
    and eating disorders in girls, 137
Social comparison theory, 124
Social influences
    on food acceptance patterns, 21–22
    on obesity prevention outcomes, 246,
        256
Social stereotypes, 56
Sociocultural Attitudes Towards
    Acceptance Questionnaire, 84–85
Sociocultural influences
    on body image in preadolescent boys,
        83–88
    on development of body dissatisfaction
        in girls, 51–52
    on eating disorders, 113–114
Sociocultural Influences on Body Image and
    Body Change Questionnaire, 85
Socioeconomic status (SES)
    in Latin America/Caribbean, 120, 121
    and obesity, 164–165
    and overweight in ethnic minority
        children, 101

Soft drinks, 162
Software, 181–182, 186
Solid foods, transition to, 19–20
Sour, rejection of, 19
South Africa, 118
Spain, 115
Speed limit enforcement, 160
Sports equipment, 245
Sports involvement, 88, 135
Sports magazines, 102
Sri Lanka, 117
SSRI (selective serotonin reuptake inhibitor), 269
Stanford Girls Health Enrichment Multi-site Studies (GEMS), 251–252
Starvation, 142
Stereotypes, 56
Steroids, 5, 77, 228
Stigmatization, 56, 249–250
Stirling Eating Disorders Scales (SEDS), 197, 203
Stoplight Diet, 291–292
Stress, 142–143
Stroke, 100
Structured Interview for Anorexia and Bulimic Disorders (SIAB), 198–199
Structured Interview for Anorexia and Bulimic Disorders for Expert Ratings (SIAB-EX), 197, 199
Structured interviews, 196–199
Structured weight management (SWM), 283, 285, 286
Student Bodies program, 223–224, 233
The Student Body project, 227
Subjective measures of body image, 179–181, 183–184
Sub-Saharan Africa, 118–119
Substance use, 311
Sugar-sweetened beverages, 162, 164, 284
Suicide, 311–313
Supplemental Nutrition Program for Women, Infants, and Children (WIC), 99, 287
Supportive environment, 166, 225
Swallowing, fear of, 43
Swallowing mechanism, 18
Swedish (language), 186
Sweet, preference for, 19
Swimming, 294
SWM. See Structured weight management
Syndrome recognition guidelines, 38

Synthesized model of development of body dissatisfaction, 53–55

T2DM. See Type 2 diabetes mellitus
Taiwan, 116, 126
Taiwanese Americans, 126
Tanzania, 118
Targeted prevention programs, 222–224
    cognitive dissonance and healthy weight programs, 222–223
    meta-analysis of, 218–219
    research on, 233
    selective vs., 216–217
Taste acceptance, 19
Taste experiences in utero, 18
Taste mechanism, 18
Taste tests, 244
TC. See Tertiary care
Teasing
    and body dissatisfaction, 87, 117
    and boys' body image problems, 138
    and eating disorders in girls, 137
    and girls' body image problems, 52, 136
    and mothers' perceptions of child overweight, 287
    and obesity prevention programs, 249–250
    and objectification of females, 144
    as predictor of overweight, 167
    preventing all forms of, 226
Teenage magazines, 102
Television commercials, 53, 163, 205
Television programming, Western. See Western television programming
Television viewing
    and adiposity, 293
    ethnic/cultural differences in, 164
    limiting, 284
    and obesity, 139, 159–161, 163
Temperament, obesity and, 139
10th International Classification of Diseases and Health Problems (ICD-10). See ICD-10
Tertiary care (TC), 283, 286
Test meals, 195, 204
Testosterone, 37–38
Thailand, 116, 117, 126
Therapeutic alliance, 274
Thin ideal, internalization of, 53, 136, 137, 144

Thinness and thinner body size
    boys' desire for, 81
    childhood preference for, 55
    cultural pressures for, 117
    gender differences with desire for,
        49–50
    and girls' body dissatisfaction, 48–49
    and menstrual status, 56
    parental values about, 22, 27
    and peer pressure, 144
    social pressure for, 120
Time for physical activity, lack of, 161
Tonga, 121
Topiramate, 142
Toxic environment, 100–101
Transnational media, 127
Trantrums, obesity and, 139
Trauma, 122, 147
Traumatic injuries, 43, 317
Treatment of eating disorders, 261–276
    anorexia nervosa, 263, 267–268, 272,
        273
    bulimia nervosa, 268–272, 275
    cognitive-behavioral, 262, 263, 266,
        269–274
    and comorbidity, 275
    and compliance, 274–275
    developmental considerations with,
        273–274
    efficacy of, 272
    family-based, 262–268, 272
    family issues with, 274
    inpatient vs. outpatient, 272–273
    Maudsley approach to, 263, 267–268
    outcomes from, 5
    and patient alliance, 274
    pharmacological, 275
Triglycerides, 8, 295
Trinidad, 121
Tryptophan, 142
Twin studies, 123, 141
Type 2 diabetes mellitus (T2DM), 281–282

Unhealthy weight control behaviors,
    247–248
United Arab Emirates, 123
United Kingdom, 38, 115, 116, 124–126
United States, 115, 116
Universal prevention programs, 216,
    332–333

Universal-selective prevention programs,
    219–222
    classroom-based, 217
    effectiveness of, 230–231
    meta-analysis of, 218
Unstructured interviews, 197
Upward mobility, 124
Urban contexts, 107, 118, 124–125
U.S. Congress, 167
U.S. Department of Agriculture, 292
U.S. Department of Education, 228
U.S. Food and Drug Administration (FDA),
    309

Vanilla, 18
Variable risk factors, 140
Vegetables, 25, 164, 244, 246, 284
Vending machines, 168, 245
Venezuela, 120
Verbal expression, 22
Very Important Kids (V.I.K.) program,
    226–227
Video distortion technique, 185
Video game characters, 86
Video games
    activity-promoting, 293–294
    playing, 102
Video projection techniques, 80
Vigorous physical activity, 159, 294
V.I.K. program. See Very Important Kids
    program
Vomiting, 43, 147, 195, 252

Walking, 294
Walking clubs, 244
Weight. See Body mass index
Weight bias, 56
Weight categories, 7, 8
Weight-change strategy(-ies)
    assessment of, 186
    and body dissatisfaction, 89
    of boys, 81
    exercise as, 159
    of Native-American children, 107
    unhealthy, 49
Weight concerns
    and eating disorders, 135, 136, 144
    and eating disorders in girls, 137
    media influences on, 85

and shape concerns, 58–69
Weight-control behaviors
    and body dissatisfaction, 5
    and obesity, 139, 167
    unhealthy, 247–248
Weight loss, significant, 38, 39, 195
Weight preoccupation, 116
Weight-related clinical disturbance, 4
Weight restoration, 262, 267
Well-being, 69
Western cultures, 51
Western Europe, 115, 116
Westernization, 114, 117, 122, 126, 127
Western media exposure, 125
Western television programming, 121, 123,
    126–127

White children
    binge eating in, 105
    overweight in, 99–100
WHO. *See* World Health Organization
WHO standards, 283
WIC. *See* Supplemental Nutrition Program
    for Women, Infants, and Children
Work schedules, parents', 102, 160
World Health Organization (WHO), 113,
    283

Yellow light foods, 291

Zimbabwe, 118, 124

ABOUT THE EDITORS

Linda Smolak, PhD, received her doctoral training at Temple University, where she obtained her PhD in 1980. She has been at Kenyon College since 1980, and she is a professor in the Departments of Psychology and Women's and Gender Studies. She has coedited two other books in the area of body image and eating disorders (*The Developmental Psychopathology of Eating Disorders*, 1996; *Eating Disorders: Innovations in Research and Practice*, American Psychological Association, 2001), and a book on prevention of eating disorders (*The Prevention of Eating Problems and Eating Disorders: Theory, Research, and Practice*, 2006). She is the author of numerous articles and chapters on the developmental psychopathology of eating disorders. She is an associate editor of *Body Image: An International Journal of Research* and is on the editorial board of *Eating Disorders: The Journal of Treatment and Prevention*. In 2007, she received the Price Family Award for Eating Disorders Research from the National Eating Disorders Association.

J. Kevin Thompson, PhD, received his doctoral training at the University of Georgia, where he obtained his PhD in 1982. He has been at the University of South Florida since 1985 and is a professor in the Department of Psychology. He has authored, coauthored, or edited four earlier books in the area of body image, eating disorders, and obesity (*Body Image Disturbance: Assessment and Treatment*, 1990; *Body Image, Eating Disorders, and Obesity: An Integrative Guide for Assessment and Treatment*, American Psychological Association [APA], 1996; *Exacting Beauty: Theory Assessment and Treatment of Body Image Disturbance*, APA, 1999; *The Muscular Ideal: Psychological, Social, and Medical Perspectives*, APA, 2007). He has been on the editorial board of the *International Journal of Eating Disorders* since 1990.